FIELDING'S
BERMUDA AND THE BAHAMAS
1989

Current Fielding Titles

FIELDING'S BERMUDA AND THE BAHAMAS 1989
FIELDING'S BUDGET EUROPE 1989
FIELDING'S CARIBBEAN 1989
FIELDING'S EUROPE 1989
FIELDING'S MEXICO 1989
FIELDING'S PEOPLE'S REPUBLIC OF CHINA 1989
FIELDING'S SELECTIVE SHOPPING GUIDE TO EUROPE 1989

FIELDING'S AFRICAN SAFARIS
FIELDING'S CALIFORNIA
FIELDING'S EUROPE WITH CHILDREN
FIELDING'S FAMILY VACATIONS USA
FIELDING'S FAR EAST
FIELDING'S HAVENS AND HIDEAWAYS USA
FIELDING'S LEWIS AND CLARK TRAIL
FIELDING'S LITERARY AFRICA
FIELDING'S MOTORING AND CAMPING EUROPE
FIELDING'S SPANISH TRAILS IN THE SOUTHWEST
FIELDING'S WORLDWIDE CRUISES 4th revised edition

FIELDING'S
BERMUDA AND THE BAHAMAS
1989

BY
RACHEL J. CHRISTMAS
AND
WALTER CHRISTMAS

FIELDING TRAVEL BOOKS
c/o WILLIAM MORROW & COMPANY, INC.
105 Madison Avenue, New York, N.Y. 10016

ABOUT THE AUTHORS

Walter Christmas, a former public relations consultant, has worked for the Ghana Information and Trade Center where he helped develop tourism for that country. He has also worked for nonprofit organizations, and in private industry. His intimate knowledge of The Bahamas and Bermuda was gained from innumerable business and vacation trips.

Now a free-lance writer, **Rachel J. Christmas** has worked as an editor at a major New York publisher. Her articles on travel and other subjects have appeared in national magazines. She is well acquainted with Spain, Mexico, the Caribbean, and Hawaii, in addition to Bermuda and The Bahamas.

The Christmases, father and daughter, live in New York City.

Copyright © 1989, 1988, 1987, 1986, 1985, 1983 by Rachel J. Christmas and Walter Christmas

All rights reserved. No part of this book may be reproduced or utilized in any form or by any means, electronic or mechanical, including photocopying, recording or by any information storage and retrieval system, without permission in writing from the Publisher. Inquiries should be addressed to William Morrow and Company, Inc., 105 Madison Avenue, New York, N.Y. 10016.

ISSN: 0739-0769

ISBN: 0-688-07132-5
ISBN: 0-340-48985-5 (Hodder & Stoughton)

Printed in the United States of America

Sixth Edition
 2 3 4 5 6 7 8 9 10

Text design by Marsha Cohen/Parallelogram

CONTENTS

WHAT'S INSIDE · · · vii

CHOOSING YOUR ATLANTIC ISLE · · · 1

BERMUDA · · · 5

   Why Bermuda? / 5
   Things to Know / 14
   Costs / 14
   Traveling with Children / 15
   Travel for the Handicapped / 15
   Special Services / 16
   When to Go / 16
   Getting There / 18
   Entry and Departure Requirements / 21
   Being There / 22
   What to See and Do / 26
   Attractions at a Glance / 26
   The Parishes and Their Sights / 29
   Tours / 64
   Sports / 65
   Night Life / 69
   Shopping / 71
   Dining Out / 73
   Where to Stay / 89
   Hotel Quick-Reference Charts / 109

THE BAHAMAS · · · 126

   Why The Bahamas? / 126
   Things to Know / 137
   Costs / 137
   Traveling with Children / 137
   Travel for the Handicapped / 138
   Special Services / 138
   When to Go / 138
   Getting There / 141
   Entry and Departure Requirements / 146
   Being There / 147
   What to Do and Where to Do It / 152
   Sports / 152

Night Life / **155**
Shopping / **155**
Tours / **156**
Dining Out / **157**
Nassau / **157**
　Attractions at a Glance / **157**
Freeport / **196**
　Attractions at a Glance / **196**
The Family Islands / **212**
　Attractions at a Glance / **213**
　The Abacos / **217**
　Acklins/Crooked Island / **230**
　Andros / **234**
　The Berry Islands / **244**
　The Biminis / **246**
　Cat Island / **251**
　Eleuthera / **255**
　The Exumas / **267**
　Inagua / **274**
　Long Island / **277**
　San Salvador / **281**
Hotel Quick-Reference Charts / **288**

INDEX · · · **311**

LIST OF MAPS

Bermuda and The Bahamas / **xii**

BERMUDA · · · 6
   City of Hamilton / **41**
   Town of St. George's / **59**

THE BAHAMAS · · · 128
   New Providence / **158**
   Downtown Nassau / **175**
   Grand Bahama / **195**
   Freeport/Lucaya / **202**
   The Abacos / **218**
   Acklins/Crooked Island / **232**
   Andros / **238**
   The Berry Islands / **245**
   The Biminis / **248**
   Cat Island / **253**
   Eleuthera / **257**
   The Exumas / **270**
   Inagua / **276**
   Long Island / **279**
   San Salvador / **284**

WHAT'S INSIDE

Sights

Throughout this book, you'll find "Attractions at a Glance" lists followed by descriptions of each area and its sights. The attractions we consider extra special are marked with an asterisk (*).

Hotel Ratings

We have used a star-rating system to give you more information about hotels. These ratings are based on our own opinions as well as those of guests and residents of the islands.

☆ hollow stars indicate comfort, variety, and quality of facilities
★ in addition to all of the above, filled stars indicate charm, atmosphere, impressive decor, and/or exceptional service

★★★★★ Top of the line
★★★★ Excellent
★★★ Very good
★★ Good
★ Plain or modest

No Stars Guest houses or housekeeping units; low-budget hotels that have limited facilities and/or services; or accommodations undergoing major renovations or other changes at press time.

Hotel Quick-Reference Charts include basic information about the accommodations we describe and highly recommend as well as about other accommodations.

Hotel Prices

Unless otherwise indicated, the average daily prices, per person, of double rooms in season are categorized as follows:

Expensive: $90 or more European Plan (EP)—no meals/$115 or more, Modified American Plan (MAP)—full breakfast and dinner
Moderate: $55–$89 (EP)/$65–$114 (MAP)
Inexpensive: Less than $55 (EP)/less than $60 Continental Plan (CP)—light breakfast
(Note that you'll save money by booking an air/hotel package deal.)

Restaurant Prices

The following prices are based on the approximate cost, per person, of a full dinner, not including liquor or tip. Lunch and breakfast will be about 15% to 25% less.

Expensive: More than $30
Moderate: $20 to $30
Inexpensive: Less than $20

Updates

During our frequent trips to Bermuda and The Bahamas, we gather the most accurate and up-to-date information possible. However, hotels, restaurants and their menus, sights, airlines, and cruise lines do change during the course of the year. We welcome any comments or suggestions about things that may have changed since our most recent visit or about the guide in general. Write to us c/o Fielding Travel Books, William Morrow & Co., Inc., 105 Madison Avenue, New York, NY 10016.

Note that all prices quoted should be considered approximate.

ACKNOWLEDGMENTS

Special thanks go to the staffs of the Bermuda Department of Tourism, and the Bahamas Ministry of Tourism.

We are grateful to American, Pan Am, Piedmont, Bahamasair, and Chalk's International for providing us with comfortable and efficient transportation.

The assistance and knowledge of the following people made an invaluable contribution to the book: Pamela H. Wissing, Charles Webbe, Eileen Fielder, Erma Grant-Smith, Nelson and Brenda Reynolds, Carmen Rolle, and Jacqueline Gibson.

We will always remember the encouragement, support, and sense of humor of the late Eunice Riedel. We are grateful to have had the opportunity to work with her.

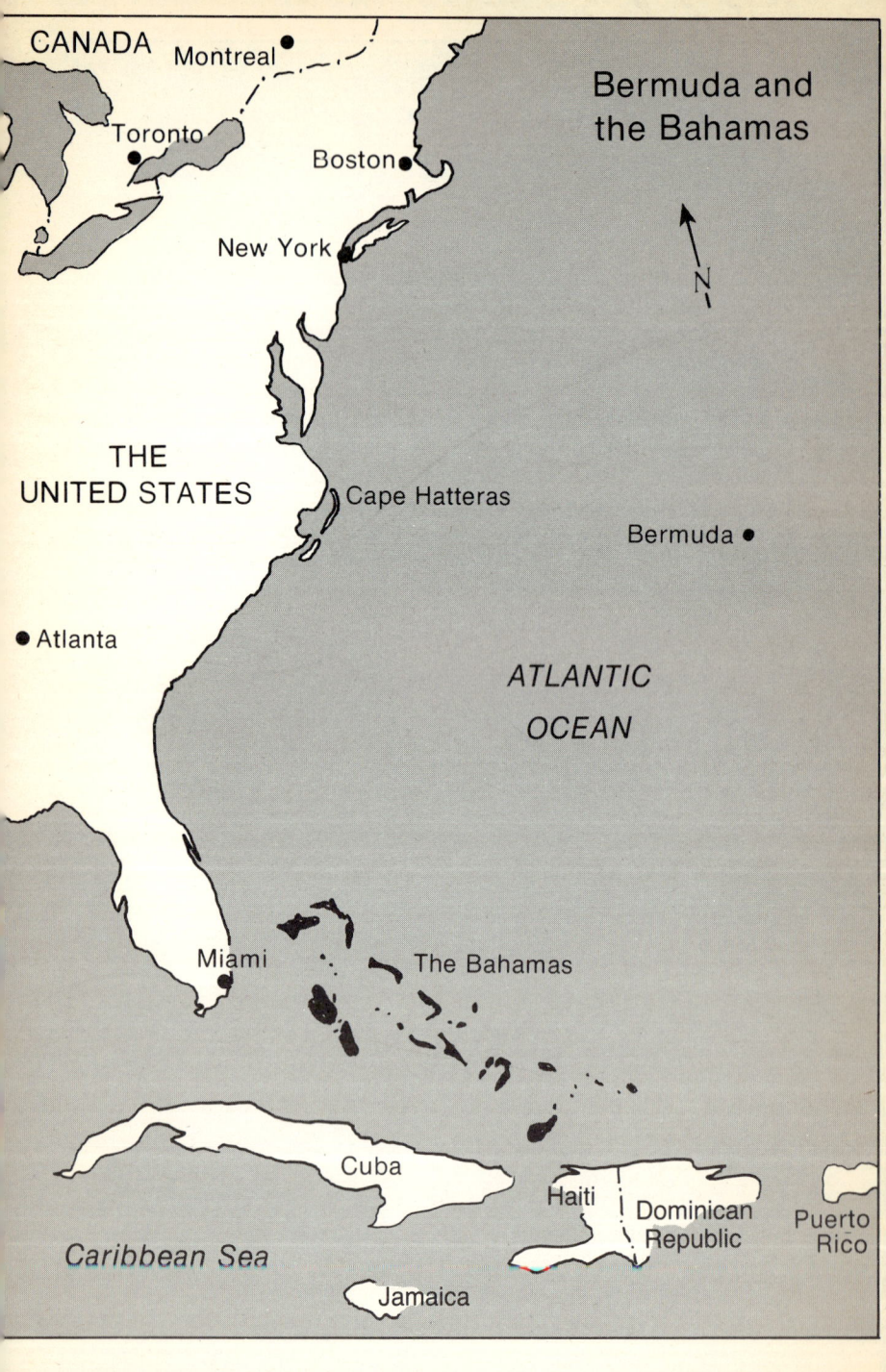

FIELDING'S BERMUDA AND THE BAHAMAS 1989

CHOOSING YOUR ATLANTIC ISLE

The tiny island of Bermuda lies isolated in the Atlantic, some 570 miles southeast of Cape Hatteras, North Carolina, the nearest land. Farther south and closer to the Caribbean, The Bahamas is 40 miles off the tip of Florida. Bermuda and The Bahamas have similarities, but it is their special differences that will determine which one you choose for your visit.

Contrary to popular belief, neither country is in the Caribbean. Bermuda—the oldest existing British self-governing colony—is some 700 miles from New York, more than 800 from Halifax, Nova Scotia, and over 900 from Nassau, the capital of The Bahamas. Actually a string of islands connected by bridges and causeways, Bermuda gives the illusion of being one long strip of land. Almost 21 square miles, it is about the size of Manhattan. It is so narrow that no matter where you are, the unbelievably blue-green sea is never more than a mile away and is rarely out of sight.

On the other hand, The Bahamas—independent from Britain since 1973—is an archipelago of more than 700 islands and islets, stretching out into the Atlantic for about 400 miles. Beginning off the coast of Florida, it almost reaches Hispaniola, the Caribbean island shared by Haiti and the Dominican Republic. The Bahamas is comprised of more than 600 cays (pronounced "keys"), 29 larger islands, and many islands no larger than rocks.

Island Highlights

Bermuda, sparkling clean, with its pastel, white-roofed houses, exudes order. Yachts, cruise ships, and other seacraft anchor in the marinas of the town of St. George's and the city of Hamilton against postcard backgrounds. Bermuda's extensive south shore is bordered by some of the world's finest beaches. In addition to comfortable living, the island offers enough sports and sights to satisfy even the most energetic vacationer.

Among the wide variety of sports facilities, the island boasts many first-rate golf courses. Groups of North American businessmen have been known to fly down just for a weekend on the green. Other attractions include underground grottos, the Botanical Gardens, and an indoor-outdoor maritime museum. There are also 17th-century forts, the oldest Anglican church in the Western hemisphere, and a historic lighthouse from which all of Bermuda is visible.

The Bahamas has the mellowed colonial charm of old Nassau contrasted with the young, modern city of Freeport, and the quiet natural beauty of the Family Islands. In Nassau, you'll see flower-bedecked villas whose walls are overgrown with lush tropical foliage. Notorious, busy Bay Street, lined with stores, boutiques, and restaurants, is the city's main thoroughfare. Cruise ships dock near bustling Rawson Square, where taxis and horse-drawn carriages await passengers. Historic sights, such as Government House and the gardens of the 19th-century Royal Victoria Hotel, are within walking distance of the square. A short ride from downtown Nassau takes you to the bridge to Paradise Island, the home of some of the more glittery hotels.

Freeport, developed in the 60s, has broad, palm-lined avenues and high-rise, balconied hotels and condominiums. It was designed to attract visitors as well as to become the center of industrial development. Here you can find everything from casinos and gourmet restaurants to the International Bazaar, Port Lucaya waterfront esplanade, and exciting night club revues.

Sparsely settled and as windswept as a Winslow Homer watercolor are the Family Islands, formerly called the Out Islands. They present a less hectic way of life than Nassau or Freeport and attract the dedicated fisherman as well as the devoted yachtsman. On many of these islands, chickens, goats, and sheep parade through yards and across winding dirt roads. Sun worshipers can find stretches of deserted, palm-shaded, pink-sand beaches where they can spend the day undisturbed. Divers can explore undersea wrecks (including a train) as well as caves and the wonders of subtropical marine life. There are also New England–like villages set against the sea and tropical foliage.

The atmosphere of the Family Islands encourages living close to nature without the formalities of attention to dress and rigid schedules. However, it is also possible to find out-island resorts where you can dress for dinner, or meet for cocktails on elegant terraces as the sun settles beyond the sea. With more tourists discovering the Family Islands, the choice of such accommodations is increasing.

Although many people consider the weather in both countries ideal at any time of year, Bermuda's most popular season is spring and summer and The Bahamas' is winter. The Bahamas is somewhat warmer than Bermuda in the winter. Bathed by the Gulf Stream, Bermuda is subtropical, with daytime temperatures from May to November in the mid-80s (Fahrenheit) and evening temperatures in the 70s. During the remainder of the year, the temperature is in the 60s and 70s in the day.

The Tropic of Cancer cuts through The Bahamas, bringing the warmest weather to the southernmost islands and cooler, Gulf Stream temperatures to the northern islands, which include Nassau and Freeport. During the winter and spring, temperatures are in the 70s, and during the summer and fall, in the 80s.

Hurricanes, which often hit the Caribbean area soon after August, seldom strike The Bahamas or Bermuda. When storms do occur, bringing dramatic cloud formations and churning waters, they are generally over quickly, followed by sun and blue skies.

During the high seasons in Bermuda and The Bahamas, accommodations are filled and the islands bustle with visitors. Accordingly, rates are higher and attractions more crowded. While off-season rates are appreciably lower, many travelers save money during the rest of the year as well by using guest houses and other small accommodations. Especially in The Bahamas' less developed Family Islands, the locally operated hotels and guest houses are much less expensive than larger hotels. Some have no more than three or four rooms. In Bermuda there is an abundance of well-maintained housekeeping apartments, most of them close to beaches, and with their own pools. If you choose housekeeping facilities, however, note that grocery prices are high since most food is imported, so you may want to bring some canned goods from home. Another way to save money is to eat at the small restaurants specializing in homestyle cuisine.

In Bermuda and in Nassau and Freeport, there is a variety of restaurants, including Italian, French, and Chinese, as well as those specializing in local cuisine. Particularly on the Family Islands, menus revolve around treats from the sea, but dishes for landlubbers are also available. Depending on where you go, you can have a steak or lobster dinner or, if feeling adventurous, sample such delicacies as cracked conch or shark hash on toast.

The Human Factor

For nearly four centuries, the cultures of Indians, Europeans, Africans, Americans, and West Indians have been melding to form the colorful ways of life unique to Bermuda and The Bahamas. While you can have afternoon tea in Bermuda and climb the Queen's Staircase in The Bahamas, you can also enjoy the influences of the African and Indian ancestors of islanders. At Christmastime, for instance, when the streets fill with the music of masked dancers dressed in bright, elaborate costumes, you can witness a 300-year-old tradition with roots in Africa. Called gombey in Bermuda, this music and dance is known as goombay in The Bahamas, and is found in various forms in a number of West Indian countries.

Getting Acquainted

Whether you are on your honeymoon, addicted to beaches, or just looking for a change of pace, you will do yourself an injustice if you do not make an effort to get to know local people and learn something about the way they live.

As you travel around the islands, you will find that people are very friendly and helpful. However, as is too often the case in countries that rely heavily on tourism, some islanders have felt slighted or taken for granted by visitors. Many Bermudians and Bahamians have expressed resentment of visitors who act as if local people exist for the sole purpose of accommodating tourists. But if you treat people as you would like to be treated, talk to clerks and cab drivers, and visit beaches, restaurants, and night spots frequented by locals, your stay will be enhanced tremendously.

Both Bermuda and The Bahamas offer programs that make meeting people extra special. In Bermuda, springtime means that you can visit a Bermudian family for a tour of their house and garden. In Nassau and Freeport, you can take part in the celebrated free "People-to-People" program where, for example, you can spend an evening at the theater with a Bahamian couple, be a guest at their home for a meal, or have tea at Government House.

For fast-moving Americans, Bermuda may more closely resemble home in regard to pace and service. At many restaurants and resorts in The Bahamas, life is slower, more relaxed, and service more casual. Visitors to either country will suffer no discomfort if they adapt to the flow and ambience of their surroundings.

No matter what you do or where you go in Bermuda or The Bahamas—whether you choose Bermuda's spectacular south shore or its busy capital, whether you crave the fast pace of Nassau or the seclusion of a Bahamian cay—you're in for a memorable visit.

BERMUDA

WHY BERMUDA?

Bermuda welcomes visitors wholeheartedly, with friendly greetings, long stretches of beach, and a host of sports and sights. If the first things you notice about this tiny island aren't its beauty and cleanliness, it will only be because you're stunned by the turquoise hues of the surrounding waters. Bermudians are proud of the island's trim appearance. Even the wildest of the colorful vegetation seems to have had a gardener's touch. You won't find any casinos, and there are only one or two fast-food restaurants. The only street vendors you might come across are the few selling fish or fruits and vegetables.

Small white-roofed homes dot the low hills. Waterside and inland roads pass patchwork farms with plots of sweet potatoes, broccoli, bananas, and onions. Pink and blue public buses, which always seem to be on schedule, peacefully coexist with mopeds and the new-looking compact cars. Ferries and cruise ships glide in and out of the harbors and some beaches even have pink sand.

The oldest existing British self-governing colony, Bermuda is anchored in the Atlantic (not the Caribbean), nearly 600 miles from Cape Hatteras, North Carolina, the closest land. Considered one island, it is really almost 150 islands, only about 20 of which are inhabited. The seven largest are connected by bridges and causeways, creating a 21-square-mile fish-hook-shaped strip about the size of Manhattan. At its widest point, Bermuda is barely two miles across.

Any time of year is a good time to visit this subtropical island tempered by the Gulf Stream. During the summer season, from May to mid-November, temperatures average 80°F (26.7°C). The rest of the year, temperatures range from the 60s to the 70s. Rainfall is evenly

Bermuda

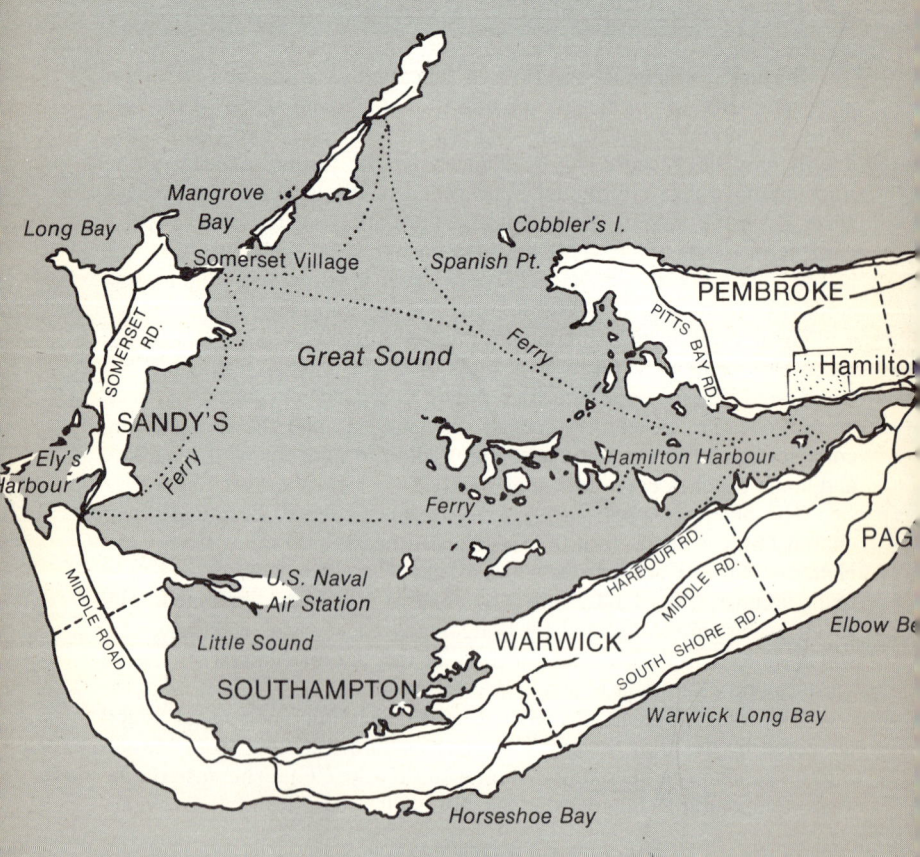

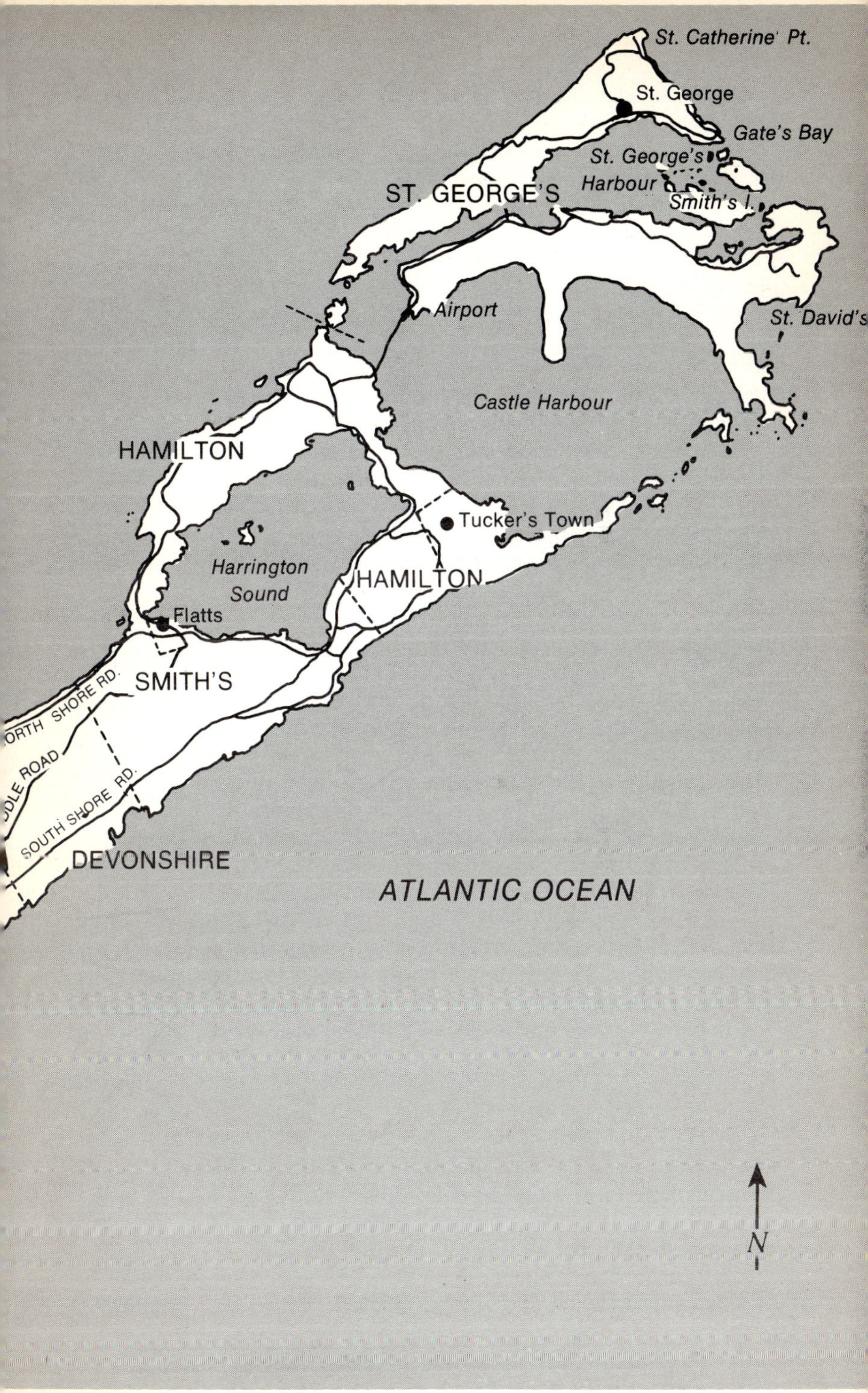

St. Catherine' Pt.
St. George
Gate's Bay
St. George's
Harbour
Smith's I.
ST. GEORGE'S
Airport
St. David's
Castle Harbour
HAMILTON
Tucker's Town
Harrington
Sound
HAMILTON
Flatts
SMITH'S
NORTH SHORE RD.
MIDDLE ROAD
SOUTH SHORE RD.
DEVONSHIRE
ATLANTIC OCEAN
N

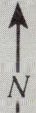

spread throughout the year, so there is no rainy season, and hurricanes are virtually unheard of.

A trip to Bermuda can mean getting to know Bermudians, who are the most important reason the island is the way it is. Visitors and locals use the same buses, eat in the same restaurants, shop in the same stores, and swim at the same beaches, the best of which are public. While walking or riding a moped, if you pause at an intersection and appear even mildly confused, someone will be sure to ask, "Lost? Need help?"

Sports

Bermuda's south shore has some of the most beautiful beaches in the world. Scuba divers, snorkelers, and those who like fishing will want to explore the reefs surrounding the top of the extinct volcano that is the island's foundation. There is more golf per acre here than in any other country—you can play on a different course each day of the week. In addition to renting boats with or without skippers, taking sailing lessons, and chartering yachts, you can waterski or learn to windsurf or parasail. Tennis buffs have 100 courts to choose from.

Sights

Exercising is only the beginning of what there is to do in Bermuda. Among other attractions, you can visit an aquarium and zoo, 17th-century churches and houses, historic forts; relax in gardens and parks; wander through nature reserves; and explore underground caves and a replica of a ship built by the early settlers. In the spring, the agricultural exhibition at the Botanical Gardens celebrates the island's farmers. Many of them are Portuguese immigrants or descendants of those who came from the Azores to fill agricultural jobs in the 1850s.

Bermuda's natural beauty is one of the most pleasing sights of all, from the roads decorated with hibiscus, bougainvillea, oleander, and morning glory to the rosy beaches with striking rock formations. Bermudians often dare visitors to find two leaves that are alike on the brown and burgundy "match-me-if-you-can" plants that are all over the island. Wispy casuarina trees that lean with the breeze are also everywhere. Since the climate is subtropical, the island has few indigenous palms. If you are visiting in the spring, amid the profusion of greenery, Easter lilies, and other flowers, you may notice trees with rust-colored autumnal leaves. These are Fiddlewoods, which got a bit confused after being uprooted from their Australian home to be grown for fuel in Bermuda. Here their leaves turn burnt orange and drop off in the spring instead of the fall, but by July they are green again.

If your itinerary includes more than basking in the sun, one of the first things you should do is get a *Handy Reference Map*, available at hotels or offices of the Visitors' Service Bureau. *Bermuda Runners' Map* and *The Bermuda Railway Trail Guide* will help joggers, walkers, and cyclists choose scenic routes.

There are no cars for rent here, and it's just as well, because the other modes of transportation are more fun. Among visitors and many Bermudians, the most popular way of getting from one place to another is by moped, which you can rent by the day or the week. Pedal bikes are also available for rent. As in Britain, driving is on the left. The island's public buses will take you almost anywhere, and you ride with Bermudians going about their daily business. Many visitors enjoy seeing the sights from horse-drawn carriages. Through most hotels or the Visitors' Service Bureau, you can arrange to take bus tours. Look for taxis with blue flags on their hoods, because the drivers are qualified tour guides who will show you the island for about $16 an hour for up to four passengers.

At night you can dance at clubs and discotheques, listen to calypso, reggae, classical, or rock music, or see a local play or revue.

The Bermudians

In culture and appearance, Bermuda bears less resemblance to its Caribbean neighbors than The Bahamas does. At first glance, this colony of nearly 60,000 people may seem like a small, warm version of its mother country. Hotels and restaurants serve afternoon tea; people play darts in pubs over English ale; barristers wear powdered wigs; and cricket and football (soccer) are national pastimes. Bermuda shorts, still worn by males from waiter to bobby (policeman), were introduced by the British military at the turn of the century.

However, on closer look the island proves to be a colorful combination of a variety of other cultures as well. The often more subtle influences of the non-British heritage can be seen in the gombey, calypso, and reggae music, with roots in Africa and the West Indies; the popularity of St. Paul's African Methodist Episcopal Church; the hoppin' john (black eyed peas and rice) also eaten by black Americans, the Portuguese red bean soup common on restaurant menus; and streets like Silk Alley and Barber's Alley, named in honor of slaves and freed blacks.

More than 60% of the population is comprised of descendants of slaves, most of whom were brought not directly from Africa, but from America and the West Indies. The rest of the people are of European background, including, most recently, Portuguese immigrants from the Azores. A small portion of the population is made up of descendants of Native Americans brought to Bermuda as indentured servants.

If you listen closely, you'll notice that Bermudians, like Bahamians, often pronounce their "w"s as "v"s—and "wice wersa." "Vhat you know?" is a common greeting and you may be asked if you are enjoying your "wacation." This pronunciation is thought to have come from 18th- and 19th-century England and America. Like the British, Bermudians often punctuate their sentences with "mate." They would say that this is "different to" (not "different from") the way Bahamians, who sprinkle many conversations with "mahn," speak. To find out more about Bermudian lingo, pick up *Bermewjan Verds,* a booklet sold throughout the island.

For an inside look at Bermudian life, take part in the Houses and Gardens tours conducted each spring. Hosts will point out traditional architectural characteristics and give you significant historical information. The pastel-colored, white-roofed houses throughout the island are identified by names, not numbers. "Wreck Hill House," "Pumpkin Patch", and even "Bacardi on the Rocks" are just a few. Buildings are constructed of limestone, coral, cement blocks, and Bermuda cedar. The stair-step roofs catch rainwater, which is stored in underground tanks. Next to some of the older homes, you will see miniature houses with pyramid-shaped roofs topped with balls. These are butteries, or cooling houses, the ancestors of refrigerators. The architecture of other buildings ranges from the simplicity of whitewashed St. Peter's Church to the Florentine detail of the Cabinet Building.

Making Merry

Traditions, whether solemn or filled with happy abandon, live long in Bermuda. Gombey dancers bounce through the streets on New Year's Day, Good Friday, Easter, Labour Day, Boxing Day (December 26), and during Heritage Month (May) and Rendezvous Time (mid-November through March). Called goombay in The Bahamas, this type of music and dance began during slavery. "Gombey" is a Bantu word meaning both rhythm and goatskin drum. The dancers' acrobatic leaps, turns, and high kicks are West African in origin. The colorful, elaborate fringed costumes are decorated with tassels, ribbons, beads, and bits of mirrors, and the feathered headdresses are sometimes four feet high. Wearing masks of distorted faces is said to have begun in order to hide the identities of the dancers. This was because the dances often represented antislavery protests. The American Indian influence was more apparent at the time when folk dramas were common, and dancers carried tomahawks and bows and arrows. Now called the captain, the "leading Indian" would go ahead of the group to chalk Indian symbols in front of homes that were receptive to the dancers. Today, crowds still follow the dancers and fall into the rhythm as they make their way around the island.

On Good Friday, gombey dancers head for Horseshoe Bay beach. This is where the most popular of the island's many kite day festivals is held. The frame of the traditional kite flown on Good Friday forms a cross, representing the one used to crucify Christ. This kite is shaped like a long, narrow diamond. Christ's rise into heaven on Easter was once symbolized by the kite's climb into the sky. The sizes and shapes of kites have become increasingly whimsical and diverse over the years and much of the religious significance is history. Nowadays, fluttering overhead will be every kind of kite from the hexagonal tissue-paper variety (considered *real* kites by purists) to the nylon ones shaped like fish, birds, sting rays, and bats. Some are a mere two or three feet wide while others span 15 feet. The sound you'll hear does not come from some strange bird, but from "hummers"—streamers that make a loud noise as the kites dip and swirl in the wind.

It has been said that more Bermudians living abroad return home for Cup Match than for Christmas. The two days in July during which these championship cricket games between St. George's and Somerset take place are public holidays. The annual event began at the turn of the century to commemorate both Sir George Somers (who stumbled upon Bermuda in 1609) and the abolition of slavery. Picture the World Series in the middle of a Caribbean carnival, and you'll have an idea of what the festivities are like. To enjoy Cup Match, you need not know a thing about cricket. Simply be prepared for serious socializing. At food stalls, the aromas of mussel pie, fish chowder, peas and rice, and other local favorites all vie for your attention. Reggae and calypso will have you moving to the beat. If you're ready to win some or lose some, take a chance with the board game called Crown and Anchor (also known as "the Stock Market"). Only during cricket championships is gambling legal in Bermuda.

Wining and Dining

Not only can you take part in traditions in Bermuda, but you can also taste them. Hot cross buns are served on Easter Sunday. Some people consider codfish with potatoes and bananas the trademark of a truly Bermudian breakfast. And cassava pie finds its way onto many a table at Christmas (the early English settlers began preparing this cassava-root crust stuffed with poultry, pork, and eggs). Bermudian specialties you can try during the rest of the year include Bermuda lobster (similar to crayfish), mussel pie, conch (pronounced "conk") fritters or stew, shark hash on toast, turtle steak, pumpkin, fish chowder spiced with black rum and sherry peppers, and Portuguese red bean soup. Wash it all down with ginger beer. Popular mixed drinks are rum swizzles (fruity concoctions that sneak up on you) and dark and stormies (made with black rum and ginger beer).

The Parishes

Bermuda's nine parishes—Sandys, Southampton, Warwick, Paget, Pembroke, Devonshire, Smith's, Hamilton, and St. George's—were originally eight districts called tribes, with St. George's being common land. The many tribe roads, the narrow rustic lanes that cross the island from north to south, are remnants of the past. Note that the old town of St. George's, the original capital, is in St. George's Parish, but the present capital, Hamilton, is in Pembroke Parish (not Hamilton Parish).

The 17th-century town of St. George's, which has changed little since it was founded in 1612, provides an exciting contrast to the more modern, bustling city of Hamilton. Each parish has a personality all its own. No matter where you decide to stay, the rest of Bermuda is only a quick ride away. Accommodations throughout the island range from self-contained resorts to small guest houses. You can even rent a room, including breakfast, in a private home. (Arrangements for this are made before arrival by contacting the Visitors' Service Bureau, Front Street, Hamilton.) Many visitors save money by staying in housekeeping apartments. Most accommodations have pools, and all are either on a beach or close by.

The Early Days

It is difficult to imagine that Bermuda was once known as the "Isles of Devils" and avoided with a passion by sailors. But long before the first settlers arrived, this remote, uninhabited cluster of islands surrounded by dangerous reefs meant disaster for ships. The mistakes of navigators can be seen in the wrecks of Spanish galleons and British vessels that have been eroding on the ocean floor for centuries. Even Shakespeare, in *The Tempest,* wrote about "the still vex't Bermoothes."

A Spanish voyager, Juan de Bermudez, is the first person on record to have come upon what is now Bermuda, where his ship was wrecked in 1503. But Spain, more concerned with seeking gold, did not claim the islands. The reefs, rocks, and inlets permitted pirates to lure trade ships and exploring vessels to wreckage. For a long period, this was the center of pirate activity.

When a later Spanish galleon struck rocks near these islands, Captain Diego Ramirez sent a small boat ashore in search of fresh water. Birds chattering in the dark of night sounded like creatures saying *"Diselo, diselo,"* Spanish for "Tell 'em, tell 'em." The frightened crew remembered tales of these devil-inhabited islands and thought that the "voices" meant that the devil was trying to tell them something. They were convinced of this when they suddenly found the boat's rudder broken. The captain ordered Venturilla, the first known black man to reach Bermuda, to go ashore to cut a piece of wood for a new rudder.

Once ashore and descended upon by flapping birds, Venturilla called out for help. When his rescuers reached him, they soon discovered that the creatures were not only birds, but also good to eat.

In 1609, the *Sea Venture,* the flagship of a fleet on its way to the Jamestown Colony from England, ran aground at what is now St. Catherine's Point in St. George's. Sir George Somers, the admiral, and Sir Thomas Gates, the lieutenant governor of Virginia, came safely ashore along with nearly 150 other men, women, and children. Here, Admiral Somers and the crew built two ships from the wreckage of their vessel. The larger of the two was christened the *Deliverance* and the voyage continued to Jamestown, where all but one of the other ships had landed.

Gates and Somers found the colony in bad shape, with many people starving. Almost a year after the wreck of the *Sea Venture,* Somers returned to Bermuda to get fish, fowl, and hogs to take back to Virginia. But Somers died before leaving Bermuda this time. His heart was buried near the garden he had planted when he was first on the island and his body was taken back to England.

Two years later another group of settlers arrived from England and in 1620 British colonial government was formally installed through the chartered company. A governor was appointed and the colony was ruled from overseas. After 1684 the colony became self-governing and is now the oldest self-governing British colony in existence. Founded in 1612, St. George remained Bermuda's capital until 1815, when the seat of government was moved to the centrally located city of Hamilton in Pembroke Parish. In 1834 slavery was abolished.

Government

Similar to that of Westminster, Bermuda's government is made up of a governor appointed by the Queen; the Cabinet headed by the premier; the Senate, or upper House of Parliament; and the House of Assembly, or lower House. All members of the Cabinet are appointed by the governor, who acts on the recommendations of the Premier, an elected official. The House, an elected body, is comprised of 40 members of parliament. The 11-member Senate is responsible for approving bills passed by the House. English law, apparent in the traditional wigs and robes of the justices, guides the Supreme Court, headed by a Chief Justice. An Appeals Court and two lower courts are also part of the judicial system.

Economy

The standard of living is high in this country that has no personal income tax, no national debt, and virtually no unemployment. Unfortunately, prices are also high, but a visit here can be worth every penny.

Before the economy settled comfortably into tourism, at various times whaling, shipbuilding, privateering, and farming thrived. At the end of the 19th century, farming flourished, especially where the Bermuda onion was concerned. Onions were exported to New York in great numbers, and Bermudians acquired the nickname "Onions." When U.S. farmers learned how to simulate Bermuda's farming conditions, the island's export onion market collapsed.

With the steamship at the turn of the century came the healthy development of tourism, which now accounts for the largest portion of the economy. The Princess Hotel, one of the island's first, was named in honor of Princess Louise, the daughter of Queen Victoria. According to one story, when the Princess was out on one of her frequent walks during a visit to Bermuda, she stopped at a cottage to ask for a drink of water. The woman of the house said she was too busy to get it because she was ironing a blouse for her trip to St. George to see the Princess. The Princess offered to iron the blouse while the woman went to get the water. After drinking it and telling her host who she was, Princess Louise finished ironing the blouse.

THINGS TO KNOW

COSTS • Although the cost of living in Bermuda is high, you will certainly get your money's worth. Accommodations range from resort hotels to rooms in private homes. In between there are small hotels, guest houses, cottage colonies, and housekeeping apartments. Most large hotels and cottage colonies have MAP rates (where the price of the room includes breakfast and dinner). Some hotels offer a choice of MAP or BP (full breakfast). During the high season (summer), cottage colonies tend to require MAP, and some also require a minimum number of nights' stay. Most of the smaller hotels offer MAP, BP, and EP (room only). Most guest houses offer EP, BP, and CP (light breakfast).

In season, from March through November, the approximate cost (per person) of a double room in a large hotel is $90–230 a night MAP. In a small hotel it is $60–140 MAP. A housekeeping apartment for two will cost $25–85 per person, per night EP. A room in a private home, including breakfast and a shared bath, is about $30 per person. During the rest of the year, when temperatures are cooler, prices are considerably lower. A service charge of about 10% will be added to the cost of your room to cover room and board tips. Some smaller hotels add an energy surcharge. All room rates are subject to a 6% government tax. *Note that most accommodations do not accept credit cards.*

In conjunction with hotels, **Pan Am** and other airlines offer money-saving packages throughout the year. Some hotels gear packages to visitors with special interests, such as tennis players, golfers, honeymooners, and families.

Riding convenient public buses or renting mopeds by the week instead of the day will also save you money. The best shopping buys are in European imports, such as china and woolens. Film is expensive, so it is best to take enough for the whole trip. There are several photo processing shops in Hamilton that will develop your film the same day or within 24 hours. Liquor prices tend to be somewhat lower than in most areas of the U.S.

Golf course and tennis court fees are reasonable, and most beaches are public. Some restaurants featuring Bermudian cuisine, particularly those emphasizing homestyle cooking, are less expensive than other restaurants.

TRAVELING WITH CHILDREN • Airlines offer discounts for children, from 10% to 75%, depending on the age of the child. Those under age two fly free.

Some accommodations have age restrictions on accepting children. Consult the **Hotel Quick-Reference Charts** or your travel agent for information about specific accommodations. Many of the larger hotels have special facilities for children, such as cribs and high chairs, as well as babysitters. They also have reduced rates for children, and offer family packages. During the summer, the Grotto Bay Hotel hosts a "day camp" for children of guests. Supervised children's programs are also run by Elbow Beach, the Sonesta, and the Southampton Princess in the summer.

There are golf and tennis tournaments for vacationers under age 18. Contact the Bermuda Golf Association, P.O. Box HM 433, Hamilton, HM BX Bermuda, or the Bermuda Lawn Tennis Association, P.O. Box HM 341, Hamilton, HM BX Bermuda.

Lee Bow Riding Centre caters to horseback riders who are age 18 and under.

The legal drinking age is 18.

TRAVEL FOR THE HANDICAPPED • Although facilities for the handicapped are not extensive in Bermuda, some accommodations, including several of the larger hotels, are well equipped for those confined to wheelchairs. Senior citizens and handicapped people who will need special assistance should contact, in advance, the accommodation where they plan to stay. For more information, get a free copy of *The Access*

Guide to Bermuda for the Handicapped Traveller from a Department of Tourism office or contact the Society for the Advancement of Travel for the Handicapped, P.O. Box HM 449, Hamilton, HM BX Bermuda.

SPECIAL SERVICES • Don't worry about falling off your diet: For up-to-date information about **Weight Watchers** meetings in Bermuda, call (212) 896-9800.

You can get information about **Alcoholics Anonymous** meetings by contacting Bermuda Intergroup, P.O. Box WK 178, Warwick, WK BX Bermuda; Tel: 295-1537.

WHEN TO GO **Weather** • The warmest season is from May through October, the official beach season. The rest of the year—when the weather can vary daily from pleasantly cool to pleasantly warm—is perfect for tennis, golf, and occasional outdoor swimming. (Some hotels and guest houses close for a few weeks in November, December, and January.) Bermuda has no rainy season and rainfall is usually brief.

Average Daily Temperatures

	Fahrenheit	Centigrade
January	68°	20°
February	67°	19°
March	68°	20°
April	71°	22°
May	75°	23°
June	80°	27°
July	85°	29°
August	86°	30°
September	84°	29°
October	79°	26°
November	74°	23°
December	70°	21°

Holidays and Special Events • Rendezvous Time, when the Department of Tourism sponsors many activities to attract visitors during the cooler weather, lasts from about mid-November through March. Among other activities, you can watch football (soccer) or rugby matches, go on a walking tour of the old town of St. George's, or see kilted bagpipers, drummers, and dancers perform the Skirling Ceremony at Fort Hamilton. The annual Bermuda Festival of the Performing Arts takes place in January and February. Performances, held either at the Ruth Seaton James Auditorium in Devonshire or the City Hall Theatre in Hamilton, feature opera, ballet, chamber music, jazz, and drama. This year's program includes cellist Lynn Harrell; pianist Emanuel Ax;

the Modern Jazz Quartet; the Summer Opera; the Hubbard Street Dancers; the West End Players in an English comedy; and the Negro Ensemble Company in *From the Mississippi Delta*. On February 6, *The Fantasticks*, New York's longest running off-Broadway show ever, will be performed as a benefit for Bermuda's proposed Cultural Centre.

Boxing Day (December 26) and New Year's Day signal the appearance of gombey dancers beating goatskin drums. Note that since Rendezvous Time is the off season, some hotels may have fewer daily activities and less frequent nightly entertainment.

During Bermuda College Weeks, in March and April, scores of moped-riding visiting students take part in weekly activities in their honor. Once a month, from April through October, except August, the Bermuda Regiment performs the Beating Retreat Ceremony on Front Street in the city of Hamilton, in St. George's, and at the Dockyard. Each year on Good Friday, the skies are ablaze with hundreds of boldly colored kites during the Bermuda Kite Festival. To join the fun, just buy a kite or bring your own. In the Peppercorn Ceremony in April, the governor collects the annual rent of one peppercorn for the use of the Old State House in St. George's. The whole island looks forward to the festivities during Cup Match each July, when cricket teams from the west and the east battle each other for the championship.

The following list of these and other events will help you decide when to visit. (Also see Making Merry, p. 10):

Bermuda Festival	January 11–February 25
Bermuda International Marathon and 10 Kilometre Race	January 14 and 15
Regional Bridge Tournament	January 28–February 5
Bermuda Open Chess Championship	end of January
Bermuda Valentine's Mixed Golf Foursome	February 12–18
Annual Bermuda Invitation Rendezvous Bowling Tournament	February 17–20
Festival for the Advancement of the Performing Arts	February 17–24
National Trust Week (includes Children's Day at Spittal Pond)	mid-February
Annual Sandys Rotary Club Invitational Golf Classic	mid-February
"Woman '88" Conference	end of February
International Championship Dog Show	March 8–12

18 · · · BERMUDA

Annual Bermuda Square and Round Dance Festival	March
Harvard Hasty Pudding Show	March
Bermuda College Weeks	mid-March to mid-April
Open Houses and Gardens Tours	mid-March to April
Beating Retreat Ceremony	April through October (except August)
Invitational International Race Week	April and May
Palm Sunday Walk	March 19
Bermuda Kite Festival	Good Friday
Peppercorn Ceremony	April
Agricultural Exhibition	April
Bermuda Game Fishing Tournament	Year round
Bermuda Heritage Month	May
Bermuda Day	May 24
Queen's Birthday Parade	June 15
Bermuda Ocean Yacht Race (Newport, RI, to Bermuda)	June (even years)
Blue Water Cruising Race	June (odd years)
Multi-Hull Ocean Yacht Race	June (odd years)
Cup Match (cricket) and Somers Day	July 30 and 31
Third Annual Triathlon*	Fall
Convening of Parliament	November
Remembrance Day Parade	November 11
Invitation Tennis Weeks	November
Rendezvous Time (special off-season events)	November 16–March 31
Bermuda Goodwill Tournament	December
Boxing Day	December 26

Other holidays are New Year's Day, Good Friday, Christmas, and Labour Day.

GETTING THERE BY AIR

From USA	*Via*
New York, Newark, Boston, Chicago	American Airlines
Boston, Atlanta	Delta Airlines

*For current information contact Patrick O'Riordan, 310 Madison Ave., New York, NY 10017, (212) 818–9800, Telex 961310.

New York, Newark, Atlanta, Philadelphia	Eastern Airlines
New York, Washington/ Baltimore	Pan Am
Tampa	British Airways
From CANADA	
Toronto	Air Canada
From UK	
London	British Airways
From OTHER COUNTRIES	
Bahamas, Caribbean, South America	British Airways

Flight time from New York is about 2 hours; from Toronto, about 2½. Transporation by taxi from the airport to your accommodation will range from about $9 if you're staying in St. George's (where the airport is located) to about $30 if you're staying in Sandys, at the far end of the island. Airport limousines (shuttle buses) are less expensive.

GETTING THERE BY SEA • A cruise is a pleasant way to reach Bermuda. Although time spent on the island may be brief, passengers can take full advantage of shipboard pampering, relaxation, and fun. Several lines, departing from New York and Florida, offer 3–7 day cruises to Bermuda with stops for sightseeing and shopping. On board are indoor and outdoor swimming pools, sun bathing decks, exercise rooms, endless dining, and many forms of entertainment. Ships such as the *Nordic Prince* even present Las Vegas–style shows. Since there is no legal gambling in Bermuda, the ships' famed casinos are a real attraction for some travelers when not in port.

While some ships carry several hundred passengers, others have space for more than 1000. Accommodations range from modest to luxurious, with well-appointed rooms and suites. Some lines offer attractive package deals that include air or land transport to the departure point. Others permit children to share staterooms with parents without additional charge. Extras generally include bar service, shore excursions, and on board tipping.

From time to time, the Respiratory Health Association and the Norwalk Hospital Better Breathing Club run an 8-day cruise on the *Bermuda Star* to Hamilton and St. George's for sufferers from diseases such as asthma and emphysema. A physician's referral is needed and sufferers are encouraged to travel with a friend or relative. Pulmonary physicians and nurses are aboard to administer medications, conduct group discussions, and hold breathing and mild physical exercise sessions. For current information on cruises, call the Respiratory Health Association in Paramus, NJ, at (201) 843–4111.

BERMUDA

Most ships dock at Hamilton, the capital. Quieter St. George's, the old capital, and the Dockyard are ports for some. These brilliant, sun-drenched ships gleaming at the foot of Hamilton's Front Street or anchored out in St. George's harbor or at the Dockyard make a thrilling sight.

Because cruise schedules change frequently from year to year and season to season, check with the cruise line or a travel agent for current sailing times, number of days, and the particular ships making the trips you want. Following are lines that currently provide cruises to Bermuda:

Cruise Line	Destination	No. Passengers	Facilities	From
Bermuda Star Line 1086 Teaneck Road Teaneck, NJ 07666 (800) 237-5361				
Bermuda Star	St. George's Hamilton	713	OP, C	New York
The Queen of Bermuda	St. George's Hamilton	860	P, C	New York
Chandris Fantasy Cruises 900 Third Avenue New York, NY 10022 (212) 750-0044, (800) 223-0848				
Amerikanis	St. George's	650	2 OP, C	New York
Galileo	Hamilton St. George's	1100	OP, C	Philadelphia, Wilmington, NC
Cunard Line 555 Fifth Avenue New York, NY 10017 (212) 661-7777, (800) 221-4770				
Sagafjord	Hamilton	589	OP, IP, C	Ft. Lauderdale
Royal Caribbean Cruise Line 903 South America Way Miami, FL 33132 (305) 379-2601				
Nordic Prince	Hamilton St. George's	1038	OP, C	New York

Key
IP Indoor Pool
OP Outdoor Pool
C   Casino
S   Spa

ENTRY AND DEPARTURE REQUIREMENTS • Travel Documents
• All visitors must have a return or onward ticket upon arrival in Bermuda. They must also have identification that will permit them to return home or visit another country. Passports are not necessary for U.S. and Canadian citizens. U.S. citizens must have *one* of the following documents: a valid or expired passport, a birth certificate, a U.S. reentry permit, a U.S. voter's registration card with bearer's signature, a U.S. naturalization certificate, or a U.S. alien registration card. Canadian citizens must have *one* of the following items: a passport, a birth certificate, or a certification of citizenship.

Smallpox vaccination certificates are required only from visitors who, within the preceding 14 days, have been in a country that is infected.

Departure Tax • A $10 tax will be collected from each adult passenger at Bermuda Airport upon departure. Children under age 12 pay $5, and those under age 2 are exempt. A $30 tax is included in the price of each cruise ship ticket.

Length of Stay • All visitors may remain in Bermuda for up to three weeks from arrival. You can obtain permission to stay longer through immigration officials at the Bermuda Airport upon arrival. To stay indefinitely, you must apply in advance to the Chief Immigration Officer, Ministry of Home Affairs, P.O. Box HM 1364, Hamilton HM FX, Bermuda.

Pets • Small well-behaved dogs and other pets are permitted at some hotels and guest houses. Permission must be obtained in advance. You will also need to obtain a permit in advance from the Department of Agriculture, P.O. Box HM 834, Hamilton HM CX, Bermuda. While airlines can carry pets as cargo or excess baggage, animals are not allowed on cruise ships. Refer to the **Hotel Quick Reference Charts** to see which hotels accept pets.

Customs • Entry—Clothing and articles for personal use, such as sports equipment and cameras, may be taken in duty free. Also duty free are 50 cigars, 200 cigarettes, 1 pound (.454 kgs) tobacco; 1 quart (1.137 litres) hard liquor; 1 quart (1.137 litres) wine; and 20 pounds of meat. Other foodstuffs may be dutiable at 5% to 20% of their value. All imports may be inspected upon arrival. Visitors may claim a $25 duty-free gift allowance.

Departure—The merchandise visitors can take back duty free is as follows. U.S. Citizens: $400 after 48 hours and every 30 days. Canadians: $100 after 48 hours and once every three calendar months, or $300 after seven days once every calendar year. U.K. citizens: £28

To take plants out, you must have prior permission from your own country. You should also check your state or country's liquor and tobacco laws before going to Bermuda.

U.S. Customs preclearance is available in Bermuda for all scheduled flights. All passengers going to the U.S. are required to fill out written declaration forms before clearing U.S. Customs in Bermuda. All Bermudian hotels, travel agencies, and airline offices provide these forms.

The duty you pay on items beyond your duty-free allowance is reasonable.

Drugs and Firearms • Importation of, possession of, or dealing with illegal drugs (including marijuana) is an offense punishable with fines up to $5,000 or three years in prison, or both. Customs inspectors may conduct body searches at their discretion.

No firearm, part of a firearm, or ammunition may be taken into Bermuda without a license granted by the Commissioner of Police. Permits will only be granted to rifle club members attending sports meetings in Bermuda.

Spearguns and similar dangerous weapons are considered firearms. Antique weapons, at least 100 years old, may be imported if the visitor can prove that they are antique. Imprisonment or heavy fines may be the consequences of importing firearms or ammunition without a license.

BEING THERE • **Language** • The language of Bermuda is English, accented with British, American, and to a lesser degree, West Indian influences. Bermudians, like Bahamians, are known for interchanging "v"s with "w"s so that "Where were you?" is pronounced "Vhere vere you?" This is thought to date back to 18th-century England and America.

Spending Money • The Bermudian dollar (BD$) is divided into 100 cents and is pegged to the U.S. dollar on an equal basis. Before 1972 it was pegged to the pound sterling. U.S. currency is widely accepted at hotels, restaurants, and stores. You will often get a combination of U.S. and Bermudian bills and coins in your change. U.S. travelers checks are accepted everywhere. Credit cards are accepted in almost all restaurants and stores, as well as some hotels. Canadian currency is accepted but it may be discounted. Exchange rates for Canadian, U.K., and other currency are subject to daily fluctuations. An **American Express** office is on Bermudiana Road, near Front Street.

Tipping—a 10% to 15% gratuity covering room, board (if board is included in the price of the room), and porter service will be added to most accommodation bills. When tips are not included, the accepted amount for restaurants and other services is 15%.

Business Hours • Stores and offices are open from 9 a.m. to 5 p.m., except in Hamilton from May through Labour Day, when many shops remain open until 9 p.m. on Wednesdays. Some of the smaller shops, such as those in hotels, close for lunch. Banks are open from

9:30 a.m. to 3:00 p.m. Monday through Friday and reopen on Fridays from 4:30 to 5:30 p.m.

Dress • Women are asked not to wear short shorts, bathing suits, bikini tops, or curlers in the street or in dining rooms, cocktail lounges, or lobbies of hotels. Men are requested to wear shirts when not on the beach or by the pool. Bare feet and short shorts are only acceptable in swim areas. Conservative sportswear is acceptable everywhere. The larger hotels have more formal dress codes than guest houses or small hotels. Dress requirements are more formal in the summer season (from Mar. through Nov.) than at other times of the year. In season, men are requested to wear jackets and ties at night. During the winter season, fall clothes will be necessary, including a lightweight coat or jacket.

Getting Around • Be sure to get a *Handy Reference Map* and public transport schedule from your hotel or a Visitors' Service Bureau office. There are no cars for rent in Bermuda, but transportation is efficient and enjoyable. Taxis or shuttle buses will take you to and from the airport. The old railroad right-of-way that runs through the island is a popular route for joggers and cyclists (see *The Bermuda Railway Trail Guide*). With the onset of cars in the late '40s, Bermuda's train was sold to British Guiana (now Guyana).

By Cycle: Motor-assisted cycles, or mopeds, are the most popular form of transportation. They can be rented (along with pedal bikes) at hotels and at less expensive independent cycle shops around the island. Mopeds begin at about $16 a day (or less if rented for several days). No driver's license is required, but moped drivers must be at least 16 years old. (You may need to leave a driver's license or a credit card as a deposit.) At all times, drivers are required by law to wear the helmets given when the moped is rented. Gas stations are open from 7 a.m. to 7 p.m., Mon. through Sat., with limited hours on Sun. and holidays. If you've never ridden before, don't worry. You'll have as much time as you need to practice in an open area before hitting the road. *Driving is on the left-hand side of the road, and the speed limit is 35 kilometers (20 miles) per hour.*

By Bus: Bermuda's pink buses are another convenient, inexpensive way to get around. At hotels and Visitors' Service Bureau offices, you can pick up the public transport schedule, which includes ferries. Bus fares range from 75¢ to $2 for adults, depending on the distance, and exact change in coins is required. Children aged 3–13 pay 50¢ and those under 3 ride free. At the Washington Street Terminal in the city of Hamilton, you can buy money-saving books of tickets. Bus stops are marked by green-and-white-striped poles.

By Taxi: All cars are compact. Taxis carry a maximum of four passengers at a time. Rates are $2.40 for the first mile and $1.20 for each additional mile. Between midnight and 6 a.m., a 25% surcharge is added to the fare. At night, be prepared to wait for a taxi, even when you call one. From the airport to Sandys, the parish farthest away, a taxi should cost from about $30 to about $35. To the city of Hamilton, in the middle of the island, it should cost about $16. To accommodations in St. George's, the parish where Bermuda's Airport, the Civil Air Terminal, is located, the fare will range from $10 to $12.

For about $16 an hour, up to four people can take a sightseeing tour in a taxi with a blue flag on its hood. The flag indicates that the driver is a qualified tour guide. Whenever you are riding blue-flagged taxis to and from hotels and restaurants, take the opportunity to ask the driver questions about the sights you are passing.

By Ferry: Ferries take scenic routes through Hamilton Harbour and Great Sound, stopping at the city of Hamilton, and Paget, Warwick, and Sandys parishes. The fare from Hamilton to Paget and Warwick is $1, and $2 from Hamilton to Sandys (often called Somerset by Bermudians). On the ferries between Somerset and Hamilton, if you arrive early enough and there is room, you can take your moped along for $2 extra. Pedal bikes ride for free. All cyclists must disembark at the first stop. You can pick up public transport schedules at hotels and Visitors' Service Bureau offices.

By Horse-Drawn Carriage: Particularly in the summer season (from March through Nov.) you will see horse-drawn carriages on Front Street in Hamilton. Some hotels will make arrangements for their guests. The cost ranges from about $7.50 to $10 per half hour.

Time • Bermuda is one hour later than Eastern Standard Time. As in the United States, Daylight Saving Time is in effect beginning in April and ending in October.

Mail • International postal service from Bermuda is efficient and airmail leaves and arrives daily. A 24-hour cable service is available, with night letter and full rates as well as an express mail service by Island Courier.

Telephones • When making calls from most public phones, be sure to have your coins ready to be dropped in as soon as (and only after) you've dialed and someone has answered.

Electricity • Electricity is 110 volts, 60 cycles A.C., so North American appliances can be used. Those from most other regions will need adapters.

Medical Concerns • Tap water in Bermuda is filtered and therefore perfectly safe to drink. Hotels and guest houses will arrange visits to doctors and dentists, if necessary. All dentists and physicians are private and fees are comparable to those in the U.S. King Edward VII Hospital is Bermuda's general hospital and it has 24-hour emergency facilities.

Newspapers • *The Royal Gazette* is Bermuda's daily paper. *The*

Mid-Ocean News and the *Bermuda Sun* are weekend papers published on Fridays. *Bermuda Times* is a monthly paper.

Visitor Information • The Bermuda Department of Tourism is located at Global House, 43 Church Street in Hamilton. The mailing address is P.O. Box HM 465, Hamilton, HM 12 Bermuda. It produces helpful free brochures, such as the *Handy Reference Map* and the *Sportsman's Guide*. *This Week in Bermuda* and *Preview of Bermuda* are other free brochures that you can pick up at hotels or stores. The Department of Tourism also has offices in the following locations:

New York
310 Madison Avenue
New York, NY 10017
USA (800) 223-6106 or
(212) 818-9800

Boston
44 School Street, Suite 1010
Boston, MA 02108
USA (617) 742-0405

Atlanta
235 Peachtree Street, N.E.
Atlanta, GA 30303
USA (404) 524-1541

Chicago
150 N. Wacker Drive
Chicago, IL 60606
USA (312) 782-5486

Toronto
1200 Bay Street
Toronto, Ontario
Canada M5R 2A5
(800) 387-1304

Los Angeles
John A. Tetley, Inc.
Suite 601, 3075 Wilshire Blvd.
Los Angeles, CA 90010
(213) 388-1151

The Visitors' Service Bureau is located at the Ferry Dock in Hamilton, and has offices in Bermuda Airport, King's Square in St. George's, and Sandys Parish. The larger hotels have social desks where sightseeing trips and tours are arranged.

Bookstores have many books by international authors as well as by Bermudians about all aspects of the country's life.

Tune into radio station VSB 1160 for tips on island activities and special events, general information about Bermuda, and local music.

WHAT TO SEE AND DO

ATTRACTIONS AT A GLANCE

BNT—A Bermuda National Trust property

	Parish	*Page*
Art Galleries		
Bermuda Arts Centre at Dockyard	Sandys	32
Bridge House	Town of St. George's	63
Bermuda Society of Arts	City of Hamilton, Pembroke	43
Churches		
*The Cathedral of the Most Holy Trinity (Bermuda Cathedral)	City of Hamilton, Pembroke	43
Cobbs Hill Wesleyan Methodist Church	Warwick	36
Old Devonshire Church	Devonshire	48
The Old Rectory (BNT)	Town of St. George's	61
St. James's Church	Sandys	33
*St. Peter's Church	Town of St. George's	61
St. Theresa's Cathedral	City of Hamilton, Pembroke	44
The Unfinished Church	St. George's	62
Forts		
*Fort Hamilton	Pembroke	46
*Fort St. Catherine	St. George's	64
Fort Scaur	Sandys	33
Gates Fort	St. George's	64
Gardens, Parks, and Nature Reserves		
*Admiralty House Park	Pembroke	46
*Botanical Gardens	Paget	38
Edmund Gibbons Nature Reserve	Devonshire	48

Gilbert Nature Reserve (BNT)   Sandys
Gladys Morrel Nature Reserve (BNT)   Sandys
North Nature Reserve (BNT)   Smith's
Paget Marsh (BNT)   Paget
*Palm Grove Garden   Devonshire
*Par-La-Ville Gardens   City of Hamilton,
                                        Pembroke

Scaur Lodge Property (BNT)   Sandys
Somers Gardens   Town of St. George's
Spittal Pond (BNT)   Smith's
Victoria Park   City of Hamilton,
                                        Pembroke

Government Buildings
City Hall   City of Hamilton,
                                        Pembroke

Old State House   Town of St. George's
*Sessions House   City of Hamilton,
                                        Pembroke

*The Cabinet Building   City of Hamilton,
                                        Pembroke

Town Hall   Town of St. George's

Historical Sights
The Bank of Bermuda Ltd. Coin   City of Hamilton,
  Collection   Pembroke
"Bermuda Journey" Show   St. George's
Black Watch Pass and Well   Pembroke
Carter House   St. George's
*Deliverance   Town of St. George's
Devonshire Dock   Devonshire
Featherbed Alley Print Shop   Town of St. George's
*Gibbs Hill Lighthouse   Southampton
*King's Square   Town of St. George's
Old State House   Town of St. George's
Palmetto House   Devonshire
Perot Post Office   City of Hamilton,
                                        Pembroke

Somerset Bridge   Sandys
Spanish Rock   Smith's
Springfield Mansion (BNT)   Sandys
*Tucker House (BNT)   Town of St. George's
*Verdmont Houe (BNT)   Smith's
Tom Moore's Tavern/Walsingham   Hamilton Parish

Libraries

The Bermuda Library	City of Hamilton, Pembroke	44
St. George's Library (BNT)	Town of St. George's	61
Springfield Library (BNT)	Sandys	32

Local Industries

Bermuda Pottery	Hamilton Parish	54
The Bermuda Perfumery	Hamilton Parish	54
Craft Market at Dockyard	Dockyard	32
Glass Blowing Studio	Tee St., Devonshire	48

Museums and Animals

*Bermuda Aquarium, Museum, and Zoo	Hamilton Parish	53
Bermuda Historical Society Museum	City of Hamilton, Pembroke	45
Blue Grotto Dolphin Show	Hamilton Parish	51
*The Carriage Museum	Town of St. George's	61
The Confederate Museum (BNT)	Town of St. George's	58
*The Maritime Museum	Sandys	31
St. George's Historical Society Museum	Town of St. George's	62

Natural Wonders

Cathedral Rocks	Sandys	33
*Crystal Caves	Hamilton Parish	54
Devil's Hole	Smith's	51
Leamington Caves	Hamilton Parish	55
Natural Arches	St. George's	63
Sea Gardens	Sandys	32

THE PARISHES AND THEIR SIGHTS FROM WEST TO EAST

SANDYS

Pronounced "Sands" or simply referred to as Somerset by Bermudians, Sandys is comprised of Ireland Islands north and south, Boaz, Watford, and Somerset islands, and the northeastern tip of the main island. Throughout their history, the people of this parish have stood out from those of the rest of the island, particularly where political opinion is concerned. For instance, while most of Bermuda aided the South during the American Civil War, many people of Sandys supported the North's Union Army. In an ongoing present-day battle between the east and the west, Sandys' cricket team fights it out with the team from St. George's every July during festive Cup Match.

To get here, you can cross the world's smallest drawbridge. Once in Bermuda's westernmost parish, you can visit two nature reserves, an 18th-century parish church, an old plantation with a mansion and slave quarters, a 19th-century fort and a maritime museum. There are two harbors, one with a striking natural coral formation. But one of the most pleasant ways to spend time in Sandys is to stroll or ride through the rural village of Somerset, in the center of the parish.

The 45-minute ferry ride from Hamilton to the Watford Bridge dock is a particularly relaxing and scenic way to reach the village, which is not far from the dock. Late in the afternoon, kids often congregate at the docks in Sandys to dive off the pier or fish. Walking to Somerset, you'll pass a military cemetery and a monument in memory of Bermudians who died of pneumonia in April 1916. In Somerset you can wander along narrow roads bordered by fragrant wild hedges, and admire peaceful bays and pretty houses with well-kept grounds. Some of the stores are branches of those in Hamilton, such as the Irish Linen Shop. Most of the stores here are a distance apart. So, unless you have a cycle, be prepared to do a lot of walking if you plan to do much shopping. The Old Market, which now sells sportswear, souvenirs, and books, was actually once a meat market. Meat hooks still hang and the various rooms have names such as "Feed Store," "Ice House," and "The Stables." For rest and refreshment, you have a choice of several restaurants and pubs, including The Loyalty Inn and Somerset Country Squire.

From the center of the village, a ten-minute walk west along Somerset Road will take you to Springfield and the Gilbert Nature Reserve, an old plantation with part of the mansion now used as a library. You'll come to Dean's Bakery and Simmons Ice Cream Factory and Variety Store on the way. Be sure to stop here if you're in the mood for exceptional rum raisin ice cream.

Bordering one side of the village is Mangrove Bay, named for the trees that line the shore. The beach closest to the center of the village is small, shady, and filled with the sounds of traffic from nearby Mangrove Bay Road. It is, therefore, not nearly as nice as other beaches in the parish or in the rest of Bermuda, but it affords a picturesque view of the cove, speckled with small boats. At Mangrove Bay Wharf, northeast along Mangrove Bay Road, arrange sailing or fishing expeditions or take sightseeing boats out to the reefs to swim or snorkel. Northwest of the wharf is Cambridge Beaches, Bermuda's oldest cottage colony. Long Bay, southwest of the cottage colony, is where you will find the parish's most beautiful beaches. Off Daniel's Head, at the southwest end of Long Bay, is Sea Gardens, the underwater spectacle of marine life on and around a sunken vessel.

The economy of the area north of Somerset Village once thrived on ship-building. The Maritime Museum, at the northernmost tip of Sandys on Ireland Island North, is located in the former Royal Navy Dockyard. You can reach the museum by public bus, cycle, taxi, or ferry. Across from the museum is the Arts Centre at Dockyard, where you'll find the works of local and international artists. After years of speculation, the extensive development of the Dockyard area has begun. Plans are in the works to make this a major cruise port, with exhibits, shops, and restaurants that rival those of St. George's and Hamilton.

South of Somerset Village, on the western side of the island are the attractive parish church of St. James's (next to the Visitors' Service Bureau) and busy Ely's Harbour, which once protected smugglers and traders alike from storms at sea. Wreck Hill and Scaur Lodge Property overlook the harbor, where you can see Cathedral Rocks, an unusual coral formation not far south of the village. On the eastern side of the island, visit the Gladys Morrell Nature Reserve, near Cavello Bay. Then stop for a picnic at Fort Scaur, which sits above Great Sound. Somerset Bridge, which joins Somerset Island to the main island, is so small that you may not notice it if you aren't paying attention when you cross it. Once past the U.S. Naval Air Station Annex, on the peninsula between Great Sound and Little Sound, you will be in Southampton.

Throughout Bermuda, the clearly marked old railway right-of-way is a serene path for jogging or walking. However, if you want to ride a moped or a bicycle along the trail, Sandys and Southampton are the places to do it, since there are no steps or other obstructions. This is also the most scenic part of the trail, which periodically joins the main road. You'll zip by high stone walls, under bridges, past a farm, between trees whose branches almost meet overhead. Views of the ocean, Gibbs Hill Lighthouse, and perhaps a cruise ship add to the beauty of the route.

***The Maritime Museum** • *at the tip of North Ireland Island; tel: 234–1418* • The Maritime Museum is a tribute to the island's 300-year nautical history. It is housed in the former Royal Navy Dockyard, once the British Empire's largest drydock. Slaves, free blacks, and convicts brought from England built the dockyard in the mid-19th century. Many of these workers died during an outbreak of yellow fever. Especially if you approach by ferry, the clock towers are an impressive sight. In sharp contrast to most of the buildings in Bermuda, which are painted pastels, the buildings at Dockyard are the natural beige of limestone. Many more stately Norfolk pines seem to grow here than in other parts of the island.

The public has enjoyed the museum's indoor and outdoor exhibits since the 1975 opening ceremony attended by Queen Elizabeth. Within the buildings that once stored munitions and served as workshops, exhibits tell you about pearl diving, boat building, and whaling. Also on display are memorabilia such as the famous Tucker Treasure, maritime maps, and sailing craft (including the 17-foot skiff in which two young Bermudians sailed some 700 miles to New York in 1935). A mounted copy of a June 19, 1937, *New York Herald Tribune* article announces, "24 Passengers Fly in Clipper to Bermuda" and an advertisement boasts, "Bermuda in Five Hours" from New York. Nearby, the menu from the "Pan American Airways flying boat" is posted. The past few decades may have shaved several hours off air time, but the filet mignon and strawberry sundae served on the inaugural flight sound a whole lot more appetizing than today's standard airborne meals. In the "Keep Yard" you will be watched over by the statue of Neptune, once the figurehead on the HMS *Irresistible,* an old British battleship.

The mansion on a hill overlooking the dockyard is the Commissioner's House, dating from the early 19th century and thought to be the most expensive home ever built on a military base. Unfortunately, this lavish example of period architecture is closed to the public, but there are plans in the works for a 1992 opening to coincide with the 500th anniversary of Columbus's landing. *Museum open daily, 10 a m – 5 p.m. Closed Christmas Day. Admission: adults—$4; children under age 12 and senior citizens—50¢.*

Craft Market • *Building 28, Dockyard, Ireland Island; tel: 234–3208* • Browse through crafts including pottery, paintings on cedar, dolls, and highly detailed miniature furniture, then see the dramatic "Attack on Washington" slide presentation. *Open daily from 11 a.m. to 4 p.m. No admission fee.*

Bermuda Arts Centre • *Dockyard, Ireland Island, Sandys; tel: 234–4280* • The striking exhibits of paintings and the displays of hand-made jewelry change periodically. *Open from 10 a.m. to 4:30 p.m,. Tuesday–Friday and 10 a.m. to 5 p.m. on Saturday and Sunday. Closed on Christmas Day and all of January. Admission: $1 adults; children under 12, students, and senior citizens, 50¢.*

Gladys Morrel Nature Reserve • *off East Shore Road, near Cavello Bay* • In memory of the woman who once owned the land, these two acres of open space were given to the Bermuda National Trust in 1973 by the Sandys Chapter of the Daughters of the Empire. *Open daily. Free admission.*

Sea Gardens • *off Daniel's Head; visits may be arranged through glass-bottom boat, scuba diving, or snorkeling tours (most Sea Gardens tours require reservations)* • Located not in Bermuda, but beneath its turquoise waters, Sea Gardens offers a clear view of the *Vixen*, a coral covered wreck. The vessel, a World War I British gun-boat, was purposely sunk to block the channel. Whether you choose to visit the site by glass bottom boat or on a snorkeling or scuba diving tour, you will see a colorful variety of coral that has found a home on the ship's hull. If you approach the gardens by boat, you'll be greeted by large swarms of angelfish, gray snapper, and chub, which have become accustomed to the dog food fed them by friendly skippers.

Springfield Library/Springfield Mansion • *Middle Road, off Somerset Road, Somerset Village; tel: 234–1980* • The nicest rooms in this well-preserved 17th-century plantation home are now the Somerset branch of the Bermuda Library. Beginning with the old arched Bermuda gateway, the mansion and its surroundings are fascinating from an architectural and historical standpoint. The outbuildings include slave quarters, the original kitchen, and a buttery—a tall shed for refrigeration, built over a stream. *Mansion open Mon. and Wed., 10 a.m.–5 p.m.; Fri. 10 a.m.–5 p.m.; closed from 1–2 p.m. and all holidays. Grounds open daily. Free admission.*

Gilbert Nature Reserve • *Middle Road, off Somerset Road, Somerset Village* • Adjoining the Springfield Library, Gilbert Nature Reserve was once part of the mansion's land. It was named after the family who owned the property from 1700 until 1973, when it was acquired by the Bermuda National Trust and the Bermuda Audubon Society. The reserve is comprised of five acres of unspoiled woodland, open space, and planting land. *Open daily. Free admission.*

St. James's Church • *between Church Valley Road and Somerset Road, near Church Bay* • Massive iron gates and a long road lead to this Anglican parish church, with its glistening needlelike spire and polished cedar doors. While the present structure was built in 1789 to replace a church destroyed by a hurricane, no one is certain when the original church was built. Aisles were added to the new church early in the 19th century; when its spire was struck by lightning 100 years later, the present spire was designed by a local architect. The bright crypts and tombstones that line the long entryway seem surprisingly cheerful. *Open daily, from 10 a.m.–5 p.m.*

Fort Scaur • *Somerset Road, near Somerset Bridge; tel: 234–0908* • On a hill above the coast of the Great Sound, this fort was built under orders from the Duke of Wellington in 1834. You can see the old bunkers, dry moats, and battlements built into the hilltop, and even search for the tunnel that leads to the ocean. Not only does the fort's location afford a view of Ely's Harbour on the other side of Somerset Island, but you can also see the rest of Bermuda (except St. David's, in the easternmost parish of St. George's). Before using the telescope to explore the islands, enjoy lunch at one of the picnic tables on the well-manicured lawns within the walks. When facing the sound, on the north side of the fort, you can see the London Milestone, a rock with "London 3076 Miles," carved into one side and "27th Regiment, R.E., 1906," inscribed on the other. On Thursdays, during Rendezvous Time (mid-November through March), join in a treasure hunt. *Open daily, 10 a.m.–4:30 p.m. Free admission.*

Scaur Lodge Property • This is a picturesque lookout point near the fort but on the other side of Somerset Island, above Ely's Harbour. It also overlooks Scaur Bay and the unusual formation called Cathedral Rocks.

Cathedral Rocks • *near Somerset Bridge* • These medieval arches and pillars are actually a natural coral formation that has been so battered by the sea that it now resembles Gothic architecture. The pink sand and small pools filled with colorful sea creatures make a visit to this spot even more worthwhile. Cathedral Rocks can be reached for picnicking or exploring by a path ¼-mile west of Somerset Bridge.

Somerset Bridge • *between the main island and Somerset Island, east of Cathedral Rocks* • This 17th-century bridge's claim to fame is that it is the smallest drawbridge in the world. The hand-operated draw is only 22 inches wide, just enough space to allow the mast of a sailboat to pass through. The shores connected by the bridge are alive with color from April to August when red, yellow, pink, and white oleanders are in full bloom.

SOUTHAMPTON

Southampton, a narrow strip of land bordered by some of the island's most spectacular beaches, stretches from the U.S. Naval Air Station Annex to Riddell's Bay. Its verdant open spaces and long sandy beaches divided by boulders and secluded coves may seem to be nature at its best. While walking, riding, or jogging along South Shore Road, you will have a wonderful view of the Atlantic shoreline below. The foaming breakers, not too far out to sea, let you know where reefs lie hidden under the blue-green waters. The public beach at Horseshoe Bay is one of Bermuda's most popular, among locals as well as visitors. South shore beaches tend to have larger waves than elsewhere on the island, and many people prefer them to those with calmer waters.

If you tire of Southampton's natural beauty, you can visit hotel shops such as those in the Sonesta Beach Hotel, Bermuda's only major hotel located directly on a beach. (Other resort hotels provide their guests with complimentary bus service to the closest beaches.) Then you can stop for a bite at one of the parish's many good restaurants such as the posh Waterlot Inn run by the Southampton Princess. At Henry VIII Restaurant & Pub (near the Sonesta Beach), waiters are dressed as if they just stepped out of the 16th century. At Tio Pepe (near the Horseshoe Bay beach entrance) the fare ranges from pizza to crab legs.

From the top of Gibbs Hill Lighthouse, the panoramic view takes in almost all of Bermuda. If the climb is not enough exercise, you can play 18 holes of golf on a championship course, the public, government-owned Port Royal Golf Course at the western end of the parish.

When Richard Norwood divided the island in the original 1616 survey, this part of Southampton was considered "overplus" land and was seized by the governor, Daniel Tucker, for his personal use. Although Governor Tucker was forced to give up most of the land when the Bermuda Company shareholders objected, members of the prominent Tucker family continued to live in this area for generations.

The cove near Southampton's border with Sandys is called George's Bay, after one of the governor's descendants. The land on which the

U.S. Naval Air Station Annex is located was formerly known as Tucker's Island. One of the most famous (or infamous) members of this family is Colonel Henry Tucker, who helped steal Bermudian gunpowder for the American colonists during the Revolutionary War. To learn more about the Tuckers and their contributions to Bermudian (and American) history, visit Tucker House in the town of St. George.

***Gibbs Hill Lighthouse** • *off St. Anne's Road; tel: 238-0524* • Before this lighthouse began operating in 1846, many ships were wrecked off the western end of Bermuda on coral reefs extending more than a dozen miles out to sea. One of the only lighthouses in the world made entirely of cast iron, it was constructed in England and shipped in sections to Bermuda where it stands 362 feet above the ocean. Once wound by hand every half hour, the machinery now runs on electricity and is fully automatic. The beam from the 1500-watt bulb can be seen by ships for 40 miles, and by planes flying at altitudes of 10,000 feet, 120 miles away. A 185-step climb to the top is well worth the exercise. From the small circular balcony, you can see almost every major landmark in Bermuda. You will certainly enjoy gazing down at the many-hued blue-green waters that blend into the deep-blue of the expansive Atlantic and surround the curving strip of land dotted with white-roofed houses. In the spring, visitors may even spot migrating whales out past the south shore reefs. *Open daily, 9 a.m.–4:30 p.m. Admission: $1; free for children under age 5.*

WARWICK

If you decide to stay in Warwick, you may find yourself quickly feeling at home. This parish offers a wide selection of housekeeping apartments in residential neighborhoods. There is also a cottage colony, as well as a few hotels and guest houses. Most accommodations have pools, and all are within walking distance of beautiful south shore beaches.

Warwick Long Bay has the longest, straightest, continuous stretch of beach in Bermuda and is known for its pale-pink sand. The beaches in the Longtail Cliffs area are also noted for the sand that is tinted by bits of shells and coral. Like Bermudians, some visitors have discovered that Jobson Cove, with its small secluded beach, is perfect for midnight skinny-dipping. The rugged cliffs overlooking the shoreline add a dramatic touch to a view of the southern coast. Toward the center of the parish is Warwick Pond, one of Bermuda's few inland bodies of water and a home for wild birds. As you wander along roads lined with flowers and thick shrubs, you will notice the contrast between newer, simple houses and larger, more elegant homes, some dating back more than 100 years.

Several Bermuda "firsts" are in this parish, which encompasses the area between Riddell's Bay Golf and Country Club and Stonehole Bay to the west, and Cobbs Hill Road to the east. From Harbour Road, along Warwick's northern shore, you will see Darrell Island to the west, a narrow strip of land with a building in the middle. Bermuda's first airport was once on this island and, during the 1930s, seaplanes bringing passengers from New York landed here. The hangars were used as movie studios during the 1950s before being demolished.

Constructed in 1922, the golf course at Riddell's Bay is the island's oldest. It is private, like Warwick's other course at the Belmont Hotel, so in order to play at either, you will need reservations or the introduction of a member. Some hotels make arrangements for their guests.

Near Longford and Ord roads, across from the Belmont Hotel and Golf Club, Christ Church is the oldest Presbyterian church (1719) in any British colony or dominion. On Morgan Road, just east of the Belmont Hotel, is Warwick Academy, the island's first school, which has been in continuous operation since 1662. Dr. Francis Patton, its best known alumnus, was Princeton University's president from 1888 to 1913.

On Cobbs Hill Road, near Paget, is Cobbs Hill Wesleyan Methodist Church, the one-room chapel planned and built in 1827 by and for slaves and free blacks who had no place to worship.

On Sunday mornings you can have a Bermudian breakfast of codfish and potatoes at Herman's, a popular spot among locals and visitors for lunch and dinner as well. The restaurant, with both indoor and outdoor dining, specializes in Bermudian homestyle cooking and is located on South Shore Road off Dunscombe Road. Down the street from Flavors discotheque and lounge is Godfrey's Bakery, where delicious wheat bread is born.

An especially enjoyable way to get to know the area is to do it on horseback. At Spicelands Riding Centre you can take lessons or rides through wooded trails leading to grassy open spaces and sandy paths by the shore. A home-cooked breakfast is served after the 7 a.m. ride along a deserted beach.

Cobbs Hill Wesleyan Methodist Church • *Cobbs Hill Road* • In the early 19th century, when they were denied places of worship, male and female free blacks and slaves (who were permitted to work only at night during their time off) spent two years building this one-room church. Edward Fraser, a slave brought from Barbados, was responsible not only for rallying fellow blacks, but also for securing the land and supplies. One of the few slaves who had been allowed to be educated, Fraser dedicated his life to helping other black people. He became a

Methodist minister, and shortly after the church was completed in 1827, he was freed. He went to England to advocate the rights of black people, and then served as a missionary in the West Indies. Many of the people who attend the church today are descendants of those who helped build it.

PAGET

Although one of the most populous parishes and with few open spaces, Paget is among the island's most attractive areas. Its north shore faces the city of Hamilton, just across Hamilton Harbour. From three landings on the harbor—Salt Kettle, Hodsdon's, and Lower—ferries go to the city and to Sandys and Warwick parishes. If you're in a car or on a moped at the last roundabout before Hamilton, you might see Johnnie Barnes, dubbed the Unofficial Greeter of Bermuda. He stands here nearly every morning, rain or shine, and waves to passing drivers. Cobbs Hill Road to the west divides Warwick from Paget, which ends just before Berry Hill Road meets Tee Street to the east. The beaches along Paget's stunning south shore are some of Bermuda's most popular.

This parish has the widest variety of all kinds of accommodations, in beautiful locations. Coral Beach and Tennis Club, Horizons and Cottages, and the Elbow Beach Hotel are in one of the most pleasant parts of the south shore. During springtime college weeks, when the island is full of vacationing students from the States, the Elbow Beach Hotel is the center of activities. On the northern shore, smaller hotels and guest houses such as Glencoe and Salt Kettle House have great views of the lively harbor.

In the center of the parish, Paget Marsh is the 18-acre home of some of Bermuda's endangered trees and plants. You can see and smell more lush foliage at the 36-acre Botanical Gardens, one of the favorite stops of visitors to the island. April's grand Agricultural Exhibition, with everything from live pigs and chickens to intricate butter sculpture, is only one of the many events that take place at the gardens during the year.

Winding roads through Paget's rolling hills afford views of luxurious country houses and estates, as well as other parts of the island. Some of the homes are often part of the spring Open Houses and Gardens Tour, such as Inwood, off Middle Road, in the Rural Hill area. It was built in 1650 and expanded in 1700 to form the shape of a cross. This kind of architecture—thought to ward off evil spirits—is typical of the 18th century. Inside are 12 powder rooms, where both men and women once powdered their wigs. On Harbour Road, not far from

Hamilton, is Waterville, an early 18th-century home that now houses the office of the Bermuda National Trust, with local and exotic trees in its garden.

A fine example of Bermuda Georgian architecture is Clermont, built in 1800, on Harbour Road near the Lower Ferry Landing. If the island's first tennis court had not been built on the grounds in 1873, people in the United States might not be playing tennis today. It was because of this court that Mary Outerbridge introduced tennis to the United States; she brought equipment and a book of rules to the Staten Island Cricket Club in 1874.

At the junction of Cobbs Hill and Middle Roads is Fourways Inn, one of Bermuda's most elegant and expensive restaurants, in a former home built in the 1720's. This Georgian-style structure of coral and Bermuda cedar is a delicious place to spend an evening. On the grounds is the island's newest cottage colony, also called Fourways.

Paget Marsh • *Middle Road* • This is the only area in Bermuda where a forest still exists much as it was when settlers first arrived. A mangrove swamp as well as some of the island's most attractive cedar and palmetto trees can be found on these 26 acres, along with other endangered trees and plants. The marsh is owned by the Bermuda National Trust and the Audubon Society. *Free admission. Arrangements to visit must be made by contacting the office of the Bermuda National Trust (tel: 2–6483).*

*Botanical Gardens • *Point Finger Road; tel: 236–5732* • Like an outdoor-living museum, this 36-acre expanse shows off Bermuda's exotic natural beauty. The 15 permanent attractions include the Woodlands, a miniature forest with twisting paths and plants of unusual shapes; the Exotic Plant House, filled with delicate rare specimens; and the Hibiscus Garden, where you can see many of the 150 known varieties of the flower that is native to China. Extra special is the Garden for the Blind, where even the sighted can enjoy the fragrances of lemon mint, spice trees, lavender, and oregano, to name just a few. Don't miss the aviary, which even contains squirrel monkeys in addition to several species of tropical birds. Seasonal displays include a grand agricultural exhibition in April (complete with chickens, pigs, cows, and handicrafts); dog shows in Feb., May, and Nov.; and periodic horse and bird shows. Stop at Tavern on the Green, in the center of the gardens, for Italian food. When there are no government functions scheduled, you can visit Camden House, the official residence of Bermuda's premier, on Tues. and Fri. (Nov.–Mar.) and Tues. and Wed. (the rest of the year), from noon to 2 p.m. You may ride onto the grounds in a car or on a cycle, but you must stay on the asphalt paths and must not exceed the 10 mph speed limit. *Open daily, sunrise to sunset. Guided tours leave from* *restaurant parking lot, Tue., Wed., and Fri. at 10:30 a.m. Free admission.*

PEMBROKE

Hamilton, the capital of Bermuda and the island's only city, is the highlight of Pembroke, a peninsula bordered by the Atlantic, the Great Sound, and Hamilton Harbour. The waterfront capital (referred to as "Town" by Bermudians) faces the bustling harbor where large cruise ships, ferries, and other craft are either docked or gliding in and out. Founded in 1790, Hamilton became the capital in 1815 when its central location was thought to be more convenient than that of the original capital, St. George's, at the extreme eastern end of the island.

The Department of Tourism, which dispenses *Handy Reference Maps*, is located in Global House on Church Street. Most of the city's many attractions are within easy walking distance of each other. Whether you take it all in from the ferry, by moped, or on foot, Front Street, full of shops and activity, is a delight. With horns blasting and colorful flags waving, cruise liners pull into the harbor on Monday mornings, remaining until they depart three days later. If you come to Hamilton by ferry, you will disembark at the western end of Front Street, by the Visitors' Service Bureau and the Bank of Bermuda, where an old coin collection is on display. The Royal Bermuda Yacht Club is behind the bank, between the U.S. Navy Shore Patrol Station and Albouy's Point, which overlooks the harbor. The yacht club sponsors the world famous Newport to Bermuda yacht race, which takes place on even-numbered years.

At this end of Front Street, a policeman directs traffic from a "birdcage." Further along there are many stores, several airline offices (Eastern, Delta, British Airways, American, Air Canada), and restaurants with balconies overlooking the harbor. Considered one of the island's most dignified public buildings, the Cabinet Building, formerly the Colonial Secretariat, takes up a block between Parliament and Court Streets.

Turning up Court Street, you'll come to Sessions House, where you can watch parliamentary debates. Churches in the area are Wesley Methodist Church, St. Andrew's Presbyterian, and St. Paul's A.M.E. This African Methodist Episcopal Church is one of Bermuda's leading black churches, and has its roots in the American abolition movement. You'll see the impressive Masjid Muhammad mosque on Cedar Avenue. On Dundonald Street East is an attractive building that was once the New Testament Church of God, and before that, the Colonial Opera

House. Inspired by 16th-century Roman architecture, its design was taken from the plans of a black carpenter and mason who had never been off the island. The carpenter's love of Roman architecture had come from books. Built at the turn of the century, the building was restored after being badly hit by the hurricane of 1926. On Church Street you can see the island's most grandiose church, the Cathedral of the Most Holy Trinity, more commonly known as Bermuda Cathedral.

Further west on Church Street is the sparkling-white City Hall, which houses a theater and art gallery. This modern building was modeled after Stockholm's city hall. The Hamilton Bus Terminal, Victoria Park, and St. Theresa's Cathedral are in this area.

A turn onto Queen Street, going back toward Front Street, will take you past the Bermuda Library, the Historical Society Museum, Perot Post Office—where the island's first postmaster made Bermuda's first stamps by hand—and pleasant Par-La-Ville Gardens.

Reid Street, parallel to Front, is Hamilton's second busiest shopping street. In several byways, you'll find a variety of small stores tucked between buildings. Going east, you will pass Washington Mall on your left and Walker Arcade on your right, both on the blocks between Queen and Burnaby Streets. Then, between Burnaby and Parliament Streets, you will come to Chancery Lane on your right, one of the island's nicest hidden attractions, even for nonshoppers. Fagan's Alley, with more small shops, runs from East Reid to Front in the block between Court and King Streets. If you're in the market for art, stop by Crisson-Hind Art Gallery, on the second floor of the Crisson Building on Front Street; The Gallery, in the Emporium Building on Front Street; or the Windjammer, at the corner of Reid and King streets.

On the eastern outskirts of Hamilton, along the harbor, is the Princess Hotel. It was named in honor of Queen Victoria's daughter, Princess Louise, who visited the island in 1883.

The headquarters of Bacardi Rum, off Pitts Bay Road, has become a favorite spot among Bermudians for taking wedding pictures. Many brides and grooms have stood in front of the waterfall and elaborate fountains with the bright glass and stone building in the background.

For a tasty, casual, homestyle meal (try the fried wahoo, pumpkin, blackeyed peas and rice), stop at the Green Lantern on Serpentine Road between Pitts Bay Road and Rosemont Avenue. Thick shrubbery along the southern part of Pitts Bay Road hides some posh private estates.

From the park at Spanish Point, at the eastern edge of Pembroke, you can look across the Great Sound to the Royal Navy Dockyard (where the Maritime Museum is located), Somerset Village, and the rest of Sandys Parish. After an early Spanish treasure galleon was caught on reefs here, the captain set up a large cross bearing directions to point future visitors toward drinking water. English settlers later mistook the

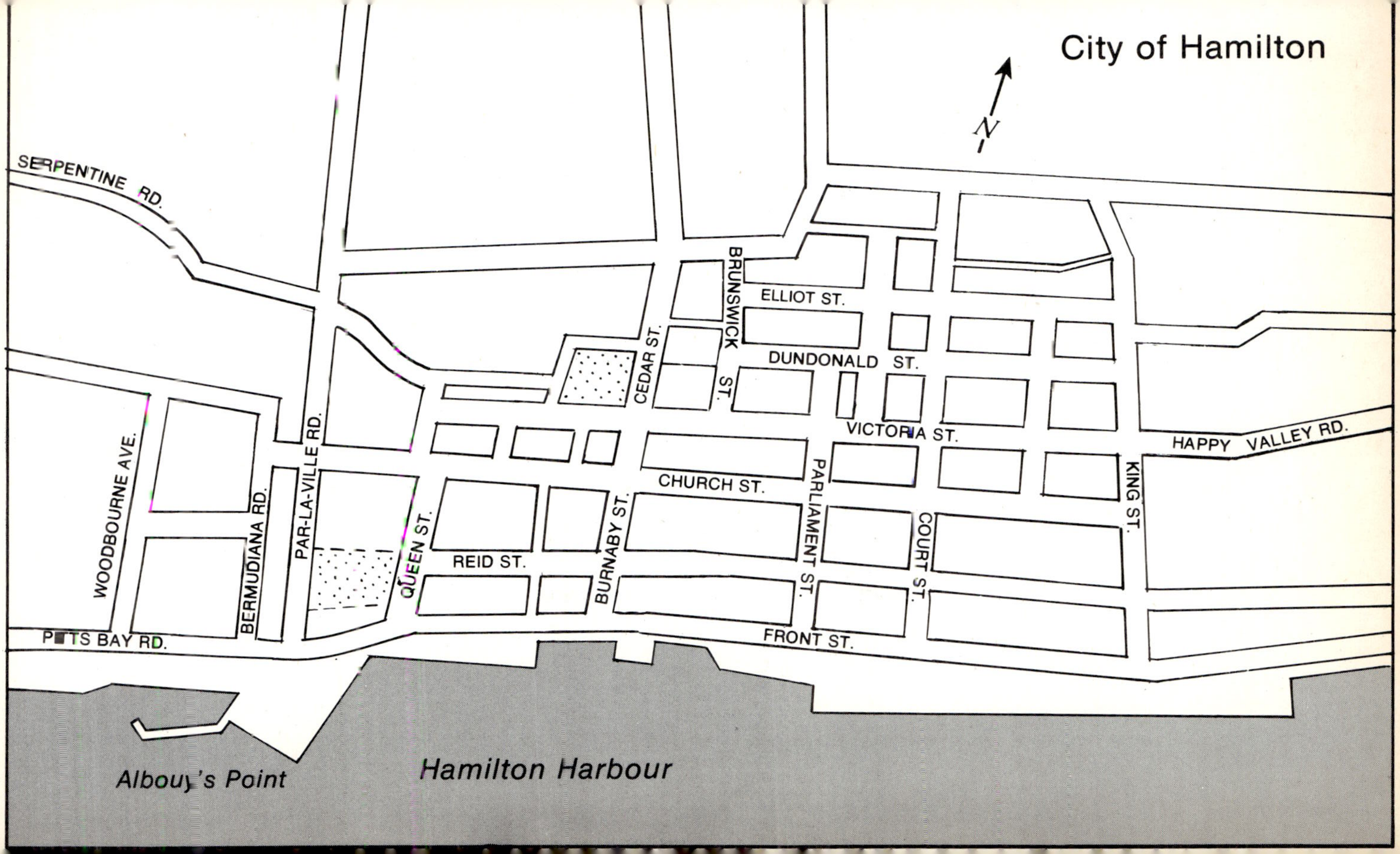
City of Hamilton
N
KING ST.
HAPPY VALLEY RD.
COURT ST.
PARLIAMENT ST.
FRONT ST.
VICTORIA ST.
DUNDONALD ST.
ELLIOT ST.
BRUNSWICK ST.
CHURCH ST.
CEDAR ST.
BURNABY ST.
REID ST.
QUEEN ST.
PAR-LA-VILLE RD.
BERMUDIANA RD.
WOODBOURNE AVE.
PITTS BAY RD.
SERPENTINE RD.
Hamilton Harbour
Albouy's Point

instructions for directions to buried treasure. This spot has been known as Spanish Point ever since. Cobbler's Island is just off the coast. It was here that executed slaves were put on display as a lesson to other black people. Admiralty House Park, a relaxing hideaway, is nearby.

Just north of Hamilton, you can visit the Government Tennis Stadium and play at the club or watch local matches. Also in this area are Black Watch Pass and Well, Pembroke's parish church (St. John's), and Government House, the official residence of the Governor.

East of the city, you can stop at Fort Hamilton for a picnic overlooking the city and harbor.

THE CITY OF HAMILTON

The Bank of Bermuda Ltd. Coin Collection • *mezzanine of the Bank of Bermuda, Front Street, near Par-La-Ville Road; tel: 295–4000* • On display are samples of 17th-century "hog money," the first coins minted for Bermuda and the earliest British colonial currency. The coins bear a picture of the *Sea Venture* on one side and a hog on the other, to commemorate the ship of the early settlers and the wild pigs they found roaming the uninhabited island. You can also see every kind of British coin minted from the beginning of the 17th century to the present, as well as Spanish coins used in colonial Bermuda, and the gold piece from 1666 stamped with an elephant in honor of the African mine where the gold was found. *Exhibition open Mon. through Fri., 9:30 a.m.–3 p.m. Free admission.*

***The Cabinet Building** • *Front Street between Parliament and Court Streets; tel: 292–5501* • This Hamilton landmark housing government offices was formerly known as the Colonial Secretariat. Completed in 1836, it is considered by many to be the island's most dignified public building. Along with the landscaped grounds, it occupies the entire block bordered by Front, Parliament, Reid, and Court Streets. Visitors are welcome to the upstairs Council Chamber where the Senate—Bermuda's upper house—meets every Wednesday at 10 a.m., except during the summer. Each November the Convening of Parliament takes place in the Chamber, and the governor gives a speech in front of a carved oak "throne" made in 1642. Similar to Britain's House of Lords, the Senate is considerably less powerful than the House of Assembly, which meets in Sessions House in the block behind the Cabinet Building. Bermuda's soldiers are honored by the Cenotaph Memorial in front of the building. Several members of royalty have visited this site, including the Prince of Wales who laid the cornerstone of the memorial in 1920 (and went on to become Edward VIII, later abdicating to marry

Wallis Simpson). *Open Mon. through Fri., 9 a.m.–5 p.m. Closed holidays. Free admission.*

*Sessions House • *Parliament Street, between Reid and Church Streets* • At Sessions House you can observe Bermuda's governing body in action. This country's parliament is the third oldest in the world, preceded by England's and Iceland's. On the second floor of the building, the lower chamber of Parliament and the House of Assembly meet (at 10 a.m. on Fri., except during the summer, and Christmas and Easter weeks). You are welcome to follow lively debates from the visitors' section of the House of Assembly. The cedarwood of the gavel used by the Speaker is more than 350 years old, and the mace carried by the Sergeant-at-Arms dates back to 1921 and is a replica of the James I Mace in the Tower of London.

When Sessions House was built in 1817, it was far less ornate than the present structure. The Jubilee Clock on the outside, along with the Florentine terra-cotta colonnade and towers, were added to commemorate Queen Victoria's Golden Jubilee in 1887.

Open Mon. through Fri., 9 a.m.–5 p.m. For further information about visiting the House, call 292–7408. Visitors are asked not to appear in jeans, shorts, or beachwear.

*Bermuda Cathedral • *Church Street, between Parliament and Burnaby streets; tel: 292–4033* • This imposing Anglican cathedral in the middle of Hamilton is an impressive example of classic Gothic architecture with a special Bermudian flair. Built largely of two of the island's few natural resources, it was constructed of limestone, and its pews were carved from cedar. Crests of shells, palm fronds, cedar shavings, and beans hang on the wall to the left of the main altar. The intricate needlepoint kneeler-cushions were all made by members of the congregation, and the stained-glass Window of Angels was designed by a local artist. The pulpit and lectern are copies of those in St. Giles Cathedral in Edinburgh, and are considered distinctive examples of ecclesiastic sculpture. In addition to the handicrafts of the Children's Chapel in the back of the church, you can see the Warrior Chapel, which honors the country's soldiers, and two throne-chairs for special occasions. Dedicated in 1894, this cathedral is the center of the Church of England in Bermuda. It stands on the site where the original church was destroyed by arson in 1884. *Open daily from 8 a.m.–7 p.m.*

City Hall/Society of Arts • *Church Street, between Wesley Street (an extension of Queen Street) and Washington Street; tel: 292–3824* • If you want to know which way the wind is blowing, look up at the wind clock and the huge weather vane (in the shape of the *Sea Venture*) that adorn the tower of City Hall. Designed by a local architect, the building was completed in 1960 and is surrounded by a small park. City Hall is more than just the headquarters of Hamilton's municipal government. It has a theater where you can attend dramatic productions, films, and concerts (although the acoustics could be better for music) as well as an art gallery where photographs and other artwork are on display. Periodically during Rendezvous Time (mid-Nov. through March), works of up-and-coming Bermudian artists are exhibited on the grounds outside. City Hall contains a time capsule that is slated to be opened in the year 2019, the colony's 500th anniversary. *City Hall open Mon.–Fri., 9 a.m.–5 p.m. Art Gallery open Mon. through Sat., 10 a.m.–4 p.m., April through November; limited hours on Saturdays December through March. Closed holidays. Free admission.*

Victoria Park • *Victoria Street and Cedar Avenue (an extension of Burnaby Street)* • In the center of Hamilton, this attractive park exemplifies the orderly beauty of the island. A favorite lunchtime spot among Bermudians as well as visitors, it has decorative shrubbery, a sunken garden, well-manicured lawns, and a gazebo where you can attend concerts during the summer.

St. Theresa's Cathedral • *corner of Cedar Avenue and Laffan Street, one block north of Victoria Park; tel: 292–0607* • The architecture and colorful walls of St. Theresa's set it apart from the more common Romanesque and Gothic styles of Roman Catholic cathedrals. Built in 1927, this church is where you can see the gold and silver chalice that Pope Paul VI gave to the Roman Catholic diocese during his visit to Bermuda in 1968. *Open daily, 8 a.m.–5 p.m.*

The Bermuda Library • *Queen Street, near Par-La-Ville Gardens, next to Perot Post Office; tel: 295–2905* • Since 1916 the Bermuda Library has been located next door to Perot Post Office, in the main house of the estate where the city's first postmaster lived with his family. Although in the early days most of the books were of a historical and scientific nature, today there is a wide selection of popular works. There is also a collection of all magazines and newspapers published in Bermuda from as far back as 1787 to the present. In the late 18th century, papers such as the *Royal Gazette* ran advertisements inviting young men looking for adventure to become privateers. For $1 a month, you can obtain a library card. The Historical Society Museum is on the first floor of this two-story former home. The large rubber tree between the library and Par-La-Ville Gardens was planted by Perot in 1847. Its branches now reach across the street. *Open Mon. through Thurs., 9:30 a.m.–6 p.m.; Fri., until 5 p.m.; Sat., until 1 p.m. Closed all holidays.*

Bermuda Historical Society Museum • *Queen Street, near Perot Post Office and Par-La-Ville Gardens; tel: 295–2487* • Don't let the small size fool you. The Historical Society Museum, on the ground floor of the old Perot mansion where the Bermuda Library is located, is full of treasures that will take you back in time. You will see antique silver, china, clothing, and Bermuda cedar furniture, as well as early coins and the sea chest that belonged to Sir George Somers, whose shipwrecked crew colonized the island. In addition to portraits of Sir George and Lady Somers that are hundreds of years old, there is a map of Bermuda thought to have been drawn by Sir George in 1610, and another map drawn several years later by Richard Norwood, who first surveyed Bermuda and divided it into the tribes that are now called parishes. On display as well are models of the three ships—*Sea Venture*, *Patience*, and *Deliverance*—that played such important roles in Bermuda's history. You can also see a copy of the letter written by George Washington in 1775 asking for gunpowder during the Revolutionary War. (Although loyal to Britain, Bermuda traded the gunpowder for food.) *Open Mon. to Sat., 10 a.m.–5 p.m. Closed 12:30 to 2 for lunch and on all holidays. Free admission, but donations are appreciated.*

Perot Post Office • *Queen Street, facing intersection with Reid Street (just north of the ferry landing and policeman's "birdcage" on Front Street); tel: 295–0880* • Bermuda's first postage stamp was printed by William Bennett Perot, Hamilton's first postmaster, who served for almost half a century. The building that bears his name was his home and the place where townspeople bought their stamps, all handmade and signed by Perot. Although he became the postmaster in 1816, it was not until 1848 that he began printing stamps. He had grown tired of finding that people who came while he was out often neglected to leave enough change with the letters they dropped off. Only 11 of the stamps that solved the problem are known to exist today. Some are part of a collection owned by Queen Elizabeth II. In 1986, a penny stamp made by Perot in 1861 was sold in a New York auction for $92,000.

The small whitewashed building that still serves as a post office was built in 1814, and stands in front of the peaceful Par-La-Ville Gardens once cared for by Perot himself. Next door, in the main house on what was called the Par-La-Ville estate, are the Bermuda Library, the Historical Society Museum, and the Bermuda Archives. *Open Mon. through Fri., 9 a.m.–5 p.m. Closed holidays.*

***Par-La-Ville Gardens** • *between Queen Street and Par-La-Ville Road* • This pleasant public park has changed little since the mid 19th century when it was designed and cared for by William Bennett Perot, the city's first postmaster. You can have a quiet picnic lunch in the shade of a palm or golden shower tree surrounded by the colorful flower beds that line the winding paths. The huge rubber tree that was planted by Postmaster Perot in 1847 is said to have disappointed Mark Twain because hot water bottles and rubber boots did not hang from its branches.

OUTSKIRTS OF THE CITY

***Admiralty House Park** • *near junction of North Shore and Cox Hill Roads* • The two small, secluded beaches here have nice views of a cove bordered by rugged cliffs. The spacious park, with lush, varied foliage, makes a trip here especially worthwhile. At the entrance are maps that outline a fitness program you can participate in while walking through the park's trail. *Free Admission.*

Black Watch Pass and Well • *intersection of Black Watch Pass and North Shore Road* • Before 1934 horses and wagons traveling between Hamilton and the north shore had to struggle over a steep hill. Now you can reach North Shore Road from the city on level ground and in no time at all by cycle or car. Driving north, you will pass through what appears to be a natural tunnel. Actually, this glistening solid archway was created by the famous Scottish regiment, the Black Watch, who cut 85,000 cubic yards of rock from the side of a cliff. During the drought of 1849, they also built a well at the northern end of the passage for the poor and their cattle. The well is still in use.

***Fort Hamilton** • *Happy Valley Road, approch from Victoria and King Streets* • Like Fort Scaur in Sandys Parish, this fort was built as part of the defense plan of the Duke of Wellington (famous for his role in Napoleon's defeat at Waterloo). Along with several others built here during this period, Fort Hamilton was outdated by the time it was finished (in 1889), and was never used to defend the island. It was restored in 1963, after having been closed for many years because of unsafe conditions. Now the well-cared-for grounds offer an exciting perch from which to gaze down on the city of Hamilton and its busy harbor. The dry moat has been transformed into a colorful, thriving garden, and the cannons, battlements, and twisting underground tunnels are a lesson in Victorian history. On the upper level, you can relax on one of the benches on the grassy slope. You can also visit the tea shop for lunch or a light snack. On Mondays at noon during Rendezvous Time (mid-Nov. through March), the fort is alive with the sounds of a skirling ceremony, the official playing of bagpipes accompanied by Highland dancers and drummers. *Open daily, except Saturdays, 9:30 a.m.–5 p.m. Free admission.*

DEVONSHIRE

Devonshire is the place to go for peace and quiet. Bordered by Paget, Pembroke, and Smith's, it is one of the more tranquil parishes. It has no restaurants or hotels, only a cottage colony and a handful of guest houses and housekeeping units. Its colorful houses are scattered throughout the green hilly countryside. The gardens, 19-acre arboretum, marshes, and nature reserve as well as the historic church are popular sights. If you are staying in a housekeeping apartment, you can buy fresh fish at Devonshire Dock, on the northern shore near Pembroke. The parish also has a public 9-hole golf course at the Ocean View Golf and Country Club.

Not far from 18th-century Old Devonshire Church on Middle Road is Devonshire Marsh, called a "brackish pond" by Bermudians. In this parish that has so much water it was once called Brackish Pond itself, a distillation plant and underground wells supply much of the freshwater for the whole island. Off South Shore Road is more marshland at Edmund Gibbons Nature Reserve, the home of various species of birds and rare plants.

The cottage colony, Ariel Sands Beach Club, is on the south shore, a short distance from Palm Grove Garden, a private garden open to the public. Walk through the Chinese Moongate for good luck, then visit the garden behind a striking old home facing South Shore Road.

Children can go horseback riding at Lee Bow Riding Centre, which caters to those aged 18 and under.

A painless way to learn about Bermuda's cultural roots is to visit Devonshire's nightclub, the Clay House Inn, on North Shore Road. Its popular show features Afro-Caribbean music and dance, including limbo and a steel band. Music ranges from lively calypso to jazz and spirited renditions of selections from Handel's *Messiah*. Popular international entertainers also appear here on occasion.

Devonshire Dock • *North Shore Road, just east of Dock Hill Road, near the border with Pembroke Parish* • In the afternoon as fishermen return from the sea, this is the perfect place to buy dinner if you are staying in a housekeeping apartment or renting a private home. If catching your own is more your style, you can buy fresh bait from the fishermen if you arrive by 10 a.m. During the War of 1812, this was the romantic spot where British soldiers and local women danced to fiddles every day. Standing at the beginning of the dock and looking out at the ocean, you will see the same view that is captured in a painting that hangs in Verdmont, the lovely old mansion you can visit in nearby Smith's Parish.

Old Devonshire Church • *Middle Road, 2 miles east of the city of Hamilton; tel: 292-1348* • From the outside, this church looks like an old Bermudian cottage. It is so small that it resembles a rectory, and the new Devonshire Church beside it is often mistaken for it by visitors. Old Devonshire Church was built of limestone and cedar in 1716 on the site of a church constructed in 1623. The huge bolts and ships' timbers inside are examples of the contributions of Bermudian shipbuilders. Because of extensive fire damage caused by an Easter Sunday explosion in 1970, what you will see for the most part is a faithful reconstruction of the early 18th-century church. Fortunately, however, a number of important relics survived the blaze, including the oldest piece of church silver in Bermuda, a beaker dating back to 1590; and the oldest chancel screen on the island. Look for the Slaves' Gallery, built by slaves themselves. Each year, on the Sunday before Christmas, you can attend a candlelight carol service here. *Open daily, 9 a.m.-5 p.m.*

***Palm Grove Gardens** • *South Road, just west of Devonshire Bay Road, near Brighton Hill Road* • These lush gardens are behind a traditional old mansion that faces South Road. Even the servants' quarters of this private estate are beautiful. In addition to caged tropical birds, there is a grass map of Bermuda growing in a pond and a wishing well. Honeymooners often walk through the Chinese moongate and make a wish. *Open Mon. through Fri., 9 a.m.-5 p.m. Closed holidays. Free admission.*

Palmetto House • *North Shore Rd.; tel: 295-9941* • This 18th-century mansion, in the shape of a cross, has three rooms on view, furnished with fine examples of Bermudian furniture and decor. *Open Thursdays only from 10 a.m. to 5 p.m. with no admission fee.*

Glass Blowing Studio • *Tee St.; tel: 295-0379* • See demonstrations of the delicate art of glass blowing. A tempting selection of glass items is on sale. *Open 10 a.m. to 6 p.m. each day, including holidays. No admission fee, but donations are accepted.*

Edmund Gibbons Nature Reserve • *South Road, west of the junction with Collector's Hill* • This marshland is the home of a variety of birds and rare species of flora native to Bermuda. The reserve was given to the Bermuda National Trust by the heirs of Edmund Gibbons, the man who preserved the land. Visitors are asked not to enter the marshy area. *Open daily. Free admission.*

SMITH'S

In Smith's, history buffs can be transported to the 17th century for a glimpse of the wealthy at home. Would-be fishermen can "catch" sharks while bird watchers wander through two nature reserves. Mystery lovers can try to figure out the origin of 400-year-old initials carved into a rock.

Along with its northern and southern oceanfronts, Smith's has a third shore on Harrington Sound, which is really a 6-mile salt water lake. If you want to stay at a housekeeping apartment, you have a few to choose from here, but there is only one hotel and one cottage colony.

Near the western border of the parish is Collector's Hill, named in honor of the tax collector who lived on it. This hill is where you will find the 17th-century mansion called Verdmont, Bermuda's most beautifully preserved old home. The Oriental Room and the nursery with its antique toys are two rooms you should not miss. This house, which is now a museum, gives the full flavor of how well-to-do Bermudians lived hundreds of years ago.

Located in the northern part of Smith's, Flatts Village, with pretty houses and tall palms, has quieted down considerably since the 17th and 18th centuries. In its heyday, the village was popular with smugglers. They would unload their ships here at night, unbeknownst to customs officials, who were in St. George's.

St. Mark's Road, which connects Verdmont and South Shore Roads, meanders over and around hills with farms, spacious estates, and great views of the south shore. On South Shore Road, just east of its intersection with St. Mark's Road, is St. Mark's Church. If you experience deja vu, you have probably been to Devonshire. St. Mark's, Smith's Parish church, is almost an exact replica of Old Devonshire Church. Spittal Pond is comprised of 60 acres near the southern shore. You may stumble onto a seafront cave here called Jeffrey's Hole, named after the runaway slave who once hid in it. The cave's opening is at the top of a cliff.

Between Spittal Pond and the shore, you will come upon Spanish Rock. For centuries, historians have been arguing whether the initials carved in the rock in 1543 are those of an early Spanish explorer or one from Portugal.

Farther east, right after Harrington Sound Road meets Knapton Hill Road, is Devil's Hole. Once a cave, it is now a deep pool where you can fish—with baited but hookless lines. You won't really catch anything—just a nibble before the fish swims away.

On the opposite shore (south shore) is John Smith's Beach. Just before the eastern border of Smith's is North Nature Reserve, at the western edge of Mangrove Lake. Here you will see a variety of animal and plant life, such as mangrove trees growing in a salty pond.

***Verdmont House** • *Verdmont Road, at top of Collector's Hill; tel: 236-7369* • This 17th-century mansion, where candelight concerts are held several times a year, is considered the most important of the Bermuda National Trust historic houses. It contains a wealth of Bermudian and English antique furniture and artifacts. Some historians believe it was built in 1662 by the three-time Bermuda governor, William Sayle, who founded Eleuthera in The Bahamas and colonized part of South Carolina. Others think that the land on which the house was to be built was bought by John Dickinson—with Arabian gold from pirateering—toward the end of the 17th century. At any rate, the house has been standing for more than three centuries, and although much of its furniture has been acquired by the Trust over the years, the mansion itself has changed little. Its last occupant was an eccentric woman who lived there for 75 years, until 1953, but never installed plumbing or electricity.

Notice the unusual double roof, the only one in Bermuda. Double chimneys at each end of the house enable all rooms to have fireplaces. The small crannies between the spacious fireplaces are called powder rooms because they were where people went to powder their wigs. The cedar staircase, held together by wooden pegs, is thought to be one of the best-made on the island. The walls of the house are decorated with oil portraits by John Green, a Bermudian official who owned the mansion during the late 18th century. You can see his smiling miniature self-portrait in the dining room on the ground floor. From the dining room doorway, the kitchen and slave quarters can be seen in separate buildings. They have been remodeled to serve as a residence for the curator.

In a chest at the foot of the 18th-century daybed in one of the upstairs rooms, you'll find a collection of antique clothing. Handpainted china is displayed in another room. The nursery, with its old toys, dolls, books, and cedar cradle, is a special treat. For a stunning view of the ocean, stand on the pleasant little second-floor balcony. You may also be able to see cattle grazing in the distance. *Open Mon. through Sat., 10 a.m.–5 p.m. Closed for lunch. Admission: $2; under age 12: 50¢.*

Spittal Pond • *South Road (just north of Spanish Rock)* • Encompassing almost 60 acres, this is considered the most impressive of the Bermuda National Trust's open spaces. It is the island's largest wildlife sanctuary, and from November to May about 25 species of waterfowl drop by for visits. Keep an eye out for the pretty bright orange and black crabs that scutter in and out of holes. *Free admission. Visitors are asked to remain on the pathways.*

Spanish Rock • *off South Road, south of Spittal Pond, about 1½ miles east of Collector's Hill Road* • On a high bluff overlooking the ocean sits a rock that caused a controversy for centuries. (Ask a Bermudian to show you the location.) Actually, it is the initials of the inscription on the rock that left historians and scholars arguing. While the cross and date (1543) were clear when the inscription was discovered by early settlers, the letters were illegible, having been badly eroded by the elements. For years the carving—which could be FK, JR, or RP—was thought by some to have been done by a 16th-century Spanish explorer. But many experts now believe that it must have been the work of one of the 32 Portuguese sailors who survived a shipwreck in 1543 on their way home from Santo Domingo in the Caribbean. The letters could be RP, for "Rex Portugaliae" and the cross, a badge of the Portuguese Order of Christ. After an unsuccessful attempt to protect the carving from further erosion, a bronze casting of it was put in its place.

Devil's Hole • *Harrington Sound Road; tel: 293-2072* • Since 1830, visitors have been coming to this collapsed cave where underground passages from the sea have created a deep pool. Soon after the owner began showing it that year, its popularity convinced him to start charging admission. Fish were stored here by the first colonists, who called it "Devil's Hole" because they thought the breeze rushing through it sounded like the devil's voice. It has been used as a natural aquarium since 1847, and now has about 400 fish, such as sharks and giant groupers, as well as moray eels and massive green turtles. You can feel the tug of one of these creatures at the end of one of the baited but hookless lines provided. Because this is a fish preserve, you cannot take any of the inhabitants home. *Open Mon. through Sat., 9:30 a.m.–5 p.m.; Sun. and holidays, 10 a.m.–5 p.m. Closed Christmas Day, Good Friday, and Jan. Admission: Adults—$3.50; children between age 6 and 12, $1.50; age 5 and under, 50¢.*

North Nature Reserve • *at the western end of Mangrove Lake (across the road from Pink Beach Club and Cottages)* • This Bermuda National Trust property is an unusual area where mangrove trees grow in a brackish (salty) pond. The pond attracts several species of birds, and is filled with water fauna and flora of special interest to scientists.

HAMILTON PARISH

There is a lot to keep you busy in Hamilton, including the popular Aquarium. Bordering most of Harrington Sound, this sprawling parish also has both northern and southern coasts on the Atlantic. Not only does Hamilton offer many attractions and a great deal of pastoral beauty above ground, but visitors can also enjoy the island's subterranean wonders.

The eastern part of the parish, along Castle Harbour, has many underground caves, several of which are open to the public. Most are known only to Bermudians, who will tell the adventurous how to slither up and down ropes and avoid poison ivy when entering. Crystal and Leamington Caves are two that are perfectly safe and are entered by stairs. At both, guides will show you clear lakes surrounded by huge, unspoiled stalagmites and stalactites, about 100 feet below the ground. At the Grotto Bay Beach and Tennis Club, one has been turned into a discotheque called Prospero's. Another, on the hotel's grounds, is Cathedral Cave, which you must crawl around in and can only see with the permission of the management. Unless you are a grotto aficionado, a visit to Crystal Caves, the most spectacular of public caves, should suffice.

To commune with monkeys, giant turtles, birds, and more than 70 species of sea animals, visit the Bermuda Aquarium and Zoo, on Sound Road. Taking North Shore Road out of Smith's, you will come to the North Shore's longest beach, at Shelly Bay, named after one of the *Sea Venture* passengers. For 200 years, beginning in the 17th century, shipbuilding flourished in this area.

Farther along the road, near Bailey's Bay, is Crawl Hill, one of the highest points in the parish. The name comes from the word "kraal," a pen used to hold captured fish and turtles before they were sold. From here you will have an eye-catching view in all directions. When you come to the top of Cottage Hill, you will be at the highest point on the road between this parish and St. George's.

Attractive estates with lush gardens are along both Fractious Street and Wilkinson Avenue. On Blue Hole Hill, you will see the Swizzle Inn, popular with cyclists who stop for Rum Swizzles—one of the island's most requested drinks. The swizzleburgers are also hot items here, along with the soups, omelets, chili, fish and chips, salads, and sandwiches on the menu. Business cards of patrons are plastered all over the restaurant. Across the street is Bailey's Ice Cream Parlour, an old-fashioned spot where homemade ice cream and even Swizzle sherbet is served.

Be careful when you come to the junction of North Shore Road, Wilkinson Avenue, and Blue Hole Road, since it is one of Bermuda's busiest intersections. This is where the Bermuda Perfumery and Gardens is located. Visitors can buy perfume after learning and smelling how it is made.

The Grotto Bay Beach and Tennis Club is worth a stop. The beautifully kept grounds are thriving with a variety of trees and smaller plants, and the view of the water is striking.

Just south of the hotel are Bermuda Pottery, the Blue Grotto Dolphin Show, and Crystal Caves. You can watch the potters at work, but the pieces for sale tend to be expensive. Children especially will like watching the dolphins doing tricks. If you get an urge to shop while at Crystal Caves, you can visit the branch of Trimingham's department store there. At Walsingham Bay is Tom Moore's Tavern, now a gourmet restaurant. Unfortunately, the famed calabash tree, under which the Irish poet Tom Moore used to write at the turn of the century, fell victim to Hurricane Emily in September 1987. At Leamington Caves you can dine at the Plantation Restaurant.

The Marriott chain has restored the fortresslike former Castle Harbour Hotel and Golf Club nearby. A new wing has been built into the hillside and the 18-hole golf course designed by Robert Trent Jones has been refurbished. Stop here for another dramatic view of the harbor.

The Southern portion of Hamilton is sandwiched between Smith's and an isolated part of St. George's. Half of the Mid Ocean Golf Course is here, as well as Mangrove Lake and Trott's Pond, two flora and fauna filled brackish ponds.

***Bermuda Aquarium, Museum, and Zoo** • *Sound Road* • Adults as well as children will enjoy this exciting assortment of marine life, tropical animals, and even an authentic sunken treasure. As you move from tank to tank in the Aquarium holding a "listening wand" to your ear, you will learn all about the creatures in their natural-looking habitats and you'll even hear some of the sounds they make. There are several hundred specimens here, about 75 species, ranging from sharks and a long moray eel to tiny seahorses, sea anemones, live coral, and sponges. Walk through the Natural History Museum with exhibits of the island's unusual geological development and ecosystem. You can admire multicolored shells, thousand-year-old fossils, a huge topographical map of Bermuda, and a treasure from a wrecked pirate ship. Animals in the outdoor zoo include cockatoos, flamingos, monkeys, and alligators. The giant tortoises from the Galapagos Islands are some of the most striking animals here. In the Children's Zoo, kids can pet small farm animals, but feeding them is prohibited. *Open daily, 9 a.m.–4:30 p.m. Closed Christmas Day. Admission. Adults–$3; children age 7–16–50¢; children under 7–free.*

The Bermuda Perfumery and Gardens • *Bailey's Bay, intersection of North Shore Road, Wilkinson Avenue and Blue Hole Hill; tel: 293–0627* • Not only is this factory located in a house two centuries old, but is also adjoined by fragrant gardens where you can see and smell the raw materials—jasmine, oleander, passion flowers, lilies. During a short guided tour, you'll learn how perfume used to be made in Bermuda (using flowers and animal fat). Then you'll have a firsthand glimpse of the modern chemical distillation process and watch the packing and bottling being done by hand. Although perfume-making in Bermuda is seasonal, ending after Easter, you can tour the factory and buy reasonably priced samples of the sweet fragrances year-round. *Open Mon. through Sat., 9 a.m.–5 p.m. Closed holidays. Free admission.*

Bermuda Pottery • *Blue Hole Hill (near the perfume factory and Blue Grotto Dolphin Show); tel: 293–2234* • A visit here allows you to watch the potters at work, or buy a sample of their craft, although pieces are on the expensive side. *Open Mon. through Fri., 8:30 a.m.–5 p.m.; Sat., 9 a.m.– 4:30 p.m. Closed holidays.*

Blue Grotto Dolphin Show • *Blue Hole Hill, close to the west end of the causeway (near the perfume factory and Bermuda Pottery); tel: 293–0864* • The natural setting makes this dolphin show special. Shaded by mangrove trees, the limestone grotto is filled by the tidal-flow through its walls. The friendly dolphins perform all sorts of tricks, from jumping through hoops and playing basketball to "shaking hands." Unlike most dolphins, these are trained to respond to voice commands instead of whistles or hand signals. Members of the audience can go on porpoise-powered boat rides. *Daily shows at 11 a.m., noon, 2 p.m., 3 p.m., and 4 p.m. including holidays, except mid-Nov. to mid-Jan. when shows are noon, 2 p.m., and 3 p.m. only. Closed Christmas Day and mid-Jan. to early Feb. Admission: Adults–$3.50; children aged 4–12 $1.50; children under age 4 free.*

*Crystal Caves • *Wilkinson Avenue, Bailey's Bay* • In and around a clear subterranean lake are millions of stalactites (hanging from the ceiling) and stalagmites (coming up from the ground). These fantastic greenish-white formations were created by eons of dripping water, which you can still hear as the process continues. As rain filters through the ground above, it picks up lime, calcium, and iron. Drops of water deposit the minerals in the caves, forming this living stone, which grows a mere cubic inch every 100 years. This eerie wonderland, 120 feet below the ground, was discovered in 1907 when two young boys lost their ball down a hole and burrowed after it. Steps and a long ramp now give visitors access. Before the wooden pontoon bridge was built over the lake, which rises and falls with the Castle Harbour tides, visitors crossed the cavern by boat. Your guide will point out formations such as one that looks a lot like a sculptured poodle. When the lights are turned off, you will see a glowing group of stalagmites resembling Manhattan's skyline. A fossil of Bermuda's only indigenous bird, the cahow, was once found here. (Cahows raise their young in burrows in the ground and are nearly extinct.) *Daily tours, 9 a.m.–4:40 p.m., including holidays, except Christmas Day. Admission: Adults–$2.50, children aged 5–11–$1; children under 4–free.*

Tom Moore's Tavern (Walsingham) • *Harrington Sound Road, Walsingham's Bay (near Leamington Caves)* • Tom Moore, the Irish poet who lived in Bermuda in 1804, visited this old house so often that many think he owned it. However, local historians say that the house, built by a relative of the Earl of Warwick in 1652, was owned by the Trott family. For quite some time it was a tavern where guests could enjoy a drink or a meal. After being closed for years, it has reopened as a gourmet restaurant. The new owners have gone to great lengths to restore it faithfully. Nearby are several small pools fed by underground streams. There is also a lake, caves, and a tiny jungle.

Leamington Caves • *Harrington Sound Road, Bailey's Bay; tel: 293–1188* • Not as large or quite as spectacular as Crystal Caves, Leamington Caves were discovered in 1908 when a boy noticed a small opening on the hillside that he and his father were preparing to plough. Ten years later the caves were opened to the public. Here you can see amber-tinted stalagmites and stalactites that look remarkably like a frozen waterfall, diving fish, and the Statue of Liberty, to name a few. Upstairs, you can have a pleasant meal or a drink at the Plantation Club. *Open Mon. through Sat., 9:30 a.m.–4:30 p.m. Closed holidays and mid-Dec. through March. Admission: Adults–$2.50; children under 12–$1.00; children under 4–free.*

ST. GEORGE'S

To understand how Bermuda got to be the way it is today, visitors can begin by absorbing the history of St. George's. In 1609, off St. Catherine's Point, at the northeastern tip of the parish, the early English settlers were shipwrecked on these uninhabited shores. Their vessel, the *Sea Venture*, was one of 7 ships headed for Virginia's Jamestown Colony when it was dashed on the reefs here. All 150 passengers were led safely ashore by the admiral, Sir George Somers, and Sir Thomas Gates. They remained long enough to build two new ships, the *Deliverance* and the *Patience,* on which they finally reached Jamestown.

Two years later, the same company sent another group of settlers on the *Plough* to this Atlantic island. In 1612 they founded a town, and called it St. George's in honor of Sir George Somers and the patron saint of England. St. George's remained Bermuda's capital until 1815 when the seat of government was moved to the city of Hamilton. After hundreds of years, the town of St. George—a striking contrast to Hamilton—is very much the way it was in the 17th century.

St. George's is the colony's most widely spread-out parish. It is comprised mainly of two large islands north of Castle Harbour that are connected to each other by a bridge, and to the mainland by a causeway. Exclusive Tucker's Town is on the southern side of the harbor. The lower of the two islands is almost completely occupied by Bermuda's Civil Air Terminal and the U.S. Naval Air Station.

On the northern island, the historic town of St. George's overlooks St. George's Harbour. A walk around the island's original capital will take you through narrow, picturesque, hilly streets with names such as Featherbed Alley, Aunt Peggy's Lane, Duke of York Street, and Shinbone Alley. According to one story, Silk Alley, also known as Petticoat Lane, was named because 17th-century women slaves used to walk up and down it rustling their petticoats. Others say the street got its name after Emancipation, when freed black women proudly showed off their newly acquired silk undergarments.

King's Square is the focal point of the town. Look out for the Town Crier in 17th-century garb. Many visitors photograph each other in the stocks and pillory, replicas of those once used to punish gossips and people who cursed. Surrounding the square are the White Horse Tavern, where diners look out on the harbor; the Confederate Museum, with exhibits that tell of Bermuda's support of the South during the American Civil War; Pub on the Square Restaurant; Town Hall, headquarters of the local government and the multimedia show called "Bermuda Journey"; and the Visitors' Service Bureau, where you can get maps and other information. Across the bridge to Ordnance Island are the ducking stool and a life-size bronze statue of Sir George Somers. On this island visitors can explore the replica of the early settlers' ship, the *Deliverance.*

Just east of the square is 18th-century Tucker House, with its collection of antique Bermuda silver and furniture. This home of the prominent Tucker family was also the home of Joseph Rainey, a freed American slave who lived in Bermuda before returning to the South to become the first black member of the U.S. House of Representatives.

After a multimillion dollar restoration of 19th-century colonial buildings, the Somers Wharf area contains shops and restaurants, as well as the Carriage Museum.

On Duke of York Street, north of King's Square, is beautiful St. Peter's Church, built on the site of what is probably the oldest Anglican church in the Western hemisphere. Many visitors find that taking pictures of this simple whitewashed building is hard to resist. On the way into St. George's from Fort St. Catherine, near Bermuda's Club Med, you will pass an overgrown church ruin where dug-up bones solved a 100-year-old mystery. This church was begun in order to replace the deteriorating St. Peter's, then abandoned when St. Peter's was restored.

In 1801 a Methodist minister was fined and sent to jail for preaching the gospel to black people in front of St. George's Historical Museum on Featherbed Alley. In addition to antique furniture, documents, and paintings, the museum contains a rare Bible and an original 18th-century kitchen.

So that Sir George Somers could be in two places at once, his heart was buried where pretty Somers Gardens are located, and his body was sent back to England. Every April at nearby Old State House, Bermudians and visitors come to see the elaborate Peppercorn Ceremony, when a rent of one peppercorn is paid to the Governor.

At Fort St. Catherine, at the northeastern tip of the parish, there are dioramas of milestones in Bermudian history. This is the largest of Bermuda's forts and overlooks the reefs where the *Sea Venture* was shipwrecked.

St. David's Island is located on the northeastern end of the parish's southern island. The people of this seafaring area live in a historically isolated community. Many of them still think of the rest of Bermuda as "up in the country." A portion of the population is made up of descendants of American Indians, mainly Pequot. Two popular local restaurants are worth a visit: the Black Horse Tavern and Dennis' Hideaway, both overlooking the water. Dennis' is known for Bermudian specialties including shark hash on toast, conch fritters, and fish chowder.

In the 19th century, Smith's Island to the west was the center of the colony's whaling activity. A story has it that a man from St. David's ended doubts about a whale's stomach being large enough to accommodate a human by crawling inside one himself. He found it quite roomy.

If you befriend a Bermudian with a boat, you might try to convince him or her to take you to Nonsuch Island in Castle Harbour, a sanctuary for the rare cahow bird. Across Castle Harbour is Tucker's Town, where half of the Mid Ocean Club and Golf Course is located. Tucker's Town was undeveloped until the 1920's when a steamship company bought some of the land to build the club and golf course. This area soon became a community for the wealthy and Bermuda's most exclusive neighborhood. Some Bermudians consider this area part of Hamilton Parish, although according to maps it is part of St. George's.

THE TOWN OF ST. GEORGE'S

***King's Square** • *center of the Town of St. George's* • Here in the center of town you can sentence yourself to a few moments of fun in the stocks and pillory, cedar replicas of those that once stood in the square. Seventeenth-century townspeople landed themselves here by being caught gossiping, nagging, missing church, or cursing. Across the bridge on Ordnance Island, you'll see the ducking stool, another 17th-century humiliating and less-than-comfortable form of punishment. This is also where you'll find Bermuda's only statue, of Sir George Somers. King's Square, which has changed little since it was built, is on the waterfront. It is bordered by buildings including the Confederate Museum, Town Hall, and the Visitors' Service Bureau.

The Confederate Museum • *Duke of York Street; tel: 297–1423* • The Globe Hotel, now the museum, was once the headquarters of the Confederate representative in Bermuda. It was from St. George's that ships filled with armaments ran the blockade to the Southern states during the American Civil War. Bermuda's slaves had been freed in 1834, three decades before abolition in the United States; however, this did not stop most of the island from supporting the Confederacy for economic reasons. (St. George's had been ailing since the capital was moved to Hamilton in 1815.) The museum contains exhibits about the short-lived period when St. George's flourished during the war. *Open Mon. through Sat., 10 a.m.–5 p.m. Closed holidays. Admission: adults–$1.50; children under age 12–50¢.*

Town Hall • *King's Square* • Built in 1782, Town Hall is faithfully restored, with a great deal of cedar woodwork and furniture. It is still used as the headquarters of the local government. The seating arrangement of the officials reflects their positions: the mayor's chair is on the highest platform, the aldermen's chairs on a lower platform, and the councilmen's chairs on the lowest. In the 19th century, townspeople were victims of a hoax when a traveling "professor" invited them to a performance of "Ali Baba and the Forty Thieves" that he said he was staging here. As the audience waited for the show to begin, the "professor" was in another part of town stealing a safe that had been left unguarded. The angry and disappointed audience was especially pleased when he was later caught.

***Bermuda Journey** • *Town Hall; tel: 297–0526* • Created by the makers of "The New York Experience" and "South Street Seaport Experience," this flashy multimedia presentation covers Bermuda's history, culture, and heritage as well as its scenic attractions. *Open Monday*

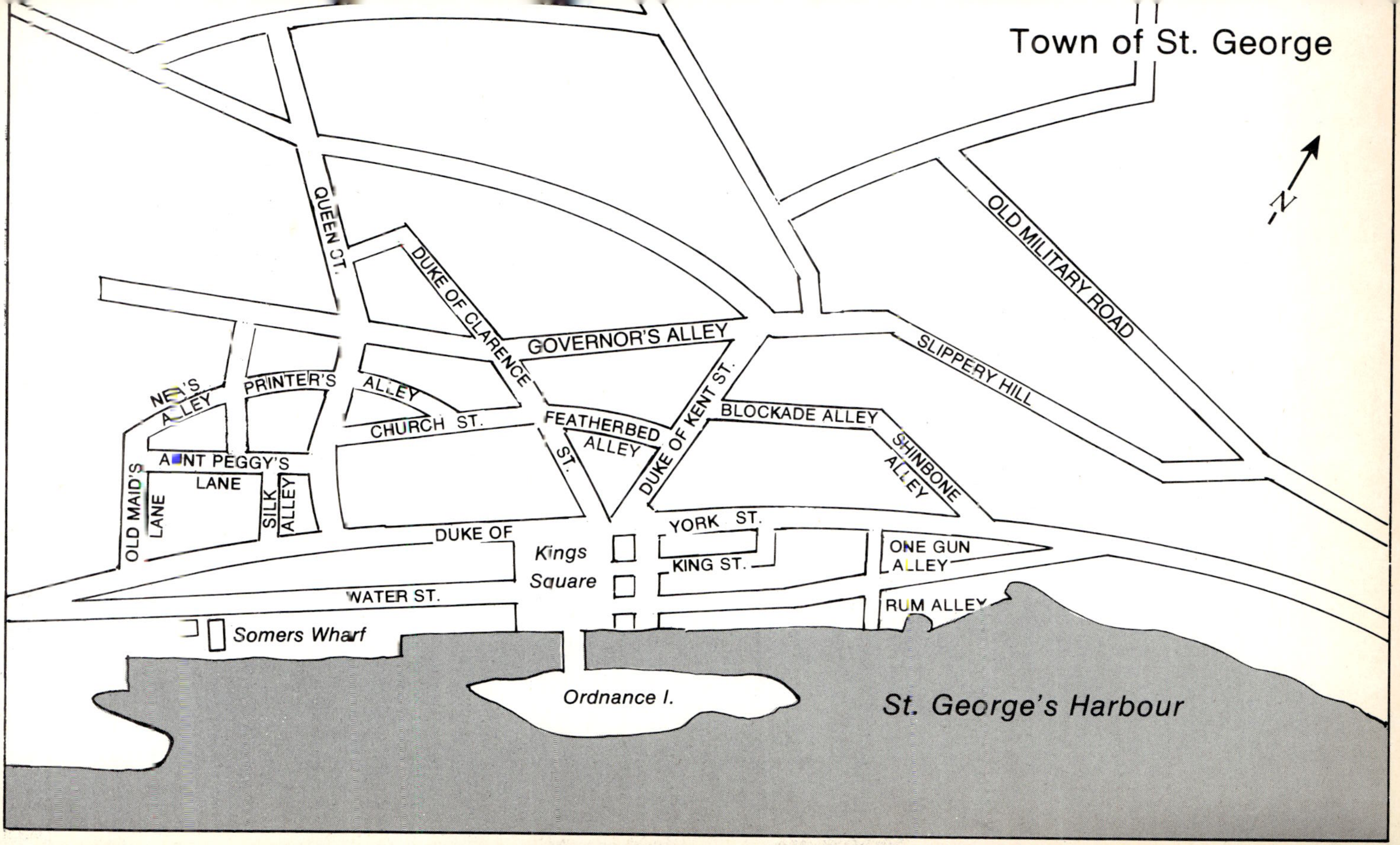
Town of St. George
N
OLD MILITARY ROAD
SLIPPERY HILL
QUEEN ST.
DUKE OF CLARENCE
GOVERNOR'S ALLEY
DUKE OF KENT ST.
BLOCKADE ALLEY
SHINBONE ALLEY
PRINTER'S ALLEY
ALLEY
CHURCH ST.
FEATHERBED ALLEY
ST.
AUNT PEGGY'S LANE
OLD MAID'S LANE
SILK ALLEY
DUKE OF
YORK ST.
KING ST.
ONE GUN ALLEY
RUM ALLEY
Kings Square
WATER ST.
Somers Wharf
Ordnance I.
St. George's Harbour

through Saturday, 9 a.m. to 4 p.m. Closed holidays. Admission: $3.50 for adults; $2 for senior citizens and children under 12.

*Deliverance • *Ordnance Island, across the short bridge from King's Square* • After Sir George Somers and his crew were shipwrecked on the island's reefs in the *Sea Venture* in 1609, they came ashore and built Bermuda's first vessels, the *Deliverance* and the *Patience*. The *Deliverance*, the larger of the two, was made on St. George's Island from materials salvaged from the *Sea Venture* as well as from local cedar. Although the *Patience* was the ship constructed on Ordnance Island, this is where you can now climb aboard a full-scale replica of the *Deliverance*. In 1610 about 150 people sailed from Bermuda to Jamestown, their original destination, in the two new ships. An exploration of the *Deliverance* replica will give you a good idea of how crowded it must have been. Inside you can see wax figures dressed in period clothing. On display are also objects the early settlers brought from England. *Open daily, 10 a.m.–4 p.m. Admission: adults–$1.50; children under age 12–50¢. From April to Sept., free refreshments every Wed., 10 a.m.–1 p.m.*

*Tucker House • *Water Street, just west of Queen Street; tel: 297-0545* • Built in 1711, this cottage became the home of members of the distinguished Tucker family in 1775. With relatives living in South Carolina and Virginia, the Tuckers were bitterly divided over the American Revolutionary War. Colonel Henry Tucker, the father of the owner of this house, tried to remain neutral. But after the American Continental Congress ordered a halt to the exportation of food to any British colonies, he decided to act against his Mother Country. Without the knowledge of Bermuda's governor (a relative by marriage), Colonel Tucker led a group of prominent Bermudians to Philadelphia to offer salt in exchange for the supplies on which Bermuda was so dependent. But because what the Americans wanted was gun powder, not salt, they were turned down. Then one summer night in 1775, a large store of gun powder from St. George's was secretly loaded onto two American warboats in Tobacco Bay. The Governor was livid, of course, when he heard about the theft, and suspected the Tucker family. However, since the island was supplied with food throughout the war, there was no serious attempt to expose those involved in the crime.

Tucker House was also the home of Joseph Hayne Rainey, a former South Carolinian slave who rented the present kitchen. During the Civil War, he came to St. George's to get away from the South. While his wife became a dressmaker, he set up a barber shop in what is now the Joseph Rainey Memorial Room. When the war ended, he returned to the United States to be elected the first black member of the House of Representatives, during Reconstruction. A lane outside the kitchen door was named Barber's Alley in his honor.

The restored interior of this Bermuda National Trust property contains antique silver and furniture, a pearl wedding necklace strung on a rope made of human hair, and a 17th-century Cromwellian lantern clock, built with only one hand on its face to point to the hour. *Open Mon. through Sat., 10 a.m.–5 p.m. Closed for lunch and holidays. Admission: Adults–$2; children under age 12–50¢.*

***The Carriage Museum** • *Water Street; tel: 297–1367* • Here on display are the elegant vehicles that Bermudians used before 1946, when the first private cars came to the island. These carriages range from a huge, high four-horse carriage to a child's two wheeler that was pulled by a pony. These predecessors of the automobile stand in stalls in much the same way as they would have been parked years ago. You can even climb into one and be transported into the past. Along with the Carriage House Restaurant and renovations of other landmarks on Somers Wharf, the museum is part of a multimillion dollar development program. *Open Mon. through Fri., 9 a.m.–5 p.m. Closed holidays. Donations accepted.*

St. George's Library • *Stuart Hall, Aunt Peggy's Lane; tel: 297–1912* • Any of this public library's cedar-beamed rooms is a relaxing place to sit and read. The library is located in a house built around 1706, and most of the furniture was made in Bermuda. *Open Mon. and Wed., 10 a.m.–6 p.m.; Sat., till 5 p.m. Closed 1–2:00 p.m. for lunch, and all holidays.*

The Old Rectory • *Broad Alley (just north of St. Peter's Church)* • Said to have been built by a reformed pirate in 1705, this timber and stone cottage served as the rectory of the Reverend Alexander Richardson, a much-loved Irish bishop. A story has it that Rev. Richardson once preached an impassioned sermon against officials who refused to pay for a stranger's funeral. The rectory is now owned by the Bermuda National Trust. *Open Tue. and Sat., 10 a.m.–5 p.m. Closed one hour for lunch. Admission: free, but donations are welcome.*

***St. Peter's Church** • *Duke of York Street (across from the Confederate Museum); tel: 297–8359* • St. Peter's stands on what is thought to be the site of the oldest Anglican church in the Western hemisphere. The first meeting of the island's Parliament took place here in 1620. In the present structure, built in 1713, you can see the original altar, first used in 1624. A silver communion service presented to the church by King William III in 1697 is still used regularly. Two bitter enemies gave the brass chandeliers hanging over the center aisle. The simple whitewashed building, with the long, wide brick staircase leading up to its rich brown cedar doors, is one of the most photographed sights in Bermuda. Look for famous names in the main graveyard, such as the American naval officer Richard Dale, who was killed in the final battle of the War of 1812; and Governor Sir Richard Sharples and his aide, Captain Hugh Sayers, who were assassinated in 1973. You can also visit the slaves' burial ground, a small area west of the main churchyard, where some of the graves bear first names only. *Open daily, 9 a.m.–5 p.m. Guide on duty, except Sun. and holidays.*

The Unfinished Church • *off Duke of Kent Street and Slippery Hill Road (on Barracks Hill)* • In 1874 this church was begun to replace the nearby deteriorating St. Peter's, the oldest church in Bermuda. When the foundations were being dug, something frightful was uncovered: the skeleton of a guard who had been murdered while on duty one summer night a hundred years earlier. He had disappeared that hot night during the American Revolution when the colony's store of gunpowder was stolen and loaded onto American ships—in exchange for food for Bermuda. But no church was ever completed above this once secret grave. Before it was finished, a means to restore St. Peter's was discovered, and the new church was left to become the verdant, picturesque ruin it is today. A local joke provides another explanation for this church's abandoned state: While it was being constructed, the minister was given a large sum of money and sent off to buy stained glass and other supplies. . . . Everyone is still waiting for him to return.

Featherbed Alley Print Shop • *Featherbed Alley, between Duke of Kent and Duke of Clarence streets; tel: 297–0009* • Located in a former home along with St. George's Historical Society Museum, the print shop contains a working 18th-century press. The printer invites visitors to help him print leaflets. *Open Mon. through Sat., 10 a.m.–4 p.m.; closed holidays. Free admission.*

St. George's Historical Society Museum • *Featherbed Alley, between Duke of Kent and Duke of Clarence Streets. (Shares the building with the print shop.); tel: 297–0423* • Built in 1725, this former home contains an original 18th-century kitchen and pantry with cooking utensils from that period hanging over the fireplace. You can also see antique furniture, china, documents, and paintings, much of which is said to have been acquired by privateers and pirates. In addition to a rare Bible printed in 1644 and a blubber cutter once used by Bermudian whalers, there are axe heads made by North American Indians, some of whom were early settlers of St. David's Island.

In 1801 John Stephenson, a Methodist missionary, was fined and imprisoned for preaching to black people in front of this building. Not giving in, he continued to preach to them from his cell window (in the basement of the building that is now the town post office). *Open Mon. through Sat., 10 a.m.–4 p.m.; closed holidays. Admission: $1; 50¢ for children under age 16. Free for children under 6. During Rendezvous Time (mid-Nov. through March), free for everyone on Mon.*

Somers Gardens • *Duke of York Street* • This small park, with its ornamental trees, indigenous flowers, and shrubbery, was once swampland. The memorial here honors Sir George Somers, whose shipwrecked *Sea Venture* crew helped him settle the island when they discovered it in 1609. Somers and his men finally reached their original destination, Jamestown, on the *Deliverance* and the *Patience,* but found the colonists there starving. Somers died in 1610, shortly after returning to Bermuda for food for the American colonists. While his body was taken back to England, his heart was buried where this quiet park is located. A life-size statue of him stands on Ordnance Island. *Open daily, 7:30 a.m.–4:30 p.m.*

Old State House • *Princess Street* • This limestone building, with mortar made of turtle oil and lime, was constructed in 1619, and is believed to be the first stone building in Bermuda. Parliament met here for years, until the capital was moved to Hamilton in 1815. Since then, the building has been rented by members of the Masonic Lodge, who pay the government a token one peppercorn a year in an elaborate ceremony every April. *Open Weds. from 10 a.m. to 4 p.m. Free admission.*

Bridge House • *Kings Square (diagonally across from Old State House)* • An art gallery can now be found in this 18th-century former home. The house got its name because a small bridge once stretched across a creek in front of it. (The creek has been filled in.) The building is owned by the Bermuda National Trust.

OUTSIDE TOWN

Natural Arches • These two 35-foot tall stone arches rise from the beach near Tucker's Town. For hundreds of thousands of years the relatively soft limestone here has been pounded by the ocean and hit by winds to create this striking natural sculpture. The arches were once caves whose walls and ceilings collapsed, weakened by centuries of powerful waves.

They are located at the end of South Road, Tucker's Town (next to the Mid Ocean Beach Club). Directions: Turn right at the bus stop near the end of South Road and follow signs to "Natural Arches" and "Castle Harbour Beach." At the end of this road, walk to the left of the building on the sandy path. Go up a slight incline for about 50 yards until you are as close as you can get to the ocean. You will see the arches below you to the right.

*Fort St. Catherine • *overlooking St. Catherine Beach; tel: 297–1920* • If you visit only one of the island's many forts, it should be this one. Not only is it the largest in Bermuda, but it also overlooks the reefs where the *Sea Venture* was shipwrecked in 1609, and the beach where the first settlers came ashore. Above and underground you can see dioramas of important moments in Bermudian history, reproductions of the British Crown Jewels, a display of guns used throughout the British Empire's history, and life-size replicas of the fort's kitchen and duty room. The walls are 8 feet thick and huge cannons point out to sea, but like many other forts in Bermuda, this one was never used to defend the island. The fort was first built of wood in the early 17th century under Richard Moore, the island's first governor. The present stone structure was built on the site in the 19th century and has been completely restored. *Open daily, 10 a.m.–4:40 p.m. Closed Christmas Day. Admission: adults–$2.50; children under age 12–free.*

Gates Fort • *intersection of Cut and Barry Roads, Gates Bay* • Like Fort St. Catherine, this restored fort is one of nine built under Bermuda's first governor, Richard Moore. It was named in honor of Sir Thomas Gates, a survivor of the shipwrecked *Sea Venture*. Gates, who later became the governor of Jamestown, is said to have jumped from the *Sea Venture* lifeboat yelling, "This is Gates, his bay!" *Open daily, 10 a.m.–4:30 p.m. Free admission.*

Carter House • *Naval Air Station, St. David's; tel: 297–1150* • This limestone former house, dating from about 1640, is one of the oldest stone buildings in Bermuda. It was built by descendants of Christopher Carter, the only *Sea Venture* crew member who remained on the island until he died. The old Carter home is now a museum celebrating Bermudian culture and U.S. military history. *Monday and Friday only. Special tours with 5 days' notice.*

TOURS

You can tour Bermuda on land or by sea—above and below the water. Bus, glass-bottom boat, or scuba diving and snorkeling tours run most frequently in the summer season (from March through Nov.). Some do not operate at all during the rest of the year.

Cruises can last anywhere from a few hours to a whole day. Rum swizzles and beer are served on some. On the Sea Gardens Dinner Cruise, visitors are taken to the Somerset Village Inn for a four-course Bermudian feast (4 hours, about $47.50, Tues.–Sun.). Sightseeing cruises include the Reef & Wreck Adventure (2 hours, about $20, sails twice daily) and the St. George's Cruise, which allows time for shopping in St. George (6 hours, about $35, Tues.–Fri.).

Bus tours, usually several hours long, cover points of interest such as the St. George's/Harrington Sound area, where you'll have a chance to visit the 17th-century original capital, the aquarium and zoo, and underground caves. Some bus tours are open only to groups.

Taxi tours cost about $16 an hour. These are usually the most fun because you visit only what you want to see.

Many hotels make bus, cruise, or taxi arrangements for their guests. Go to the tour or social desk at your hotel, or a Visitors' Service Bureau for the most up-to-date information about prices and tours offered.

SPORTS

Beaches • The island's most attractive beaches are public, and the south shore, especially in Southampton and Warwick, has some of the nicest in the world. Waves tend to be bigger on the south shore than on the north. **Horseshoe Bay** in Southampton, with unobtrusive changing facilities and a snack bar, is probably the most popular beach. Along with **John Smith's Bay** in Smith's, Horseshoe Bay now has lifeguards during the summer. Also in Southampton are isolated **Church Bay,** with many reefs and an abundance of marine life, and quiet and secluded **West Whale Bay,** a tiny cove at the bottom of a cliff. Beaches at both **Warwick Long Bay** and the **Longtail Cliffs** area are noted for their pink sand, colored by bits of coral and shells. Warwick Long Bay, where bathers dive off the boulders that jut out of the water, attracts many snorkelers. **Jobson Cove** in Warwick can be nice for skinny dipping after dark. On the private **Tucker's Town Beach,** you can see the 35-foot-tall Natural Arches. **Long Bay** in Sandys is also picturesque.

Bermuda International Marathon and Ten-Kilometer Race • In January, runners flock to the Bermuda International 10-kilometer race beginning at the National Stadium. The route offers views of oleander, hibiscus, palms, and the dark-blue-and-turquoise ocean. The next day is the International Marathon, where runners go through downtown Hamilton twice, and along the scenic north shore for 10 miles. For entry forms and more information, contact the Bermuda Track and Field Association, P.O. Box DV 397, Devonshire DV BX, Bermuda.

Boating • Most large hotels have watersports facilities available to their guests as well as to people staying elsewhere. In Hamilton Parish, Bermuda Water Sports (293–2640, ext. 1938) at the Grotto Bay Hotel, for example, has sunfish, pedaloes, and yak boards (which are somewhere between a surfboard and a paddleboard). You can rent various kinds of boats from the following places: Tobacco Bay Beach House, St. George's (293–9711); Rance's Boatyard, Pembroke (292–1843); Robinson's Charter Boat Marina, Somerset Bridge, Sandys (298–9408 or 294–0709); Salt Kettle Boat Rentals, Paget (236–4863 or 236–3612); and Mangrove Bay Marina, Sandys (234–0914).

Prices for boats that you sail yourself range from about $20 to $65 for a half day, and $35 to $100 for a full day. You can also rent boats for one or two hours. Outboard motor boats without skippers cost from about $50 to $80 for a half day, and from $80 to $110 for a full day.

Sailing lessons are given at Salt Kettle Boat Rentals. In Salt Kettle you can also charter a powerboat with a licensed skipper. Yachts with licensed skippers can be chartered at Bermuda Water Tours, in the city of Hamilton (295–3027); Bermuda Caribbean Yacht Charter in Sandys (234–0497); Chicane Charters in Hamilton (235–0775, days; 236–7278, eves.); Somerset Bridge Cruise in Sandys (234–0235); Starlight Sailing Cruises in Pembroke (292–1834); Ocean Yacht Charters in Hamilton (295–1180), and Salt Kettle Boat Rentals in Paget (236–4863).

Bowling • If you want to keep that arm in shape, you can bowl on one of 16 lanes at the Bermuda Bowling Club & Warwick Lanes (236–5290), open Mon. through Fri., from 6 p.m.–midnight; Sat. and Sun., 2 p.m.–midnight. In February, the Annual Bermuda Invitation Rendezvous Bowling Tournament is held here. *$1.75 per game; shoes 50¢ per pair.*

Fishing • Many avid anglers consider Bermuda one of the world's greatest fishing areas, particularly for light tackle fishing. Fishing is best from May through November. The kinds of fish caught in different locations are as follows:

Deep sea—Wahoo, amberjack, almaco jack, rainbow runner, barracuda, dolphin, blue marlin, white marlin, blackfin tuna, yellowfin tuna, and skipjack tuna.

Reef—Greater amberjack (school size), almaco jack, barracuda, little tunny, Bermuda chub, gray snapper, yellowtail snapper, and assorted bottom fish.

Shore—Bonefish, pompano, gray snapper, and barracuda.

Spearfishing is not allowed within one mile of any Bermuda shore and spear guns are not permitted in the country. No lobsters at all can be taken from April 1 through the end of August.

Shore fishing equipment can be rented at Bermuda Water Sports (293–2640) at the Grotto Bay Hotel, Fly Bridge Tackle in the city of Hamilton (295–1845); Four Winds Fishing Tackle Co., also in Hamilton (292–7466); Robinson's Charter Boat Marina in Somerset, Sandys (238–9408 or 234–0709); Salt Kettle Boat Rental in Paget (236–4863 or 236–3612); and Capt. John Shirley Boat Rentals in Mangrove Bay, Sandys (234–0914 or 234–1889). Charter boats can be rented for deep-sea fishing through Bermuda Sport Fishing Association Booking Office (295–2370 or 295–1986) or Bermuda Charter Fishing Boat Association Booking Office (292–6246).

Golf • Bermuda has more golf per acre than any other country. Golf is played here year-round. Public courses are Ocean View Golf and Country Club (292–6758), Port Royal Golf Course (234–0974), and St. George's (297–8067), the island's newest. Others, including those at the Mid Ocean Club, Riddells Bay Golf and Country Club, and the Belmont, Marriott's Castle Harbour, and Princess hotels, require introduction by a member or that arrangements be made through your hotel. The Mid Ocean Club in swanky Tucker's Town is considered the cream of the crop. All courses are 18 holes except the Ocean View Golf and Country Club, which is 9 holes. If you bring your own clubs, check with the airline you use, since some include them in the free baggage allowance while others charge a special rate.

Helmet Diving • From May through November, visitors may walk on the ocean floor at a depth of 10–14 feet without getting their hair wet. Even nonswimmers and those wearing glasses can try helmet diving, which allows them close-up views of marine life without the skill required for scuba diving or snorkeling. Touching fish, coral, and other marine life is part of the fun. Once participants have descended a ladder and are in the water up to their necks, 70-pound lead helmets are placed on their heads. Air pumped in by tubes allows them to breathe during the 30 minutes they spend underwater. These guided tours, which are perfectly safe for children, are conducted by the Hartley Helmet Diving Cruise in Smith's (234–2861) and Hartley's Under Sea Adventure in Somerset (234–2861 or 234–1556). *Cost: $28 per person.*

Horseback Riding • Spicelands Riding Centre in Warwick (238–8212) conducts trail rides several times a day and offers private, semi-private, and group lessons. Beginning at 7 a.m., the early-morning 2-hour ride along a beach is followed by a home-cooked breakfast (about

$25 during the winter season and $30 during the summer). Regular trail rides (about $15 for one hour) are along wooded routes perfumed with flowers and paths with dramatic views of south-shore beaches below.

Lee Bow Riding Centre in Devonshire (232–4181) is especially for children age 18 and under and has use of a 15-acre cross-country course. Here young people take trail rides or lessons for about $20 an hour. Junior event riders may attend equestrian workshops.

Jogging • *The Bermuda Runner's Map,* which you can pick up at hotels or Visitors' Service Bureaus, will tell you the distances and features of various attractive routes. It also gives you the dates of races in Bermuda throughout the year. Most people jog along the main roads, the beaches, and the railroad-right-of-way in Southampton and Sandys (see *The Bermuda Railway Trail Guide*). From November to March, joggers gather at the Botanical Gardens in Paget on Sunday mornings for one, two, and four-mile runs for a 25¢ fee. From April to October, these runs take place on Tuesday evenings. For information, call Sportseller, Washington Mall, Hamilton; 295–2692.

Scuba Diving and Snorkeling • Diving lessons and trips are conducted from March through January. Snorkeling trips run from May through November. Most of the large hotels have facilities for scuba diving and snorkeling available to guests as well as to those staying elsewhere. Masks, snorkels, weight belts, air tanks, fins, and other equipment can be rented at hotels or bought in sporting goods stores. Warwick Long Bay on the south shore is an exceptionally attractive area for snorkelers. Hotel tour desks will have details of snorkeling and diving excursions. Hartley's Under Sea Adventure, 234–2861, provides diving suits for seabed walks. Other diving operations are: South Side Scuba, Ltd., 293–2915, Nautilus Diving, Ltd., 238–2332, and Skin Diving Adventures & Blue Water Divers 234–1034.

Spectator Sports • You can watch tennis matches as well as cricket (May to September), rugby (September to December), and football (soccer—October to April).

Squash • Four squash courts are available to visitors at the Bermuda Squash Racquets Club in Devonshire (292–6881). Courts are open from 10 a.m.–4 p.m. and must be reserved.

Tennis • Tennis came to the U.S. from Bermuda, which now has about 100 courts at hotels and other locations. At many hotels, courts are free to guests. Tennis attire is preferred at all courts, except the Government Tennis Stadium, where tennis whites are mandatory. The following have courts lit for evening play: Ariel Sands, Belmont Hotel,

Bermudiana Hotel, Marriott's Castle Harbour, Coral Beach & Tennis Club, Elbow Beach Hotel, Government Tennis Stadium, Grotto Bay Hotel, Hamiltonian Hotel, Port Royal Tennis Courts, Sonesta Beach Hotel, and the Southampton Princess. All year, there are tournaments you are welcome to watch.

Waterskiing • Arrangements to waterski can be made through Bermuda Water Sports at the Grotto Bay Hotel in Hamilton Parish (March–November; 293–2640); Bermuda Waterski Centre in Somerset (late-April–end-October; 238–9408); and Somerset Bridge Cruises (year round; 234–0234); as well as through other hotels.

Windsurfing • To try this thrilling combination of surfing, sailing, and skiing, contact Hugh Watlington's Windsurfing Bermuda (236–6218), the first such school in Bermuda, which will teach the rudiments of this sport in a 1½-hour session. Salt Kettle Boat Rentals (236–4863 or 236–3612) also provides lessons and equipment.

NIGHT LIFE

Clubs with shows, music, and dancing are found at many of the larger hotels and some of the smaller ones. **The Gazebo Lounge** at the Hamilton Princess and **Le Cabaret** at the Inverurie, for instance, present shows for about $28 per person including two drinks and gratuities. Except on Sundays, the **Empire Room** at the Southampton Princess hosts a dinner show for $40 per person, not including drinks. Sometimes live bands or singers will entertain at restaurants. Pubs, mostly along or near Front Street in Hamilton, are usually filled with ale-drinkers, dart-players, and young folks trying to meet each other. **Rum Runners** and **Robin Hood** are two of the most popular. When there is a cover charge at a discotheque or night club, it is generally between $5 and $8. Note that during Rendezvous Time (mid-November through March) some hotels and restaurants offer less frequent entertainment or none at all.

CITY OF HAMILTON

The Forty Thieves Club • *Front St.; tel: 292–4040* • After spending several years as Disco 40, drawing a wild, young crowd, this club has changed its personality and returned to its original name. The theme now is tropical and the nightly shows feature Bermudian calypso bands, Caribbean steel bands, and limbo. As we go to press, the manager has plans for weekly comedians, hypnotists, and impressionists. For the full show and a table, the cost is $27.50 per person, including two drinks and gratuities. Those who come to dance after the show will pay $12, including two drinks. Closed Sundays.

The Club • *Bermudiana Rd.; tel: 295–7799* • This popular disco is packed on weekends and often during the week as well. On Sunday nights it becomes a jazz club, filled with the sounds of the live band that also plays at the Sparrow's Nest. Admission is free if you dine at the first-floor Little Venice restaurant, Tavern on the Green in the Botanical Gardens, the New Harbourfront on Front Street, or La Trattoria on Washington Lane in Hamilton.

Oasis • *Front Street's Emporium Building; tel: 292–4978* • This nightclub is bright with exotic plants and unusual artwork. The Bambu Lounge features quieter music.

The Spinning Wheel • *Court St.; tel: 292–7799* • At this triplex disco, people party 'til dawn, then have a pre-sunrise breakfast of codfish and potatoes. Truly a local hangout, it is located "back a' town," as Bermudians say. Some visitors may feel less like outsiders if they go with Bermudians.

Sparrow's Nest • *Reid St.; tel: 293–9161* • On Saturday nights, this club, open 'til 3 a.m., showcases Bermuda's best jazz musicians.

The Coral Rock Cafe • *Reid St.* • Through music and old posters, Sam and Dave, Wilson Pickett, Otis Redding, and other greats come to life at this bar, which features the sounds of the 50s, 60s, and 70s. The Coral Rock Cafe is one of Hamilton's newest nightspots and is located near the Forty Thieves Club.

Casey's • *Queen Street* • With music throbbing from the juke box, this local bar is always "packed out." Friday nights draw the largest crowd. This is the kind of place where you're likely to meet a lawyer in a suit chewing the cud with a construction worker with concrete dust on his boots.

Place's Cafe, on Dundonald Street, and the **Captain's Lounge** and **Triangle's Golf Club,** both on Reid Street, are three other after-hours spots to try if you're looking for local color.

DEVONSHIRE

Clay House Inn • *North Shore Rd.; tel: 292–3193* • During the summer, this club caters to the cruise ship crowd. The mainly Afro-

Caribbean revues feature limbo, glass-stomping, fire eating, and a steel band that also plays European classical music. A major jazz club during the 50s and 60s, Clay House Inn has been graced by the likes of Hazel Scott and Chuck Mangione. Jazz bands and international entertainers such as Roberta Flack appear from time to time during the off season.

The Anchorage • *North Shore Rd.* • Next door to the Clay House Inn, this is a *very* local after-hours hangout.

HAMILTON PARISH

Prospero's • *Grotto Bay Hotel; tel: 293–8333* • The big band music and the location—in a cave!—are definite lures. Open until 1 a.m.

SOUTHAMPTON

The Touch Club • *Southampton Princess Hotel; tel: 238–8000* • This crowd-pleasing disco plays all kinds of music, from snuggle up to shake it up.

Lillian's • *Sonesta Beach Hotel; tel: 238–8122* • People stay on after dinner or come from other restaurants for night caps, coffee, desserts, and dancing.

WARWICK

Flavors • *Middle Rd. in Riddell's Bay; tel: 238–1498* • This disco and lounge is one of the island's oldest nightspots. Dancing is upstairs from 10 p.m. to 3 a.m. The lounge downstairs, where a live band plays in the evenings, is open from 4 p.m. to 3 a.m.

The Golden Hind • *South Rd.; tel: 236–5555* • Comedian Jimmy Keys performs his patented cabaret act here. Plan to spend about $35 per person for the a la carte dinner show. You can also watch the show from Jimmy's Pub, the bar, where snacks are served starting at 10:30 p.m.

SHOPPING

The island's three main shopping areas are the city of Hamilton, St. George's, and Somerset Village. Most stores are in Hamilton, Bermuda's capital, where the larger stores have main branches. The best bargains are European imports, which generally cost 25% to 50% less than in the U.S. Among such items are Italian, German, and French knitwear; European textiles, bone china, and crystal; Swiss watches; Norwegian enameled jewelry; Spanish, Italian, and British shoes; Burberry rainwear; British teas, chutneys, and marmalades; Icelandic wool knits; French perfumes; Porthault linens; and Florentine stationery. Now that duty rates on imported jewelry have been reduced, prices for good gold and silver are competitive with those on most Caribbean islands. Film tends to be more expensive than in the U.S.

Crafts made of cedar are popular, such as bookends, candlesticks, lamps, and handbags with cedar handles. Bermuda's trademark black rum is a good buy, along with other liquor at "in-bond" prices (sold to be consumed only outside Bermuda). For a delicious way to chew your rum, sink your teeth into a buttery slice of **Horton's Bermuda Black Rum Cake,** sold in decorative tins throughout the island.

You'll come across a surprisingly wide and colorful selection of sweaters in the larger shops, including **Archie Brown & Son, Smith's,** and **The Scottish Wool Shop. Constables of Bermuda** has a variety of Icelandic sweaters, jackets, coats, and blankets. **Trimingham's** department store, with branches throughout Bermuda, sells reasonably priced imports from Europe and the Far East, as well as clothing, cosmetics, and perfumes. Sheets and pillowcases used by Queen Elizabeth II are on display at the **Irish Linen Shop** on Front Street in Hamilton.

At the Somerset branch of **Wilson's Fine Jewelers,** you can watch the artisans at work. **Astwood Dickinson** on Front Street was the first jewelry store to produce a line of 14-carat gold "Bermuda Collection" pendants. They come in shapes including a spiney lobster, a cedar bough, a Bermuda onion, a longtail, and the *Deliverance*. Other shops in Hamilton include **Heritage House,** selling antiques, on Front Street West and **Rhubarb,** a needlepoint shop, on Queen Street. Many boutiques line Hamilton's Chancery Lane and Fagan's Alley, both between Front and Reid streets. With three stories of shops selling clothes, jewelry, antique coins, and artwork, the Emporium Building on Front Street always buzzes with activity. In St. George's, **Bridge House Straw Market** has bags, hats, and dolls, as well as bangles and T-shirts. **Frangipani,** also in St. George's, carries handmade dresses, sweaters, and shawls imported from Greece. **The Old Market** in Somerset Village has a collection of brass, copper, sportswear, antiques, and African woodcarvings. The chopping blocks and meat hooks here date back to the time when this shop was actually a meat market.

In addition to the gallery in City Hall, the following are among the art galleries in the city of Hamilton: **Pegasus** (across from the Princess Hotel), which has the largest collection of prints in Bermuda; **Thistle Gallery** (Park Street), with exhibits by Bermudian and visiting artists; **Wells Art Gallery** (Washington Mall), the **Windjammer Gallery** (corner of Reid and King streets), which has the largest collection of local art and photographs and also sells handmade jewelry; and Crisson-Hind (Front Street). Elsewhere on the island are **Art House** (South Shore Road in Paget, near the Paraquet Restaurant); and **Minstrel's Gallery** (Flatts Hill in Smith's), owned by Desmond Fountain, a sculptor.

DINING OUT

Bermuda's many restaurants offer visitors choices that range from a candlelit continental feast at Once Upon a Table in Pembroke to a sampling of local specialties in the casual, eclectic surroundings of Dennis' Hideaway in St. David's. You can stop at an English pub for fish and chips or a Chinese restaurant for shrimp in Szechuan sauce. Bermuda is far from lacking in Italian restaurants, and visitors can also satisfy cravings for Spanish food. At Tio Pepe in Southampton, crab legs are on the menu along with pizza. The Bombay Cycle Club has a variety of vegetarian Indian dishes. When you're in the mood to break the bank, head for Waterlot or Fourways, known as much for their good food as for their very steep prices. Although we have not yet been able to sample two of the island's newest restaurants, we've been hearing good things about them. Joining the growing number of other national cuisines is Tivoli Gardens, a Danish restaurant that readers tell us has a lavish smorgasbord. Reports are also favorable for the Ristorante Primavera, called very Italian, very chic. Look for more details in next year's edition of the book. In Hamilton, several restaurants have balconies facing the harbor. Unfortunately, however, the stunning view of the water is often blocked by cruise ships in port.

For the most part, the best (and freshest) Bermudian food comes from the sea. Much of the meat (and shrimp, surprisingly) is imported. Two delicacies are Bermuda lobster (crayfish from island waters from September through March, and lobster from Maine the rest of the year) and rockfish. There are many other kinds of fish to try, including yellowtail, hind, wahoo, and grouper. The "Bermuda fish" on many menus is simply whatever local fish was caught that day.

Get to know the real Bermuda (and save money) by eating in local restaurants specializing in home-style cuisine, such as The Green Lantern in Pembroke. At Herman's, a family restaurant in Warwick, you can have a traditional Bermudian breakfast of codfish, potatoes, and bananas.

Although most restaurants, in and outside of hotels, emphasize international cuisine, many serve at least one Bermudian specialty (see "Wining and Dining," p. 11). A 15% gratuity will be added to your bill at some restaurants. Especially during the summer season, most require reservations for dinner or Sunday brunch, and request that men wear jackets in the evening. At this time of year, you may even have to make reservations at the more expensive dining spots several days in advance. Many restaurants are closed or have limited hours on Sundays.

Combined as the Bermuda Collection, seven small hotels and cottage colonies (Cambridge Beaches, Glencoe, Lantana Colony Club, Newstead, Pompano Beach Club, The Reefs, and Stonington Beach) offer guests year-round dining exchange privileges. Those taking advantage of the program will treat themselves to some of Bermuda's finest dining in some of its most attractive settings, and in different parts of the island. Other hotels offering dining exchange privileges are the Princess and the Southampton Princess; and the Belmont and the Bermudiana. Evening diners may be discouraged by the steep cab fares between some of the hotels; however, you can save money in some cases by catching the last bus or ferry instead of taking a taxi both ways. While many visitors and Bermudians ride mopeds at night, we don't recommend it.

During Rendezvous Time (mid-November through March), 23 restaurants take part in another dine-around program, one that is quite economical. The restaurants range from the informal, such as the Reid Street Cafe and Ye Olde Cock & Feather, to the elegance of the Margaret Rose and the New Harbourfront. The set menus are available in different price categories, depending on the restaurant, from about $18 to $30 per person (not including drinks) for each three-course meal. Ask for sample menus at your hotel or see the Rendezvous Time packet handed out at the airport when you arrive. Be sure to make reservations at the participating restaurants, which are indicated by the abbreviation RDA in the following descriptions.

SANDYS

EXPENSIVE

Lantana Colony Club • *Somerset Bridge; tel: 234–0141* • All of the dining areas, indoors and out, are arranged and decorated to make eating here a memorable experience. The main dining room, with its glass roof and polished cedar tables, is an especially pleasant place. Homegrown flowers and plants, paintings, and sculpture are everywhere. The extensive menu changes daily, ranging from well-presented, delicate hors d'oeuvres to entrees such as veal in an apple brandy sauce, wahoo with lemon butter, and roast duck. An array of desserts is served from the trolley. On Mondays dress is informal for the set sirloin dinner. There is dancing on Tuesdays, Thursdays, and Saturdays. Reservations are recommended. *No credit cards.*

MODERATE–INEXPENSIVE

Somerset Country Squire • *Mangrove Bay Rd., Somerset Village; tel: 234–0105* • This tavern near the Watford Bridge ferry dock specializes in English and Bermudian fare. Featured are steak-and-kidney pie, sausages and mash, fish and chips, and Bermuda onion soup. Diners come miles for the curried mussel pie. You can eat outside on the terrace overlooking Mangrove Bay or downstairs in the dining room, where there is entertainment six nights a week. Dinner reservations are recommended. *No credit cards.* RDA.

The Village Inn • *Watford Bridge, Somerset; tel: 234–2449 or 238–9401* • The emphasis here is on seafood, featuring international and local cuisine. With a nice view of the water, this is the first restaurant you'll see if you arrive at Somerset by ferry. *Major credit cards.*

Il Palio • *Main Rd., Somerset; tel: 234–1049 or 234–2323* • This casual Italian restaurant about a 10-minute walk from Somerset Village serves lunch and dinner and has take-out service. The spiral staircase from the downstairs bar leads up to the main dining room where northern and southern Italian food is served. The take-out pizza is popular with the young crowd. In addition to a variety of pasta, the menu includes veal, steak, roast duckling, and seafood. Reservations are suggested. Closed on Tues. *No credit cards.* RDA.

Freeport Gardens • *Dockyard area; tel: 234–1692* • A short stroll from the Maritime Museum, this makes a good lunch stop. Try the peas and rice and the crispy wahoo, which is so nice and dry that it seems to have been deep fried without touching the oil. Dinner menu items include veal cordon bleu, strip steak, and jumbo shrimp. Near the bar, the walls are decorated with colorful paper currency from such disparate countries as Ceylon, Jamaica, Vietnam, Bolivia, Botswana, and Indonesia. One bill even bears these words: "The Japanese Government—Five Pesos." *No credit cards.*

The Blue Foam • *Somerset Bridge Hotel; tel: 234–2892* • When the excavation was being done for this site, workers dug up a well-preserved cedar sign carved with the words "Blue Foam"—hence the name of this popular restaurant. We've sampled some of the island's best fish chowder with black rum and sherry peppers here. The grilled fish is also delicious. Other menu items include Cornish hen, sirloin steak with garlic butter, and pizza.

INEXPENSIVE

Loyalty Inn • *Mangrove Bay, Somerset Village; tel: 234-1398* • As popular with locals as with visitors, this inn specializes in seafood, and is a 5-minute walk from the Watford Bridge ferry dock. At lunch time, eat on the patio overlooking Mangrove Bay. Menu selections include shrimp, lobster, omelets, burgers, and peas and rice. A 250-year-old Bermuda home was converted into this restaurant. *No credit cards.*

Woody's • *Ireland Island* • Near the West End Sail Boat Club, this local hangout serves excellent Bermuda fish and chicken dishes.

SOUTHAMPTON

EXPENSIVE

Lillian's • *Sonesta Beach Hotel; tel: 238-8122* • Popular during and after dinner, Lillian's serves everything from raw shrimp, oysters, and Florida stone crab claws to double veal or lamb chops and spring chicken with rosemary butter. A peek at the desserts before ordering dinner will convince you to leave room. "Mile High Ice Cream Pie," "Viennese Sacher Torte," strawberry shortcake, and black forest cake are among the killer sweets. For a delicious finish, choose from the assortment of international coffees with liqueurs. Then dance away the calories to the music of the live band. *Major credit cards.* RDA.

Henry VIII • *South Shore Rd.; tel: 238-1977 or 238-0908* • Across from the Sonesta Beach Hotel and right below Gibbs Hill Lighthouse, this friendly (sometimes noisy) Tudor pub and restaurant has a strolling minstrel (Wednesday nights). During Sunday brunch and all evenings (except Wednesdays), guests can join the singer-pianist for sing-alongs. Waiters are dressed in 16th-century costumes. Traditional English dishes include roast beef and Yorkshire pudding and roast prime sirloin. Bermuda mussel pie and seafood newburg are also on the menu. The Royal Sunday Brunch consists of hot and cold entrees, salads, and desserts. Men are asked to wear jackets for dinner. *Major credit cards.* RDA.

Newport Room • *Southampton Princess; tel: 238-8000* • For that elegant, no-holds-barred dinner out, the Newport Room is probably the place. In a room decorated to resemble a luxury yacht, all gleaming brass and polished teak, guests dine on Wedgwood china, drink from Waterford goblets, and use heavy English silver and fine linen napkins. The menu is continental with a touch of nouvelle cuisine and a bow to Bermudian tradition. The elegantly clad staff provides discreet and excellent service. A refreshing sherbet is served between courses. Reservations are a must. *Major credit cards.*

Waterlot Inn • *Middle Rd.; tel: 238-0510* • Eleanor Roosevelt, Mark Twain, Eugene O'Neill, and James Thurber are some of the more famous patrons of this historic inn that began as a tavern at the turn of the century. It is now owned by the Princess Hotels. Dinner here could easily set you back $50 per person. (Much to the annoyance of forward-thinking patrons, women who dine with men are given menus without prices.) Diners may come to the private north shore pier by boat, and eat on an outdoor terrace. Before descending to the indoor dining room, they can have drinks by the cedar bar. A model ship enclosed in glass is above the tiled cedar fireplace. Downstairs, below sloping dark beam ceilings, you can try such entrees as Guinea chicks (spiny lobster, a house specialty) or curried chicken breast stuffed with banana and pimentos. The Caesar salad prepared at tableside comes with a wonderfully spicy dressing. Soft background music played on the baby grand by the bar floats downstairs. In addition to dinner served daily, the inn also has a good Sunday brunch. Reservations are essential and men are asked to wear jackets and ties in the evenings. *Major credit cards and Princess Hotels cards.* RDA.

Whaler Inn • *East Whale Bay, off South Shore Rd.; tel: 238-0076* • This informal restaurant at the Southampton Princess beach club overlooks the south shore coast. Guests may eat in the dining room or on the outdoor terrace. Sunday brunch is popular here. After dinner, you can dance on the terrace until midnight.

MODERATE TO EXPENSIVE

The Greenhouse • *Sonesta Beach Hotel; tel: 238-8122* • At this pleasant indoor and outdoor restaurant overlooking the pool and Boat Bay, unusual dishes include pompano with macadamia nuts and boned pheasant stuffed with cognac-soaked fruit and cooked in a puff pastry crust.

The Reefs • *South Shore Rd.; tel: 238-0222* • Dinner reservations are mandatory for the main dining room in this small hotel overlooking the beach. The menu changes daily, offering dishes such as honeydew melon with Parma ham, French onion soup, coq au vin, roast leg of lamb, Dover sole, and cheese with fruit. A band plays during dinner. Try to make the weekly Saturday night buffet. With a dramatic ocean view, this bright, attractive dining room is an especially pleasant place for lunch. Midday selections include salads, hamburgers, tuna melts, and other sandwiches. Coconuts, down by the water, is the hotel's more casual restaurant.

Pompano • *Pompano Beach Rd.; tel: 234–0222* • Many visitors talk as much about Pompano's good food as they do about the friendly, efficient service. Aimee Southworth, wife of the manager and a member of the family that owns the Pompano Beach Club hotel, is heavily involved in designing the menus, which change daily. One of her elaborate dinner creations is Bermuda fish filet stuffed with pistachios and truffle and scallop mousse, wrapped in spinach, and steamed with watercress sauce. Another night you might try beef stroganoff or seafood in a pastry shell, followed by raspberry cheese cake or Crepe Suzette. Reservations recommended. *No credit cards.*

MODERATE

Tio Pepe • *South Shore Rd.; tel: 238–1897* • This casual Italian and Spanish seafood restaurant near the entrance to Horseshoe Bay has everything from crab legs to take-out pizza. Closed on Tuesdays, Tio Pepe is a good family restaurant for lunch or dinner. *Mastercard, Visa, and Diner's Club.*

INEXPENSIVE

Port Royal Golf Club Restaurant • *off Middle Rd.* • From the bar and lounge of this large restaurant you can see both the ocean and the golf course. Only breakfast and lunch are served.

Riddell's Bay • *Middle Rd.; tel: 238–1090* • This informal roadside restaurant serves breakfast all day; also sandwiches, salads, beef and mussel pie, hamburgers, and fish cakes. Alcohol is not served.

Traditions • *Middle Rd.* • Popular with golfers, this casual restaurant serving homestyle breakfast, lunch, and dinner is across from the Port Royal Golf Course. Salad plates and sandwiches are on the menu as well as pork chops, fish, and collard greens. Cyclists can order from the take-out window.

WARWICK

EXPENSIVE

The Golden Hind • *Discovery Bay, South Shore Rd.; tel: 236–5555* • Lunch or Sunday brunch here isn't complete without a swim before or afterward. On a cliff overlooking the beach, the Golden Hind makes changing rooms available to diners, who eat on a breezy terrace high above the water. At night, Jimmy Keys has the crowd rolling with his cabaret dinner show. The $35 one-price-fits-all dinner menu includes an appetizer, soup or salad, the main course, dessert, and tea or coffee. Drinks, gratuities, and a few menu items are extra. Popular selections are spinach and oyster soup; sirloin with green, pink, and black peppercorn sauce; and breast of chicken with herb butter. Men are asked to wear jackets in the evening. *Major credit cards.*

Miramar • *Mermaid Beach Club; tel: 236–5031* • In this split-level dining room at the water's edge, dinner is table d'hote, with a limited a la carte menu. Lunch is also served. Specialties include veal curry, baby lamb chops, filet mignon, and chateaubriand. RDA.

INEXPENSIVE

White Heron Country Inn • *Riddell's Bay Rd.; tel: 238–1655 or 238–1617* • The dining rooms in this old manor house on the Riddell's Bay waterfront are relaxed and informal. Fish and chips wrapped in newspaper are on the rotating menu, along with stuffed shrimp and steak. Sunday is barbecue night. You can enjoy live entertainment at the pub. This is a good place to meet locals.

Herman's • *Dunscombe and South Shore rds.; tel: 238–9635* • Wonderful for a Sunday brunch of codfish and potatoes, this indoor and outdoor family restaurant specializes in home-style cooking. The omelets, soups, chowders, veggie burgers, hamburgers, pasta, seafood, sandwiches, salads, and other selections are popular among locals as well as visitors. Colorful framed posters decorate the walls. Near the counter at the entrance, you can buy everything from film and candy to magazines and sunglasses. High chairs for tots are available. Herman's is open from 7 a.m. to 11 p.m.

PAGET

EXPENSIVE

Fourways Inn • *Cobbs Hill and Middle rds.; tel: 236–6517* • French and Bermudian treats are specialties of this elegant and very expensive restaurant. Don't be surprised if you end up spending more than $60 per person for dinner. Fourways was built in 1727 as a private home and later became a pub. The original kitchen, with its spacious fireplace, has been converted into the bar. The menu includes caviar, French goose liver pate, escargot, cold salmon soup with chives, mandarin duck with orange sauce, lamb, rockfish, and steak tartar. There is also an extensive wine cellar. The small courtyard, with a fountain, is a romantic place to dine. A pianist entertains with soft classical and popular music. On Thursdays and Sundays, try the gourmet brunch. *Major credit cards.*

Tavern on the Green • *Botanical Gardens; tel: 236-7731* • After wandering through the Botanical Gardens, you may find this casual Italian restaurant (located on the grounds) a pleasant place to stop. You can dine inside or outside, surrounded by greenery, and you will be able to see the south shore. In the evenings, a guitarist plays and sings. Dinner here entitles you to complimentary admission to The Club disco in Hamilton. *Major credit cards.* RDA.

The Norwood Room • *Stonington Beach Hotel; tel: 236-5416* • The elegant table settings, chandeliers, and tall fanlight windows facing the water and lush greenery make this restaurant especially appealing. By day, the room is bathed in sunlight. By night, it is filled with soothing piano music. The imaginative continental cuisine is as attractively presented as it is delicious. *Major credit cards.*

Glencoe • *Salt Kettle; tel: 296-5274* • A two-minute walk from the Salt Kettle ferry stop, this small hotel restaurant is not far from the city of Hamilton. You can sit inside, or outside near the lively bar and watch the activity in Hamilton Harbour. The menu includes Bermudian and international selections. *Major credit cards.*

INEXPENSIVE

Mungal's • *Middle and South Shore rds.; tel: 236-8563* • Also known as Chicken Coop, this late-night spot near the Harmony Club hotel features fried chicken, soup, and hamburgers, along with Indian specialties such as roti, curried chicken or goat with rice, dhall, and mango chutney. While Mungal's is open from 6 p.m. until 6 a.m., only light snacks are served after 2 a.m. *No credit cards.*

Paraquet • *South Shore Rd.; tel: 238-9678* • Three meals a day are served at this local restaurant specializing in home-style food. This is a perfect spot for families. No alcohol. *No credit cards.*

PEMBROKE

HAMILTON

EXPENSIVE

The New Harbourfront • *Front St.; tel: 295-4207* • On the second story of a building right across from the ferry landing, this upscale restaurant is a good choice for a special night out. Candles flicker in glistening hurricane vanes inside and on the balcony. Lanterns adorn the walls. The long mahogany-trimmed granite bar is so attractive that you may want to linger there, chatting with the bartender, before your meal. To start, try the breast of duck in pineapple sauce or seafood ravioli. The chilled cream of broccoli soup, pastas, and soft shell crabs are all good choices. The piano bar remains open until 1 a.m. After dining here, you'll be admitted at no charge to The Club, the after hours spot around the corner. Men are asked to wear jackets and ties at dinner. *Major credit cards. RDA.*

Lobster Pot • *Bermudiana Rd.; tel: 292-6898* • This small informal restaurant decorated with lobster traps and fishnets is one of the city's most popular dining spots, particularly among locals. The menu consists of a wide variety of seafood dishes, as well as steak and chicken. *Major credit cards. RDA.*

Penthouse • *Front St.; tel: 295-3410 or 292-3414* • Located above Burnaby's and Longtail, this intimate gourmet restaurant has an extensive menu and a large wine cellar. The mushroom crepe in cheese sauce is especially good. The atmosphere is elegant and relaxed. Since space is limited, be sure to make reservations well in advance. *Major credit cards. RDA.*

Romanoff • *Church St.; tel: 295-0333* • This continental restaurant, serving everything from crepes filled with sherried seafood to an assortment of coffees, stirs up visions of old Europe. The owner's award-winning specialty is Turnedos Alexandra (beef tenderloin flambeed with cognac at your table). Mirrored walls reflect red carnations and the warm burgundy decor. Save room for something from the dessert trolley. *Major credit cards.*

The Little Venice • *Bermudiana Rd.; tel: 295-3503* • This popular Italian restaurant serves such imaginative entrees as salmon trout baked with olives, tomatoes, capers, and dry sherry; veal scaloppine with artichokes; and filet mignon cooked in red wine. Jacket and tie required for dinner. Complimentary admission to The Club, the disco upstairs. *Major credit cards.* RDA.

MODERATE TO EXPENSIVE

Fisherman's Reef • *Burnaby St.; tel: 292–1619* • Located upstairs from the busy Hog Penny Pub, this cozy, nautical restaurant is a convenient and pleasant place for lunch or dinner in the center of Hamilton. The extensive menu includes cold appetizers such as avocado and prawns, smoked salmon, and scallops cocktail royal; hot appetizers such as seafood crepes, champagne oysters, and escargots; and entrees such as guinea chicks, sharks, pepper steak, and filet mignon. Banana fritters and peach melba are on the dessert menu. There is a choice of special coffees. *Major credit cards.* RDA.

The New Queen • *Par-la-Ville Rd.* • This restaurant is run by a Chinese family that has been in Bermuda for more than seventy years. After a dramatic facelift, the New Queen is no longer a fast-food eatery. It now has a completely new menu (with much higher prices) that includes gourmet Szechuan selections. *No credit cards.*

Loquats • *Front St.; tel: 292–4507* • Ask to be seated on the balcony, with its long cedar bench running along the sides and front. The eclectic menu at this restaurant across from Number Six Passenger Terminal includes items such as corn and pumpkin chowder, Bahamian conch marinated in chili sauce with sherry peppers, souvlaki, baby back ribs, and grilled wahoo with honeyed mushrooms and bananas. Try the hot fudge brownie a la mode or pecan pie for dessert. Nightly entertainment adds to the warm atmosphere. *Major credit cards.* RDA.

The Conch Shell • *Second level, Emporium Building, Front St.; tel: 295–6969* • Asian and continental cuisine are featured at this restaurant with a balcony overlooking the harbor. You can have anything from teriyaki shrimp and fried rice to coquille St. Jacques and poached Bermuda fish with ginger sauce. *Major credit cards.*

MODERATE

Burnaby's • *Burnaby St.; tel: 292–0095* • A comfortable and informal restaurant, Burnaby's serves morning coffee, breakfast, lunch, afternoon tea, and an early dinner. *Major credit cards.*

The Longtail • *Front St., opposite the flagpole; tel: 293–9297* • Among the menu items at this casual restaurant are fish chowder, spinach salad, smoked salmon, escargots, chicken parmigiana, wiener schnitzel, vegetarian or seafood crepes, and burgers. Early bird specials are served from 6–8 p.m. *Major credit cards.*

Bombay Bicycle Club • *Reid St., Hamilton; tel: 292–0048* • This is a new-to-the-scene upscale Indian restaurant featuring spicy, northern cuisine by cooks from Delhi. There is an array of Tandoori dishes as well as curries and breads. Vegetarians can revel over more than 15 well-seasoned selections. Lunch, from Monday to Friday, is from noon to 2:30 p.m. and served buffet style, with dinner from 6:30–11 p.m.

The Balcony • *In A. S. Cooper, Front St., Hamilton; tel: 295–3961* • For the convenience of the department store's hungry shoppers, breakfast is served from 10 a.m., soon after A. S. Cooper opens. The continental dishes, bordering on the gourmet, are reasonably priced, with Japanese *sushi* a daily luncheon special. A traditional tea is served from 3 to 4:30 p.m., complete with finger sandwiches and scones.

Ram's Head Pub • *Reid St. East; tel: 295–6098* • Try the bangers and mash, steak and kidney pie, or sandwiches at this English-style pub and steakhouse. *Major credit cards.*

Showbizz • *Reid and King sts.; tel: 292–0676* • With black-and-white tile floors and walls hung with entertainment posters, this attractive cafe has an extensive menu (although several items weren't available during our last visit). Good choices include the chicken wings with sweet and sour sauce, gazpacho, avocado crab salad, burgers, onion rings, fish cakes, and coconut shrimp. Open for lunch and dinner Monday to Friday. Dinner only on Saturday and Sunday. Closes 1 a.m. *Major credit cards.*

Hog Penny Pub • *Burnaby St.; tel: 292–2534* • Downstairs from Fisherman's Reef, this is another good place for lunch during a trip to the city. This British-style pub is popular with locals, and offers traditional pub fare such as steak-and-kidney pie. There is entertainment at night. Lunch and dinner are served daily except on Sundays, when only dinner is served. *Major credit cards.*

INEXPENSIVE TO MODERATE

M. R. Onions • *Par-la-Ville Rd. North; tel: 292–5012* • M. R. Onions serves up barbecued chicken and ribs, sandwiches, ice cream sodas, and alcoholic beverages. Children aged 10 and under choose from a special menu in the "Kidds Korner." Closed for lunch on Saturday and Sunday. *Major credit cards.* RDA.

Portofino • *Bermudiana Rd.; tel: 292–2375 or 295–6090* • Behind a wrought-iron gate is Portofino, where you can dine in or take out freshly made original Italian specialties including 13 varieties of pizza. Phone at least 15 minutes ahead to place take-out orders. *No credit cards.*

La Trattoria • *Washington Lane, between Reid and Church sts.; tel: 292–7059* • This casual Italian restaurant is popular with families. If you've never had "pizza Pekinese" (made with snow peas, chicken, and sweet and sour sauce), here's the place to try it. The gelato is also good. Thursday is buffet night. Take-out service is available. After dinner here, you'll be admitted at no charge to The Club, the disco on Bermudiana Road. *Major credit cards.* RDA.

Ye Olde Cock & Feather • *Front St.; tel: 295–2263* • This friendly pub is a good place to chat with Bermudians over a beer, fish and chips, or a game of darts. You can stay up late here, dancing to the live music after dinner. *MasterCard and Visa for dinner only.* RDA.

Robin Hood • *Richmond Rd.; tel: 295–3314* • This former private home has the atmosphere of a country inn. A British-style pub and restaurant, Robin Hood is an unofficial expatriate's club, which also attracts a young crowd. Evenings include sing-alongs and games of darts. The upstairs wine bar and the hamburgers, in many varieties, are both popular. *No credit cards.*

Rum Runners • *Front St.; tel: 292–4737* • Here you can sit on a balcony overlooking Front Street and the harbor while you eat lunch or dinner. Though serving mostly pub fare, the restaurant offers a more formal ambience in the Lord Halifax Dining Room. *Major credit cards.*

INEXPENSIVE

The Botanic Garden Tea Room • *Trimingham's; tel: 295–1183* • Take a break from shopping at this Front Street department store by stopping at this greenery-filled oasis for morning coffee, a light lunch, or afternoon tea.

The Red Carpet • *37 Reid St.* • Reservations are not necessary in this casual restaurant that serves sandwiches, cold plates and salads, along with a variety of coffees and exotic drinks. The Red Carpet is located in the old Armoury. It is closed on Sundays and on Saturdays only dinner is served. *No credit cards.*

Lorraine's Checkerboard Diner • *Brunswick St.; tel: 292–5582* • You can sample Bermudian specialties at this casual and homey restaurant.

Prego • *Reid St.; tel: 292–1279* • Vying for distinction among Bermuda's good Italian restaurants is Prego. It offers an outstanding Vesuvio pizza as well as eggplant parmigiana and calamari. The service is quick and efficient.

Rendezvous • *Front St.; tel: 295 5373* • Breakfast, lunch, and dinner are served in this take-out and eat-in restaurant that is decorated with paintings by Bermudian artist Alfred Birdsey. Selections range from codfish cakes on buns and deep-fried scallops 'n chips to steak-and-kidney-pie and homemade chicken pie. Closed Sundays and holidays. *No credit cards.*

The Spot • *Burnaby St.; tel: 292–6293* • What this restaurant lacks in atmosphere it certainly makes up for in good cooking. Try the delicious homemade soups, such as split pea, black-eyed-pea, vegetable barley, or yellow pea. Breakfast, lunch, and dinner are served. No alcohol is on the menu. *No credit cards.*

Turkey's Rancho Grande • *Victoria Street* • The home-style meals here are plentiful and popular among locals. Chef and owner Turkey Barnes has cooked on ships and in hotels around the world.

Mac Williams • *Front St.* • Three meals a day are served at this pleasant restaurant near Waterloo House. For lunch, try the sandwiches, codfish cakes, pasta salad, peas and rice, or crabmeat on an English muffin with melted cheese. For dinner, chicken, veggie burgers, and lasagne are good choices.

The Reid Street Cafe • *Williams House, Reid St.,; tel: 292–4704* • Near many of Hamilton's stores, this cafe makes a good stop for weary shoppers. Dinner is served on Thursday, Friday, and Saturday nights only. RDA.

Angle Street Deli • *Angle and Court sts.* • You'll get generous portions of ribs, sausage and beans, meat loaf, and other hearty selections at this Mom and Pop–style deli. Bermudians know that this is one of the best places to find good home-baked desserts, such as apple or peach cobbler.

OUTSKIRTS OF HAMILTON

EXPENSIVE

Harley's • *Princess Hotel; tel: 295-3000* • A long wine list accompanies the menu of European specialties. A pianist entertains in the evenings. Lunch is served daily, and dinner is served every evening but Monday.

Once Upon A Table • *Serpentine Road; tel: 295-8585* • This former home, beautifully decorated with Victorian touches, has rounded archways, a sofa, and lace curtains. The atmosphere and service are warm and friendly. You'll be given sherbet between courses and sweets at the end of your meal. In addition, wine stewards, candlelit tables, and plentiful food make this continental restaurant one of the island's most pleasant places to dine. Stop by for afternoon tea with cucumber and watercress sandwiches, strawberries with cream, hot scones with jam, and homemade pastries. Once Upon a Table is closed on Mondays. *Major credit cards.* RDA.

INEXPENSIVE

The Green Lantern • *Serpentine Road, between Pitts Bay Road and Rosemont Avenue; tel: 295-6995* • For some local flavor, stop by this casual, friendly restaurant for fish and chips, peas and rice, broiled fish, chicken, or pork chops. No alcohol is served. The Green Lantern is closed Wednesday afternoons.

Richardson's • *North Shore Road; tel: 293-9577* • Open since 1924, this busy restaurant featuring home-style cuisine has been soaring in popularity over the past few years. It is known for its wonderful curry dishes, as well as its fish cakes, stews, soups, and beef pies. No alcohol is served.

DEVONSHIRE

Restaurants are limited to dining rooms in the cottage colony and guest houses.

SMITH'S

MODERATE
Palmetto Hotel • *junction of Flatts Hill, North Shore, and Harrington Sound Roads; tel: 293-2323* • While visiting the eastern side of Bermuda, you may want to stop at the small restaurant here for a lunch that includes a salad bar.

HAMILTON PARISH

EXPENSIVE
Plantation Club • *Harrington Sound Road; tel: 3-1188* • When you surface from a visit to Leamington Caves, stop at this restaurant. Its reputation as a *real* Bermudian dining place has grown dramatically. The menu includes steaks, chops, chicken, and seafood. You can dine outdoors in the summer and inside by a log fire on cool evenings. Dinner is served every night except Sunday and the restaurant closes from mid-December to the end of February. *Major credit cards.*

MODERATE TO EXPENSIVE
Tom Moore's Tavern • *Harrington Sound Road, Walsingham's Bay (near Leamington Caves)* • The scenic grounds surrounding this gourmet restaurant are maintained by the Bermuda National Trust. Named after the Irish poet who lived on the island in the early-19th century, the tavern was built in 1652 as a private home. *Major credit cards.*

INEXPENSIVE
Half Way House • *Flatt's Village; tel: 293-9200* • This popular spot was named for its location between the city of Hamilton and St. George's. Not far from the Aquarium, it is across from the sprawling, pink, former Coral Island Hotel. The menu includes hamburgers, sandwiches, soups, fish cakes, chicken legs, and fountain drinks.

Bailey's Ice Cream Parlour • *Blue Hole Hill* • In this Victorian style spot, you can cool off with homemade ice cream. Across from the Swizzle Inn, this ice-cream parlor also serves swizzle sherbert.

Swizzle Inn • *Blue Hole Hill* • This is a favorite stop among cyclists traveling between the city of Hamilton and St. George. Patrons have plastered their calling cards all over the restaurant. The home of the rum swizzle, a fruity drink that is more powerful than it tastes, the inn also serves swizzle burgers, shepherd's pie, sandwiches, and omlets, as well as Bermudian coffee (with Bermuda Gold liqueur). *Mastercard and Visa.*

ST. GEORGE'S

IN TOWN

EXPENSIVE

The Carriage House • *Water St.; tel: 297–1730 or 297–1270* • In the same building as the Carriage Museum, this restaurant is on the waterfront in the newly renovated plaza. The bare brick walls and arches retain the flavor of the 18th-century warehouse it once was. Beef and seafood dishes are on the menu. There is also a large salad bar. This is a good place to bring the family, especially for Sunday brunch. *Major credit cards.*

※ **The Margaret Rose** • *St. George's Club; tel. 297–1200* • This elegant hilltop restaurant overlooks the town and harbor of St. George's. Men are requested to wear jackets at dinner, which is served by candlelight. Menu selections might include fresh smoked river trout with cranberry cream, mushroom caps with tomato and herb stuffing, cream of onion soup, broiled double lambchops, or roast duckling. Reservations are suggested. The Margaret Rose is open daily for lunch and dinner. *Major credit cards.* RDA.

MODERATE TO EXPENSIVE

Fisherman's Wharf • *Somers Wharf; tel: 297–1515* • This seafood restaurant serves many island specialties such as fish cakes with peas and rice, conch or fish chowder, and curried Bermuda mussels straight from Harrington Sound. There is a sandwich board for lunch, and wine lists and dessert menus are given at dinner. *Major credit cards.*

MODERATE

Clyde's Cafe and Bar • *tel: 297–0158* • People come from all over the island for the fish sandwiches, fish and chips, and cole slaw served up in this neighborhood pub. Choose from the selection of beers and ales or try a dark and stormy (black rum and tangy ginger beer). Clyde's is open from noon until 1 a.m., except Tuesdays. *No credit cards.*

INEXPENSIVE
Pub on the Square • *King's Sq.; tel: 297–1522* • This British-style country pub serves sandwiches, pizza burgers, fish and chips, and has live entertainment at night. It's a good place to stop for lunch. *Major credit cards.*

White Horse Tavern • *King's Sq* • The location on the harbor makes this extra special. A casual restaurant with indoor and outdoor dining, this is St. George's oldest tavern. The building was originally Government House. *Major credit cards.*

OUTSIDE TOWN
MODERATE
Fort William • *Government Hill; tel: 297–0904* • One of St. George's unusual restaurants, this was once a gunpowder cavern. The menu includes filet mignon, lamb chops, veal, chicken, and seafood. Children's portions are available on request.

INEXPENSIVE TO MODERATE
Dennis' Hideaway • *St. David's Rd.* • You will be hard-pressed to find two pieces of furniture that match in this casual, family-operated restaurant on the water. Many locals and visitors have found this an ideal place for fresh Bermudian dishes such as turtle steaks, seafood stews, conch fritters, and shark hash. No alcohol is sold.

INEXPENSIVE
Black Horse Tavern • *between airport and St. David's Lighthouse; tel: 293–9742* • Not far from Dennis' Hideaway, this is another friendly local seafood restaurant specializing in home-style cuisine. *No credit cards.*

WHERE TO STAY

Not only does Bermuda offer a wide variety of accommodations from simple to luxurious, but it is also difficult to find a place to stay that is not well-kept, comfortable, and convenient to the rest of the island. No matter where you stay, you'll be close to beaches, water sports, tennis, golf, sightseeing, shopping, and restaurants.

Rooms in most guest houses, cottage colonies, and small hotels are individually decorated. These homelike touches reflect the personal attention guests can expect from staff. In addition, evidence of Bermuda's rich history is apparent in the architecture and surroundings of many of these accommodations.

Many guest houses, which can be quite economical, are in former private homes in garden settings. Most have pools and some are on the waterfront. Some serve breakfast and other meals, but many don't have dining rooms. Visitors can also save money by renting rooms in private homes. Make arrangements by contacting the Visitors' Service Bureau, Front Street, Hamilton, Bermuda.

Housekeeping cottages and apartments, with full cooking facilities and limited maid service, are popular with families and those who want privacy as well as comfort. Cottage colonies are like housekeeping units, except that they have main clubhouses with dining rooms, lounges, and bars. Their kitchen facilities may be used for light snacks but not for full-time cooking. Most cottage colonies are on private beaches and have pools. During the summer season, some require a certain number of nights minimum stay and room rates generally include breakfast and dinner.

Bermuda has two luxurious private clubs, Coral Beach and Tennis Club and the Mid Ocean Club. Both require the introduction of a member. Visitors can investigate time-sharing at the Hamiltonian Hotel & Island Club and St. George's Club.

While resort hotels may be more impersonal than other accommodations, they offer the greatest number of facilities, including private beaches, indoor and outdoor pools, golf courses, tennis courts, scuba diving, waterskiing, snorkeling, sailing, bars, restaurants, night clubs, international and local entertainment, and planned activities. Many have cycle liveries, stores, barber shops, beauty salons, games rooms, and taxi stands on the premises. Though with less extensive facilities, smaller hotels all have beaches and/or pools. While most establishments will help guests make arrangements for babysitters, and some have high chairs, large hotels may be best for children since many also have shallow pools and other recreational facilities for children.

All hotels and most guest houses are fully air-conditioned. (You may pay a daily surcharge, however, to use the air conditioners at some guest houses and housekeeping apartments.) The larger hotels have social desks where you can make arrangements to go on tours, or to take part in activities such as golf and scuba diving when they are not available at your accommodation. Most hotels and cottage colonies and some guest houses have nightly entertainment. Most will make arrangements for sports activities not available on the premises. Many serve complimentary high tea.

Most hotels and cottage colonies have MAP rates (Modified American Plan: the price of the room includes a full breakfast and dinner). Some hotels, particularly during the winter season, also offer BP (Bermuda Plan: full breakfast), and EP rates (European Plan: no meals). Except in a few cases, housekeeping apartments offer EP only. Guest houses offer MAP, BP, EP, and CP (Continental Plan: light breakfast). A daily service charge of about 10% (in lieu of tips) and a 6% government tax will be added to the cost of your room. *Note that most accommodations, even some large hotels, do not accept credit cards.* Some guest houses and hotels close for a few weeks during November, December, and January. See ''Hotel Quick Reference Charts'' for specifics.

RENTING PRIVATE HOMES

Those who would like to rent private homes can contact the Secretary of the Bermuda Chamber of Commerce Real Estate Division, c/o Visitors' Service Bureau, Front Street, Hamilton 5-31, Bermuda; (809) 295–4201. The following are some of the real estate agents you can also contact:

- Bermuda Realty Company Ltd., P.O. Box HM 724, Hamilton 5, Bermuda; (809) 295–0294
- L. P. Gutteridge, P.O. Box HM 1024, Hamilton 5, Bermuda; (809) 295–4545
- Kitson & Company, P.O. Box 449, Hamilton 5, Bermuda; (809) 295–2525
- Joy Lusher Estate Agent, Darrell's Wharf, Harbour Road, Warwick 7-17, Bermuda; (809) 296–5120 or (809) 296–0108
- Penboss Associates Ltd., P.O. Box HM 271, Hamilton 5, Bermuda; (809) 295–3927

In the **Hotel Quick-Reference Charts,** you'll find more information about the following accommodations, which we highly recommend, as well as details about additional establishments.

RESORT HOTELS

☆☆ **The Belmont Hotel Golf and Country Club** • *Warwick* • On a 110-acre estate overlooking Hamilton Harbour, this resort also has wonderful views across Great Sound. There is a large pool, and the hotel provides complimentary transportation to its south shore beach club. Electric golf carts are used on the private 18-hole championship golf course. Three all weather tennis courts are lit for evening games. The ferry to the city of Hamilton, just a few minutes away, sails from the Belmont dock. Guests are offered exchange privileges with the Harmony Club and the Bermudiana Hotel. (Expensive)

☆☆ **The Bermudiana Hotel** • *Pembroke* • This large, modern hotel on the edge of Hamilton is surrounded by subtropical gardens. Rooms overlooking Hamilton Harbour have balconies. There is an outdoor garden pool as well as an indoor pool. Complimentary transportation is provided to the hotel's south shore beach club. Facilities include tennis courts and turkish baths. Guests have exchange privileges with the Harmony Club and the Belmont Hotel. Hotel is likely to be sold before your visit.

★★★★★ **Marriott's Castle Harbour Resort** • *Tucker's Town* • This impressive luxury hotel stands on a high bluff overlooking Castle Harbour and Harrington Sound. Behind the unpainted limestone walls, which are truly castlelike, lies the beautifully elegant round lobby, with gleaming marble and terracotta tile floors. The 250 acres of well-tended grounds include an 18-hole Robert Trent Jones golf course, seven tennis courts, three heated swimming pools, and two sandy beaches. Guests are able to indulge in a number of water sports such as windsurfing, waterskiing, and snorkeling. Sunfish and mopeds can also be rented on premises. Guests rooms, suites, and public spaces are decorated with Queen Anne and Chippendale furnishings. Most rooms, some of which have balconies or patios, face the ocean. The Harbour Wing spills down a steep cliff to the waterside. At the entrance, the arresting view of the ocean through the tall windows is overwhelming. Instead of taking the elevator *up* to your room, you'll ride *down*. The six restaurants include Bermuda's only Japanese restaurant, The Mikado. Blossom's is the resort's popular night club. Guests not wanting to go into Hamilton for shopping will find that branches of some of the city's best shops are located in the hotel for the same prices as in town. (Expensive)

☆☆ **Elbow Beach Hotel** • *Paget* • On a private section of one of Bermuda's most popular beaches, this south-shore hotel is centrally located, only 10 minutes from downtown Hamilton. Guests can stay in balconied rooms in the main hotel, duplex cottages, lanais overlooking the free-form pool and ocean, and surfside lanais. Some ground-floor guest-rooms in the main building may be noisy since they are on a main hallway with stores and much activity. A third of the hotel's rooms have been redecorated, and new rooms have been added by the pool. Another addition is a shopping promenade. The pool is heated and has a fountain and a shallow play area for children. Two of the five tennis courts are lit for evening games and there is a health club. Note that Elbow Beach is the center of activities during College Weeks in March and April. (Expensive)

★★★ **Grotto Bay Beach Hotel & Tennis Club** • *Hamilton Parish* • The 21 acres of beautifully landscaped hillside on the water's edge make this a particularly pleasant place to stay. Located in nine cottages, all rooms have balconies with panoramic sea views. New rooms have color TV, refrigerators, coffee makers, and hair dryers. The decor throughout is bright and attractive, especially the sunny garden room where guests can have breakfast. There are two beaches, a pool, tennis courts, and a putting green. Prospero's, a night club, is only one of the illuminated grottos on the property and there are nightly shows in the Rum House Lounge. Grotto Bay has many activities for children including a summer "day camp." (Moderate)

☆☆ **Inverurie Hotel** • *Paget* • This centrally located low-rising hotel sprawls along the edge of Hamilton Harbour. Some of the balconied rooms overlook the water, where guests can sail, waterski, or swim from the main terrace. Other rooms have views of the large pool. The hotel has tennis courts, and provides a complimentary bus to a private beach club. On the wall in the coffee shop, a drink menu transports guests to 1927, when a martini could be had for 35¢ and Spanish sherry cost $3 a quart. Off the lobby is a comfortable sitting room with a fireplace. Nightly entertainment includes leading bands and international performers. (Expensive)

★★★★ **The Princess** • *Pembroke* • This luxury resort on Hamilton Harbour is at the edge of the city's main drag. The Princess is one of the island's first hotels. A few of the more famous guests during its 100-plus years of service have been Mark Twain, Prince Charles, and Muhammad Ali. From the elegant lobby, a marble staircase leads up to an indoor balcony with a striking view of the harbor. Hotel photos and menus dating back to the 19th century decorate the balcony wall. People having drinks in the back of the lobby can gaze at a fish-filled pond bordered by trees, moss, and small waterfalls. Floor-to-ceiling windows surround most of the Gazebo lounge. Many rooms have private balconies. There are two oceanside pools—one freshwater, the other salt. Guests have exchange privileges with the Southampton Princess, and complimentary transportation is provided to the private south-shore beach club and 18-hole golf course.

Special arrangements are made for repeat guests, such as business travelers. Through the Princess Club, members are guaranteed rooms and take advantage of express check-in and check-out. They receive a corporate rate, complimentary continental breakfast, and afternoon wine and cheese. Rooms for club members have TV sets, terry robes, toiletry kits, suit and skirt hangers, and desks with telephones. Golf- and tennis-playing executives are given a discount and there is same-day laundry and cleaning service. Checks up to $200 may be cashed and companies may be billed directly. Applicants may call (809) 295-2254. (Expensive)

★★★★★ **Sonesta Beach Hotel** • *Southampton* • This modern, beach front hotel is located on 25 acres of landscaped grounds. All rooms have balconies with views of the ocean. One of the three beaches is enclosed in a sheltered bay. Popular with honeymooners, the Sonesta Beach has a moongate through which newly married couples walk for good luck. The lawn overlooking cliffs and crashing surf is a dramatic place for sitting and relaxing. There are two pools—one enclosed in a bubble; the other, outdoors, is heated. In addition to tennis, windsurfing, scuba diving, and snorkeling, guests can play shuffleboard, croquet, and Ping-Pong. Golf can be arranged at nearby courses. The European health spa has a universal gym and separate facilities for men and women including exercise and massage rooms, whirlpools, saunas, and steam baths.

Lillian's offers dining and dancing. The Greenhouse Restaurant is for fine, gourmet dining. Four-course dinner cruises with cocktails on a glass-bottom boat are held twice a week with transportation to the dock and then to a restaurant. Nightly barbecues are held on the terrace and there is a weekly pirate's night. (Expensive)

★★★★★ **The Southampton Princess Hotel** • *Southampton* • A luxurious Georgian-furnished hotel on a 60-acre estate, the Southampton Princess has two pools, one indoors and the other outdoors, a nearby private beach club (transportation provided), an 18-hole executive golf course, and 11 tennis courts. It is perched on a hill and the spacious rooms with walk-in closets all have balconies with panoramic views. In addition to its gourmet restaurants, the hotel has other rooms for dining, as well as for dancing and entertainment. The Whaler Inn, a restaurant at the south shore beach club, and the Waterlot, a more formal dining spot on the north shore, are both run by the hotel. Transportation is provided. Inquire about the 54-room Newport Club, with special amenities for guests, which has opened in a wing of the 6th floor. Guests can take advantage of exchange privileges with the Princess Hotel just outside Hamilton. (Expensive)

SMALL HOTELS

★★★ **Glencoe** • *Paget* • Many guests, particularly avid boaters, return year after year to this waterfront owner-operated hotel. The main house is more than two centuries old. There are two heated freshwater pools and a (very) small manmade beach. With water on three sides, Glencoe is perfect for those who want to go windsurfing (lessons are given), deep-sea fishing, scuba diving, waterskiing, and sunfish sailing (free to guests). The bar on the large patio overlooks the small inlet where boats always seem to be coming and going. Guests eat meals on the lively patio or in the attractive indoor dining room. Meals range from pepper pot or chilled avocado soup to codfish cakes with banana chutney, roast duckling, and chocolate brioches with raspberry cream. Small winding outdoor stairways lead to guest rooms, each refreshingly distinct, on different levels. The colorful rooms and suites have sitting areas or living rooms, patios or balconies, wicker furniture, and old-fashioned dark exposed-beam ceilings or high wooden tray ceilings. Some also have fireplaces, double balconies, and round bathtubs. In the newest wing, the conference room has a view of the second pool, which doubles as a Jacuzzi. Located in scenic Salt Kettle, where salt was stored during the 1800s, Glencoe is a short walk from the ferry. Guests receive discount ferry tickets to Hamilton as well as complimentary copies of the *Royal Gazette,* Bermuda's daily newspaper. The hotel provides a free taxi ride to the cycle livery for those who want to rent mopeds. (Moderate)

★★★ **Harmony Club** • *Paget* • Now catering to couples, this all-inclusive resort was formerly the Harmony Hall Hotel. Although the clientele is much younger these days, one thing hasn't changed: the gorgeous flowerbeds throughout the grounds. The rate covers three meals a day, unlimited drinks, afternoon tea, evening cocktails, and one two-seater moped per room for your entire stay. You'll be greeted with a bottle of champagne when you arrive. Rooms, luxuriously decorated with Queen Anne furniture, are equipped with terry-cloth bathrobes or kimonos, hair dryers, and other welcome amenities. Recreational facilities include tennis courts, a swimming pool, whirlpool, and sauna. Guests have complimentary use of the facilities at the Discovery Bay Beach Club, where the Golden Hind restaurant is located. They are also admitted free to Oasis and The Club discos in nearby Hamilton. Many take advantage of exchange dining privileges at the Bermudiana and Belmont hotels. (Moderate)

☆☆ **Mermaid Beach Club** • *Warwick* • During spring break, the boisterous College Weeks crowd descends on this beachfront hotel that also has a pool. Individual rooms as well as two- and three-bedroom suites with kitchens are available. Most of the bright, sunny units have balconies, and some have televisions. Miramar Restaurant is on the grounds and guests have exchange dining privileges with the Jolly Lobster restaurant.

★★★ **Newstead** • *Paget* • Especially during spring and summer race weeks, sailing enthusiasts flock to this harborside hotel. With the sparkling pastel buildings of Front Street just across the water, the city of

Hamilton is a brief ferry ride away. From the patio where lunch is served, guests have a perfect view of waterfront activity. In addition to the heated salt-water pool, where playful dolphins are frozen in a sculpture, there are two all-weather tennis courts, a putting green, and sauna baths. Two private docks are good for deep-water swimming. One of Newstead's most arresting public rooms is the bar/lounge in the main house, a 19th-century mansion. With blood red walls and plush black couches and chairs, this room is a pleasant place to relax. Tea is served every afternoon and English antiques, oriental rugs, a grand piano, and wing chairs decorate the spacious living room and library. Dark cabinets and ceiling beams are set off by stark white walls in the dining room. Guest rooms are in the main house and in surrounding former private homes. The two huge guest rooms in the main house have sitting areas, large patios, and panoramic views of the water. Two fanlight windows are at the foot of the stairs that lead up to these rooms. Some of the rooms in other buildings share sitting areas and face the gardens or road. Many are decorated with an oriental theme: handsome teak and rosewood chests and chairs from Hong Kong, lamps with abacuses as their bases, Chinese wall hangings. Framed *Vogue* posters from the twenties and earlier add to the visual feast. Rooms have coffee makers and hair dryers. Refrigerators will be provided upon request at an additional cost. Newstead's guests have exchange privileges with the private Coral Beach Club, and with Waterloo House and Horizons and Cottages. (Moderate to Expensive)

☆ **Palmetto Hotel & Cottages** • *Smith's* • Sailing, snorkeling, and other watersports are available at this hotel on Harrington Sound that has a small manmade beach, a pool, and a sun terrace. From the entrance to the main house, where a sprawling 200-year-old mahogany tree stands, there is a fabulous view of boat-studded Flatts Inlet. The hotel's original buildings were once a vicarage. A circular staircase near the lounge in the main house leads to small guest rooms decorated with wicker furniture. Rooms are also in cottages. One unit has a tiny extra room that is good for a child. Free transportation is provided to a nearby south-shore beach. Unlike in most small hotels, room service is available. Located at the edge of pretty Flatts Village, Palmetto Hotel is a 10-minute ride from downtown Hamilton. The aquarium and zoo are within walking distance, and other sightseeing attractions are also nearby. (Moderate to Expensive)

★★★ **Pompano Beach Club** • *Southampton* • This family-owned and -managed hotel is a cluster of pink, white-roofed buildings on a bluff overlooking the Atlantic. Pompano opened as Bermuda's first fishing club almost forty years ago. Fishing from the private dock is still popular here (particularly bone fishing) and sailing is available. While

Pompano is the only completely American-owned hotel in Bermuda, it has a personalized Bermudian atmosphere, from the friendly, helpful staff to the Bermuda cedar in the clubhouse. The managers make a special effort to get to know their guests by name. Viewed from the dining room, bar/lounge, or any of the guest rooms (which all face the ocean), the sunsets are a real treat. For a front-row seat, slip into the Jacuzzi, overlooking the Atlantic. Two late check-out rooms are nearby, each with private bath and telephone. The bay windows in the dining room look out to a cliff above the water and the neighboring golf course. Breakfasts are really special here, with waffles topped with kiwi fruit, honey, coconut, and whipped cream; shrimp and guacamole omelets; kippered herrings; and chocolate chip muffins. Enclosed by rocky cliffs, the small beach makes for ideal swimming and snorkeling among coral reefs in the clear depths. (Just be careful as you enter the water, since rocks are hidden by the waves.) At low tide guests can walk 250 yards out to sea on a smooth sandbar. There are 5000 feet of waterfront property. The kidney-shaped pool, with a mosaic pompano on the bottom, overlooks the ocean. A championship clay tennis court is on the premises and the Port Royal Golf Course is right next door. In separate cottages in the hilly grounds, rooms are decorated in a variety of styles, all with patios or balconies. They are available as studios, cabanas, and suites. Even the smallest studios are more than comfortable in size. Terra cotta tiles and floral bedspreads and curtains are features of some rooms. Others are decorated with area rugs on parquet floors, Queen Anne furniture, oak nightstands, and ginger jar lamps. Some have fireplaces and dressing rooms. There are telephones, clock radios, irons and ironing boards, and refrigerators in all. Complimentary transportation is provided from the bus stop down the hill from Pompano. (Moderate to Expensive)

★★★ **The Reefs** • *Southampton* • This hotel is built into a cliffside overlooking its private, secluded south-shore beach. The pool is heated, and guests can fish or play tennis and shuffleboard. All facing the water, rooms are lanai and cabana-style, with wicker furniture, dressing areas, and ceiling fans. Many guests enjoy having tea in the attractive, comfortable lounge filled with natural rattan furniture. Lush hanging plants adorn the dining room, which has a sloping exposed-beam ceiling. On Saturday nights, the Reefs is alive with guests dancing to a combo in the lounge, drinking at the brass-trimmed cedar bar in the adjoining room, and feasting on the elaborate weekly buffet. The music floats through the louvered doors into the main dining room, where the spread might include curried chicken, ribs, pates, steamed mussels, smoked salmon, and a variety of salads. Coconuts is the name of the casual open-air waterview restaurant. On a bulletin board near the front desk, the names of arriving guests are posted along with names and photos of the friendly staff. For guests whose planes leave much later than check-out time, there are five courtesy rooms with showers so that they can spend more time on the beach. (Moderate to Expensive)

☆☆ **Rosedon** • *Pembroke* • Although several wings with modern rooms have been added, the main building at Rosedon has retained the feeling of an old mansion. On a hill across from the Princess, it is often mistaken for a private home. Overlooking beautifully manicured flowerbeds, the tiled veranda in the front is the locale for weekly cocktail parties. The four guest rooms with the most character are in the original mansion. The rooms in the new wing, around the large heated pool out back, are more motel-like and don't get much light. Guests may have breakfast in their rooms or on the shared balcony outside their doors. Lunch, tea, and light suppers are served in sitting rooms in the old part of the hotel, where rounded floor to ceiling windows border the stairway. Lawns and gardens surround this small hotel, which is in easy walking distance of Hamilton's shops, ferry, and restaurants. Guests have the use of the beach and facilities at the Elbow Beach Hotel in Paget. (Inexpensive to moderate)

☆☆ **Somerset Bridge Hotel** • *Sandys* • Water enthusiasts are attracted to this family-run housekeeping apartment hotel because it offers a dive package and has a freshwater pool. In addition, there is a popular restaurant and bar, the Blue Foam. All guest rooms are air conditioned and have balconies overlooking the bay. Close by are the Hamilton ferry (each guest receives one complimentary round-trip ticket), glass bottom boat tours to Sea Gardens, and the unique Somerset bridge. (Inexpensive)

★★★ **Stonington Beach Hotel** • *Paget* • Just a 10-minute ride from downtown Hamilton, this luxury hotel overlooks a beautiful private south-shore beach. Facilities include a freshwater pool and tennis courts. The public rooms and guest rooms are a pleasing combination of the modern and the traditional. At the entrance, sunlight filters through the fronds of a palm in a tiled atrium. Wicker furniture adorns the modern airy lobby, with its arched windows and high open-beam ceilings. Tea is served every afternoon, and the comfortable library, decorated with an oriental rug, has a wood-burning fireplace. The Norwood Room, with its chandeliers and elegant table settings, is one of Bermuda's best restaurants. Guests who are so inclined may help prepare memorable dishes in the kitchen. Ceiling fans, cedar furniture, refrigerators, and balconies or patios are features of guest rooms. The best views of the ocean are from those on the second floor. One of the island's newest hotels, Stonington has a guest room and special walkways designed for people in wheelchairs. Visitors may be surprised to learn that nearly half the staff members are students of the Bermuda Department of Hotel Technology. (Expensive)

★★ **Waterloo House** • *Pembroke* • An intimate hotel filled with antiques, Waterloo is on the harbor just outside downtown Hamilton. The entrance is an archway that leads to an inviting, greenery-filled courtyard. Tea is served in a cozy sitting room. The elegant dining room has high-backed chairs, chandeliers, and china cabinets. Sunny hallways in the main building look out to flower-filled courtyards. One sitting area is decorated with white rattan chairs, straw mats, and summery floral wallpaper. All air-conditioned, guest rooms have modern baths, attractive area rugs, and large closets. Most have dressing rooms and some have porches and sitting areas with comfortable couches. Televisions will be provided upon request. There is a small heated pool and a private dock. Guests are transported free to a private south-shore beach. Tennis and golf can be arranged. (Moderate)

COTTAGE COLONIES

☆☆ **Ariel Sands Beach Club** • *Devonshire* • Guest cottages sit along a slope that leads to the long private beach. In the clubhouse, a wrought-iron gate separates the dining room from the spacious sitting room, which has a piano, a large fireplace, and oriental rugs. Guests may dine inside or on the sunny indoor/outdoor patio that faces the pool and the ocean. Small comfortable rooms, some with two double beds, have large closets and modern baths, and come equipped with coffee makers. Entertainment includes calypso singers, piano music, and weekly barbecues during the summer season. Ariel Sands has three all-weather tennis courts. (Moderate to Expensive)

☆☆☆ **Cambridge Beaches** • *Sandys* • Tucked away on a peninsula in the pastoral western end of the island, Cambridge Beaches is on a 25-acre garden estate. This was Bermuda's first cottage colony and some guests have been returning here for more than 20 years. The cottages, one of which was built three centuries ago by a pirate, overlook Mangrove Bay, Long Bay, and the Atlantic. The sitting rooms in the main building, with a wonderful view of the boats in the water, are separated by archways and have antiques and fireplaces. With vinyl furniture in some, the guest rooms are not as attractive as the public rooms, but they are comfortable nonetheless. Over the years, some guests have found the food here unexceptional at best. However, the management has now hired a French chef to make meals memorable for the right reasons. The long strips of private beaches have secluded coves. Sailing, waterskiing, fishing, and other watersports are available along with tennis courts and a large heated pool. Mangrove Bay and Somerset Village are within walking distance and Hamilton is a ferry ride away. Room service is now available from 7 a.m. to 6 p.m. (Moderate)

☆ **Flamingo Beach Club** • *Warwick* • As we go to press, a swimming pool is being added to this modest cottage colony where the atmosphere is relaxed. Most of the handful of units face the beautiful south-shore beach. Rooms are air conditioned, and all have refrigerators. The Jolly Lobster restaurant here is popular. (Moderate)

★★★ **Fourways Cottage Colony** • *Paget* • Guests of this posh harborview cottage colony don't have to travel far to dine at one of the island's most celebrated restaurants. Intimate Fourways Cottage Colony is located on the grounds of popular Fourways Inn. Continental breakfast is served in the cottages. The ground-floor suites can be connected to the double rooms upstairs. You'll find fresh flowers; mini bars; balconies or patios; remote control color television; radios; telephones with extensions in the baths; and kitchenettes stocked with orange juice, milk, tea, and coffee. The huge baths have "his" and "hers" sinks, and terry-cloth robes are provided. Marble floors in all rooms add to the elegance. Room service is available for three meals and snacks, and there is nightly turn-down service. You can also arrange to have your laundry done. Although not on a beach, Fourways has a freshwater swimming pool, near the exercise room, and guests may use a private beach club. (Expensive)

★★★ **Horizons and Cottages** • *Paget* • A circular driveway around a towering cedar leads to the entrance. In the main building, a former mansion, guests are cooled by a ceiling fan while they check in and out at the glistening cedar front desk. The homelike sitting rooms have wing chairs, handsome side tables, a grandfather clock, china cabinets, and Victorian love seats. A game room is to the right of the entrance. Overlooking the pool and the ocean is a grassy patio with weathered wooden tables, where lunch is served. Guests also eat in the dining room, decorated with hanging plants, or just outside on the brick patio with cast-iron tables and chairs. Horizons is Bermuda's only *Relais et chateaux*. Since it is set into a hillside, there's a breathtaking view of white rooftops nestled in trees, a plot of farmland, and the Atlantic in the distance. Some of the wonderfully attractive guest rooms are more modern than others. Over a dozen have fireplaces. Rooms in the cottages are larger than those in the main house. Done in pinks and other pastels, they have appointments including white wicker furniture, terra cotta tiles, dressing areas, and large closets. Most are air conditioned. Visitors staying in cottages have breakfast served on their terraces. Nightly turn-down service is a special plus. Sports facilities are 3 all-weather tennis courts, a 9-hole pitch-and-putt golf course, and an 18-hole putting green. (Expensive)

★★★★ **Lantana Colony Club** • *Sandys* • This family-run hideaway is among the most sumptuous resorts in Bermuda. Plush cottage units, done in pastel colors, have private quarry-tiled patios, aromatic cedar chests, and extensive views of the Great Sound. There are split-level suites as well as units with separate living rooms and two bedrooms. All have the latest in baths. Guests staying in the Pool House cottage may use the owner's private pool. Those who forgo continental breakfast served in their cottages may have a full breakfast in the clubhouse. The main dining room, with ceiling beams hand-painted in floral designs, is where guests eat when they first arrive. After they have spent several days at Lantana, they'll be seated in the dazzling solarium dining room, where sunlight spills over plants, antiques, and polished Bermuda cedar tables. The menu, which changes daily, might include dishes such as steamed asparagus, gazpacho, and sauted calves liver with apple rings and onion. After dinner, guests move to the lounge, decorated with oil paintings, for demitasse or liqueurs. On land that was once a Bermuda onion farm, Lantana's 22 acres are rich in spectacular plantings, including orchids, antheriums, and other tropical flowers, all growing around fountains and life-size bronze sculpture. The Canary Island date palms resemble overgrown pineapples. Many people are amused by the bench where there's a statue of a woman reading a newspaper. The umbrella of a huge almond tree provides a shady spot for relaxing. Another highlight of the property is a bridge over the old railway right-of-way now used only by joggers, cyclists, and, occasionally, horses. In addition to tennis courts, a freshwater pool, a small beach, and a private dock where watersports are available, there are a croquet lawn and a shuffle board. The Port Royal Golf Club is not far away. Guests may take a complimentary 40-minute ferry ride to Hamilton for sightseeing and shopping. (Expensive)

★★★ **Pink Beach Club** • *Smith's* • The two south-shore beaches make Pink Beach Club an especially pleasant place to stay. And, yes, the sand really does have a pink cast, from pulverized coral and shells. The club was built as a home by Americans during the Depression and opened as a hotel in 1947. Some of the friendly staff members have worked here for more than 25 years. Hilly pathways lead through the hotel's extensive gardens. Guests may relax in wing chairs in the lounge, which has a fireplace. The spacious main dining room, with a menu that changes daily, overlooks the water and guest cottages. The longer guests stay, the closer they are seated to the picture window when they dine. A full breakfast is served in the dining room or in the cottages. While some rooms get little light, they are attractively decorated with dark wood furniture and have modern baths. They all have radios, televisions, and balconies or patios, and some have views of the boulders in the ocean. When the water is clear, parrot fish are visible. Sports facilities include a large freshwater pool and three tennis courts. Golf can be arranged at the nearby Mid Ocean Club. Nightly entertainment takes place by the pool or the bar. The club does not take children under 5. (Expensive)

★★★ **The St. George's Club** • *St. George's* • This combination cottage colony/time-sharing resort sits on a hill overlooking the town of St. George and its picturesque harbor. Modern one-bedroom cottages are available along with two-bedroom, two-bath duplexes. In the two-bedroom units, you'll dine on Wedgwood china and crystal. Terra cotta tiles the kitchen, which is separated from the living room by a cedar bar. The spacious living room is decorated with Haitian cotton couches and dark wood tables and chairs. Off the living room and guest room is a patio. Upstairs, the plush master bedroom makes lingering easy. Two steps up are all that divides the bedroom area from the huge sunken tub, by a window, and the two sinks. The toilet and stall shower are enclosed, however. Bright lights trim the vanity mirror. Ceiling fans or air conditioners cool the air. At night, curl up in bed with a book from the selection of *New York Times* best-sellers. In addition to Margaret Rose, the gourmet restaurant, there are a pub, a lounge, and a gourmet food shop. Sports facilities include three freshwater pools, complimentary transportation to a private beach, all-weather tennis courts, and an 18-hole golf course. (Expensive)

☆☆ **Willowbank** • *Sandys* • To enter this cottage colony, guests pass through a stone moongate. Although Willowbank is an international Christian retreat, with daily devotional hours and no bar service, anyone is welcome. (Guests may have their own liquor in their rooms.) In the main building, the fireplaces, cedar-paneled walls, high ceilings, and well-worn comfortable furniture give the library and lounges a homelike feeling. The guest rooms are somewhat plain. Facilities include two beaches, tennis courts, and a freshwater pool. Except on barbecue nights during the summer, guests are asked to wear formal attire to dinner. Some have complained that portions at meals are far from generous. (Inexpensive to Moderate)

INEXPENSIVE
LARGE GUEST HOUSES

Archlyn Villa • *Pembroke* • The Bermudian owners of this comfortable former home live on the property, and are available to provide guests with sightseeing and dining information. The closest beach is only a 5-minute walk away and a bus stop is also nearby. Overlooking Mills Creek, Archlyn Villa has a spacious garden area, a pool, and a sunny breakfast room. All rooms are air-conditioned.

Loughlands • *Paget* • This gracious mansion built in 1920 is set on nine flourishing acres. The tennis court sits on the terraced front lawn. White cast-iron garden furniture decorates the front porch and the entrance is shaded by a balcony. Enter the wide foyer and you'll be stepping back in time. The grandfather clock is over a century old. In the lounge, whose floors are covered with thick carpets brought from China, you'll see a mirrored Victorian chest and a hearth where cedar fires burn on cool winter nights. Breakfast is served in the dining room, across from the lounge. A window seat on the landing halfway up the stairs may tempt you to sit a while on your way to your room. Many guests admire the old tapestry and paintings on the walls. Most of the rooms contain English antiques. All have coffee makers and radios. Some share baths. A bus stop is nearby and Elbow Beach is a 10-minute walk away.

Royal Palms • *Pembroke* • This large old Bermudian home is in a quiet, residential neighborhood within walking distance of downtown Hamilton. The shuttered windows and the tall curving palm trees out front in the lush, colorful gardens set Royal Palms apart from the surrounding houses. There is a restaurant and a bar off a patio where weekly barbecues are given during the summer season. Most of the spacious guest rooms have two double beds.

Sugar Cane Hotel • *Sandys* • At first glance, this small, white house with a balustraded porch and set upon a lawn appears to be a family home. At press time, it is undergoing a major renovation and expansion. Mangrove Bay is just a few steps away, and restaurants and other conveniences are in the nearby town of Somerset. Good beaches are not far.

White Heron Inn • *Warwick* • Guests can stay in twin rooms or self-contained suites in this old manor house. There is a small pool and full dining facilities. Boating, fishing, and scuba diving are available from the private dock.

SMALL GUEST HOUSES

Ashley Hall • *Devonshire* • Some guests have been returning to Ashley Hall for more than two decades. Set in a garden in the center of the island, this modern guest house is not far from Devonshire Bay. It has a large pool and is convenient to Hamilton. Rooms all have private baths and are air conditioned. The closest beach is within walking distance. Mopeds can be delivered to guests.

Canada Villa • *Pembroke* • A 15-minute walk to Hamilton, this guest house has large bedrooms, a large pool, and sun terrace. Guests are welcome to use the kitchen for breakfast and lunch.

Edgehill Manor • *Pembroke* • This beautiful colonial-style mansion with high ceilings and a handsome wooden staircase is in a residential area on the outskirts of the city of Hamilton. Each bright, airy room has its own character. Most have balconies and two have their own kitchens. Some are air conditioned, while others are cooled by ceiling fans. You can have breakfast served in your room or in the cheerful dining room. Arriving guests are greeted with pots of English tea. The personal attention of the owner and staff makes a stay here particularly pleasant. Set in a secluded garden, Edgehill Manor has a small freshwater swimming pool.

Fordham Hall • *Pembroke* • If you're looking for convenience and a relaxed setting, consider Fordham Hall. Although breakfast is the only meal served here, restaurants and stores in Hamilton are within easy walking distance. Staying here will put you close enough to the capital to take advantage of downtown attractions whenever the spirit moves you, yet you'll feel pleasantly removed from city life. While eating your morning meal on the glass-enclosed veranda, you'll be able to watch the activity in Hamilton Harbour. Some of the comfortable, homey rooms, cooled by ceiling fans, also have views of the water. The harborview corner rooms, with their lacy curtains fluttering in the breeze, are popular with guests who've stayed here before. Although the sound of mopeds, cars, and horse-drawn carriages can be noisy at times, the view is excellent.

Greene's Guest House • *Southampton* • Half of the eight warmly decorated rooms, which vary in size and decor, look out to the water. All are equipped with refrigerators, telephones, coffee makers, TV, and VHS. The cozy dining room where breakfast is served adjoins the large open kitchen. Known for her curried goat and rice, Ms. Greene (originally from Trinidad) will prepare dinner on request for an additional charge. Across from the dining room, a short staircase leads past a plant-filled passageway to the large sitting room. Here you'll find a radio, books, and a working fireplace. Nearby is a games room with a dart board. A large swimming pool and bar are out back. A five-minute walk will take you to the beach.

Hillcrest Guest House • *St. George's* • A family-operated guest house more than two centuries old, Hillcrest is on the edge of the 17th-century town of St. George's. It has spacious verandas, lawns and gardens, and is convenient to restaurants and shopping. From the balcony off the upstairs sitting room, there is a breathtaking view of the town and St. George's Harbour, where yacht races take place. Although no meals are served here, Hillcrest is within walking distance of the restaurants in town. This eclectically furnished home has been in the family of its current owners since 1914. The owners, who boast a lot of repeat business, give guests as much personal attention as they need.

Hi-Roy • *Pembroke* • Just off North Shore Road, Hi-Roy is located in the residential Princess Estate. You'll get a lot for your money at this six-room guest house run by Hyacinth ("Hi") and Everard ("Roy") Jones. Rates include breakfast and dinner, served in the petite window-enclosed dining room. Hi-Roy is popular with visiting college students. The shared refrigerator is used to store lunch fixin's and snacks. At least one room (all have private baths) has a closet in the bathroom—so there's no need to worry about ironing your clothes! All rooms come with satellite TV. Guests have the run of the house. Mr. Jones, a jazz lover, says that sooner or later most visitors find their way to his sound room. He welcomes company as he listens to music and watches one of his 300 video tapes of concerts featuring jazz greats such as John Coltrane, Dizzie Gillespie, Miles Davis, and Milt Jackson. Bus stops are nearby.

Little Pomander Guest House • *Paget* • On the edge of Hamilton Harbour, this old Bermuda cottage has a waterfront patio with a barbecue, and is close to beaches, as well as to downtown Hamilton.

The Oxford House • *Pembroke* • This old townhouse is within walking distance of downtown Hamilton. The entrance to the handsome building is bordered by two columns supporting a small balcony over the arched doorway. A gracious curving staircase just inside leads to comfortable spacious rooms. This family-operated guest house has the atmosphere of a friendly private home.

Pleasant View Guest House • *Pembroke* • Located in the residential Princess Estate off North Shore Road, Pleasant View has a pool and six comfortable bedrooms of varying sizes. You'll find books in all rooms and refrigerators in some. All have private baths, ceiling fans, telephones, clock radios, and televisions. Guests are welcome to use the washer, dryer, iron, and ironing board. Making visitors feel like part of the family, owner Uriel Griffin serves a full breakfast in the homelike dining room.

Royal Heights • *Southampton* • At the top of a driveway that would almost be vertical if it were any steeper, Royal Heights is aptly named. Not far from Henry VIII Restaurant, this guest house is poised high on a hill. Balconies run the width of the three-story, crescent-shaped house. The view of the surrounding hills and houses and the boat-studded Great Sound is so breathtaking that you'll feel as if you're seeing it for the first time every time you look. Continental breakfast is served in the handsomely furnished dining room with wide windows. Nearby is the comfortable living room with a decorative fireplace. A circular staircase leads down to pool-level rooms. With two double beds and a long balcony, room #3 is the largest of the seven guest rooms. The sunken tub and the walk-in closet help make it extremely popular among repeat guests. All rooms have televisions, refrigerators, and clock radios. Russell and Jean Richardson are your amiable hosts. Royal Heights is near south-shore beaches.

Salt Kettle House • *Paget* • This quiet, modern guest house with cottages is just across the road from the harbor and has a private dock. Some rooms have kitchenettes. Close to the ferry, Salt Kettle boasts 80% repeat guests. Discount ferry tickets and room service are provided.

LARGE HOUSEKEEPING COTTAGES AND APARTMENTS

Arlington Heights • *Smith's* • These modern cottage units and apartments on a garden estate have balconies and terraces and surround a large swimming pool.

Astwood Cove • *Warwick* • In a residential neighborhood near south-shore beaches, these well-kept apartments provide maximum privacy and comfort. The cluster of attractive buildings surrounding a pool are painted sparkling white. The main house dates back to about 1710 and was part of a dairy farm before guest apartments were built in the 1960s. Facilities include a sauna.

Clairfont Apartments • *Warwick* • Close to bus stops, entertainment, and restaurants, Clairfont is in a residential area and has a pool and sundeck.

Clear View Suites • *Hamilton Parish* • Overlooking a rocky shore where guests can swim, these cottages are also near a sandy beach. There are two pools on the premises. Joggers take advantage of the picturesque trail along the water. The large balconied guest rooms, some with kitchenettes and sitting areas, all have high ceilings and are equipped with radios and televisions. Cribs and high chairs are available. A bus stop right outside the entrance makes transportation around the island very convenient. Clear View is midway between Flatts Village and the town of St. George.

Longtail Cliffs • *Warwick* • These cheerful apartments on the south shore all have balconies with ocean views. Rooms are appointed with white wicker upholstered furniture and straw mats on the tiled floors. Most units have two bedrooms, two baths, and a kitchen. There is a swimming pool, and guests can use Mermaid Beach facilities. The beaches in this area are pale pink.

Munro Beach Cottages • *Southampton* • Getting to this quiet locale is part of the fun. The road snakes through the wonderfully scenic Port Royal Golf Course. Perched high above the water, the eight cottages house the 16 plain but comfortable air-conditioned units. Each has a modern full kitchen, a couch, table and chairs, a ceiling fan, phone, and clock radio. Sliding glass doors open to patios facing the ocean and great sunsets. Guests may arrange to have groceries delivered at no extra charge. Have breakfast at the Port Royal Club House when you're not in the mood to cook. The Port Royal tennis courts are a five-minute walk away. A path leads down to the beach.

Pretty Penny • *Paget* • Near Fourways Inn, Pretty Penny is a good choice for travelers who like privacy in a personalized setting. Four cottages house nine upscale guest rooms, all with private patios and kitchenettes. Hibachis are also provided. Varying in size and decor, the units are accented with throw rugs, tile floors, and wicker or cane furniture. Two have fireplaces, one of which works. Weekly cocktail parties take place on the wooden deck surrounding the small pool. White cast-iron garden furniture and a plant-covered archway make the flourishing grounds even more pleasant.

Rosemont • *Pembroke* • This group of housekeeping units has a large pool area with a stunning view of Hamilton Harbour and the Great Sound. The grounds are nicely landscaped with colorful flowers and thatch palms, and there is a citrus orchard. Each self-contained unit has a private entrance and some have private balconies. Double beds will be provided upon request. Some apartments have been specially designed to accommodate wheelchairs. Rosemont is within walking distance of downtown Hamilton. Guests are given complimentary newspapers.

The Sandpiper • *Warwick* • In a residential neighborhood of South Shore Road, these attractive apartments have a garden and pool. Buses, beaches, hotels, and entertainment are all nearby.

SMALL HOUSEKEEPING COTTAGES AND APARTMENTS

Burch's Guest Apartments • *Devonshire* • With a small garden, these apartments have panoramic views of the north shore and are close to Hamilton by bus.

By Faith Apartments • *Southampton* • Close to popular Horseshoe Bay Beach, these units have private terraces. Some are air conditioned. Free newspapers and airport transportation are provided.

Granaway • *Warwick* • Built in 1734, the seaside Granaway sits with its back to the water. This is because the captain who built it had spent his life at sea and wanted the house to face the gardens. Through the years, the house has been a wedding gift from a privateer to his daughter and has been rented to artists, writers, and schoolteachers who took in "wayward" boys. Noel Coward, a frequent guest of one of the owners, liked staying in the "Slaves Quarters," a small cottage adjacent to the main house. With its own fireplace, kitchen, and solarium, this cottage is still a popular unit. Guest rooms have exposed cedar ceiling beams. One room has a kitchen-style fireplace and bread oven. Breakfast is served in the rooms on trays, with china that matches each room's color scheme. Another special touch is the silver tea/coffee service. The two Bermuda stone love seats are popular with honeymooners, and there is good swimming and snorkeling.

Marley Beach Cottages • *Warwick* • This secluded cluster of cottages and studio apartments is set among lawns and gardens. You can arrange to have groceries delivered prior to your arrival. From the small pool, you'll have a striking view of the south shore and the rocks below. The owners are proud of the fact that the movie *The Deep* was filmed here. Marley Beach is more expensive than most housekeeping accommodations. Nearby is Astwood Park where you can relax on benches overlooking the south-shore beach.

Ocean Terrace • *Southampton* • Located at Scenic Heights, Ocean Terrace has three modern, air-conditioned units. They all have full kitchens, ceiling fans, satellite TV, clock radios, and telephones. There is a pool on the premises and Horseshoe Bay beach is about a 10-minute walk away. Hop on a moped, and the shops and restaurants at the Southampton Princess are five minutes away.

Robin's Nest • *Pembroke* • You'll find this quiet guest house up a hill near the juncture of Cox Hill and North Shore roads. The three units have full kitchens, and are appointed with wicker headboards, ceiling fans, air conditioners, telephones, TV, and clock radios. The pool patio, where owner Milton Robinson plans to build more units, is a good place to relax. A glossy Bermuda cedar door leads to the two-bedroom apartment, complete with an eat-in kitchen with a window over the sink.

HOTEL QUICK-REFERENCE CHARTS

Key

Facilities

BP	Beach Privileges: complimentary transportation to a private beach	L	Laundry (washing machines available)
BT	Boating	P	Swimming Pool
F	Fishing	MP	Mopeds rented on premises
G	Golf	S	Waterskiing
PB	Private Beach	M/D	Marina-Dock
SC	Scuba	Ba/B	Barber-Beauty Salon

Meal Plans

MAP	Modified American Plan: Full breakfast and dinner	CP	Continental Plan: Light breakfast
BP	Bermuda Plan: Full breakfast	EP	European Plan: Room only

Credit Cards

A	American Express	M	Mastercard
C	Carte Blanche	V	Visa
D	Diners Club		

Note that the following hotel room prices are approximate.

Resort Hotels
Prices are MAP unless otherwise indicated.

Page	Establishment, Mailing Address, Telephone	Meal Plans Offered	No. Rooms	Price of double (per person, in season)	Credit Cards	Facilities	Other
91	The Belmont Hotel Golf and Beach Country Club (Warwick) P.O. Box WK 251, Warwick WK BX Bermuda/Tel: (809)236–1301 Toll free from U.S.: (800)223–5672; from NYS: (800)442–5886; in NYC: (212)541–4400	MAP, BP, EP	154	$110–150	M, V, D, A, C	BP, R, Ba/B, G, T, P, BT, F, S, M/D, MP	shops, games room, nightly entertainment, transportation to private beach club, exchange privileges with Bermudiana Hotel
92	The Bermudiana Hotel, Tennis and Beach Club (Pembroke) P.O. Box HM 842, Hamilton 5, Bermuda/Tel: (809)295–1211	MAP, BP, EP	233	$110–150	M, V, D, A, C	BP, G, T, 2P, BT, F, S, M/D, Ba/B, MP	Likely to be sold.
92	Elbow Beach Hotel (Paget) P.O. Box HM 455, Hamilton HM BX Bermuda/Tel: (809)236–3535/ 800–223–7434	MAP, BP	298	$110–220	M, V, A, D, C	PB, P, T, Ba/B, MP	shops, games room, pool w/ shallow play area for kids, beach club, nightly entertainment
93	Grotto Bay Beach Hotel & Tennis Club (11 Blue Hole Hill) Hamilton CR 04, Bermuda/Tel: (809)293–8333/ 800–225–2230	MAP, BP	171	$110	none	2PB, P, G, T, BT, M/D, L	games room, library, caves, summer "day camp" for children
93	Inverurie Hotel (Paget) P.O. Box HM 1189, Hamilton HM CX Bermuda/Tel: (809)296–1000	MAP	134	$120–160	none	BP, P, T, BT, S, Ba/B	gift shop, nightly entertainment

92	Marriott's Castle Harbour Resort (Tucker's Town, Hamilton Parish) P.O. Box HM 841, Hamilton HM CX Bermuda/Tel: (809)293-2040	MAP, BP, EP	415	$120–190	M, V, A	2PB, G, T, 3P, BT, M/D, Ba/B, S, SC, MP	shops, nightly entertainment, yacht club & marina, Japanese restaurant, TVs
93	The Princess (Pembroke) P.O. Box HM 837, Hamilton HM CX Bermuda/Tel: (809)295-3000 or (800)223-1818	EP	456	$120–152	M, V, D, A	FB, P, SC, T, G, 2P, BaB, MP	shops, games room, beach club, miniature golf, nightly entertainment, 5 min walk Hamilton, exchange privileges w/Southampton Princess
94	Sonesta Beach Hotel (Southampton) P.O. Box HM 1070, Hamilton HM EX Bermuda/Tel: (809)238-8122 or (800)343-7170	MAP	403	$110–170	A, M, V, D	2P, 3PB, T, SC, Ba/B, MP	shops, games room, nightly entertainment, shuffleboard, croquet, ping-pong, windsurfing, European health spa
94	The Southampton Princess Hotel (Southampton) P.O. Box HM 1379, Hamilton HM FX Bermuda/Tel: (809)238-8000	MAP	600	$145–195	M, V, D, A	PB, 2P, G, MP, Ba/B	shops, games room, nightly entertainment, exchange priv. w/ Princess Hotel, comp. transport to close beach club

Small Hotels

Prices are MAP unless otherwise indicated.

Page	Establishment, Mailing Address, Telephone	Meal Plans Offered	No. Rooms	Price of double (per person, in season)	Credit Cards	Facilities	Other
94	Glencoe (Paget) P.O. Box PG 297, Paget PG BX Bermuda/Tel: (809)236–5274 800-468–1500	MAP, BP	41	$95–125	M, V, A	P, BT, S, PB, F	near ferry, free sunfish sailing, some entertainment
	The Hamiltonian Hotel and Island Club (Pembroke) P.O. Box HM 1738, Hamilton HM GX Bermuda/Tel: (809)295–5608	MAP, EP, BP	75		M, V, A	P, T, M/D	time-sharing units available; hotel operating license has been suspended
95	Harmony Club (Paget) P.O. Box PG 299, Paget PG BX Bermuda/Tel: (809)296–3500	3 meals daily	72	$150 (all-inclusive)	M, V, D, A, C	P	comp. transport. to prv. south shore beach club, one free moped per room, unlimited drinks, exchange privileges with Belmont and Bermudiana hotels, TVs
95	Mermaid Beach Club (Warwick) P.O. Box WK 250, Warwick WK BX Bermuda/Tel: (809)236–5031/ (809)236–5031	MAP (EP & BP Nov. through Mar.)	67	$100–130	M, V, A, D	PB, P	gift shop, French cuisine in restaurant

95	Newstead (Paget) P.O. Box PG 196, Paget PG BX Bermuda/Tel: (809)296-6060 (800)468-4111	MAP, BP	50	$80–125	none	P	heated pool, sauna, deepwater swimming, near ferry
96	Palmetto Hotel and Cottages (Smith's) P.O. Box FL54, Smith's FL BX Bermuda/Tel: (809)293-2323 (800)982-0026	MAP, BP	42	$90–120	A	PB, P, M/D,	water sports, coffee machines in rooms
96	Pompano Beach Club 32 Pompano Beach Road Southampton SB 03 Bermuda/Tel: (809)294-0222/ 800-343-4155	MAF, BP, EP, CP	56	$110–125	none	PB, P, BT, M/D, SC	fresh-water pool, games room
97	The Reefs (Southampton) 56 South Road, Southampton SN 01 Bermuda/Tel: (809)238-0222	MAP, BP	64	$110–140	none	PB, P, T	heated pool, fishing, nightly entertainment, children on advance request only
98	Rosedon (Pembroke) P.O. Box HM 290, Hamilton HM AX Bermuda/Tel: (809)295-1640 Cables: Rosedon Bermuda	BP, EP	43	$65–85 BP	none	P	near ferry, tv room, comp. transport. to beach, no children under age 10, use of Elbow Beach Hotel facilities.
98	Stonington Beach Hotel (Paget) P.O. Box HM 523, Hamilton HM CX Bermuda/Tel: (809)236-5416	MAP, BP	64	$140–150	M, V, D, A, C	PB, P	staffed by hotel training students supervised by professional management team

Small Hotels (cont.)

Prices are MAP unless otherwise indicated.

Page	Establishment, Mailing Address, Telephone	Meal Plans Offered	No. Rooms	Price of double (per person, in season)	Credit Cards	Facilities	Other
99	Waterloo House (Pembroke) P.O. Box HM 333, Hamilton HM BX Bermuda/Tel: (809)295–4480/ 800-468–4100	MAP, BP	32	$80–120	none	P, BP	heated pool
	White Sands and Cottages (Paget) P.O. Box 174, Paget PG BX Bermuda/Tel: (809)236–2023	MAP, BP, EP	35	$90–120	M, V, A	P	family-owned

Cottage Colonies

Page	Establishment, Mailing Address, Telephone	Meal Plans Offered	No. Rooms	Price of double (per person, in season)	Credit Cards	Facilities	Other
99	Ariel Sands Beach Club (Devonshire) P.O. Box HM 334, Hamilton HM BX Bermuda/Tel: (809)236–1010 (800)468–6610	MAP, BP	45	$98–135 (MAP)	none	PB, P, T	heated pool
99	Cambridge Beaches (Sandys) 30 King's Point, Sandys MA 02 Bermuda/Tel: (809)234–0331 (800)468–7300	MAP	75	$120–185	none	PB, BT, S, F, P	heated pool, some nightly entertainment, pets allowed on request
100	Flamingo Beach Club (Warwick) P.O. Box 466, Hamilton HM BX Bermuda/Tel: (809)236–3786	MAP	11	$75–85	M, V	PB	good restaurant
100	Fourways Cottage Colony (Paget) P.O. Box PG 294, PG BX Paget, Bermuda (809)236–6517	CP	10	$120–145	A, M, V, D	P	freshwater pool; 1- and 2-BR suites

100	Horizons and Cottages (Paget) P.O. Box PG 198, Paget PG BX Bermuda/Tel: (809)236-0048	MAP, BP	50	$95–150 (MAP)	none	P, G	most units air-conditioned, heated pool, children under age 6 on request
101	Lantana Colony, Club (Sandys) P.O. Box SB90, Sandys SB BX Bermuda/Tel: (809)234-0141 (800)468-3733	MAP	65	$120–160	none	P, PB, BT, S, M/T	complimentary ferry to Hamilton, children under age 10 on request; closed Jan.–mid-Feb.
101	Pink Beach Club (Smith's) P.O. Box HM 1017, Hamilton HM DX Bermuda/Tel: (809)293-1666	MAP	72	$120–150	none	PB, P	no children under age 5
102	St. George's Club P.O. Box GE 92 St. George's GE BX Bermuda 809)297-1200	EP	61	$260 EP	V, M, A, D	P, G, T, BP	time share units available
102	Willowbank (Sandys) P.O. Box MA 296, Sandys MA BX Bermuda/Tel: (809)234-1616	MAP	57	$60–80	none	2PB, P	optional daily devotional time

Large Guest Houses

102	Aechlyn Villa (Pembroke) P.O. Box HM 220, Hamilton HM AX Bermuda/Tel: (809)292-1405	CP, EP	12	$50 (EP)	none	P, MP	5-min. walk to beach

Small Hotels (cont.)
Prices are MAP unless otherwise indicated.

Page	Establishment, Mailing Address, Telephone	Meal Plans Offered	No. Rooms	Price of double (per person, in season)	Credit Cards	Facilities	Other
103	Loughlands Guest House (Paget) 79 South Road, Paget PG 03 Bermuda/Tel: (809)236–1253	CP	25	$50	none	P	some shared baths
103	Royal Palms Club Hotel (Pembroke) P.O. Box HM 499, Hamilton HM CX Bermuda/Tel: (809)292–1854	MAP	12	$80	none		
103	Sugar Cane Hotel (Sandys) P.O. Box MA146 Sandys MA BX Bermuda/Tel: (809)234–0989	MAP, BP, EP			M, V, A	P, PB	near ferry and Somerset Village, undergoing renovations & expansion
103	White Heron Inn (Warwick) P.O. Box WK 235, Warwick WK BX Bermuda/Tel: (809)238–1655/1617	MAP, BP	11	$90 BP	M, V, D, A	P, BT, F, SC, M/D	full dining facilities
103	Woodbourne/Inverness (Pembroke) P.O. Box HM 977, Hamilton HM DX Bermuda/Tel: (809)295–3737	CP	14	$50	none		children on advance request only

Small Guest Houses

103	Ashley Hall (Devonshire) P.O. Box DV 204, Devonshire DV BX Bermuda/Tel: (809)236-3533	CP	7	$50	none	P	mopeds delivered, air conditioned
104	Canada Villa (Pembroke) P.O. Box HM 1864, Hamilton HM HX Bermuda/Tel: (809)292-0419	EP	5	$24-32	none	P	kitchen privileges, children age 12 and above only, some shared baths
104	Edgehill Manor (Pembroke) P.O. Box HM 1048, Hamilton HM EX Bermuda/Tel: (809)295-7124	CP	9	$50	none	P	some rooms air-conditioned, others with ceiling fans
104	Fordham Hall (Pembroke) P.O. Box HM 692, Hamilton HM CX Bermuda/Tel: (809)295-1551	CP	10	$50	M, V		children on advance request only
104	Greenbank and Cottages (Paget) P.O. Box PG 201, Paget PG BX Bermuda/Tel: (809)236-3615	EP	9	$85	none	M/D	swimming, water sports, near ferry, air-conditioning on request, pets on request
104	Greene's Guest House (Southampton) P.O. Box SN 395, Southampton SN BX Bermuda/Tel: (809)238-0834	MAP, BP, EP	6	$80 (MAP)	none		
105	Hilcrest Guest House (St. George's) P.O. Box GE 96, St. George's GE BX Bermuda/Tel: (809)297-1630	EP	11	$40	none		children on advance request only

Small Guest Houses (cont.)

Page	Establishment, Mailing Address, Telephone	Meal Plans Offered	No. Rooms	Price of double (per person, in season)	Credit Cards	Facilities	Other
105	Hi-Roy Guest House (Pembroke) 22 Princess Estate Road, Pembroke HM 04 Bermuda/Tel: (809)292–0808	MAP, BP	6	$55 (MAP)	none		children on advance request only
105	Little Pomander Guest House P.O. Box HM 384 Hamilton HM BX Bermuda/Tel: (809)236–7635	CP	5	$50	none		
105	Mazarine-By-The-Sea (Pembroke) P.O. Box HM AX, Hamilton HM AX Bermuda/Tel: (809)292–1659	EP	7	$50	none		good deepwater swimming from cliffs
105	Oxford House (Pembroke) P.O. Box HM 374, Hamilton HM BX Bermuda/Tel: (809)295–0503	CP	10	$50	none		children on advance request only
105	Pleasant View (Pembroke) P.O. Box HM 1998 Hamilton HM HX Bermuda/Tel: (809)292–4520	BP, EP	6	$45–60	none	P	
106	Royal Heights Guest House (Southampton) P.O. Box SN 144, Southampton SN BX Bermuda/Tel: (809) 238–0043	CP	6	$55	none	P	children on advance request only

106	Salt Kettle House (Paget) 10 Salt Kettle Road Paget PG 01 Bermuda/Tel: (809)236-0407	BP	6	$30–35	none	some kitchen facilities
	Seven Arches Guest House (Smith's) P.O. Box 247, Smith's FL BX Bermuda/Tel: (809)292-4718	CP	4	$30	none	no children under age 12; dock with deep water swimming
	Tallent Villa (Pembroke) P.O. Box HM 446, Hamilton HM BX Bermuda/Tel: (809)292-0163 or (809)293-1913	BP	4	$25	none	no children under age 7

Small Guest Houses—Fewer than 12 Beds

Limbar Terraces (Pembroke) P.O. Box HM 855, Hamilton HM DX Bermuda/Tel: (809)252-0468	BP	3	$30	none	no children under age 8
Que Sera (Paget) P.O. Box HM 1, Hamilton HM AX Bermuda/Tel: (809)235-1998	EP	3	$30–35	none	P
Sound View Cottage 9 Bowe Lane Southampton SN 04 Bermuda/Tel: (809)238-0064	EP	3	$30	none	3 housekeeping apts.
South View (Warwick) P.O. Box HM 515, Hamilton HM CX Bermuda/Tel: (809)236-3382	EP	3	$35–55	M, V	sun deck on roof, apts.; one air-conditioned apt., two with fans

Small Guest Houses (cont.)

Page	Establishment, Mailing Address, Telephone	Meal Plans Offered	No. Rooms	Price of double (per person, in season)	Credit Cards	Facilities	Other
	Wainwright (St. George's) 2 Point Lane, St. George's GE 02 Bermuda/Tel: (809)297–0254	EP	4	$35	none		

Large Housekeeping Cottages and Apartments
Prices are EP unless otherwise indicated.

Page	Establishment, Mailing Address, Telephone	Meal Plans Offered	No. Apartments	Price of double (per person, in season)	Credit Cards	Facilities	Other
106	Arlington Heights (Smith's) P.O. Box FL 2, Smith's FL BX Bermuda/Tel: (809)292–1680	EP	10	$50	none	P	
106	Astwood Cove (Warwick) 49 South Road, Warwick WK 07 Bermuda/Tel: (809)236–0984 Telex: 3298 (ACOVE BA)	EP	15	$45–60	none	P	sauna
	Banana Beach Ocean Front Apartments (Warwick) P.O. Box HM 1039, Hamilton HM EX Bermuda/Tel: (809)236–5121	EP	27	$40–65	none	P, PB	heated pool
	Belljori (Warwick) P.O. Box WK 217, Warwick WK BX Bermuda/Tel: (809)238–1985	EP	11	$80	none		

106	Blue Horizons (Warwick) 43 South Road, Warwick WK 10 Bermuda/Tel: (809)236-6350	EP	11	$37–50	none	P	near public pool
106	Clairfont Apartments (Warwick) P.O. Box WK 85, Warwick WK BX Bermuda/Tel: (809)238-0149	EP	8	$33–42	none	P	sun deck
106	Clear View Suites Sandy Lane Hamilton Parish CR C2 Bermuda/Tel: (809)293-0484 (800)468-9600	EP (MAP and BP on request)	38	$45–55 EP	none	P	cribs and highchairs available; close to beach
107	Longtail Cliffs (Warwick) P.O. Box HM 836, Hamilton HM CX Bermuda/Tel: (809)235-2822	EP	12	$155	none	P	use of Mermaid Beach facilities
107	Munro Beach Cottages P.O. Box SN 99, Southampton SN BX Bermuda/Tel: (809)234-1175	EP	16	$70	none	PB	better for couples than singles
107	Paraquet Guest Apartments (Paget) P.O. Box PG 173, Paget PG BX Bermuda/Tel: (809)236-5842/3962	EP	9	$40–55	none	R	good home-style restaurant
107	Rosemont (Pembroke) P.O. Box HM 37, Hamilton HM AX Bermuda/Tel: (809)292-1055	EP	44	$55–60	none	P	roof sun deck, near ferry
108	Sandpiper Apartments (Warwick) P.O. Box HM 685, Hamilton HM CX Bermuda/Tel: (809)236-7093	EP	8	$50	M, V, A, D	P	

Large Housekeeping Cottages and Apartments (cont.)
Prices are EP unless otherwise indicated.

Page	Establishment, Mailing Address, Telephone	Meal Plans Offered	No. Rooms	Price of double (per person, in season)	Credit Cards	Facilities	Other
	Sky Top (Paget) P.O. Box PG 227, Paget PG BX Bermuda/Tel: (809)236–7984	EP	11	$45–55	M, V		
98	Somerset Bridge Hotel (Sandys) P.O. Box SB 149 Sandys SB BX Bermuda/Tel: (809)234–1042 (800)468–5501	EP, BP, MAP	24	$90 (MAP)	M, V	P, PB, M/D	watersports, near ferry, pool w/Jacuzzi
	South Capers Cottages P.O. Box PG 273, Paget PG BX Bermuda/Tel: (809)236–1222/1987	EP	18	$55–70	none	2P	
	Surf Side Beach Club (Paget) P.O. Box WK 101, Warwick WK BX Bermuda/Tel: (809)236–7100	EP	36	$70	none	P	coffee shop
	Waterville Vacation Apartments 174 Middle Road, Southampton SN 03 Bermuda/Tel: (809)238–1582	EP	12	$45	none	P	

Small Housekeeping Cottages and Apartments

Prices are EP unless otherwise indicated.

Angel's Grotto P.O. Box HS 62, Smith's HS BX Bermuda/Tel: (809)293–1936	EP	6	$40	none	snorkeling, swimming
Barnsdale Guest Apartments P.O. Box DV 628, Devonshire DV BX Bermuda/Tel: (809)236–0164	EP	4	$45–55	none	
108	Burch's Guest Apartments (Paget) 110 North Shore Road, Devonshire FL 03 Bermuda/Tel: (809)292–5746	EP	10	$40	none	no children under age 3
108	By Faith Apartments (Southampton) P.O. Box SN 41, Southampton SN BX Bermuda/Tel: (809)238–1166	EP	5	$30–35	none	some air conditioning, children on advance request only
Cabana Vacation Apartments P.O. Box FL 40 Smith's FL BX Bermuda/Tel: (809)236–6964	EP	8	$45	none	P	club room, 200-year-old home, transportation from airport with tour
Garden House (Sandys) 4 Middle Road, Somerset Bridge, Sandys SB 01 Bermuda/Tel: (809)234–1435	EP	6	$35	none	P	deepwater swimming; air conditioning at extra charge

Small Housekeeping Cottages and Apartments (cont.)

Prices are EP unless otherwise indicated.

Page	Establishment, Mailing Address, Telephone	Meal Plans Offered	No. Apartments	Price of double (per person, in season)	Credit Cards	Facilities	Other
	Glenmar Holiday Apartments (Paget) P.O. Box PG 151, Paget PG BX Bermuda/Tel: (809)236-2844	EP	6	$30	none		
	Granaway Guest House and Cottages P.O. Box WK 533, Warwick WK BX Bermuda/Tel: (809)236-1805	EP, CP	8	$45 (CP)	M, V	M/D	close to ferry
	Grape Bay Cottages (Paget) P.O. Box PG 137, Paget PG BX Bermuda/Tel: (809)236-1194	EP, BP	10	$85 (EP)	none		some cottages on Grape Bay Beach
108	Marley Beach Cottages (Warwick) P.O. Box PG 278, Paget PG BX Bermuda/Tel: (809)236-1143	EP	13	$65-90	none	PB, P	
108	Middleton Cottages P.O. Box PG 48, Paget PG BX Bermuda/Tel: (809)236-2954	EP	8	$35-40	none		
108	Ocean Terrace P.O. Box SN 501, Southampton SN BX (809)238-0019	EP	3	$50		P	

Hillar-Ville P.O. Box SN 2, Southampton SN BX Bermuda/Tel: (809)238-0445	EP	8	$30–35	none	some air conditioning, children on advance request only
107	Pretty Penny Guest House P.O. Box PG 137, Paget PG BX Bermuda/Tel: (809)236-1194 (800)247-2447	EP	7	$50–55	none	P	near ferry, complimentary newspapers, family-run
109	Robin's Nest Apartments (Pembroke) 10 Vale Close, Pembroke HM 04 Bermuda/Tel: (809)292-4347	EP	3	$40	none		not air-conditioned; each unit has fan, heater, TV, radio
	Syl-Den Apartments (Warwick) 8 Warwickshire Estate South Road, Warwick WK 02 Bermuda/Tel: (809)238-1834	EP	5	$40	none	P	sun terrace
	Valley Cottages (Paget) P.O. Box PG 214, Paget PG BX Bermuda/Tel: (809)236-0628	EP	18	$45–50	none		no children under age 12

THE BAHAMAS

WHY THE BAHAMAS?

The variety of islands, breathtaking coastlines, and different lifestyles is what makes The Bahamas special. From the international city of Freeport and its neighboring Lucaya to the pink sand beaches of tiny Harbour Island, The Bahamas offers a wide choice of vacations. It sprawls southeast from the tip of Florida to the fringes of the Caribbean. Unlike Bermuda, much of which can be seen by moped in a day, The Bahamas, with its many islands and cays, could take months of exploration.

Contrary to a widespread impression, The Bahamas, a country of more than 200,000 people, is in the Atlantic Ocean, not the Caribbean. Its islands and islets are an archipelago strung out on the northern side of Cuba, Hispaniola, and the Lesser Antilles, those islands that arc toward South America to enclose the Caribbean Sea.

Visitors looking for the excitement and conviviality of casinos, a vibrant night life, and varied dining opportunities have Nassau and the adjoining Paradise Island, as well as Freeport. Some of the larger resorts here are quite self-contained and cater to guests not interested in exploring much beyond their hotels. Vacationers who do wish to get to know Nassau and Freeport during their stay can begin with bus or taxi tours available through hotels and the tourist bureau. Those with a more adventurous spirit can attempt tours on their own using local transportation. This can be fun and gives the flavor of what life is like for residents.

Through its popular People-to-People Program, which operates in Nassau, Freeport, and now Eleuthera, the government sponsors a means of getting acquainted with its citizens. This free program enables visitors to meet Bahamians, go to their homes, and take part in local activities that would otherwise be missed by most tourists.

Visitors seeking a slower pace, fewer fellow tourists, and more serene surroundings should definitely consider one of the Family Islands. Once called the "Out Islands," these more reclusive spots are often striking in their beauty. They bring visitors closer to the natural wonders of Bahamian land and sea and introduce them to friendly people not jaded by the tourist trade.

For all, there is swimming, tennis, boating, fishing (including big game), diving, snorkeling, windsurfing, parasailing, and, especially in Nassau and Freeport, golf. Those whose idea of a vacation is to sit lazily on a terrace, read, sunbathe, or beachcomb can also find desirable hideaways to suit these quieter pursuits. Through some hotels and resorts, you can even arrange to be "marooned" on your own "X-rated" island beach, where you and a friend, well provisioned, are left alone all day.

If you like to explore, the islands abound in caves, deserted and pristine beaches, old churches, mysterious ocean holes, plantation ruins, early local architecture, undersea caves, wrecks and marine life, lacy gingerbread manor houses, bird sanctuaries, salt flats, eerie pine forests, old fortresses, international research centers, sun-drenched lighthouses, wild boars, and much more. None of the above is ever too far from the incredibly colored and ever-changing sea.

Nassau/Paradise Island and Freeport/Lucaya

The best-known city in The Bahamas is Nassau, the capital. It is located on the island of New Providence, where more than 135,000 Bahamians live. In the past it was one of the playgrounds for the international rich. Just before World War II, the Duke and Duchess of Windsor were in residence, while the duke served as governor general. Their presence helped to attract the world's affluent, especially Americans. International conferences and meetings are frequently held in Nassau and jet-setters, entertainers, and politicians still find their way here to enjoy the beaches, posh hotels, secluded hideaways, and casinos. Some, such as British royalty, find seclusion in more remote spots, like Windermere Island and some of the private cays.

Nassau is also full of the nation's history. Visitors can explore the sites of both intact and crumbling fortresses and see legendary homes and monuments. They can wander through settlements such as Grant's Town, Carmichael, Adelaide, and Fox Hill, founded by or for freed slaves after emancipation. They can bask on beaches where buccaneers once strolled and see rocky coasts where ships were deliberately wrecked for plunder. At the New Year, the Junkanoo Festival, with roots reach-

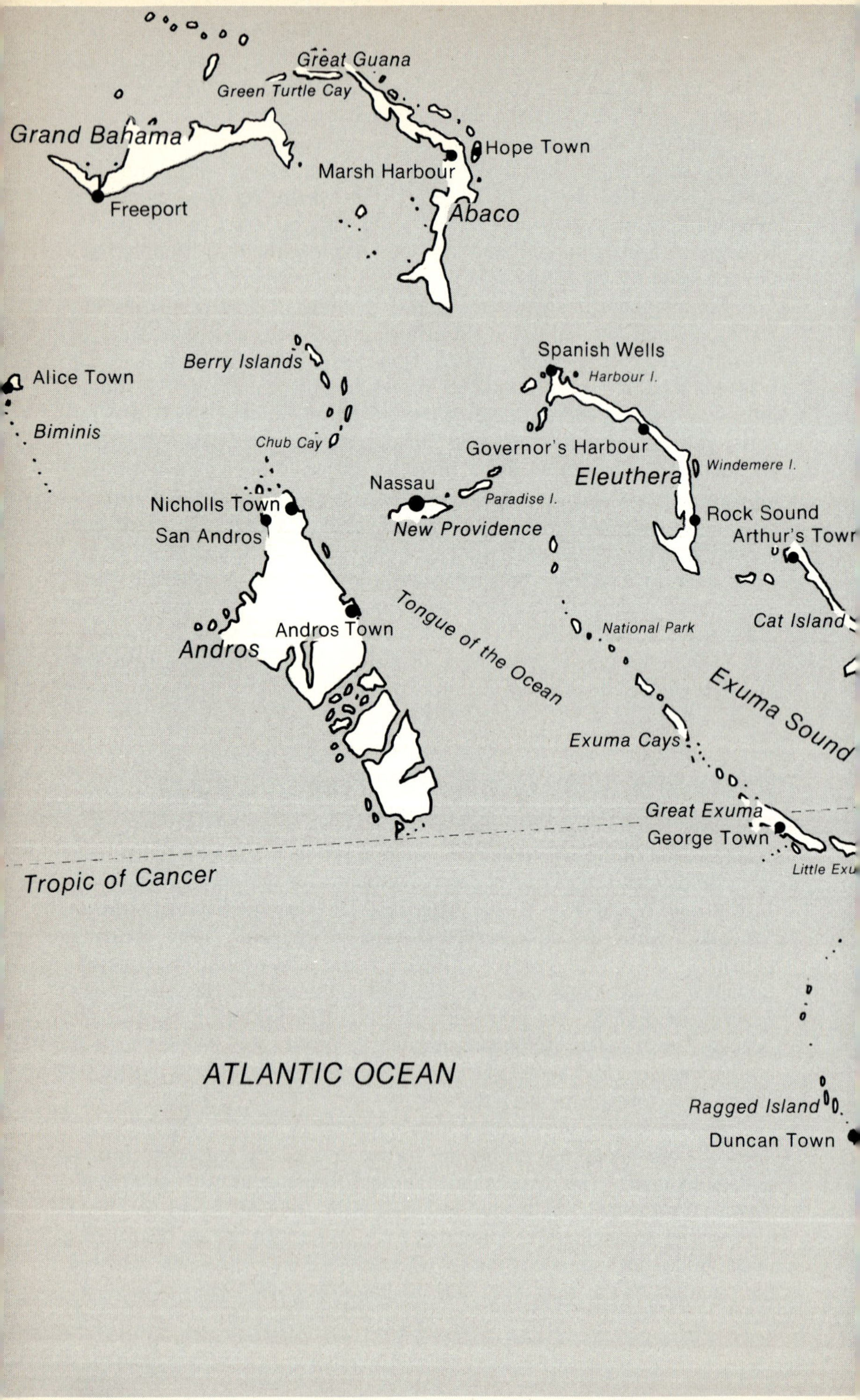

Great Guana
Green Turtle Cay
Grand Bahama
Hope Town
Marsh Harbour
Freeport
Abaco
Spanish Wells
Berry Islands
Harbour I.
Alice Town
Biminis
Chub Cay
Governor's Harbour
Windemere I.
Eleuthera
Nassau
Paradise I.
Nicholls Town
San Andros
New Providence
Rock Sound
Tongue of the Ocean
Andros Town
Andros
National Park
Cat Island
Exuma Sound
Exuma Cays
Great Exuma
George Town
Tropic of Cancer
ATLANTIC OCEAN
Ragged Island
Duncan Town

The Bahamas

ATLANTIC OCEAN

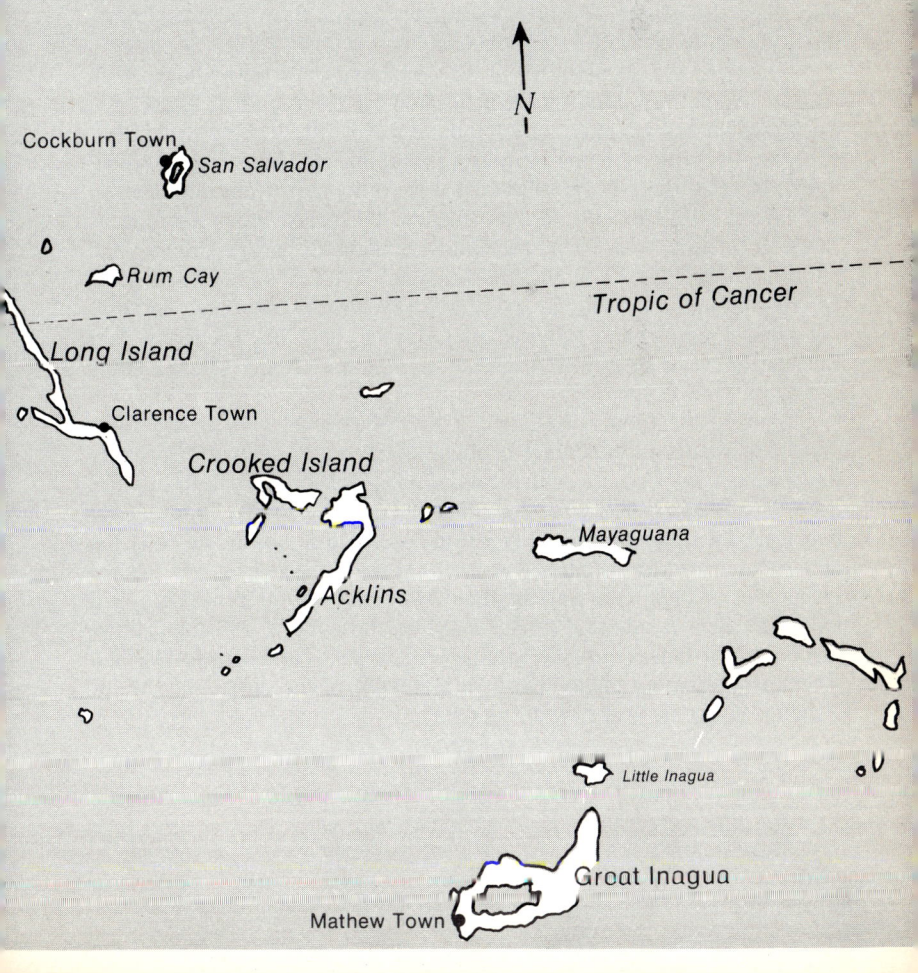

N

Cockburn Town — San Salvador

Rum Cay

Tropic of Cancer

Long Island

Clarence Town

Crooked Island

Mayaguana

Acklins

Little Inagua

Great Inagua

Mathew Town

ing back to slavery, erupts throughout the islands, but nowhere as sizzlingly as in downtown Nassau.

For shoppers, Bay Street and some of its tributaries in downtown Nassau are full of stores with bargains in linens, woolens, china, crystal, perfumes, cameras, and watches. The Straw Market offers a wide variety of "native" crafts. Bahamians often surprise visitors by their use of the word "native" to describe their food, crafts, and some customs. Visitors are cautioned not to use the word themselves in describing Bahamians, as some people consider it demeaning.

Nassau has enough restaurants to satisfy the dining whims of any visitor. The cuisine available ranges from continental to local, and from elegant to inexpensive and homelike. Settings range from seaside to poolside.

Connected to Nassau by an arched toll bridge, Paradise Island is a long, narrow sand bar with many hotels and restaurants, a casino, and a variety of nightspots. Communities of condominiums and private homes also share the island. The beaches attract visitors from the island's hotels and condos as well as from Nassau.

Freeport, the second city of The Bahamas, has fewer hotels than Nassau and is less compact. It is located on the island of Grand Bahama, which has a population of about 35,000. Built during the sixties, Freeport lives in its dazzling present, making its history now, since, unlike Nassau, there is very little evidence of its past. Carefully planned and landscaped, the city adjoins Lucaya, the beach area, merging as Freeport/Lucaya, with wide, palm-lined boulevards and gleaming white buildings. The island's main attractions are the casinos, one of which is entered through a domed, Moorish archway, the two shopping and dining plazas, the 10-acre International Bazaar, and the waterfront Port Lucaya, and The Dolphin Experience, a program through which visitors can swim with Flipper's cousins.

Outside the Central Mall and Lucaya beach area, there are some good restaurants in appealing settings at the water's edge. Especially toward the West End are settlements of local Bahamians whose families have lived on the island since long before an American, Wallace Groves, began its development. Wealthy individuals with financial stakes in the area have created tourist attractions such as the Garden of Groves, named for Groves and his wife, and the Rand Memorial Nature Centre. Beyond the resort area, in addition to the waterfront restaurants and small settlements, you'll come across oil refineries, pharmaceutical factories, and other manufacturing plants that give a glimpse of the day-to-day life of Bahamians not associated with tourism.

The Family Islands

Except for some game fishermen, confirmed boaters, and dedicated divers, most visitors know little of The Bahamas beyond Nassau and Freeport. But away from those bustling tourist centers is the serenity, calm, and beauty of the Family Islands, where 40,000 Bahamians live and work in more sparsely settled communities. Some residents, young and old, have never been to Nassau. Still also called the "Out Islands," the Family Islands are largely undeveloped. Only a handful have tourist accommodations. Many are breathtaking reminders of Winslow Homer watercolors. They make no demands for activity, and you can organize your day or let it go to pot with no pangs of guilt.

Many of these islands have few large trees. The thick vegetation that stretches for miles between towns consists mainly of shrubs and bushes. The flat terrain of many of the smaller islands encourages walking when venturing out to explore and see the sights. You may come upon unexpected settlements, discover a small fishing colony, or be awed by a natural wonder peculiar to the islands such as a cave or an inland pool teeming with sea creatures or unusual flora. You'll see chickens, donkeys, sheep, and goats wandering freely through yards and on roads. Should you find nature too close, you can always flee to one of the islands' more up-to-date resorts with comfortable and often posh appointments, and services for the less rugged.

Visitors may find that, even in the larger resorts, tap water tastes a bit salty and brief power "outages" are not uncommon, but hotels supply filtered or bottled water for drinking and guest rooms usually have candles. Some Family Island accommodations close for several weeks during the off season. Although many of the hotels and guest houses have little or no air conditioning, most visitors are perfectly comfortable with fans and sea breezes. Most Family Island restaurants are in hotels and guest houses, although there are some good, locally operated eating spots.

Since Family Island towns are small, it is easy to meet and socialize with locals, most of whom are farmers, fishermen, craftspeople, or service workers at resorts. With tourism a seasonal business, many islanders combine resort service with one or more other occupations. Some of the older people will say "God bless you" instead of good-bye. The numerous churches (there is at least one in even the tiniest of towns) are another indication of the importance of religion here. While the majority of people adhere to Christianity, on the more remote islands some still practice the voodoo or obeah of their African ancestors.

The buildings in the islands' villages and settlements, formerly constructed of wood, limestone, and coral, are now mainly of concrete block. You may see some that seem abandoned, with weeds, grass, and shrubs growing within the windowless, roofless walls. These are homes in progress, which grow as their owners can afford building materials. When the house is finally finished, the owner is secure in an unmortgaged home.

Some villages seem transported from New England, such as Dunmore Town on Harbour Island and Hope Town on Elbow Cay. Striking examples of colonial manor houses and native thatched-roof stone houses remain. You can see outdoor ovens for baking bread in Gregory Town in northern Eleuthera. There are underwater caves, grottos, and reefs to attract divers, including one of the longest reefs in the world. Many divers are fascinated by the sunken railroad train parts off Eleuthera.

Especially in the Family Islands, visitors will encounter islands called "cays," pronounced "keys" as in Florida's Key West. Chub Cay, Pigeon Cay, and Green Turtle Cay are just a few of these islets.

A Bit of History

In his 1492 voyage to the New World, Christopher Columbus is said to have landed at San Salvador. Later research has placed the landing at Samana Cay, farther south. This southerly Family Island was once known as Guanahani by the Indians who lived there. The Bahamas was first called the Lucayans, after the Indian tribe that, with the Arawaks, inhabited the islands. The name was later changed to Bahama, derived from "baja mar," meaning shallow water or shallow sea in Spanish.

The islands remained in the possession of the Spanish until 1647, when what is now Eleuthera was taken over by a group of English refugees in search of religious freedom. Later, another band of British, who were fleeing Bermuda and also escaping religious restrictions, arrived here. They chose the name "Eleutheria," meaning freedom in Greek. As time went on, the "i" was lost.

During the next two centuries, The Bahamas, near the much-used shipping lanes connecting Europe with the New World, became a lucrative haven for pirates seeking treasure. The marauders found endless hiding places, entrapments, and points of attack among the many inlets and cays. Piracy was not suppressed until 1718, when Woodes Rogers, a much more ruthless governor than those who had preceded him, was able to bring about order and stop the plunder.

As the American Revolution came to a close, thousands of Americans, loyal to the British crown, settled with their slaves in The Bahamas. Also seeking a new life, freed American slaves found these shores as well. As in Bermuda, slavery was abolished in 1834 in The Bahamas, almost 30 years before Emancipation in the United States.

After years of racial, political, and economic strife, the accumulation of grievances in this predominantly black country came to a head during the fifties and sixties. Bent on majority rule, black leaders formed the Progressive Liberal Party (PLP) in 1953. When the new International Airport opened in 1957, taxi drivers were furious over the government's plan to provide low-cost buses to take tourists to hotels. Drivers parked their cars on roads leading to and from the airport, closing it down for several days. But the drivers' demands were not met and trade union leaders called a general strike. After three weeks, the unionists won. Bolstered by the surge in the power of workers, people joined black political parties in droves. You'll note that there is still no public bus service to and from the airport.

In 1961, those who did not own property were finally granted the right to vote, and women won the right to vote for the first time. Eight years later, the islands became a commonwealth nation and PLP leader Lynden Pindling became the country's first prime minister. Despite reluctance on the part of Her Majesty's government and resistance by the "Bay Street Boys," independence from Britain was gained in 1973.

Government

Now a member of the British Commonwealth of Nations, The Bahamas is a parliamentary democracy with a two-chamber parliament, an independent judiciary, and a government headed by a Prime Minister. The British Queen appoints the Governor General. The first Bahamian-born Governor General was appointed in 1977. In 1979, the government of The Bahamas celebrated its 250th year of uninterrupted parliamentary democracy.

Economy

Tourism accounts for the greatest part of the Bahamian gross national product, about 70%. Oil and pharmaceuticals, based on Grand Bahama, are also important contributors to the GNP. Other significant areas supporting the economy are finance, based primarily in Nassau, and to a lesser degree, fishing and agriculture. Bahamians pay no sales tax or income tax.

The Bahamians

In a country that is more than 80% black, it was not until 1956 that black Bahamians could legally patronize theaters, hotels, and restaurants. The populations of several islands (Spanish Wells, Man-O-War Cay, and Elbow Cay among them) are still exclusively or predominantly white. However, it can now be said that Bahamians of all colors like to regard themselves simply as Bahamians. Some will assure you that animosities and prejudices based on race are behind them and that, as a nation, they are moving confidently forward to a more enlightened time.

With tourism the major industry, black people, historically the poorest members of the nation, were once restricted to service jobs. Since independence, increasing numbers of black people have found their way into hotel administration and management. Some have opened their own small hotels and guest houses. Young Bahamians continue to leave the Family Islands, attracted to Nassau and Freeport by employment opportunities in the nation's largest industry. The heritage of British habits and culture persist, along with African, Caribbean, and traces of indigenous Indian influences.

When spoken by Bahamians, English, the national language, may sound West Indian to some ears. But it actually has its own lilt, intonation, syntax, and idiom. You'll hear accents ranging from upper-class British to those where the letters "v" and "w" are interchanged. "So you wisitin', eh?", translates into "So you're visiting, are you?" Some words even sound as if they were imported from Brooklyn: "woik" is what you do "fuh" a living and a waiter will "soive" you.

If a Bahamian tells you he's going "spilligatin'," he means that he is planning to "carry on bad." In short, he intends to "party," "paint the town red," or have an all-out good time. Some Bahamians, Harbour Islanders and people from Abaco, for example, add or drop *h*s. Harbor becomes " 'Arbor" and the name Anderson becomes "Handerson."

The church plays a major role throughout The Bahamas. Churches, representing the leading religions and their denominations, are very visible. Structures run the gamut from almost cathedral in size to one-room shacks. Great numbers of the smaller churches are scattered throughout the poorer residential neighborhoods. On the Family Islands, no village or settlement is complete without at least one place of worship. As in small towns of the American south, Sunday mornings bring the comforting sounds of hymns and gospel from the islands' many churches. Itinerant preachers travel from island to island for local services as well as large revival meetings.

It is against the law for Bahamian citizens to gamble in the country's casinos. Some visitors have suggested that this is paternalistic, that adults should be able to decide for themselves whether or not to gamble. However, most Bahamians seem to agree that the law is good, especially since the purpose of casinos is to bring in new money, not to recirculate Bahamian money. Besides, they add, Bahamians who want to gamble find other means: witness the many domino games, regattas, and other sporting events where more than a few bets are placed.

Meeting the People

The free People-to-People Program, sponsored by the government in Nassau and Freeport through the Bahamas Tourist Bureau and with hundreds of volunteers, gives visitors unique opportunities to meet, socialize with, and get to know Bahamian families and individuals. Besides meeting Bahamians in their homes, visitors can participate in local social and cultural events.

Visitors can be invited to activities such as performances of the local theater group, civic and sporting events, and local receptions not generally open to tourists. On several occasions, visitors have gained access to behind-the-scenes political events. What you do and see depends on you and your host.

Information about the People-to-People Program is available at the Bahamas Tourist offices on Market Square in downtown Nassau and at Prince George Dock. Other offices are on Rawson Square, just west of the fountain, and at the arrival and departure points of Nassau International Airport. In the Freeport/Lucaya area, you can make arrangements to participate at the International Bazaar tourist office.

Music and Festivals

Most of the music you will hear on the radio and in discos and night clubs will be calypso (sometimes called meringue), reggae, and American pop or rock. One type of indigenous Bahamian music, played with goatskin drums and West African rhythms, is called "goombay." (The Bermudian version is "gombey.") The name has been adopted for the July and August "Goombay" festival, with its street dancing, music, and other activities for tourists during the off season.

The biggest and most popular of the Bahamian festivals is Junkanoo, celebrated on Boxing Day (Dec. 26), and on New Year's Day. As in pre-Lenten carnivals in the Caribbean, celebrants dance through the streets in colorful and fantastic costumes, masks, and intricate headdresses, blowing whistles and jangling bells, creating Junkanoo music. In Nassau, Bay Street truly comes alive during Junkanoo celebrations. The parade begins at 4 a.m., followed by a "boil fish" and johnny cake breakfast at 9:00.

The origin of Junkanoo remains in dispute. It is variously attributed to West Africa, indigenous Indians, and the American south, among other sources. Some say the name comes from a West African called "Jananin Canno," others, the American folk hero "Johnny Canoe," and still others, someone called *l'inconnu,* meaning "the unknown" in French. Whether this figure was a god, a slave, a Mayan Indian, or an African prince, there is a move to develop Junkanoo into the primary Bahamian music.

Eating and Drinking

The ubiquitous sea is the main source of Bahamian food. Chief among the varieties of fare available is conch, pronounced "conk." High mounds of discarded conch shells indicate that the meat has gone into delicacies such as cracked conch (beaten and fried), conch salad, (raw, with vegetables and lime juice), and conch fritters. You can watch fishermen on docks prepare scorched conch, eaten raw from the shell after being spiced with salt, hot pepper, and lime.

Fish, especially grouper, which turns up for dinner, lunch, and even breakfast, is also a staple, along with varieties of shellfish. Lobster is usually what Americans call crayfish. Minced lobster, a favorite, is shredded crayfish cooked with tomatoes, green peppers, and onions, then served in the shell. Among other local specialties are crab and rice, chicken and dough (dumplings), mutton, turtle steak, wild boar, and souse (pig's feet, chicken, sheep's tongue, or other meat in a savory sauce). Everything comes with heaping portions of peas and rice, potato salad, or cole slaw—sometimes all three. Mildly sweet johnny cake is also often on the side.

Don't let the various ways of preparing seafood confuse you. "Boil fish" (a popular breakfast item served with grits) is cooked with salt pork, onions, green peppers, and spices. Also eaten as the day's first meal, stewed fish has a rich brown gravy. Steamed fish (which may sound bland, but is far from it) isn't eaten before noon and is cooked with a tomato base. Of course, you'll also find beef, lamb, and pork, but they are imported.

Guava duff, a rich and delicious dessert, is to Bahamians what apple pie is to people in the U.S.A. It is made by spreading guava jelly on dough, rolling it, boiling it for about 90 minutes, then topping the warm slices with a white sauce.

Because most food is imported, it tends to be expensive. Restaurants serving Bahamian specialties and Bahamian diners can save you money and introduce new tastes. Salads and greens are not much in evidence, but you'll also discover such dishes as roti, curried chicken, and plantain, inspired by Caribbean neighbors.

While local restaurants, especially in the Family Islands, stress traditional Bahamian fare, American and continental cuisine are available almost everywhere. Thirst is quenched with beer, beer, and more beer—most of it imported directly from Germany and the Netherlands—as well as with fruity concoctions such as Goombay Smashes, Bahama Mamas, and Yellowbirds, all with a rum base.

THINGS TO KNOW

COSTS • In season, from December through April or May, double-room rates, per person, range from $25 per night at a small guest house to $100 or more including meals at a resort. Off-season rates are appreciably lower. Meal plans offered by hotels are FAP (room and three meals), MAP (room, breakfast and dinner), FB (room and full-American breakfast), CP (room and light breakfast), and EP (room only). If you plan to stay at an accommodation where you can prepare your own meals, you should be aware that although supermarkets may be nearby (in Nassau and Freeport), food prices may be quite high. This is because many foods are imported.

Travel agents can advise you on economic package deals, such as those offered by **Pan Am** to Nassau and Freeport. Many packages have specific requirements for day and time of departure and return, and a limited choice of hotels and locations. **Eastern Airlines** offers hotel package deals to a few Family Islands as well as to Nassau/Paradise Island and Freeport. However, particularly if you plan a trip to the more remote Family Islands, you may want to design your own vacation. The accommodations charts in the back of the book will help you make your own reservations should you choose to do so.

Hotels add a 6% tax on rooms throughout The Bahamas. There is no sales tax. Most restaurants and hotels add a 15% service charge to cover gratuities for food and drink. The smaller, locally operated restaurants specializing in homestyle cuisine are the least expensive and serve better food than some hotel dining rooms. Taxi drivers and tour guides are also given tips of at least 15%. Bellmen and porters are tipped 50¢ to $1 for each bag.

It is best to arrive with enough film and books to last for the duration of your stay. Film and imported books are sold at inflated prices compared to those back home.

TRAVELING WITH CHILDREN • Ships, planes, and hotels all go out of their way to help make traveling with children as simple, safe, and enjoyable as possible. Most hotels offer free accommodations for children up to about age 12, provide small-fry menus, and, sometimes, special recreation programs, as well as baby-sitting. Some of the larger hotels, such as the Holiday Inn and Princess Towers in Freeport, have small playgrounds.

The minimum drinking age is 21.

TRAVEL FOR THE HANDICAPPED • With rising concern for improving and extending leisure-time facilities and services for the physically disabled, many hotels in The Bahamas, including some resorts in the Family Islands, have made their accommodations more accessible to this group of visitors. Nassau's Cable Beach Hotel & Casino, for instance, has set aside a number of specially designed rooms for people confined to wheelchairs. The Bahamas Paraplegic Association, based in Nassau, has made a survey of hotels and resorts throughout The Bahamas where ramps, elevators, dining areas, baths, and other facilities can also serve those with limited mobility. Contact the association at (809) 322–2393 or (809) 323–1392.

SPECIAL SERVICES • Members of **Weight Watchers** need not postpone or forego a trip for fear of interrupted regimens. For the latest information on Weight Watchers programs in The Bahamas, call (212) 896–9800.

Chapters of **Alcoholics Anonymous** meet in The Bahamas in the following areas: Nassau; Freeport; George Town, Exuma; Hope Town, Abaco; and Moxey Town, Andros. For specific information, contact Alcoholics Anonymous at 468 Park Avenue South, New York, NY, 10016; Tel: (212) 686–1100.

WHEN TO GO Weather • The winter season (from December through April) is considered the ideal time to visit The Bahamas. Daytime temperatures average in the 70s with cooler evenings. Swimming is often comfortable in January and February, but some days and most evenings may be quite cool, making a jacket or heavy sweater necessary. While there is more rain at times during the summer, rates are lower and the government sponsors enjoyable "Goombay" festivities. Showers are usually brief and the temperature averages in the 80s.

Most hotels have air conditioning, but trade winds make it unnecessary in some hotels. On the Family Islands, some visitors prefer the more romantic and relaxing ceiling fans that stir the already refreshing air. Nassau and Freeport, both north of the Tropic of Cancer, are in the cooler climate zone. Warmer weather is found in the more southerly islands.

Holidays and Special Events • Junkanoo and Goombay are two festivals that may help determine when to visit The Bahamas. Junkanoo is a festival that occurs during the Christmas/New Year's season. Goombay is an annual series of special events to attract visitors during

	Average Temperature Fahrenheit/Centigrade		Average Rainfall Inches
January	70°	21°	1.9
February	70°	21°	1.6
March	72°	22°	1.4
April	75°	24°	1.9
May	77°	25°	4.8
June	80°	27°	9.2
July	81°	27°	6.1
August	82°	28°	6.3
September	81°	27°	7.5
October	78°	26°	8.3
November	74°	23°	2.3
December	71°	22°	1.5

the summer season, when the weather is hotter and somewhat wetter. Other special events such as those for boaters, sports fishermen, and divers will also help you decide when and where to go.

In anticipation of the 500th anniversary of Columbus' arrival in the New World, a fall promotion called "Discover It," lasts from September through December, previewing the all-out celebration in 1992. Events include culinary festivals, walking tours, and tea parties at Government House.

Event	Month	Location
Junkanoo Parade*	Jan. 1	All Islands
Supreme Court Opening	2nd Wed. in Jan.	Nassau
Annual Miami-Nassau Boat Race	Feb.	Nassau
Annual Nassau Yacht Cup Race	Feb.	Nassau
Marlboro Championship Sailors' Regatta	Feb.	Nassau
International 5.5 Metre World Championships	Mar.	Nassau
Annual Bacardi Snipe Winter Championship	Mar.	Nassau
Annual Abaco Fishing Tournament	Apr.	Abaco
Family Island Regatta	Apr.	George Town Exumas

THE BAHAMAS

Event	Month	Location
Supreme Court Opening	1st Wed. in Apr.	Nassau
Annual Walker's Cay Billfish Tournament	May	Walker's Cay Abaco
Long Island Sailing Regatta	June	Long Island
Cat Cay Billfish Tournament	June	Cat Cay
Bimini Big Game Blue Marlin Tournament	June	Bimini
Labour Day Parade	1st Fri. in June	Nassau & Freeport
Supreme Court Opening	1st Wed. in July	Nassau
Independence Day	July 10	All Islands
Pepsi-Cola Independence Open Golf Tournament	July	Nassau
Commonwealth Exhibition and Fair	July	Nassau
Chub Cay Blue Marlin Fishing Tournament	July	Chub Cay Berry Islands
Emancipation Day	Aug. 4	All Islands
Bimini Local Fishing Tournament	Aug.	Bimini
Cat Island Regatta	Aug.	Arthur's Town Cat Island
Fox Hill Day Celebration	2nd Tues. in Aug.	Nassau
Supreme Court Opening	1st Wed. in Oct.	Nassau
Discovery Day Regatta	Oct.	Nassau
Discovery Day	Oct. 12	Nassau
Remembrance Day	Nov.	Nassau
Abaco Week	Nov.	Abaco
Annual Bahamas Bonefish Bonanza	Nov.	George Town Exumas
Annual International Pro-Am Golf Championship	Nov.	Nassau
Boxing Day Junkanoo Parade*	Dec. 26	All Islands
Adam Clayton Powell, Jr. Memorial Fishing Tournament	Dec.	Bimini

*Visitors may join in the Junkanoo Parades by applying before Dec. to the Bahamas Tourist Office.

THE BAHAMAS · · · 141

GETTING THERE BY AIR Airlines fly to The Bahamas from the U.S., Canada, the Caribbean, Great Britain, and Europe. Some small airlines in addition to those listed below fly from Florida to Freeport, Abaco, Eleuthera, and Exuma.

Private Planes and Yachts: Private planes and yachts are free to enter and leave The Bahamas at their own convenience. Aircraft pilots, however, should contact the Bahamas Tourist Office for the Air Navigation Chart or Flight Planner Chart, or contact the Bahamas Private Pilot Briefing Center at 1 (800) 327-3853.

Private plane pilots must also file declaration forms with customs

Airline	From	To
AeroCoach	Ft. Lauderdale; West Palm Beach	Marsh Harbour, Treasure Cay (Abaco); George Town (Exuma); North Eleuthera
Air Canada	Toronto; Montreal	Nassau; Freeport
Air Jamaica	Chicago; Toronto	Nassau; Freeport
Bahamasair	Newark; Miami; Tampa; Atlanta; Ft. Lauderdale	Nassau; Freeport; Family Islands*
Braniff	New York	Nassau
British Airways	London; Bermuda; Kingston, Jamaica	Nassau; Freeport
Chalk's International	Miami; Ft. Lauderdale; West Palm Beach	Paradise Island; Bimini; Cat Cay
Delta	Atlanta; Boston; Chicago; Detroit; New York; Newark	Nassau; Freeport
Eastern	Atlanta; Baltimore; Ft. Lauderdale; Miami; Philadelphia; Washington, DC; New York	Nassau; Freeport
Gull Air	Palm Beach	Nassau
North American	Ft. Lauderdale; West Palm Beach	Freeport
Pan Am	New York	Nassau; Freeport
Piedmont	New York; Baltimore; Richmond	Nassau

Airline	From	To
Trans Air	Miami; Ft. Lauderdale; West Palm Beach	Marsh Harbour, Treasure Cay (Abaco); N. Eleuthera; Nassau; Freeport
United	Chicago	Nassau; Freeport

*Bahamasair has daily flights from Nassau to the Abacos, Andros, Eleuthera, and Exuma. Flights to other Family Islands leave from Nassau several times a week.

officials. A copy is retained by the pilot as a cruising permit when visiting other islands. U.S. Airmen's Certificates are recognized flying credentials in The Bahamas, but an extension of the aircraft's insurance may be needed to include the islands. Declaration forms are obtainable from Fixed Base Operators at points of departure, or at Bahamian ports of entry.

Charter Planes: Charter flights are frequently used to reach resorts not served by regularly scheduled airlines. Charter planes are available for hire in several southern Florida cities. Following are some Bahamian inter-island charter services:

Pinders Charter Service
Nassau International Airport
P.O. Box N–10456
Nassau, Bahamas
(809) 327–7320

Norman Nixon Charter Service
Nassau International Airport
P.O. Box SS–5980
Nassau, Bahamas
(809) 327–7184

Trans Island Airways, Ltd.
Nassau International Airport
P.O. Box N–291
Nassau, Bahamas
(809) 327–8329

Helda Charter Service
Freeport International Airport
P.O. Box F–3335
Freeport, Grand Bahama
(809) 352–8832

Lucaya Air Service
Freeport International Airport
P.O. Box F–2521
Freeport, Grand Bahama
(809) 352–8885

GETTING THERE BY SEA • An increasingly popular way of traveling to The Bahamas is to go by cruise ship. For those who don't live near a departure point, some lines include bus or air transport to the port as part of the cruise package. Small children are often put up in their parents' stateroom without additional cost. Some ships have recreational areas, baby-sitters, and special activities for youngsters.

The well-appointed ships that cruise to The Bahamas have so many amenities that travelers need never leave the vessel. In response to the current physical fitness vogue, exercise rooms, jogging areas, and spas have burgeoned. Now more than ever, sumptuous and almost continual dining, formal as well as in snack bars and soda fountains, is a feature of shipboard life. Young people can dance until all hours in discos, and some ships even put on lavish nightclub extravaganzas. Passengers with the itch can visit the ships' casinos. Those who prefer a more relaxed trip have the choice of libraries, lounges, in-cabin television, sun decks, and indoor and outdoor pools.

A hallmark of ships of the Royal Caribbean Line, Viking Crown Lounges are glass-enclosed public rooms circling the ships' funnels, to give a 360-degree, panoramic view of the sea and the decks below.

A very different and delightful way to reach Eleuthera and Exuma, two intriguing Family Islands, is to sail from Miami on a real sailing ship, the 440-foot *Windstar*. This 150-passenger ship has a mere 74 staterooms, all outside, giving carefree passengers the feel of a luxury yacht. That feeling is enhanced even more when travelers find that they can eat when they want and make their own recreation and entertainment.

Another line, SeaEscape, Ltd. (1080 Port Blvd., Miami, FL 33132; tel: (800) 327-7400), offers a one-day cruise from Miami or Fort Lauderdale to Freeport for a day of shopping, gambling, or hitting the beach.

Ships carry from several hundred to more than 1000 passengers. Some ships tend to be sedate, while others encourage continual activity. Carnival Cruise Lines, for example, calls its vessels "Fun Ships" and tends to attract a younger and more budget-conscious crowd. However, on the same ships, Carnival also offers posh suites with private decks. For all lines, extras usually include bar service, sightseeing tours, and on-board tipping.

Some cruise lines have added Cashphones, so that passengers may call the United States as well as other countries. On most lines, calls to the U.S. range from $11 to $15.50 per minute, with calls to other countries costing more.

Except for military personnel, the U.S. Immigration and Naturalization Service has imposed a $5 inspection fee for all U.S. cruise passengers arriving in the U.S. on ships that have stopped at foreign ports. In most cases, the fee is collected from the cruise line, which adds it to the passenger fare.

Embarking points for The Bahamas are primarily Miami, Fort Lauderdale, and Port Canaveral. One line, American Canadian, departs from Nassau in The Bahamas for a 7-day cruise to cays in the Family Islands. Because most Bahamian cays do not have landing docks, the line's 72-

passenger *New Shoreham II* has a landing ramp in its bow permitting direct access to the cays and their beaches.

Because schedules, ships and prices change from season to season, it is advisable to call the ship line or check with your travel agent when planning a cruise.

Following are lines that provide service to The Bahamas:

Cruise Line	Destination	No. Passengers	Facilities	From
American Canadian Lines P.O. Box 368 Warren, RI 02885 (401) 247–0955, (800) 556–7450				
New Shoreham II	Family Islands	72		Nassau
Carnival Cruise Line 5225 N.W. 87th Avenue Miami, FL 33166 (305) 599–2600				
Mardi Gras	Freeport Nassau	906	2 OP, IP, C	Ft. Lauderdale
Carnivale	Freeport Nassau	950	4 OP, IP, C	Miami
Chandris Fantasy Cruises 900 Third Avenue New York, NY 10022 (800) 621–3446				
Britanis	Nassau	1100	OP	Miami
Galileo	Nassau	1100	OP, C	Miami
Costa Cruises 1 Biscayne Tower Miami, FL 33131 (305) 358–7330, (800) 447–6877				
Costa Riviera	Nassau	1000	OP, C	Ft. Lauderdale
Dolphin Cruise Line 1007 North American Way Miami, FL 33132 (305) 358–2111				
Dolphin IV	Freeport Nassau	664	OP, C	Miami

THE BAHAMAS · · · 145

Cruise Line	Destination	No. Passengers	Facilities	From
Holland America Lines, Westours 300 Elliott Avenue West Seattle, WA 98119 (206) 281–3535				
Noordam	Nassau	1214	2 OP, C, CPh	Ft. Lauderdale
Rotterdam	Nassau	1114	OP, IP, C	Ft. Lauderdale
Norwegian Caribbean Lines 1 Biscayne Tower (Suite 3000) Miami, FL 33131 (305) 358-6670, (800) 327-7030				
Norway	Nassau	1864	IP, 2 OP, C, CPh	Miami
Skyward	Stirrup Cay	790	OP, C, CPh	Miami
Southward	Nassau	764	OP, C	Miami
Sunward II	Nassau, Freeport	696	OP, C	Miami
Princess Cruises 2029 Century Park East Los Angeles, CA 90067 (213) 553–7000				
Sun Princess	Samana Cay	686	OP, C	Miami
Premier Cruise Lines P.O. Box 573 Cape Canaveral, FL 32920 or 101 George King Blvd., Port Canaveral, FL (305) 783–5061, (800) 327–7113				
Oceanic	Nassau Salt Cay	1500	2 OP, C	Port Canaveral
Royale	Nassau Salt Cay	1100	3 OP, C, W	Port Canaveral
Royal Caribbean Cruise Line 903 South America Way Miami, FL 33132 (305) 379–2601				
Nordic Prince	Nassau	1038	OP, C	Miami
Song of America	Nassau	1414	2 OP, C	Miami
Sun Viking	Nassau	728	OP, S	Miami
SeaEscape, Ltd. 1080 Port Blvd. Miami, FL 33132 (800) 327–7400	1-day cruises Miami, Fort Lauderdale			Freeport

THE BAHAMAS

Cruise Line	Destination	No. Passengers	Facilities	From
Sitmar Cruises 10100 Santa Monica Blvd. Los Angeles, CA 90067 (213) 553–1666				
Fairsky	Nassau	1212	2 OP, S, YC, C	Ft. Lauderdale
Fairwind	Nassau	925	2 OP, YC, C	Ft. Lauderdale
Windstar Sail Cruises 7415 N.W, 19 ST. Miami, FL 33126 (800) 258–SAIL				
Windstar	Eleuthera, Exuma	150		Miami

Key
IP   Indoor Poor
OP   Outdoor Pool
C   Casino
CPh   Cashphone
S   Spa
YC   Youth Center
T   Theater
W   Whirlpool

ENTRY AND DEPARTURE REQUIREMENTS • Travel Documents •

To enter the Bahamas, you must have proof of citizenship and an onward-bound ticket. While Bahamian Immigration accepts either a valid passport, birth certificate, voter's registration card, or driver's license as proof of citizenship, the U.S. government now requires that you have a passport to reenter the country.

Citizens of Canada and the United Kingdom visiting for three weeks or less may enter upon showing a passport or the same items required for U.S. citizens. Citizens of Commonwealth countries do not need visas for entry.

All visitors must fill out and sign immigration cards. Vaccination certificates for smallpox and cholera are needed only for people coming from areas where such diseases still occur.

Departure Tax • Upon departure by air, adults are required to pay a $5 tax and children under 12, $2.50.

Customs • Although no written declaration is required, baggage is subject to customs inspection. For dutiable items such as furniture, china, and linens, a declaration is necessary. New items should be accompanied by sales slips. Any used household items are subject to assessment by the Customs Officer.

Each adult visitor is permitted 50 cigars or 200 cigarettes or one pound of tobacco and one quart of alcohol duty free, in addition to personal effects. Purchases of up to $25 are allowed all incoming passengers.

Duty-Free Allowances • United States residents, including children, may take home duty-free purchases up to $300 in value if they have been out of the United States for more than 48 hours, and have not taken such an exemption within 30 days. The exemption includes up to 32 ounces of alcohol per person over 21, and families may pool their exemptions.

Canadians absent from their country for 48 hours or more may take home up to $50 (Canadian) worth of duty-free merchandise, which must accompany the passenger.

Personal items such as jewelry, cameras, and sports equipment may be brought in duty-free.

Pets • The Bahamian Ministry of Agriculture and Fisheries, with headquarters in Nassau, requires a permit for all animals entering the country. Written applications for permits should be submitted to the Ministry of Agriculture and Fisheries, P.O. Box N–3208, Nassau, telephone (809) 32–21277. Forms are available at the Bahamas Tourist Offices. Although most hotels exclude pets, several accept them when arrangements are made in advance and a permit has been obtained.

Drugs and Firearms • Possession of marijuana or other drugs is an extremely serious and punishable offense. Under no circumstances may firearms be brought in without a Bahamian gun license.

BEING THERE • **Language** • The language of The Bahamas is English, accented with West Indian, Scottish, and Irish influences. Like Bermudians, Bahamians often substitute "w" 's for "v" 's. This is thought to date back to 18th-century English.

Dress • In The Bahamas, dress is generally casual although, in season, most hotels and restaurants request that men wear jackets and ties for evening meals. Dress is more relaxed during the off season. At some of the larger hotels and posher resorts, long skirts are preferred for women during the evening. Out in the Family Islands, dress is much more casual, except in one or two resorts.

Beachwear is discouraged in the public rooms of hotels, and wearing short shorts is frowned upon for both men and women.

Business Hours • In Nassau, banks are open 9:30 a.m.–3 p.m. Monday through Thursday, and on Friday from 9:30 a.m.–5 p.m. Stores are open 9 a.m.–5 p.m. every day except Sunday and holidays.

Banks in Freeport are open 9 a.m.–1 p.m. Monday through Friday, then again from 3–5 p.m. on Friday. Most stores are open 9 a.m.–6 p.m. except Sundays and holidays. Many shops in the International Bazaar and Port Lucaya stay open until 9 p.m. on Saturdays during the winter season. Some banks on the Family Islands are open only several days a week, with limited hours. Many stores close for an hour or two for lunch.

Accommodations • The large hotels and resorts have daily activities and many facilities such as shops, restaurants, large dining rooms, cycle rental stations, and water sports equipment. Most also have nightly entertainment. When not located on a beach, many provide complimentary transportation. Most establishments that have few or no sports facilities will arrange sporting activities for their guests elsewhere. All large accommodations are fully air conditioned. Smaller hotels and guest houses have fewer facilities and many are partially air conditioned, if at all. Particularly in the Family Islands, many establishments rely on fans and trade winds. Some of the smaller guest houses are in former private homes and have shared baths. In the Family Islands, with power generators in wide use at hotels, visitors may sometimes find themselves without electricity for short periods of time. It is therefore a good idea to note the location of candles that are put in most guest rooms.

Hotels add a 6% room tax to rates. Many also add a 15% service charge. High season runs from about December through April. During the summer (or ''Goombay'') season, rates are about 20% to 50% lower.

In the **Hotel Quick Reference Charts** at the back of the book, you'll find more information about the accommodations described in each island section as well as details about other establishments.

Renting Private Homes • Following are some real estate agencies that handle private homes throughout The Bahamas:

- Caribbean Management, Ltd.
  P.O. Box N–1132, Nassau, The Bahamas; (809)322–8618/1356
- Ingraham's Real Estate
  Hospital Lane North, P.O. Box N–1062, Nassau, The Bahamas; (809)325–2222/3433/8930
- Jack Isaacs Real Estate Co., Ltd.
  George Street, P.O. Box N–1458, Nassau, The Bahamas; (809)322–1069/325–6326
- G. Knowles & Co.
  P.O. Box N–10757, Nassau, The Bahamas; (809)322–4187/4188
- Plot Realty Co., Ltd.
  P.O. Box N–1492, Nassau, The Bahamas (809)322–2460

Money • Bahamian money is pegged to the American dollar, with the same designations for bills and coins and exchanged at the same rate. Visitors are likely to receive change in mixed American and Bahamian dollars and coins. Travelers checks are accepted throughout the islands and are cashable at banks and hotels. However, banks and some restaurants will add a service charge. Credit cards are widely accepted.

In Nassau and Freeport, commercial banks are open from 9:30 a.m. to 3 p.m., Monday through Thursday, and until 5 p.m. on Friday. Most banks will cash verifiable personal checks. Nassau's American Express office for check cashing and cash advances is conveniently located downtown at the Playtours office, upstairs at the intersection of Shirley and Parliament streets. In Freeport, American Express is located in the Kipling Building, off Kipling Lane in Churchill Square.

Getting Around • *By Taxi:* Taxis are available in New Providence, Grand Bahama, and most of the Family Islands. In Nassau and Freeport, as well as the Family Islands where there are no tour buses, drivers will serve as island guides. The rates, often negotiable, are about $16 an hour. Some Family Island roads are not in the best of repair. A bumpy ride with a friendly driver can be an adventure in itself.

In Nassau and Freeport, taxis, which are metered, wait for passengers at airports and hotels. From Nassau International Airport to a hotel on Cable Beach, two people should expect to pay about $9; from the airport to Paradise Island, the ride will be about $18, including the $2 bridge toll. From Freeport's International Airport to the hotel districts, the fare will range from about $5 to $8. Taxis in the Family Islands are not metered and tend to be more expensive than in Nassau or Freeport. On most Family Islands taxis (sometimes simply the cars or vans of local residents) meet planes. However, to be on the safe side, check with your accommodation about land transportation before arrival.

By Car: Visitors with valid U.S. or Canadian driver's licenses can rent cars in the Bahamas. *Note that driving is on the left.* Daily rates range from about $45 to $72. You'll save renting by the week. Rental agencies in Nassau and Freeport are at airports, hotels, and downtown locations. During high season, a reservation is suggested before leaving home. In addition to local companies, Avis, Budget, Dollar Rent-A-Car, and National also have offices in The Bahamas. An Avis agency is in back of Nassau's Sheraton British Colonial Hotel and National agencies are on nearby Marlborough Street and at the Cable Beach Hotel. You'll also find an Avis office in Freeport's International Bazaar. You can rent cars in the Family Islands (sometimes from taxi drivers), but many of the models are battle scarred by years of use on bumpy roads. Be sure to check your car's condition before pulling off. You can import your car for touring, duty-free, for up to 6 months. A deposit of up to 70% of the vehicle's value may be required, but it is refunded if the car is shipped out within 6 months. The value is assessed by Customs upon arrival.

By Cycle: Cycles are a popular mode of travel in The Bahamas and visitors take to them with a passion. At most hotels and resorts, you can rent mopeds on the premises or at nearby cycle shops if you are 16 or older. No driver's license is necessary. Wearing a helmet, which you are given with the moped, is required by law. Until you become accustomed to motorized bikes, it is best to practice driving in a low-traffic area. Renting a moped ranges from about $10 a day, $6 a half day to about $25 a day, $18 a half day, including insurance. You'll be asked to leave a deposit of about $20. Bicycles are about $10 a day. *Remember, Bahamians drive on the left.*

By Bus: Visitors can take advantage of public transportation in getting around Nassau and Freeport. Bahamians will come to the rescue with directions if you seem uncertain. Nassau has 50¢ jitneys you can pick up at bus stops, and they go to Cable Beach, downtown Nassau, public beaches, and other points in the city. To go east, toward the Paradise Island bridge, pick up jitneys downtown at Frederick Street at the corner of Bay Street; to go west to Cable Beach, pick up jitneys in front of the Sheraton British Colonial at Bay Street. Some hotels run complimentary buses to downtown Nassau and to the casino on Cable Beach. Buses on Grand Bahama (65¢) connect Freeport with Lucaya and all hotels with beaches, the International Bazaar, and Port Lucaya.

By Ferry: Ferries run between downtown Nassau and Paradise Island from Prince George Dock. These "water taxis" also operate in the Family Islands to various offshore cays.

By Mail Boat: Inter-island mail boats travel between Nassau and the Family Islands. The mail boats leave for the outer islands from Potter's Cay, next to the Paradise Island bridge, East Bay Street in Nassau. Boats leave once a week, stopping at one or two islands, in a trip that takes almost a day, and is usually made overnight.

Mail boats are an economical way of traveling, if only for the more adventurous visitor. Decks are crowded with local commuters, freight, varieties of cargo, produce, and livestock. Schedules are constantly revised and there are often postponements. Passage cannot be arranged in advance. Bookings can only be made after arrival.

Information on mail boats may be obtained at the Dock Master's office on Potter's Cay in Nassau (809) 323-1064.

Casinos • Gambling at the casinos of The Bahamas is legal for all visitors over the age of 21. Bahamian citizens, however, are not permitted to play. Two casinos are located in Nassau: one on Paradise Island, and the other on the mainland in the Cable Beach Hotel. Two more are found in Freeport, Grand Bahama—one between the Princess Tower Hotel and the International Bazaar, the other at the Lucayan Beach Resort and Casino.

Time • Eastern Standard Time is in use throughout The Bahamas. Eastern Daylight Saving Time is used during the summer months coinciding with the U.S. changes, so when it is noon in New York, it is noon in The Bahamas, year round.

Electricity • American electrical appliances can be used in The Bahamas without adapters.

Medical Concerns • There are excellent medical services in The Bahamas. Hospital, public and private medical facilities, and personnel are available in Nassau and Freeport. There are also health centers and clinics in the Family Islands. In medical emergencies, patients are brought to Princess Margaret Hospital, a government operated institution in downtown Nassau. The water throughout The Bahamas is potable. However, on most Family Islands it is best to drink bottled water, if only because tap water can be quite salty.

Newspapers • Nassau's two newspapers are the *Nassau Guardian*, published Monday through Saturday, and the *Tribune*, an afternoon periodical. Freeport's paper is the *Freeport News*, published Monday through Friday. *The New York Times*, the *London Times*, the *Daily Telegraph*, and *The Wall Street Journal* are available at most of the larger hotels and newstands, but sometimes a day late.

Visitor Information • The address of The Bahamas Ministry of Tourism is P.O. Box N-3701, Nassau, The Bahamas. Contact the Family Islands Promotion Board at 255 Alhambra Circle, Suite 420, Coral Gables, FL 33134 (305) 446-4111, or The Grand Bahama Promotion Board, P.O. Box F650, Freeport, Grand Bahama. Following are the locations and phone numbers of The Bahamas Tourist Offices in the United States and Canada:

Atlanta
1950 Century Boulevard, NE
Atlanta, GA 30345
(404) 633-1793

Chicago
875 North Michigan Avenue
Chicago, IL 60611
(312) 787-8203

Dallas
2050 Stemmons Freeway
World Trade Center P.O. Box 581408
Dallas, TX 75201
(214) 742-1886

Los Angeles
3450 Wilshire Boulevard
Los Angeles, CA 90010
(213) 385-0033

Coral Gables
255 Alhambra Circle
Coral Gables, FL 33134
(305) 442-4860

Toronto
85 Richmond Street West
Toronto, Ontario M5H2C9
(416) 363-4441

New York
150 E. 52 St.
New York, NY 10022
(212) 758-2777

Boston
1027 Statler Office Building
Boston, MA 02116
(617) 426-3144

Philadelphia
437 Chestnut St.
Philadelphia, PA 19106
(215) 925-0871

Michigan
26400 Lahser Road
Southfield, MI 48034
(313) 357-2940

District of Columbia
1730 Rhode Island Avenue, NW
Washington, DC 20036
(202) 659-9135

Montreal
1255 Phillips Square
Montreal, Quebec H3B3G1
(514) 861-6797

Vancouver
470 Granville Street
Vancouver, British Columbia
　V6C1V5
(604) 688-8334

WHAT TO DO AND WHERE TO DO IT

For most visitors, having a good time in The Bahamas revolves around watersports and just being outdoors. Because the islands are surrounded by some of the clearest, most beautiful, and game-stocked waters in the world, fishing, boating, and undersea exploration are very popular. Nassau, the adjoining Paradise Island, and Freeport offer lively nightlife, including their casinos, and the Family Islands are paradise for those looking for real escape. For more specific information on sports, nightlife, shopping, tours, or dining, refer to the individual islands.

SPORTS

You can get further information about exactly where and when various sports are available before leaving home. Contact The Bahamas Sports Information Center at 1 (800) 32-S.P.O.R.T. for answers to any sports-related question.

Bare Boating • The marinas, ports, and harbors of almost every island are thronged with pleasure boats making use of the extensive

Bahamian boating facilities. Sailors have a wide choice of marinas throughout the Family Islands as well as in New Providence and Grand Bahama, where Nassau and Freeport are located. Visitors without boats can charter bare boats and, if needed, a captain and crew. Provisions, fuel, and instruction are all at hand on the islands. Ask at your accommodation how to make arrangements.

Game Fishing • The Bahamas cannot be mentioned without a discussion of fishing. Its Bimini Islands are known as the fishing capital of the world, and locals as well as visitors are addicted to this pastime. Scores of world-record catches have been made in The Bahamas. Fishing tournaments are held throughout the islands at various times of the year and attract fishing enthusiasts from around the world. Even those not aspiring to take part in tournaments can be bitten by the fishing bug on almost any island. Arrangements can be made through your accommodation.

Golf • Most courses are in and around the cities of Nassau and Freeport/Lucaya. Courses designed by such luminaries as Robert Trent-Jones and Dick Wilson are also in the Cotton Bay Club in Eleuthera and Treasure Cay in the Abacos. Grand Bahama's Lucayan Park Golf and Country Club is the oldest in the country. The newest is at the Cable Beach Hotel in Nassau. The best is said to be the South Ocean Golf Club, which is private. The Emerald Course in Grand Bahama is considered less challenging than the Ruby Course. Bahamian courses play host to several tournaments, including an annual Pro-Am, and an Open to celebrate Independence Day.

Horseback Riding • In Freeport you can go horseback riding at Pine Tree Stables and in Nassau, at the Paradise Island Riding Stable.

Jogging • For some barefoot joggers, the hard-packed sand near the waterline of beaches throughout The Bahamas can be sufficient. Those who run in shoes, however, prefer places like the wide, tree-lined, traffic-free esplanade of Nassau's Cable Beach area. There is also the cool, tree-vaulted Casuarina Walk on Paradise Island that leads to the dock and to Chalk's seaplane terminal. In Grand Bahama's Freeport/Lucaya area, there is a choice of streets in a broad, landscaped, well-paved network. The Bahamas Princess Resort & Casino has a 10 km (6.2 mile) jogging course, dedicated to world marathon champion Grete Waitz. On the Family Islands, most joggers blaze their own paths, using either the beaches or the paved roads.

Parasailing • If you've ever had the urge to be strapped to a brightly colored parachute that is tied to a boat, then gently lifted into the air as the boat takes off, parasailing is for you. In Nassau, you can enjoy this sport at the Cable Beach Hotel & Casino, the Ambassador Beach Hotel, and the Nassau Beach Hotel; on Paradise Island, at the Sheraton Grand Hotel and at Paradise Island Resort and Casino, and in Freeport, at the Atlantik Beach Hotel and Holiday Inn.

Scuba Diving and Snorkeling • The Bahamas' magnificent undersea attractions have helped to encourage the growth of scuba and snorkeling. Centers such as the Underwater Explorers Society (UNEXSO) in Freeport and Treasure Cay, Abaco, have sprung up for trained divers as well as beginners. The centers give instruction and lead expeditions to the undersea wrecks, special marine life, and coral formations. UNEXSO offers a week-long course in underwater photography. It also hosts The Dolphin Experience (in Freeport), a program that allows people to swim with several of those friendly mammals.

Most hotels will make arrangements for snorkeling and diving if facilities are not on the premises. The Family Islands are major attractions for those fascinated by underwater spectacles such as the sunken train off Eleuthera. One of the largest barrier reefs in the world is just off the coast of Andros. Excellent diving programs are run by Small Hope Bay Lodge in Andros; Brendal's Dive Shop at the Green Turtle Club in the Abacos; the Stella Maris Inn on Long Island; at Riding Rock Inn on San Salvador; and at the Rum Cay Club, on a tiny island between Long Island and San Salvador (see San Salvador).

By merely donning a helmet, novice divers of any age can take an undersea walk to see fish, coral, and other marine life through Hartley's at the Nassau Yacht Haven.

Tennis • Nassau and Freeport have many courts and you can also play on a number of Family Islands, such as the Abacos, the Berry Islands, Eleuthera, and Exuma. The larger resorts have pro shops for players. The first-class tennis facility at the Cable Beach Hotel & Casino has 10 courts, five of them lighted, as well as a stadium for tournament and exhibition games. Next door is an indoor complex with three courts each for **squash** and **racquetball.** A junior national tennis championship for youngsters 10–18 years old is sponsored annually in Nassau to encourage the sport among young Bahamians.

Waterskiing • This sport is available at most large beach hotels throughout The Bahamas.

Windsurfing • Seeing several windsurfers at once is as thrilling as watching one of The Bahamas' popular regattas. In addition to Nassau and Freeport, windsurfing is available in Walker's Cay, Treasure Cay,

Marsh Harbour, and Elbow Cay in the Abacos; Nicholls Town in Andros; and Harbour Island and Rock Sound in Eleuthera.

NIGHTLIFE

Nassau and Freeport/Lucaya are the places to see and enjoy Bahamian nightlife in its most elaborate and sophisticated form. Entertainment tends to run to what Bahamians refer to as "native." Native shows include some elements common to countries in the Caribbean like calypso, limbo dancing, and steel drums. A difference is that a goombay beat alters these rhythms, transforming them into Bahamian music.

The larger hotels have discos and present revues and single acts in their night clubs, lounges, and sometimes in dining-room areas. Performances can be loud, lavish, and brassy as some are on Paradise Island, or smooth, refined, or intimate as when a single player strums a guitar and softly croons songs of the tropics.

Discos and nightclubs are also found away from the hotels in places such as the Bay Street area in Nassau and the Mall area in Freeport. Visitors should venture out for Bahamian entertainment away from their hotels and resorts for another aspect and flavor of life in the islands.

On the Family Islands you can see the same kind of entertainment, but on a smaller scale. Some performances are so understated that they gain even more in overall effect.

The Bahamas' casinos are located in Nassau, Paradise Island, and Freeport, and are open until all hours.

SHOPPING

Although The Bahamas is not a duty free territory, bargain hunters can be roused by the wares offered along Nassau's Bay Street, in some Paradise Island shops, and in Freeport. Prices can be 25 to 45% lower than in the U.S. for things such as crystal, china, woolens, linens, perfumes, watches, clocks, cameras, and liquor. You don't even have to leave the larger hotels to dip into your purse or wallet. Many have arcades filled with tempting shops and boutiques. Most visitors agree, however, that it's more fun to venture out and rub elbows with other shoppers.

Seeming to jostle for attention, shops line Bay Street, Nassau's main thoroughfare and several tributary streets on both sides. Arcades such as the International Bazaar, Beaumont House, and Colony Place run from Bay Street out to Wodes Rogers Walk.

For Seiko and Rolex watches, clocks; jewelry; English, Meissen and Limoges porcelain, and much more, stop in at **John Bull** between East Street and Elizabeth Avenue. The **Brass and Leather Shop,** on Charlotte Street off Bay, sells wallets, belts, Bottega Veneta luggage, and the like.

French, American and local perfumes are available at the **Bahamas Fragrance and Cosmetic Factory** on Charlotte Street, which makes its own, and at **Lightbourn's** on Bay Street. **Marlborough Antiques,** across from the Sheraton British Colonial on the street of the same name, has beautifully displayed antique items, and **Balman Antiques** specializes in old maps.

In Freeport, many shops, boutiques, and restaurants are clustered in the International Bazaar. **Midnight Sun** is where you'll find a wide selection of Scandinavian bargains, and the **Discount Bazaar** is worth checking out. The new, multimillion dollar **Port Lucaya** is an exciting shopping, dining, and entertainment complex, across from the Holiday Inn and the Lucayan Beach Resort & Casino.

Handmade straw goods are sold on most Bahamian islands, but the greatest variety is found in Nassau and Freeport. The largest straw market in The Bahamas is on Bay Street in Nassau. On Nassau's Cable Beach, a straw market is located across from the Ambassador Beach and Cable Beach hotels. Shoppers can pick up straw hats to keep the sun off, or straw bags for overflow on the way home. Don't be shy about bargaining—no one expects you to pay the first price quoted.

Throughout The Bahamas you'll find bright resort wear made of Androsia batiks. These colorful bathing suits, shirts, shorts, shifts, head ties, and dresses come from the factory begun by the owners of Small Hope Bay Lodge on Andros. At the Andros Beach Hotel in Nicholl's Town on Andros, the proprietor in the on-premises boutique will run you up a shirt or a dress overnight made of an Androsia fabric or another material.

TOURS

In Nassau and Freeport, bus, taxi, and boat tours can be arranged at hotel tour desks, or at Bahamas tourist offices. From Rawson Square in Nassau, you can also take 45-minute horse-drawn carriage tours for about $5 per person. Horses rest from 1 p.m. to 3 p.m. from May to

October and from 1 p.m. to 2 p.m. November through April. In the Family Islands, taxi tours can be arranged through resorts or guest houses. Bus, boat, and horse-drawn carriage tours run most frequently during the winter season.

DINING OUT

Especially in Nassau and Freeport, restaurant reservations are generally required for dinner during the winter season. Men are expected to wear jackets at night at the more expensive restaurants. Off season, these requirements are relaxed at most places. While Nassau and Freeport have many restaurants, those in the Family Islands are mainly limited to hotel and resort dining rooms and small locally operated restaurants. On some islands, such as Abaco, there are individuals who prepare elaborate Bahamian feasts for visitors who call ahead. Hotel staff members and other residents can tell you how to find these chefs.

NASSAU

ATTRACTIONS AT A GLANCE

	Place	Page
Forts		
*Fort Charlotte	Off West Bay Street	174
Fort Fincastle	Bennett's Hill	174
Fort Montagu	East Bay Street	174

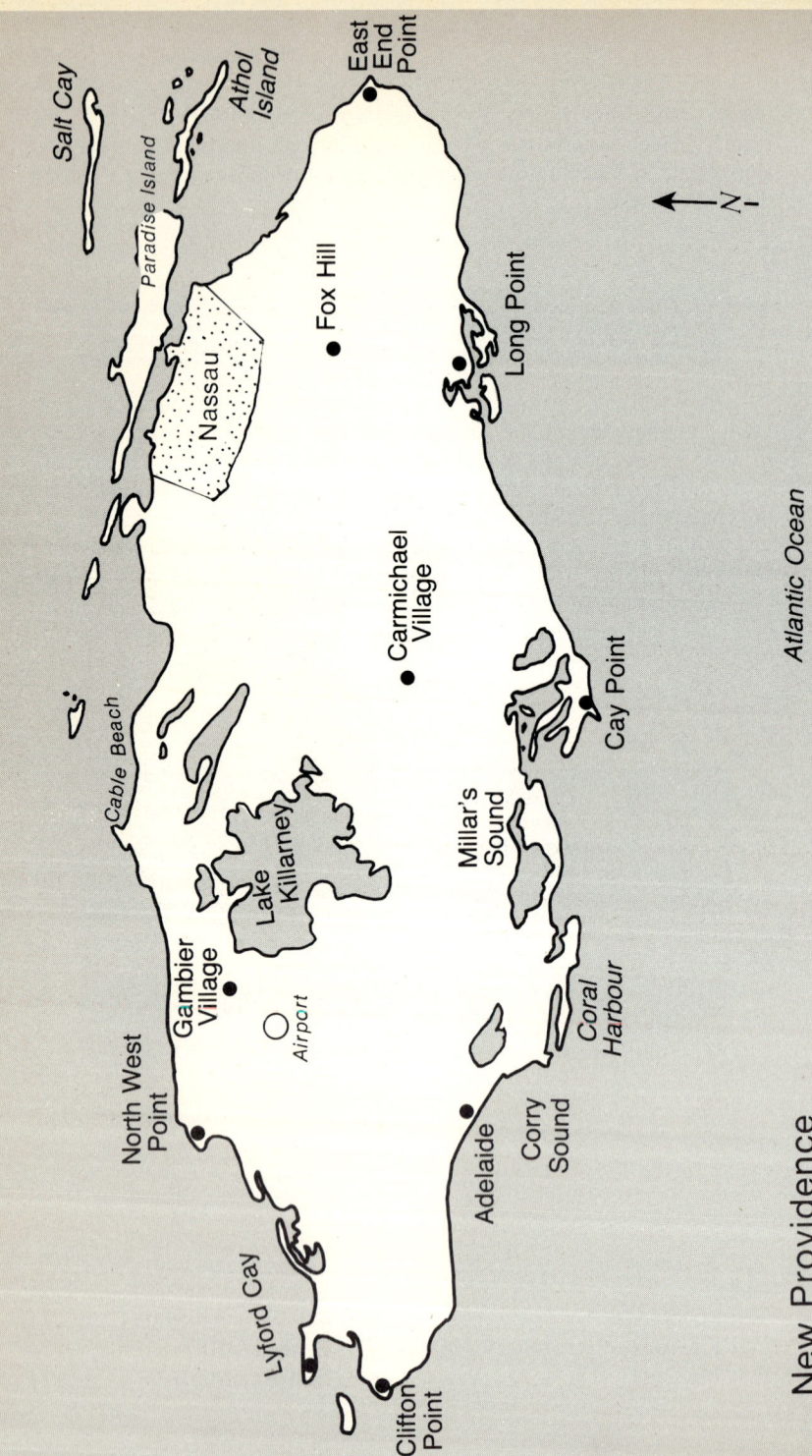

New Providence

Flatt's Inlet, Hamilton Parish, Bermuda

CREDIT: BERMUDA NEWS BUREAU

King's Square, St. George's, Bermuda   CREDIT: GORDON CHRISTMAS

Horseshoe Bay, Southampton, Bermuda   CREDIT: BERMUDA NEWS BUREAU

City Hall in Hamilton, Bermuda's capital city   CREDIT: BERMUDA NEWS BUREAU

Shopping area in Hamilton, Bermuda   CREDIT: GORDON CHRISTMAS

Gibbs' Hill Lighthouse, Southampton, Bermuda   CREDIT: BERMUDA NEWS BUREAU

A surrey ride, Nassau, Bahamas   CREDIT: BAHAMAS NEWS BUREAU

CREDIT: RACHEL J. CHRISTMAS

Entrance to the International Bazaar, Freeport, Bahamas

Garden of the Groves, Freeport, Bahamas

CREDIT: RACHEL J. CHRISTMAS

Harbour Island, Bahamas

CREDIT: RACHEL J. CHRISTMAS

Potters Cay Dock, Nassau, Bahamas

CREDIT: BAHAMAS NEWS BUREAU

Congo Town, Andros, Bahamas

CREDIT: WALTER CHRISTMAS

THE BAHAMAS · · · 167

	Place	Page
Gardens, Parks, & Nature Reserves		
Ardastra Gardens	Near Fort Charlotte	172
Royal Victoria Gardens	Near Government House	176
*Versailles Gardens	Paradise Island	
*Botanical Gardens	Near Fort Charlotte	173
Government Buildings		
*Government House	Blue Hill Road	174
Other Government Buildings	Parliament Square	174
Historical Sights		
Blackbeard's Tower	Fox Hill Road	173
Queen's Staircase	Shirley Street	176
Gregory Arch	Near Government House	176
Ex-Slave Settlements	Directions at Tourist Office	173
Museums & Animals		
*Seafloor Aquarium	Near Ardastra Gardens	177
Roselawn Museum	East Street & Bank Lane	176
*Sea Gardens	East End of Nassau Harbor	177
*Coral World	Silver Cay	173
*Hartley's Undersea Walk	East Bay Street	177
Local Sights		
*Bay Street	Off Waterfront	173
Water Tower	Bennett Hill	177
Potters Cay	Under Paradise Island Bridge	176
Straw Market	Market & Bay Streets	177
*Rawson Square	Bay St. & Prince George Dock	176
Statue of the Bahamian Woman	Prince George Dock	177

First Impressions

One of the first places most visitors see upon arrival in The Bahamas is the 7-by-21-mile island of New Providence, where Nassau, the capital, is located. The island has an international airport, and gleaming white cruise ships dock at its busy harbor. Some of the largest and most luxurious hotels and restaurants serve its visitors, and the city is rich in Bahamian beauty and history. If you arrive at the International Airport, your taxi takes you along a scenic drive, with glimpses of surf, exotic blossoms, ancient trees and leafy, overhung roads, dappled with sunlight. You see pastel-colored, shuttered houses, some from colonial times, with flowers and shrubs spilling in abundance over their walls. Then come the condominiums and hotels along Cable Beach, followed by historic downtown Nassau. If you're bound for one of the Paradise Island hotels, your taxi turns off notorious Bay Street and takes you over the toll bridge.

Unfortunately, too few visitors venture much beyond Cable Beach, downtown Nassau, or Paradise Island. To see more of New Providence you can take part in the popular free **People-to-People Program,** where Bahamians will be your hosts. You might be taken on a personalized sightseeing tour. Your host might also give you the opportunity to join in some local event to which visitors are seldom privy, such as a church picnic or local beach party. In any case, you will learn about The Bahamas from people who know the islands intimately. Arrangements can be made through one of the Bahamas Tourist Bureau offices.

Some Bahamians and visitors get to know each other in another way: it's been all the rage in the last few years for visiting women to have all or part of their hair cornrowed by Bahamian women on the beach or in the straw markets. Depending on the number of braids, this can take anywhere from a few minutes to over an hour. The price, which varies greatly from braider to braider, is negotiable. Be forewarned: If you don't have much melanin in your skin, put some sunscreen on the exposed scalp between braids!

A Bit of History

New Providence was settled in 1656 by a colony of Britons, some of whom came from Bermuda, looking for a better way of life. The new colony was supposedly ruled from the Carolinas on the North American mainland, but supervision was lax and the new and remote Bahamians were pretty much on their own.

Spain, in an effort to end the incessant and irksome raids on its ships by pirates based in the Bahamas, attacked the settlement called Charles Town, named for Britain's Charles II. Spain's occupation of the town was short lived and she left almost immediately, because there was a new king in England. The settlement was renamed Nassau, after William III, of Orange-Nassau.

The pirates, notably Blackbeard, the alias for Edward Teach, remained there along with his cohorts, "Calico" Jack Rackham, Major

Bonnet, a Frenchman, and the notorious women pirates, Mary Reed (who was eventually hung) and Anne Bonney, Rackham's mistress.

The marauders were not driven out until the ruthless Captain Woodes Rogers was appointed governor. In tribute to his feat, a statue stands before the Sheraton British Colonial Hotel, and a waterfront road bears his name.

Nassau was once an acknowledged playground for the rich. The height of that period was probably during the tenure of the Duke of Windsor, the abdicated King of England, just before World War II. The wealthy still come to Nassau, many finding their way to Lyford Cay, a private resort.

Cable Beach

With one of the most beautiful (but busy) strips of beach in The Bahamas, this area was named in 1892 after the laying of a telegraph cable from Jupiter, Florida, to The Bahamas. For the first time, messages could be sent directly from The Bahamas to the United States and England. Horse racing, all the rage with officers of the British West India Regiment stationed in Nassau, was once Cable Beach's prime attraction. In 1933 an annual racing season began, lasting until 1975 when the track closed. In the past, pineapples to be exported to the United States were grown in much of the Cable Beach area.

Nassau's first luxury beach resorts began springing up here after World War II. The refurbished Royal Bahamian is now one of the most lavish hotels in the area. A 700-room government owned resort, the more modern Cable Beach Hotel & Casino has a plush first-class sports complex.

Runners jog along tree- and flower-lined West Bay Street in front of the hotels. **Delaporte Beach,** at the western end of the area, is never crowded. **Goodman's Bay,** on the way to downtown Nassau, is another pleasant beach, and is popular with locals for cookouts as well as swimming.

Downtown Nassau

Bay Street, full of all sorts of shops and restaurants, is in the heart of Nassau. Here you'll find bargains in a variety of items from china to liquor, and you can visit Nassau Art Gallery By the Waterfront. At one end of the street is the dignified Sheraton British Colonial Hotel, where an ice cream parlor makes a stop refreshing. The busy straw market in the open-air Ministry of Tourism building sells T-shirts and jewelry in addition to countless straw products. Nearby Rawson Square is really a palm-shaded circle full of bright flowers where horse-drawn carriages wait to give tours.

Also called a wharf, Prince George Dock, off Rawson Square, is the busiest point in Nassau. Cruise ships dock here. Freighters, tugs, charter boats, sightseeing boats, pleasure boats, fishing craft, and mail boats to the Family Islands all use this wharf. It teems with pedestrians coming and going, mirroring the activity of the harbor. Woodes Rogers Walk is a colorful place for a stroll.

Off Bay Street on Frederick Street you can catch local jitneys or minibuses to Cable Beach, the Paradise Island bridge, and elsewhere. Small boys with sacks slung over their shoulders will sell you peanuts through the window of your bus as you wait for it to take off. While taxis are available and some of the larger hotels provide complimentary bus service to and from downtown Nassau, riding these jitneys is much more fun. For about 50¢, with the radio playing reggae or calypso, you'll pass sights most visitors miss—tiny churches, homes with lush banana trees growing in their front yards, local stores and bars, wide-trunked silk cotton trees, a bakery decorated with huge red polka dots. If you call out "Bus stop!" as you approach your destination, you might even pass for Bahamian. As well as being the capital and the seat of government, Nassau is the financial center. It is also the hub of air and boat traffic to the outer islands. Visitors can watch ceremonial parades in Parliament Square or attend the solemn opening of the nation's Supreme Court. The annual Junkanoo Parade, rivaling Caribbean carnivals and New Orleans' Mardi Gras, passes rhythmically along Bay Street.

Sections of the city seldom seen by tourists are just over the ridge from downtown Nassau. The local name for the area is Over-the-Hill, and it contains settlements or neighborhoods including Gambier Village, Adelaide, Bain Town, Carmichael, and Grant's Town. Gregory Arch, which can be seen from Bay Street, just west of downtown, is one of the historic gateways to the area.

Adelaide, for example, is named for Queen Adelaide, consort of William IV of England. Its first settlers were Africans captured by the Portuguese in the early 1800s and headed for enslavement. Their vessel, the *Rosa,* was taken by the British, and the nearly 200 Africans were landed in Nassau as free men, since slavery had been abolished in the British colonies.

Carmichael Village is another 19th-century settlement of free Africans. Founded by James Carmichael Smith, the village's residents worked as laborers and domestics in nearby Nassau. Bain Town and Grant's Town run into one another and are difficult to define as separate units. A 19th-century black Bahamian businessman, Charles H. Bain, purchased a land grant from its previous owner to found the town bearing his name.

Tourists can see some of these areas by taking a jitney ride. The rides are inexpensive and the vehicles make their circuits and return to the point of departure.

Paradise Island

Paradise Island is connected to New Providence Island by a dramatic arching bridge that gives a spectacular view of the harbor. As you cross the bridge (25¢ by foot, 50¢ by bike or moped, $2.00 by car, round trip), you will see colorful fruit and vegetable stands on the Nassau side next to piles of conch shells.

Ferries run between downtown Nassau and Paradise Island (about $1.50 to $2 each way, depending on your hotel location). Shuttle buses (about 50¢) connect Paradise Island hotels and restaurants.

Lavishly landscaped and stocked with deluxe hotels, restaurants, sports facilities, condominiums, and a transplanted ruin, Paradise Island went by the unglamorous name of Hog Island when it was farmland.

The original concept to develop Hog Island came from a Swedish millionaire, Axel Wenner-Gren. He purchased the old Lynch estate on the island and set about digging canals to connect a lake with the Nassau harbor. He then proceeded to rebuild the estate, the former home of the Mr. Lynch of Merrill, Lynch fame. During World War II, it was discovered that Mr. Wenner-Gren's munitions works in Sweden were allied with and partially owned by the Nazi-controlled Krupp works. Despite a boycott, the war made him even wealthier, but he sold his Hog Island holdings to another millionaire, Huntington Hartford, the A&P heir.

After a few false starts, the island's serious development was begun again by Hartford, who planned to make it a millionaire's showplace. A medieval cloister had been dismantled earlier and brought stone by stone from France by William Randolph Hearst and stored with the rest of his Old World treasures. Hartford took it off Hearst's hands and had it reassembled in Versailles Gardens, where it now stands, an ancient attraction for the new Paradise Island.

The island continued its ascent toward prestige and glamour even after the departure of Hartford. Other hotels sprang up to take advantage of the new space and its attractive beaches. World renowned statesmen, politicians, jet setters, and European royalty came to sample the enticements of this fashionable new playground.

The casino, operated by Resorts International, is connected to the Britannia Towers and the Paradise Towers, part of the Paradise Island Resort. Between the towers are many shops and boutiques, the Folies Bergere–like Cabaret Theatre, and a selection of pleasant places to dine and drink.

Guests from nearby hotels as well as those from adjacent and more remote island locations find their way to the casino, including those at the island's self-contained Club Med. The only visitors who seem to shun the casino are patrons of the Yoga Retreat, who prefer contemplation, vegetarianism, exercise, and work.

A shopping center, Paradise Village, serves hotel guests as well as residents of the island's apartment hotels and condominiums. The center includes a bank, fast-food shops, and the inevitable souvenir stores.

The Ocean Club, one of the small luxury hotels, began as a vacation home for Hartford. Operated by Resorts International, it remains one of the preferred hostelries for those with deep pockets. Not far away is quiet, secluded Cabbage Beach.

Restaurants that have achieved the widest reputations are the Cafe Martinique, the Courtyard Terrace of the Ocean Club, the Villa d'Este, and Julie's in the Grand Hotel. Because of confusion with the Courtyard Terrace and the Terrace at the Britannia Towers, the Terrace Restaurant in downtown Nassau has added its address, 18 Parliament Street, to its name.

Athletic-minded visitors at Paradise Island resorts take advantage of an almost unlimited choice of sports. Windsurfers and parasailers splash the landscape with the bright colors of their sails and parachutes. Fringed with beaches, the island has many swimming pools, an 18-hole golf course, and tennis courts. Romantics who have dreamed of going horseback riding along a beach can have that fantasy come true at the stables near the Ocean Club.

Chalk's International Airlines, another Resorts enterprise, has an amphibious terminal on the island for flights to Bimini, Cat Cay, and Miami. While waiting for your plane, try some fresh conch salad or have a drink at the Island Restaurant.

WHAT TO SEE AND DO

SIGHTS

New Providence is one of the Bahamian islands that was settled early and has a number of points of historical interest, most of which can be reached in a day's tour. Nassau, as the seat of government, has reminders of former British rule, and remnants of slavery.

Ardastra Gardens • *Near Fort Charlotte off Columbus Avenue and Chippingham Road (323–5806)* • The national bird of The Bahamas, the flamingo, is used to put on a show for visitors to the gardens. Among the attractions is a precision parade of the pink birds to the command of their trainer. Visitors are invited to pose for photographs with the birds. *Open 9 a.m.–4:30 p.m. Admission $7.00. Children under 12, $3.50.*

*Bay Street • *Off the waterfront, from Cumberland, east to Church Street* • Bay Street is Nassau's downtown shopping area. It brings back memories of the "Bay Street Boys," a group of notorious businessmen who ruled The Bahamas from Nassau, and are alleged to have divided the spoils among themselves and their enterprises. The Duke of Windsor was tainted by their scheming during his tenure as wartime governor. Today the street, and some others running into it, is the tourist mecca for bargains in linens, woolens, cameras, crystal, china, and liquors. Lately some chic shops for both men and women have opened on some of the side streets off Bay.

Blackbeard's Tower • *East of Fox Hill Road* • The climb to Blackbeard's Tower is worth the trip if only to view the sweep of the Nassau harbor and the city stretching east and west. However, what remains of the tower itself is not as spectacular. The structure was supposedly used as a lookout point by the pirate Edward Teach, alias Blackbeard, to watch for approaching ships during the period when he was a marauder in Bahamian waters.

*Botanical Gardens • *Near Fort Charlotte, off Columbus Avenue* • This protected area has 18 acres of 600 species of tropical flowers and plants. There is a lily pond, a cactus garden, and a children's playground. *Open daily 9 a.m.–4 p.m. Admission: Adults $1, Children 50¢.*

*Coral World • *Silver Cay, between Cable Beach and downtown Nassau (328–1036)* • Allow at least a couple of hours to take in this marine park not far from Fort Charlotte. Built by the same folks who developed Coral World in the U.S. Virgin Islands, the Bahamian version also has a natural underwater observatory. A fresh water well at the ocean's edge may have been dug by pirates. At the Pearl Bar, select an oyster guaranteed to contain a pearl. Flamingos, parrots and other rare birds flutter on the grounds. The shark tank can be seen from above and below. There are morays, rays, parrot fish, huge sea turtles, and many others. A souvenir shop, a snack counter and a restaurant are on the grounds. Groups of giggling Bahamian school children on education excursions are admitted at no charge. *Open daily 8.30 a.m. to 6 p.m., with extended hours during Daylight Saving Time (Apr.–Oct.); admission: $12, adults; $8, children aged 3 to 12; free for children under 3; a round-trip boat departs from Woodes Rogers Walk every half hour, $18, including admission.*

Ex-Slave Settlements • *Locations and directions available at the Tourist Office, (809) 322-7500* • When Bahamian slavery was abolished in 1834, black people set up homesteads in Adelaide, Gambier Village, Carmichael Village, and Fox Hill, among others. These Over-the-Hill settlements, some outside Nassau proper, are accessible by bus or taxi. Every August, Emancipation Day and Fox Hill Day celebrations draw crowds to the village green and the park in Fox Hill.

*Fort Charlotte • *Off West Bay Street overlooking Nassau harbor* • This is the largest fort in The Bahamas. Built in 1788, it guards the entrance to Nassau's harbor. Like Blackbeard's Tower, it also affords a panoramic view of the harbor. Of special interest are its moat, dungeon, and gun emplacements. The guide often waits to collect a group and expects a tip at the tour's end. *The tourist office in Nassau has information on the frequency of tours, since they are not regularly scheduled; tel. 2–7500.*

Fort Fincastle • *On Bennett's Hill overlooking Nassau harbor* • This bow-shaped fort also sits above downtown Nassau overlooking the busy harbor. It served primarily as a signal tower and is now largely in ruins. Nearby is a souvenir shop.

Fort Montagu • *Off East Bay Street* • Fort Montagu is the oldest of Nassau's remaining forts. Facing the eastern entrance to the harbor, it was built in 1741 to ward off an attack by Spaniards that never came. The fort, however, was occupied for a short time by Americans during the Revolutionary War. The nearby park, with lawns, shade, and vendors, is a pleasant place to stop.

Government Buildings • *Parliament Square across from Bay Street* • By crossing Bay Street from Rawson Square, you come upon Parliament Square where a cluster of official buildings surrounds a statue of a slim, young Queen Victoria. Housed in these colonial structures, from which The Bahamas is governed, are the House of Assembly, the Supreme Court, the office of the Colonial Secretary, the Tourist Information Office, the Central Police Station, the Garden of Remembrance with its monument honoring the war dead, and the Public Library, a former prison.

*Government House • *Off Blue Hill Road* • The official residence of the British-appointed Governor General stands on one of the island's highest points. In front of the colonial mansion is a statue of Christopher Columbus wearing a broad-brimmed hat, draped in a cloak, and carrying a staff. Every other Saturday morning, the changing of the guard takes place here. The mansion's grounds are thick with lush tropical foliage and plants. Visitors can sign the guest book in a small house located near the exit gate.

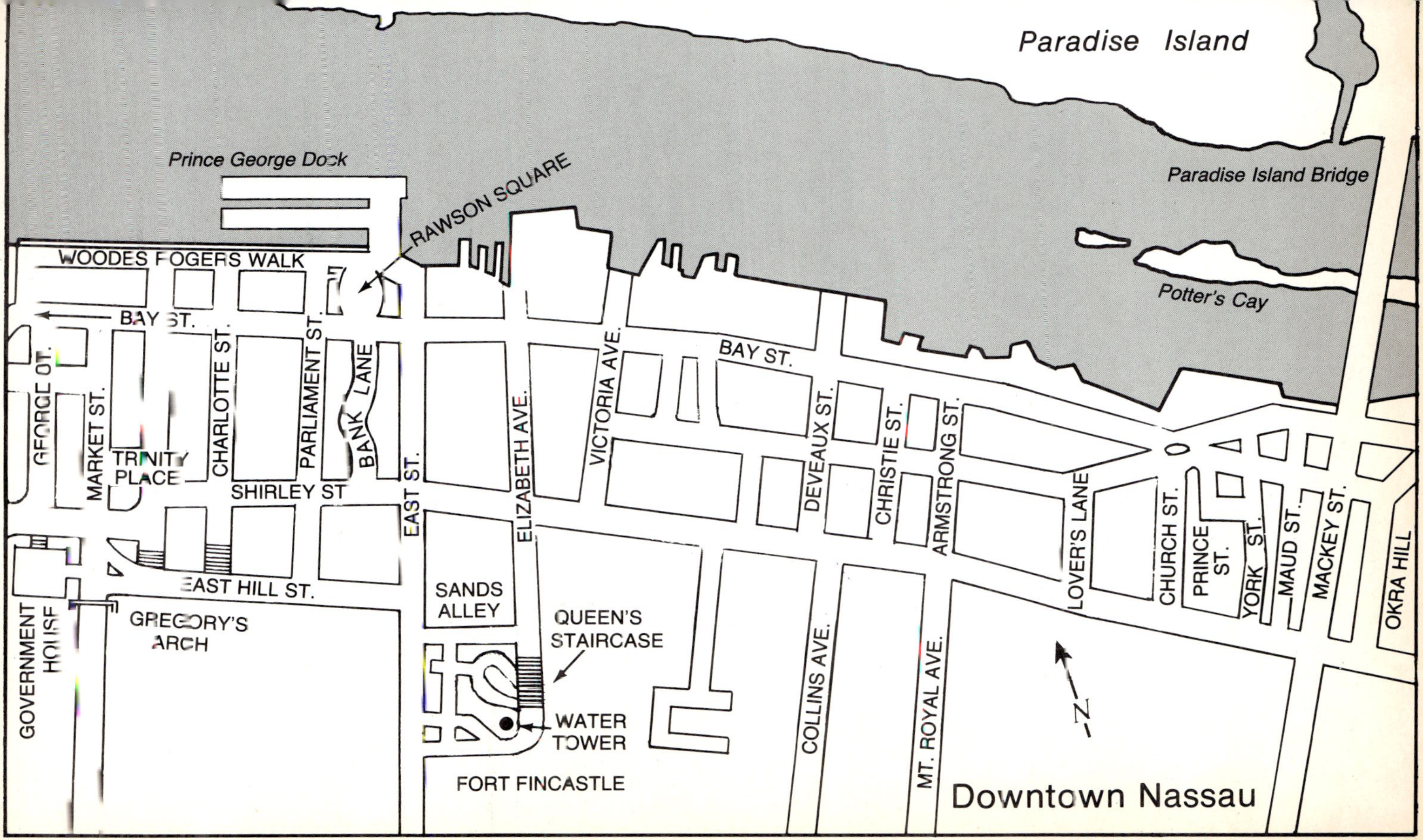
Paradise Island
Paradise Island Bridge
Potter's Cay
Prince George Dock
RAWSON SQUARE
WOODES ROGERS WALK
BAY ST.
GEORGE ST.
MARKET ST.
TRINITY PLACE
CHARLOTTE ST.
PARLIAMENT ST.
BANK LANE
SHIRLEY ST
EAST ST.
EAST HILL ST.
GOVERNMENT HOUSE
GREGORY'S ARCH
ELIZABETH AVE.
SANDS ALLEY
QUEEN'S STAIRCASE
WATER TOWER
FORT FINCASTLE
VICTORIA AVE.
BAY ST.
DEVEAUX ST.
CHRISTIE ST.
ARMSTRONG ST.
COLLINS AVE.
MT. ROYAL AVE.
LOVER'S LANE
CHURCH ST.
PRINCE ST.
YORK ST.
MAUD ST.
MACKEY ST.
OKRA HILL
N
Downtown Nassau

Gregory Arch • *East of Government House at Market Street* • This arch marks the entrance to Grant's Town, just over the ridge from the Nassau harbor. The town was established at Emancipation on land given to ex-slaves to build homes and set up farms.

Potters Cay • *Under Paradise Island Bridge* • At this colorful market, you can buy fresh fish, fruit, and vegetables, and watch fishermen shell conch.

Queen's Staircase • *Across Shirley Street, toward the rise away from the harbor and beyond Princess Margaret Hospital* • These 65 steps-of-stone have come to represent the number of years Victoria ruled the British Empire. One hundred and two feet high, the staircase is said to have been hewn by slaves from solid limestone, and leads to the now crumbling Fort Fincastle at the top. When the weather and/or water supply permit, a cascade spills down next to the staircase, causing an iridescent mist when the sun hits the enclosure. At the top of the stairs, small boys wait to give you the well-memorized history of the staircase in exchange for a small fee.

***Rawson Square** • *Just off Prince George Dock at Bay Street* • This lively square faces Prince George Dock in one direction and the government buildings across Bay Street in the other. Visitors from cruise ships pour out into the square heading for restaurants and bargains on Bay Street. Tourists from town compete with the cruise passengers for the taxis and surreys that line up in the square. The 45-minute surrey trips are about $5 per person.

Roselawn Museum • *East Street and Bank Lane* • In a house built in 1820, The Roselawn museum displays memorabilia from Nassau and the Family Islands, including Bahamian coins, maps, stamps, parts of shipwrecks, old bottles salvaged from the sea, and Junkanoo costumes. *Open 9 a.m.–5 p.m. Free admission.*

Royal Victoria Gardens • *Across Shirley Street and up toward Government House* • The sprawling Royal Victoria Hotel was built during the American Civil War and was used as the headquarters of Bahamians who ran arms for the Confederacy. Part of the building is now used for government offices. In its time, the hotel was the showplace of The Bahamas, and its gardens reflected its grandeur and opulence. The gardens contain about 300 kinds of tropical plants. Although the grand old hotel was closed in 1971 and rumors of its reopening persist, the gardens remain open to the public.

*Hartley's Undersea Walk • *Nassau Yacht Haven, East Bay St.; tel: 325-3369* • This 3½-hour cruise on the yacht *Pied Piper* includes a safe, escorted undersea walk to see varieties of tropical fish, coral formations, and other undersea life. Even kids, the elderly, and nonswimmers can enjoy the experience. The trick is the helmet you wear. Take a bathing suit. The yacht leaves at 9:30 a.m. and 1:30 p.m. daily. Check-in time is a half hour before departure. *$28 per person.*

*Sea Gardens • *Eastern end of Nassau harbor* • This fantastic underwater attraction covers 40 acres of coral, fern, and all the colorful marine life found in tropical waters. *($15 from Prince George Dock)*

*Seafloor Aquarium • *West of Columbus Avenue near Ardastra Gardens* • Also close to downtown Nassau, the aquarium presents underwater tropical marine life including giant turtles, sharks, manta rays, and myriads of sea creatures that inhabit coral reefs. A performance is put on by trained sea lions and dolphins. Tortoise-shell jewelry, made on the premises, is for sale along with other Bahamian souvenirs. *Open 9 a.m.–5:30 p.m. Shows every 2 hours weekdays. Closed Sun. Admission: Adults $5, children $2.50.*

Statue of the Bahamian Woman • *Prince George Dock* • Facing the water is a statue by Randolph W. Johnson of Little Harbour, Abaco, in tribute to the Bahamian woman. It was dedicated in 1974 by the prime minister, and the inscription begins, "In grateful tribute to the Bahamian woman whose steadfast love and devotion sustained our nation through countless years of adversity."

Straw Market • *Bay and Market Streets* • Everything that can be rendered in straw—plus much more—is on sale here. Market women may beckon you to examine their handicrafts. They may quickly slip a necklace over your head in an attempt to convince you to buy. The wares include hats and baskets, which are much in evidence, along with objects of shell, bead jewelry, wood sculpture, and T-shirts. Many items are fashioned on the spot. The merchants are aggressive and bargaining is spirited.

Water Tower • *On Bennett Hill near Fort Fincastle* • While on Bennett Hill seeing Fort Fincastle, also stop at the Water Tower. It is the highest point on New Providence, 216 feet above sea level. An elevator takes you to the observation deck for an unusual view of Nassau and points beyond. *Open 9 a.m.–5 p.m. Admission: 50¢.*

SPORTS

Diving • Make diving arrangements through your hotel or by contacting Bahama Divers (326–5644), Nassau Dive Supply (2–4869), South Ocean Beach Hotel & Golf Club (326–4391/6), Sun Divers (326–3301), or Underwater Tours (326–3285).

Fishing and Boating • Arrange fishing and boating trips through your hotel or by contacting Bayshore Marina (326–8232); East Bay Yacht Basin (326–3754); Lyford Cay Marina (326–4267); Nassau Harbour Club (322–1771); or Nassau Yacht Haven (322–8173), all in Nassau; or Hurricane Hole Marina (326–5441) on Paradise Island.

Nassau offers a variety of sightseeing **cruises** as well as sailing trips to other islands for swimming and snorkeling. For example, the *Keewatin* sailing schooner, which departs from the Sheraton British Colonial dock at 9:45 a.m. and the Loew's Harbour Cove dock on Paradise Island at 10:15 a.m., goes to Rose Island for **snorkeling,** swimming, and lunch (about $30; 326–2821). The Sea Island Adventure excursion goes to another Family Island and also includes snorkeling, swimming, and lunch (325–3910).

Glass-bottom boats go from Prince George Dock to Paradise Island for all-day swimming. A catamaran cruise, with a Goombay band and a picnic lunch, also leaves from this dock, as well as daily schooners. *Hotel tour desks have further details.*

Golf • Courses are at the Ambassador Beach Golf Club, 18 holes, (327–8231); the Coral Harbour Golf Club, 18 holes, (326–1144); the South Ocean Beach Hotel & Golf Club, 18 holes, (326–4391); and the Paradise Island Golf Club, 18 holes (326–5925).

Horseback Riding • *Paradise Island* • Rates at the Paradise Island Riding Stables are about $20 an hour (326–1433).

Tennis • Most of the large hotels have tennis courts. The sports complex at the Cable Beach Hotel has **squash** and **racquetball courts** as well. You can also play these sports at the Nassau Squash and Racquet Club (Independence Drive; 322–3882).

Parasailing • Enjoy this sport on Cable Beach at the Ambassador Beach Hotel, the Cable Beach Hotel, and the Nassau Beach Hotel, and on Paradise Island at the Grand Hotel.

Waterskiing • Most of the larger beach hotels offer waterskiing.

Windsurfing • The Ambassador Beach Hotel, the Cable Beach Hotel, and Coral Harbour Beach Villas all have windsurfing.

NIGHT LIFE

At the Cable Beach Hotel, visitors can see elaborate musical productions in the 1000-seat theater. Many other hotels have night clubs and discos. **Club Pastiche** in Paradise Island's Casino and **Trade Winds Lounge** in the adjoining Paradise Towers attract many Bahamians as well as visitors, and feature rock and roll, disco, and sometimes Bahamian music. **The Paon,** in the Sheraton Grand, has a computerized sound system that will shame any New York disco.

In Nassau, **Peanuts Taylor's Drumbeat Club** on West Bay Street features an Afro Bahamian Revue with a fire ritual and limbo. Dinner is served during the first show of the evening. **The Palace** on Elizabeth Avenue has a live band that plays a mix of calypso, reggae, and disco. **Confetti's** is an indoor/outdoor disco at **Captain Nemo's Restaurant.** Another popular disco is **Club Waterloo,** on East Bay Street. A new club, **Sparkles,** on West Bay Street was formerly called Ronnie's Rebel Room. **Club Mystique** hosts a well-attended Friday happy hour, but it is closed on Sunday. It's located in the Cable Beach Inn.

The casinos in Nassau and Paradise Island are two of the most popular places to be after dark—and for some, during the day as well. The Cable Beach casino gives visitors a bright, modern alternative to the more traditional-looking Paradise Island Casino. Glittery Las Vegas–style performances are put on in the Paradise Island Cabaret Theatre.

DINING OUT

Cable Beach/Nassau

EXPENSIVE

Baccarat • *Royal Bahamian Hotel, Cable Beach; tel: 327–6400 •* This main dining room of the hotel is reached by walking across the hotel's courtyard and through the Palm Bar, and is open for dinner only. Tall arched windows look out on the lovely landscaped pool terrace and at night reflect the sparkling chandeliers. The tables are draped in lace and set with Wedgwood china and crystal. The atmosphere, from furnishings to cuisine, is French, and the menu features an extensive selection of France's traditional gourmet specialties. The staff knows just what wines to recommend and the cellar is abundant. Reservations are required. *Major credit cards.*

Sole Mare • *Cable Beach Casino; tel: 327–6200* • Although this gourmet restaurant is located in the casino building, you don't have to be a gambler to enjoy the delicious Northern Italian food. The Sunday buffet brunch is popular. Seafood and veal are served in addition to a variety of pasta dishes. *Major credit cards.*

The Regency • *Cable Beach Hotel; tel: 327–6000* • This gourmet French restaurant is located on the fourth floor of this vast hotel. Guests are greeted by candlelit tables. Only dinner is served and guests are asked to dress up. The wine list covers a varied selection. Reservations are suggested. *Major credit cards.*

The Riveria • *Cable Beach Hotel; tel: 327–6000* • Also located on the hotel's fourth floor, the Riviera is somewhat more casual than the Regency. The cuisine is continental and much is made of adapting local Bahamian dishes. The restaurant is open for dinner only, and reservations are suggested. *Major credit cards.*

Tsunami • *Ambassador Beach Hotel, Cable Beach; tel: 327–8231* • Those seeking a good Chinese-Polynesian restaurant as well as some Japanese specialties will enjoy this unique dining place on Cable Beach. The dining room is open every evening except Wednesday from 6 to 11 p.m. Men are required to wear jackets, and reservations are suggested. *Major credit cards.*

Buena Vista • *Delancy St., Nassau; tel: 322–2811* • A circular driveway leads to the gourmet restaurant in an old mansion. The candlelit dining areas are decorated with paintings and hanging plants. At night, a pianist plays. *Major credit cards.*

Roselawn • *Bank Lane, Nassau; tel: 325–1018* • This restaurant is a stone's throw from Rawson Square. Pasta is made on the premises and Bahamian seafood as well as Continental cuisine is served. There is entertainment at dinner. Roselawn is closed on Sunday, and reservations are a must. *Major credit cards.*

Cafe de la Ronde • *Nassau Beach Hotel, Cable Beach; tel: 327–7711* • This room is the Nassau Beach Hotel's setting for its Continental menu. All pink, candlelight, and Louis Quinze, it is an appealing place for a special evening. *Major credit cards.*

Da Vinci • *10 West Bay St., Nassau; tel: 322-2748* • For good Italian and French cuisine not far from the main drag, Da Vinci, which serves dinner only, is the place to go. It has a fine cellar to match its excellent Italian entrees. *Major credit cards.*

Frilsham House • *West Bay St., next to the Nassau Beach Hotel; tel: 327-7639* • Just east of the Nassau Beach Hotel and under the same management, set back from the road among lush foliage, this restored mansion is now an exciting restaurant. The tasteful decor that greets you upon entrance heralds the impressive dining that follows. Diners are immediately thrust into comfort and ease, beginning with deep, enveloping lounge chairs covered in pale crewel, burnished brass, and dark and gleaming Chippendale chairs. There is no stinting on the ample drinks served while you order seated in the drawing room or the coral-hued bar through the archway. Fresh flowers adorn low tables, and an excellent young woman singer strums a soft, pleasing guitar and never intrudes.

When your order is ready you are escorted into one of the three dining rooms where snowy linen, sparkling crystal, and flashing silverware greet you. Some tables are completely covered in frosty linen while others reveal their sheen through batistelike, delicately embroidered placemats with generous matching napkins. The artfully prepared continental dishes include a number of house specialties fashioned by the chef, formerly of London's Grosvenor House Hotel. Bahamian dishes and ingredients also grace the menu, creatively transformed and given a continental touch in such delights as whole grouper done in a butter pastry, pan-fried filet of red snapper in a mushroom sorrel sauce, and breast of chicken filled with crayfish and truffles. The wine cellar, one of the most complete in Nassau, meets the demand of almost any meal or palate. The summery latticed veranda can be opened to fine weather. Parties of up to 20 may dine *en famille* in the Board Room, which looks like a richly appointed dining room in an elegant home. Frilsham House serves dinner daily beginning at 6:30 p.m. and reservations are a must. *Major credit cards.*

Graycliff • *West Hill and Blue Hill Rd., Nassau; tel: 322-2796* • This is considered one of the finest restaurants in The Bahamas. It is located opposite Government House in a beautiful old mansion, and meals are served in charming and tasteful settings that include antiques, Royal Copenhagen china, and British silverware. Although the cuisine is elegantly Continental, the chef also knows his way around Bahamian cooking. Visiting celebrities as well as ordinary mortals beat a path to

Graycliff's at least once before leaving the island. Reservations are required. *Major credit cards.*

Sun And . . . • *Lakeview Ave., off East Shirley St., Nassau; tel: 323–1205* • In an old mansion not far from Fort Montague, this restaurant serves French and Bahamian dishes including conch chowder, braised duckling, and sweetbreads with asparagus tips. Guests, who are asked to dress up, may dine al fresco or on a palm-shaded patio or in the indoor-outdoor areas around the pool. Sun And . . . is closed on Mondays. Reservations are requested. *Major credit cards.*

MODERATE

Admiral Dining Room • *Pilot House Hotel, East Bay St.; tel: 322–8431* • This dining room has a fine waterfront view. Diners look out on the hotel's marina and off to the busy harbor with its cruise ships. The service is prompt, the food is both Bahamian and American, and the atmosphere is cheerful. Lunch is the best time to enjoy the harbor. *Major credit cards.*

Poop Deck • *East Bay St.; tel: 322–8173* • The busy water traffic of Nassau's harbor can entertain while you dine outdoors. There is also a bar inside if you are just stopping for a drink. If you are not in the mood for a heavy lunch, a burger or a bowl of sea food chowder might be satisfying.

Corona • *Hotel Corona, Bay St. and Dunmore Lane, Nassau; tel: 326–6815* • This restaurant is fast gaining a reputation for tasty Bahamian dishes at moderate prices. It is conveniently located in the thick of downtown activity and is well worth a try. The lunchtime buffet draws Bahamians from all over the island. Upstairs is a lounge for drinks, and there is entertainment in the evening.

The Lobster Pot • *Nassau Beach Hotel, Cable Beach; tel: 327–7711* • This indoor-outdoor seafood restaurant features mussels mariniere, baked red snapper flambed with Pernod, and paella Valenciana, among other dishes. *Major credit cards.*

Tony Roma's • *West Bay St., Nassau and Cable Beach; tel: 325–2020 or 325–6502* • An informal chicken and ribs restaurant, Tony Roma's chain has two locations, one overlooking Saunders Beach, the other near the Paradise Island bridge. Try a side order of a loaf of onion rings. Other items on the menu include London broil and grouper. Tony Roma's is open until 2 a.m. on Fridays and Saturdays, and until midnight Sunday through Thursday. *Major credit cards.*

Bon Homme Richard • *Nassau Harbour Club; tel: 323-3771* • British favorites like steak and kidney pie are found at the Bon Homme Richard. The restaurant also caters to those who like Bahamian or Continental dishes.

Europe Restaurant • *Ocean Spray Hotel, Nassau; tel: 322-8032* • The Europe Restaurant, in the small, downtown Ocean Spray Hotel, is as intimate as the hotel. At night it is warmly lighted, and the American and Bahamian dishes are well-served. The restaurant is proud of its German specialties. It has a good selection of wines and, of course, beer. *Major credit cards.*

Green Shutters • *Parliament St. Nassau; tel: 325-5702* • Located downtown, Green Shutters has all the flavor of an English pub. From its decor to its fish and chips, steak and kidney pie, and beer, it is all British and good for a luncheon stop. *Major credit cards.*

Round House • *Casuarinas Apartment Hotel, Cable Beach; tel: 327-7921* • With the owners on the premises, the restaurant does admirable Bahamian cooking, and capably ventures into other cuisines. *Major credit cards.*

The Terrace (18 Parliament Street) • *Parliament Hotel, Nassau; tel: 322-2836* • Because of confusion with two other Nassau restaurants with similar names, this downtown establishment has added its address to its name. In the evening, torches flare at the entrance to the outdoor dining area. Candlelit tables are covered in bright African prints and the waiters wear colorful dashikis. The managers emphasize Bahamian cuisine. *Major credit cards.*

Marietta's Restaurant and Lounge • *Marietta's Hotel, Okra Hill, Nassau; tel: 322-8395* • Not far from the Paradise Island bridge, this warm, friendly restaurant is certainly worth a visit, if only to sample the crab soup, the house specialty. Other Bahamian dishes are just as delicious.

MODERATE TO INEXPENSIVE

The Swank Club • *Cable Beach Shopping Center; tel: 327-7495* • A casual restaurant serving 20 varieties of pizza, the Swank Club will deliver anywhere in Cable Beach or nearby. Other entrees such as lasagne and spaghetti are also on the menu. A second Swank pizzeria is located in downtown Nassau on Woodes Rogers Walk at Frederick Street (326-7069), another in the Paradise Island Shopping Plaza (326-2765), and a fourth is on Horseshoe Drive in Oakesfield (325-1398). All of the restaurants serve breakfast, lunch, and dinner.

Androsia Restaurant • *Henrea Carlette Hotel on Cable Beach; tel: 327-7805* • The restaurant is a pleasant room with wicker chairs and napkins rolled in tall glasses. There are ship's lanterns on the walls and other reminders of the sea. Among the house dishes are lobster thermidor, conch chowder, gazpacho, veal, and duck. *Major credit cards.*

INEXPENSIVE

Basil's • *Blue Hill Road, Nassau* • Basil's, slightly off the beaten track, caters very much to a local clientele. Visitors would do well to sample its conch fritters.

The Fish Net • *Ernest Street, Nassau; tel: 323-2568* • Just a step off Bay Street, this is another restaurant that caters to locals, but visitors would do well to stop by to get a taste of what Bahamian cooking is all about.

Larry's Pub No. 2 • *Thompson Blvd.: tel: 322-3800* • This spacious restaurant and bar is popular for lunch accompanied by television soap operas. The food is tasty and plentiful. House specialties include such dishes as steamed and cracked conch, lobster salad, okra soup, most of which come with side dishes of peas and rice and fried plantain. To get here from the Cable Beach area, take a jitney going downtown. You can also go from downtown, but you'll have to go all the way through Cable Beach before arriving. *American Express.*

Mondingo Restaurant & Lounge • *Mondingo Inn, Nassau Village; tel: 324-3333* • Mondingo's is across Prince Charles Street. This is an area that visitors often miss. The walk can be worth it since the Bahamian dishes offered are the ones cooked for locals.

Piggily Viggily • *Gambier Village; tel: 327-7439* • This restaurant's name plays with the way Bahamians pronounce the letter "w." There is no playing with the way good, inexpensive food is served up, accent and all, in this relaxed local restaurant.

The Palm • *Bay St. opposite John Bull, Nassau; tel: 323-7444* • This bright restaurant is done in greens giving a crisp, cool feeling to diners. The pleasant waitresses also wear green. The Palm can be a cheerful, inexpensive place to stop for a snack during shopping. Start with a refreshing tall iced tea and finish with a scoop or two of their delicious ice cream for dessert. Breakfast is now served. *Major credit cards.*

Traveller's Rest • *West Bay St., near airport; tel: 327-7633* • Very good Bahamian food, especially from the sea, is served at this indoor-outdoor restaurant overlooking the Atlantic. It likes to call itself the home of the banana daiquiri. *Major credit cards.*

Other good casual restaurants specializing in homestyle cooking are the **Bahamian Kitchen** on Trinity Place off Market Street; **F & S** in Beaumont House on the Waterfront; **Frank's Place** on Mackey Street South; **Grand Central** on Charlotte Street off Bay; **Lum's** on Bay Street; **Three Queen's** on Wulff Road; and **The Shoal** on Nassau Street, which serves the best "boil fish" around, according to residents. **Coco's Cafe & Restaurant,** a bright, new, dining spot on Marlborough Street, across from the Sheraton British Colonial, takes all major credit cards.

Paradise Island

EXPENSIVE

Cafe Martinique • *opposite Britannia Towers; tel: 326-3000* • As its name implies, the cuisine emphasis is French. The popular restaurant is situated in a palm-shaded spot across from the Britannia Towers. With glimpses of the sea, the setting invites dining at what some consider one of the best Continental restaurants in The Bahamas. The candlelight, the linens, and the romantic music add to the elegant atmosphere. *Major credit cards.*

Julie's • *the Grand Hotel; tel: 326-2011* • This is the Grand Hotel's formal dining room and it opens every night for dinner only. Reservations are necessary for dining in this room decorated with paintings, fresh flowers, and eighteenth-century French pieces. Although French cuisine is stressed, Bahamian specialties are also available. *Major credit cards.*

Courtyard Terrace • *the Ocean Club; tel: 325-7501* • Dine al fresco in the elegant surroundings of this quiet haven. The terrace is especially inviting at night when the stars and candles accompany the wine and continental cuisine. The service matches the other charms of the restaurant. *Major credit cards.*

Villa d'Este • *Britannia Towers; tel: 325-5441* • This restaurant, serving delicate Italian specialties, is situated in the casino area. It is open for dinner nightly and features entertainment. It attracts much of the casino crowd. *Major credit cards.*

Le Cabaret Theatre • *Britannia Towers; tel: 326-3000* • Here the show is more exciting than the food. The nightly revue, much like the Folies Bergere, presents women dancers, often innocently bare-breasted, in spectacles with performers ranging from comedians and acrobats to animals. *Major credit cards.*

MODERATE

Boat House • *opposite Britannia Towers; tel: 326–3000* • Next door to the Cafe Martinique, the Boat House is also open only for dinner. It has gained a reputation for steaks and seafood Bahamian-style. Food is cooked on grills at your table and the decor, as the name implies, has the sea as its theme. *Major credit cards.*

Coyaba • *Britannia Towers; tel: 326–3000* • For lovers of Polynesian and Chinese cuisine, this room in a South Pacific design with impressive rattan furniture sets the proper atmosphere. The drinks echo the tropical mood of this restaurant, which is open only for dinner. *Major credit cards.*

Neptune's Table • *Holiday Inn; tel: 325–6451* • Patrons are enthusiastic about the seafood and hearty Bahamian specialties of this restaurant. It is the Inn's top dining place and features gourmet delicacies. *Major credit cards.*

The Terrace • *Britannia Towers; tel: 325–5441* • This indoor-outdoor dining spot overlooks the quiet and pleasant lagoon. Quick meals are available, enabling guests to get back to whatever pleasures were being pursued. It is also possible to enjoy a more leisurely meal while people-watching and enjoying the view. *Major credit cards.*

WHERE TO STAY

Nassau's variety of accommodations gives visitors a wide choice. There are hotels, housekeeping apartments, and guesthouses to suit almost any need and pocketbook. Places to stay are located along Cable Beach, in downtown Nassau, out on Paradise Island, and at a sprawling, self-contained resort at the island's southwestern end. The Cable Beach, Nassau Beach, and Ambassador Beach hotels are all within easy walking distance of each other. The Sheraton British Colonial is the only downtown hotel on a beach. During spring break, the more modest hotels in Cable Beach, downtown Nassau, and Paradise Island often cater to the American high-school and college student crowd. Unless you plan to join the (often noisy) fun, this may not be the best time to book a room at these hotels.

Two newcomers: Replacing the Emerald Beach, one of Nassau's oldest hotels, the 750-room **Crystal Palace** on Cable Beach is scheduled for completion in the winter of 1989. On a much smaller scale, the **Coral World Hotel,** also due to open this year, will have a mere 20 rooms.

Cable Beach

EXPENSIVE

☆☆☆**Wyndham Ambassador Beach** • Across from the Cable Beach golf course, this modern 385-room hotel is a sister to Wyndham's Royal Bahamian and Cable Beach hotels. The spruced up and inviting public rooms have been done in subdued pastels and the pleasant guest rooms with ample baths are cheerfully and sunnily redone with new carpeting and tiled baths and dressing areas. Guests have a choice of restaurants and bars, which are also being redone, including a new dining room with Italian cuisine. Sun worshipers gravitate either to the pool or step out to the hotel's beach. Water sports facilities are shared with neighboring Cable Beach Hotel. Guests can perfect their tennis, raquetball or squash skills at the Sports Centre.

☆☆☆ **The Cable Beach Hotel & Casino** • This huge government-owned resort spreads along one of The Bahamas' nicest beaches. To some, the beige buildings look more like a modern factory than a hotel; 700 rooms, all oceanfront, are located in two wings, one on each side of a bright, spacious lobby overlooking the pool area. (Corridors are *very* long, so depending on where your room is, you may be in for a lot of exercise.) Watersports include parasailing, windsurfing, diving, sailing, and fishing. The Sports Centre across the street, where guests can play free, features 10 tennis courts (5 clay and 5 all-weather), 3 squash courts, 3 racquetball/handball courts, a health bar, a fully stocked pro shop, rental equipment, and lockers. Nearby is an 18-hole golf course. The casino is connected to the hotel by an extensive shopping mall as well as a gallery displaying colorful Bahamian art and lore. In the theater, which seats 1000, musical extravaganzas are performed. Service in hotel restaurants tends to be slow, even by Bahamian standards. Trivia buffs take note: the Cable Beach Hotel has the only escalator in The Bahamas.

Crystal Palace Resort & Casino • This hotel will be Carnival Cruise Line's lavish presence on Cable Beach. The new resort rises from the ashes of the old Emerald Beach Hotel and is slated to open in the winter of 1989. It will have 872 rooms in 5 towers. This is not to mention meeting rooms and other special facilities for guests. The present casino, shared with the next-door Cable Beach Hotel, is being enlarged and refurbished. It was ready for action before the Palace. (First things first.) Six theme restaurants are promised, a 300-seat buffet restaurant, and a 114-seat Chinese deli. Of course, there will be pools and spas and tennis, racquetball, squash and golf also.

★★★ **Nassau Beach Hotel** • This lavish hotel has well-appointed and decorated rooms, its own beach, pool, a small spa, and a landing dock, the latest in watersports, tennis, and a pro shop. A number of dining rooms cater to varied tastes, and Cinnamon's, a night club and disco on the premises, can provide an evening on the town. The hotel has opened a gourmet restaurant, Frilsham House, located next door in a restored colonial home. It should not be missed. A renovated wing has been added for an all-inclusive program called the Palm Club. Guests are met at the airport by limousine and taken to the hotel where a chilled bottle of champagne awaits and a concierge handles any entertainment and/or recreational needs.

★★★**The Royal Bahamian** • For a pampered stay in a serene and posh setting without the hordes and noise of a large hotel, this is the place. The columned six-story pink main house with its marble-floored, Georgian-furnished entrance lobby opens onto a courtyard with a fountain. One end of the paved courtyard leads to an area of pink villas, some with their own pools, set among attractive landscaping. The pampering continues with plush rooms, some with balconies overlooking the sea and the hotel's secluded private beach. There are "his" and "her" closets, dressing areas, and an array of toiletries. Beds are turned down at night, and a helpful concierge is at hand to take care of any special needs. Afternoon tea is served off the lobby of the main building. Guests can have drinks in the Palm Bar or on its terrace, followed by dinner in the elegant Baccarat Room. Breakfast and lunch are served either indoors or outside on the patio of the Cafe Royale, which is adjacent to the pool. Luncheon drinks are available at the Pool Bar, which also has sandwiches. Tennis courts are on the grounds, and guests have access to the facilities of nearby Cable Beach Hotel, including the casino. Complimentary transportation is provided to that hotel as well as into town. The Royal Bahamian's Spa has the latest in the universal gym equipment and exercise rooms, which are free to guests. Massages and mud baths, arranged by appointment, are the only spa services for which there is an extra charge.

INEXPENSIVE

☆☆ **Cable Beach Inn** • *across from Cable Beach Inn villas* • This 7-story, gray building has suites on the top floor, and a painted horse and carriage give welcome out front. The impressive lobby has a marble-topped front desk and is furnished Federal style. The main dining room is ballroom size and the Fox and Hound bar is just off the lobby.

After the lobby the plain, motel-like rooms are a disappointment. There is television, and the baths have ample counter space. There are two swimming pools, one circular and the other rectangular, and a small, manmade beach. Casuarinas is next door, and both hotels are about a 10-minute walk to Swank's Pizza, a liquor store, and other shops located in a shopping center.

☆☆**Cable Beach Manor** • This pink, 2-story apartment hotel surrounds a swimming pool. All rooms and suites have housekeeping facilities, and a shopping center, including a restaurant, is across the street. Daily maid service is available and, for small children, baby-sitting. There are 34 apartments and the hotel has its own beach. The dining in the neighboring hotels and restaurants is varied and, of course, there is the nearby casino. The hotel is convenient to the airport as well as to downtown Nassau, either trip taking about 15 minutes.

☆☆**Casuarinas** • Located on two sides of the road, Casuarinas has a flower-filled courtyard and a small pool out back. Paintings of local and island scenes decorate the lobby walls and the adjoining bar. There are 1- and 2-bedroom units with kitchenettes, and some studios also have kitchens. Albrion's restaurant serves three meals. At its back are more rooms and another swimming pool. Albrion's serves light meals such as conch fritters, fish and chips, pizza, omelets and hamburgers. On the oceanside is the Round House, the other restaurant, which is open for dinner only and closed on Tuesday.

Downtown Nassau

EXPENSIVE

★★★**Graycliff Hotel** • This historic mansion, set behind a wall opposite Government House, has become a sought-after accommodation. The columns at the entrance, the wide porch, and the latticework set it apart from the run-of-the-mill hotel. It houses a five-star restaurant that boasts a world-wide reputation. A plaque celebrating its five stars and its *relais et chateau* designation, is affixed to its outside wall. Staying as a guest in one of the 12 rooms is like accepting an invitation to the home of a wealthy friend. Each large room is different and each bears a name, such as Pool Cottage, Yellowbird, or Hibiscus. Some have walk-in closets and dressing rooms, and many have beautiful tile floors. All are furnished with a melange of comfortable, eye-pleasing pieces, including well-polished antiques. The varied bathrooms are commodious and invite lingering showers or bubble baths. An old stone walkway and lush greenery surround the pool. The hotel seems to have endless dining areas, including porches, patios, terraces, and poolside. One dining room off the main sittng room has bamboo growing outside the window.

MODERATE

☆☆☆**Sheraton British Colonial** • The largest downtown hotel and the only one directly on a beach, the Sheraton British Colonial is an impressive-looking structure. It stands at the end of Bay Street and spreads over eight acres of gardens. The large rooms face the city, the harbor, and the ocean. The private beach is great for watching incoming and departing cruise ships. The hotel is a vivid reminder of Blackbeard, the pirate, who lived on the site when it was Fort Nassau and hid from the Royal Navy in a well that is still on the grounds.

☆ **The Pilot House** • For being in the center of things, the Pilot House is the place. Just across the bridge from Paradise Island, this hotel has a harbor view and is steps away from the action on the island and in the square. It was erected on the site of a pilot house which had stood for 150 years. Guests have an ever-changing view of the harbor's activity.

INEXPENSIVE

★★**Buena Vista** • After crossing the veranda of this nineteenth century mansion near Government House, and entering the reception area, it seems as if you have stepped into a comfortable, lived-in, private home and well-used living room. Everything spells comfort. A staircase leads up to the second floor and six, spacious, eclectically furnished rooms. The Buena Vista dining room rivals the best and most elegant of eating places, ranging from candlelight to fine china and crystal in the several dining areas hung with paintings and plants.

★**The Parliament** • *18 Parliament Street* • For those who dislike large, bustling hotels, the Parliament, at the hub of town, may be the answer. Located across the street from Government buildings, near the venerable Victoria Gardens and the Cenotaph, it has pleasantly decorated rooms. No two are alike and all 11 are comfortable in size. The hotel has its own restaurant, The Terrace—18 Parliament Street, which attracts visitors as well as the hotel's guests. It is several blocks from a beach. Bay Street shopping and Rawson Square and its attractions are also nearby.

☆ **Lighthouse Beach Hotel** • Formerly the Mayfair, the Lighthouse Beach is a comfortable hotel that is right across the street from a beach, yet close to the heart of downtown Nassau. While the rooms are small, they are pleasantly decorated and have color satellite TVs. Some have ocean views and private balconies. A swimming pool is on the roof. In addition to the weekly manager's cocktail party, a moonlight cruise and a Rose Island picnic several times a week are complimentary to guests. In the lobby, the sign on the door that leads to Franco's Original Italian Restaurant and Pizzeria reads, "No shoes, no shirts, no service."

The New Olympia Hotel • Within walking distance of Bay Street shopping and the beach, the Olympia has comfortable rooms that vary in size. They overlook the beach, Paradise Island across the harbor, and the street. The back rooms are quietest. All are air conditioned and most have balconies. The five rooms on the main floor are good for the elderly or wheelchair-bound (there is a ramp at the entrance for wheelchairs). The small, dimly lit English-style pub serves pizza and sandwiches, and guests can watch satellite TV or play darts or backgammon. The Olympia is next door to Da Vinci restaurant.

☆ **Ocean Spray Hotel** • Many Europeans have been coming to this hotel for years. Located across the street from Peanuts Taylor's Drumbeat Club, a popular nightspot, Ocean Spray is fully air conditioned and has a sun roof. The beach and the stores of downtown Nassau are short walks away. The cozy Europe restaurant/bar serves continental and Bahamian food.

☆ **El Greco Hotel** • Despite its Spanish decor, with its huge ornate wrought-iron chandelier in the lobby, El Greco serves excellent Bahamian and European food. Its restaurant, Del Prado, opens at 5 p.m. There are 26 rooms and a pool. The hotel faces a beach and is within walking distance of Bay Street shopping.

☆ **Marietta's Hotel** • Marietta's is near the Paradise Island bridge and the Potter's Cay fish and vegetable market. Rooms are plain and practical. The restaurant is a magnet for guests and outsiders looking for exceptional Bahamian cooking. Marietta's was begun by a former hotel maid. Some of the better known guests have included Count Basie's band.

Harbour Moon Hotel • This is a modestly priced, small hotel along Nassau's Bay Street. Although there is a restaurant, the hotel offers guests no meal plan. The rooms were recently redone, and Harbour Moon is a stone's throw from the Paradise Island bridge.

☆☆**Dolphin Hotel** • Across West Bay Street from the beach, this hotel does a land-office business during spring break. The students descend upon Nassau, and life is not the same for those nearby. The rooms all have balconies and look out to the beach. The lobby is modern with ceiling fans and paneled in horizontally laid wood.

Paradise Island

EXPENSIVE

☆☆ **Holiday Inn** • This high rise structure looms over the casuarinas and palms of Paradise Island and serves as a landmark for wanderers. The huge, somewhat overcrowded lobby with its grand chandelier is furnished in rattan made comfortable with floral cushions. There is a bar, restaurants and a variety of shops. The free-form pool has a bar, reached by a bridge for those who are clothed and by water for swimmers. An outdoor restaurant overlooks the pool. All sports are at hand and the hotel bustles with much leisure time activity organized by its enthusiastic staff.

★★★★★**Ocean Club** • This posh resort was once the home of A&P heir, Huntington Hartford. Guests checking in are offered rum punches in crystal goblets while seated at an antique desk. From there, the concierge escorts them to their rooms. Rooms are furnished with double beds, television, dining areas, patios or balconies and ceiling fans for those who eschew air conditioning. Some rooms have garden views while others face the ocean. Villas are also available, some of which have whirlpool baths. The Courtyard Terrace can be a romantic dining spot at night. The lavishly landscaped grounds bring vistas that include medieval Versailles Gardens and a filagree gazebo overlooking the harbor. Teatime is every afternoon except Sunday. The white sand beach is dreamlike and water sports are always on tap for the energetic.

★★★★**Paradise Island Resort & Casino** • The two main buildings of this lavish resort were once separate hotels. Paradise Towers and Britannia Towers are part of the largest resort/gaming complex in the world. The busy, sprawling lobbies of the buildings connect with the 30,000-square-foot casino. A short walk to the beach takes guests to the pool, shuffleboard, afternoon balloon dances, and snorkeling. Offshore are windsurfers, parasailers, and pleasure boats making for a lively and colorful tropical vista. Ferries to downtown Nassau pick up and drop off at Britannia Towers. The casino is open from 11 a.m. until 4 a.m., but the slot machines go on forever. A Las Vegas type revue at Le Cabaret Theatre plays every night except Sunday. A new, beachfront building has recently been completed for *Club Paradise* guests. This luxury, all-inclusive-rate program provides airport transportation, breakfast at a selection of dining places and dinner at any one of 12 Resorts restaurants. Wine is served with meals and there are amenities from open bar cocktail parties to hot and cold hors d'oeuvres in the Lounge.

For the athletically minded there are unlimited greens fees, tennis clinics, complimentary use of health club and aerobic classes. Guests receive terry robes in the *Paradise Concierge* program, $20 in match play chips for the casino, newspapers in rooms, and they can book vast suite with a matching price tag of $3000 per night during the winter season, complete with a butler. Note that throughout the year, weekday room rates are lower than weekend.

☆☆☆**Sheraton Grand** • All rooms in this beige high rise have balconies which look out to the ocean. The lobby's focus is a fountain and waterfall which empty into a pool surrounded by lush foliage and other plantings. High backed rattan chairs are arranged before the floor-to-ceiling windows and there are hanging baskets and lazily revolving ceiling fans. Last visit, the plastic cushions were in need of replacement but, in all, the lobby is impressive and welcoming. The rooms are tastefully decorated and the latest disco innovations lure stay-up-late guests from other Paradise Island evening attractions, most of which are within walking distance. An excellent beach stretches in front and all water and other sports are on tap, including tennis. Julie's, the gourmet restaurant and the Rotisserie serve dinner only. Two upper floors are given over to luxury living. For an unmentionable price, those guests are provided with a limousine, a maid and butler, a private elevator, an outdoor jacuzzi and a sunken bath tub with gold fixtures.

MODERATE TO INEXPENSIVE

☆☆ **Bay View Village** • The rooms in these red roofed white buildings with dark wood balconies are more plain than the flower-filled grounds might lead you to expect. There are rental units as well as units for sale. There is a mini-market for those who cook in and lunch and snacks are served at the bar of one of the three pools. Tennis is free during the day and one dollar for 45 minutes at night. Paths through the grounds are planted with a profusion of blossoming flowers and fruit trees. There is bougainvillea and more than 20 varieties of hibiscus. The villas and duplexes are 1, 2 and 3 bedroom units, each with a terrace or patio garden. There are even some penthouses with roof gardens.

★★ **Club Land'or** • The main focus of this resort is time sharing, but some hotel rooms are available. Affiliated with the Xanadu Hotel in Freeport, it is a part of Resorts Condominiums International. All units have living-dining areas and kitchenettes and rattan furnishings. Some of the rooms have balconies. The beach is about 10 minutes away, and from the pool which overlooks the lagoon, the twice-a-day dolphin show of Resorts International can be seen. Each day except Sunday there is a happy hour in the Oasis Lounge and the Blue Lagoon restaurant serves breakfast and dinner on the third floor. There is a once a week trip to

Rose Island and the ferry to Nassau or the island tour boat are just outside.

☆☆☆ **Loew's Harbour Cove** • This hotel stands tall, just south of the humpbacked Paradise Island bridge to overlook all of Nassau and its waterfront bustling with cruise ships, pleasure and excursion boats, ferries, and the spectacular sight of Chalk's seaplane as it takes off and lands. Cabbage Beach is a stone's throw and the palm shaded pool overlooks the harbor. All water sports can be had along with such games as tennis, table tennis, and shuffleboard played near the hotel's petite, man-made beach. All rooms, furnished in wicker, have two double beds, television, and some have balconies. The Buccaneer Lounge is a popular night spot. A complimentary water taxi takes guests to Nassau every day except Wednesday and Sunday.

☆☆ **Paradise Paradise** • The atmosphere of this 100-room hotel is relaxed. Rooms have mini bars, television, and double or king-sized beds. Some have balconies. Young people in pink T-shirts with the letters AE (for achievers of excellence) are ever-present to see to your needs. Because the emphasis is on sports here, the ratio of activity directors to guests is higher than at the larger hotels. There is a bicycle tour every morning and all activities are included in the room rate. The inviting beach is seldom crowded and changing rooms are at the disposal of guests who arrive early or stay around after check-out.

Southwestern New Providence

EXPENSIVE

☆☆☆ **Divi Bahamas Beach Resort & Country Club** • Formerly the South Ocean Club, this sprawling resort is about a 10-minute drive from the airport. By 1992 the hotel is expected to have over 1000 rooms. Right now, there are just over 100. New guests are greeted with rum punches as they enter the circular lobby decorated with potted ficus, banana trees, and exotic, colorful birds in domed cages. Rooms are smartly decorated with wicker and dark wood. Most have louvered doors leading to balconies or patios. However, those on ground level, whether facing the pool-area cafe or the gardens, have little privacy and can be noisy if you want an afternoon nap. It is best, therefore, to request a second-story room. The glass-enclosed Papagayo restaurant overlooks the golf course and is a pleasant alternative to the rather standard main dining room. Papagayo is Italian/American gourmet. Video tapes are for rent to play in your room, and the hotel has an extensive video library. The in-room safe-deposit boxes are good for passports, tickets, jewelry, and cash, but too small for 35mm cameras and the like. Front-desk safes are available for a small fee. There are 4 tennis courts and scuba certification courses as well as windsurfing and other watersports.

Room keys come on rubber coils that fit your wrist for swimming. Complimentary transportation is provided to downtown Nassau (about 30 minutes each way). This is a good thing, since taxi drivers either groan or quote exhorbitant rates upon discovering that you want to go all the way to Divi. The last hotel shuttle leaves Nassau at midnight. You can also take the local jitney for about $1.75 each way. Divi owns the nearby beachfront Sandpiper timeshare units and, as we go to press, 168 additional hotel rooms were under construction on the beachfront..

Silver Cay

Coral World • *on Silver Cay, between downtown Nassau and Cable Beach* • This new hotel, at the Coral World Undersea Observatory and Marine Park, is not yet open at press time. Its 22 rooms will all have private patios, each with its own free-form swimming pool and kitchenette. One other end of each suitelike room opens to decks and the ocean. A bridge takes you over to Silver Cay, but the hotel promises free daytime ferry service to downtown Nassau and buses to Cable Beach as well as boats to Paradise Island.

FREEPORT

ATTRACTIONS AT A GLANCE

	Place	Page
Shopping and Dining Plazas		
International Bazaar	Torii gate at West Sunrise Highway	201
*Port Lucaya	Lucaya	201
Local Industries		
Straw Market	Next to International Bazaar	203

	Place	*Page*
Perfume Factory	West End Road	201
Bahamas Arts and Crafts Market	near International Bazaar	199
Gardens, Parks, and Nature Reserves		
*Rand Memorial Nature Centre	West End Road	201
*Garden of the Groves	West End Road	200
*Lucayan National Park	Eastern End	201
Hydroflora Garden	East Beach Drive	200
Bird Sanctuary	West End	199
Museums		
Underwater Explorers Society Museum	Across from Lucayan Beach Resort	203
Grand Bahama Museum	Garden of the Groves	200
Animals		
*The Dolphin Experience	UNEXSO Dock, Lucaya	200

The Second City

Freeport, with an array of restaurants, clubs, sports, and two vast casinos, is located inland on Grand Bahama. This island of about 35,000 people has taken its place after New Providence as the second most important in the Bahamas chain. An orderly city with excellent roads and broad, landscaped highways bordered by stately palms and pines, Freeport is not even three decades old. Since it is shy on historical attractions and sightseeing meccas, those who thrive on sunbathing, watersports, fishing, golf, gambling, dining, and nightlife will find it made to order. For theatergoers, the Regency Theatre on West Mall presents local and imported plays.

Gleaming high-rise hotels, apartment buildings, condominiums and time-sharing complexes stand against the cerulean sky and sparkling waters. Residents of Freeport and adjoining Lucaya, which is on the coast, have attractive homes surrounded by well-kept lawns and flowering shrubs. The many Europeans, Canadians, and Americans now living in Freeport/Lucaya make it a truly international city. The late American band leader Count Basie lived in Bahamia, an exclusive neighborhood popular with sightseers.

As you enter Freeport along West Sunrise Highway, the lofty Princess Tower Hotel, now combined with the Princess across the road into the Bahamas Princess Resort & Casino, and the casino next door become unmistakable landmarks. Through Moorish domes, minarets, and intricate tilework, they strive for the exotic. Unlike other hotels that are not located on the beach, they provide complimentary transportation.

Alongside the Princess Resort's tower, a Japanese torii gate welcomes you to the sprawling International Bazaar with its shops and decor representing countries around the world. Visitors may purchase international wares and dine on a wide selection of international cuisines. The Bahamas Tourist Office is in a tranquil, shaded plaza in the busy bazaar. Here, through the government's free **People-to-People Program,** you can arrange to do things with individual Bahamians or families who volunteer their time to make your stay more enjoyable. Whether or not you participate in the People-to-People Program, you may want to check the local newspaper for the weekend barbecues or beach parties sponsored by churches, lodges, or schools to raise money. There is always music as well as spirited domino games, and you'll have an inexpensive home-cooked meal of treats such as conch fritters, curried chicken, and ribs.

If you're staying somewhere with cooking facilities, you can buy fresh seafood at the Harbour Fish and Lobster House in Freeport's downtown industrial area. Fresh fruits and vegetables are sold in the market outside the grocery store in the downtown shopping area and fresh-baked goods can be found at Mum's and Western bakeries.

In the Lucaya area, across from the Lucayan Beach Resort & Casino, the Atlantik Beach Hotel and the Holiday Inn, is a new shopping complex called Port Lucaya. Spread along the waterfront are 12 buildings of shops, a marina, restaurants, a bandstand, and other attractions. At UNEXSO, near Port Lucaya, a not-to-be-missed experience for visitors is swimming with playful dolphins.

Local buses running between Lucaya and Freeport's Mall area, where the International Bazaar is located, and downtown Freeport cost about 65¢. Near Pub on the Mall restaurant you can get a bus to the Holiday Inn beach for windsurfing or waterskiing. Rent a car or a moped through a hotel for a short trip to one of the uncrowded Lucaya beaches, such as beautiful Taino and others off Midshipman Road. The 40-acre Lucayan National Park, about 25 minutes by car east of downtown Freeport, has a wide, secluded beach with high dunes. The lush Garden of the Groves is also worth a visit. Another pleasant nature reserve is the Rand Memorial Nature Centre, not far from the Mall area. A drive

Grand Bahama

along the western coast will take you through tiny old settlements and to restaurants overlooking the ocean.

The Early Days

Until the sixties, Grand Bahama had developed in fits and starts, beginning at its west end. Then Wallace Groves, an American from Virginia, saw trade and other growth possibilities. With loans and the enthusiastic encouragement of the colonial government, he began building the city of Freeport and developing its deepwater harbor for the expected boom in trade and commerce. Since the 1964 opening of its first tourist hotel, the Lucayan Bay, Freeport/Lucaya has blossomed with hotels and resorts. Sensing that his new city could not thrive on tourism alone, Groves set out to attract industry as well. His foresight has resulted in an industrial area that now supports oil refineries, cement production, pharmaceuticals, and other types of manufacturing.

Most of what little history there is can be found in the small settlements such as Pinders's Point, Eight Mile Rock, and Seagrape, along the western coast. Before the advent of tourists, and when there was Prohibition in the United States, this section of Grand Bahama was notorious. It was an important operating point for smugglers and rum runners who used the area much as their predecessors, the pirates, did.

When it appeared that tourism would develop at the western end of the island, the Grand Bahama Hotel and Country Club was erected. This expansive resort with lush plantings, a golf course, tennis courts, a giant pool, a marina, and countless other amenities, fell upon hard times when growth took place at Freeport, some 25 miles to the east. Now resurrected, it is called Jack Tar Village.

WHAT TO SEE AND DO

SIGHTS

Bahamas Arts and Crafts Market • *Behind the International Bazaar* • The various booths here sell locally made jewelry, paintings, and other crafts. This market, too often overlooked by visitors, deserves a stop.

Bird Sanctuary • *West End near Jack Tar Village* • This natural haven welcomes hundreds of species of tropical birds, as well as others using it as a stop-off point during their annual migration.

Bus Tours • A number of buses take visitors on tours of Freeport/Lucaya and the vicinity. Tour attractions are celebrity homes, the historical West End, several beaches, nature reserves, and the industrial area. Some tours stop for shopping and lunch or a snack. One of the tours is aboard a red, double-decker bus from London. *Prices range from about $10 to $15 for adults. Check hotel tour desks for details.*

*The Dolphin Experience • *At the UNEXSO dock across from the Lucayan Beach Resort & Casino; tel: 373–1244* • Few animal lovers pass up the chance to swim with the dolphins in this special program. You get right into the water with these playful acquatic mammals, who allow you to stroke and hug their powerful 6- or 7-foot bodies, caress their smooth skin, and hitch rides across the water while hanging on to their dorsal fins. Children are welcome. After a 15-minute orientation, up to six participants swim with the dolphins for about 20 minutes. Participants wear flippers. Life jackets, masks, and snorkels are also available. Afterwards you can view your performance on video and purchase a copy for about $30. Originally from Mexico, the dolphins now reside in a large pen at the UNEXSO dock. They are part of an experiment in human/dolphin interaction. Once they learn to follow a boat back and forth between their enclosure and a reef a mile away, they will be released into the open sea every day to swim with scuba divers. The trainers will test the dolphins' ability to use sonar and to retrieve objects from the divers. *Call for reservations. $50 per swim session; $5 for orientation only; $95 to spend day as an assistant trainer.*

*Garden of the Groves • *West End Road* • This 12-acre garden is named for Freeport's founder, Wallace Groves, and his wife. The garden has a thousand species of flowers, ferns, shrubs, and trees. Among its attractions are waterfalls and hanging gardens. *Open daily 9:30 a.m.– 5 p.m. Free admission.*

Grand Bahama Museum • *Garden of the Groves* • This museum is just inside the entrance to the Garden of the Groves. Here you'll find artifacts of the Lucayan Indians, who came by canoe from South America and inhabited the island when Columbus arrived. You'll learn that English words such as canoe, hurricane, potato, and barbecue were taken from the Lucayan language. Also on display are colorful costumes worn for the Bahamian traditional Junkanoo parades on New Year's Day, Boxing Day, and Independence Day. *Admission: $2.00 for adults; $1.00 for children.*

Hydroflora Garden • *East Beach Drive* • This garden demonstrates hydroponics, the growing of plants in water. Visitors are given complimentary Bahamian flowers, and they learn the history of the conch shell, which has its own museum here. *Open daily 9:30 a.m.–5 p.m. Admission: Adults, $1, Children under 12, 50¢.*

*Lucayan National Park • *Eastern End* • This 40-acre park made up of four different ecological zones has coca plums, seagrape, ming trees, wild tamarind, mahogany, and cedar, among many other types of vegetation. Gold Rock Creek flows through the park to the ocean and there is a beautiful, wide, secluded beach. Two cave openings are accessible by stairways and ramps, and there is over a mile of footpaths and elevated walkways. *Free admission.*

International Bazaar • *Entrance through Torii gate on West Sunrise Highway, next to Princess Tower Hotel and casino* • This is a vast complex of international shops, boutiques, and restaurants with architecture, goods, food, and souvenirs reminiscent of a variety of countries. All Freeport/Lucaya visitors find their way to the bustling bazaar, either for exotic bargains or just to look and be overwhelmed. *Open daily (except Sundays) until midnight. No admission charge.*

Perfume Factory • *Eight Mile Rock. Follow signs on West End Rd.* • Perfumes, made from local flowers, are manufactured here, and the entire process may be seen in operation. Visitors may make purchases, selecting from among several fragrances.

*Port Lucaya • *Near UNEXSO dock* • Pleasing to the eye, Port Lucaya is a cluster of pastel, shingle-roofed buildings filled with shops and restaurants. Guests dine and relax on balconies overlooking the surrounding water. Food ranges from Chinese to English pub and Bahamian. Strolling through, you can buy everything from imported gold jewelry and perfumes to handmade crafts. Count Basie, the legendary jazz pianist and band leader, who lived on Grand Bahama until his death, first had the idea for this attractive plaza and promenade. Live music spills out of a lacy gazebo both by day and night. A steel band plays every evening except Sunday. Many of the shops and restaurants stay open late and can be pleasant spots for sunset watching.

*Rand Memorial Nature Centre • *Off West End Road* • Named for and financed by James H. Rand, a former president of Remington-Rand, this 100-acre park has 200 species of birds, and more than 400 varieties of plants. On the guided tour, you are followed by friendly birds. You can photograph the national bird, the pink flamingo, in all its glory at a tropical pool. You will also learn where the "straw" at the straw markets really comes from, and you'll see how bubble gum grows. *Open Mon. through Fri. and Sun. Guided tours at 10:30 a.m., 2 p.m., and 3 p.m. and on Sun., 2 p.m. and 3 p.m. $2.00.*

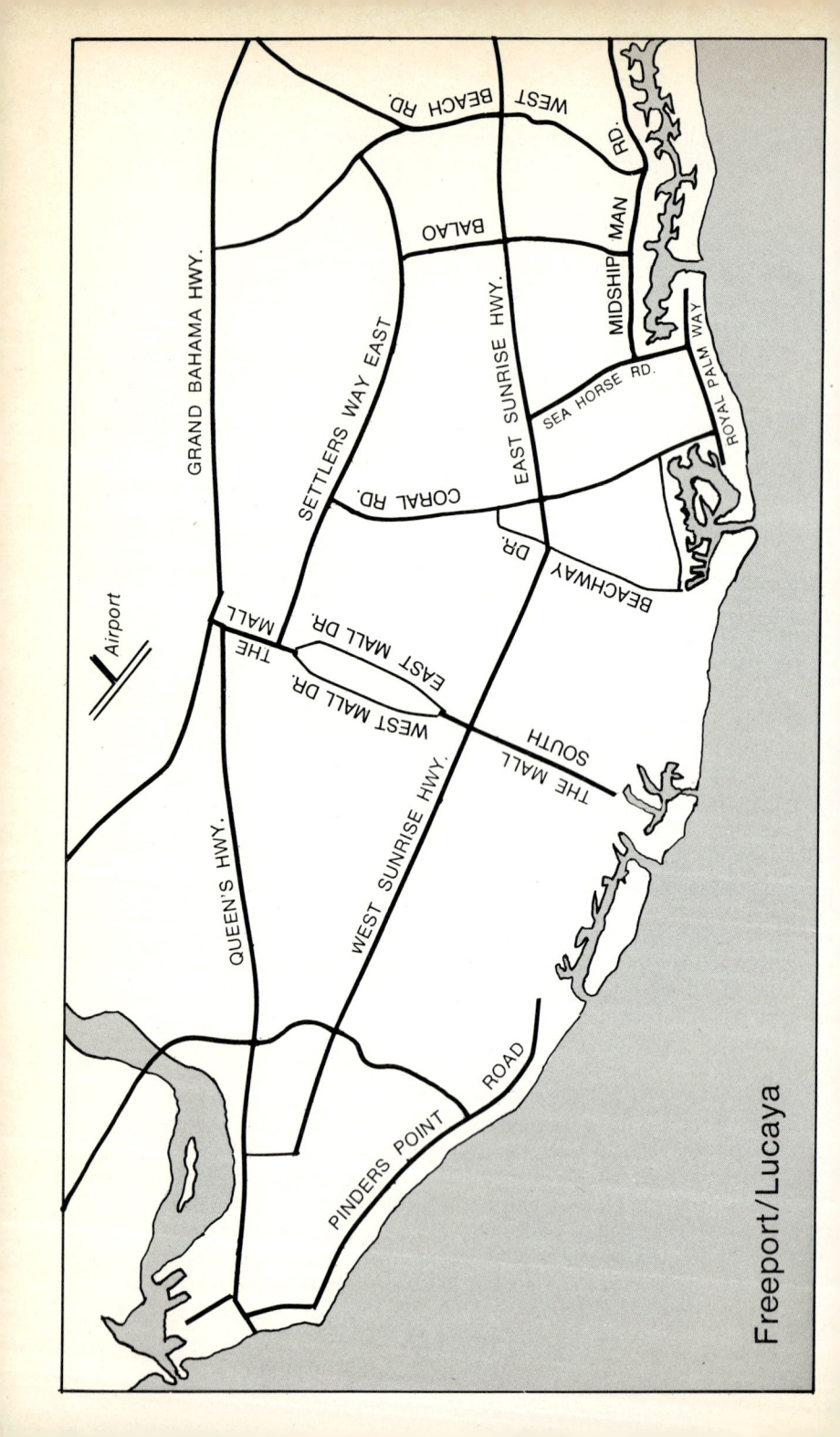

Freeport/Lucaya

Straw Market • *Next to the International Bazaar* • Freeport/Lucaya's Straw Market carries the same kinds of handcrafted items found in straw markets throughout The Bahamas. Items include hats for both sexes, baskets, and place mats, as well as wood carvings, necklaces, and a variety of objects fashioned from the ubiquitous conch shell. *Open daily.*

SPORTS

Diving • Divers gravitate to Freeport/Lucaya to take advantage of the services and facilities offered by the Underwater Explorer's Society (UNEXSO), which gives diving lessons, leads expeditions to several diving sites, operates a diving museum and library, and runs a snack bar where visitors can grill their own hamburgers. Across from the Lucayan Beach Resort & Casino, UNEXSO offers a course in underwater photography. UNEXSO personnel are happy to give advice on diving sites on other islands. The "resort course" is about $80 and the 5-day certification course runs about $295. A single dive in the tank will be about $30. Dive packages range from about $75 for 3 dives to about $200 for 10 dives. (Call UNEXSO at (809)373-1244 in the Bahamas, (305)761-7679 in Florida; and 1-800-992-DIVE toll-free from the rest of the U.S.)

Fishing and Boating • For deep-sea fishing, boats leave daily from the marina adjacent to the Lucayan Bay Hotel at 9 a.m. and 1 p.m. Bait and tackle as well as soft drinks and ice are included in the price. Make reservations through your hotel tour desk or bell captain. The cost is about $40 (or $20 for spectators).

Cruises include sightseeing trips as well as **snorkeling** excursions for beginners or those with experience. The *Mermaid Kitty,* said to be the world's largest glass-bottom boat, leaves from the Lucayan Bay Hotel dock at 10 a.m., noon, and 2:30 p.m. and visits tropical fish-filled coral reefs and a shipwreck. You can also see a diving show. The cost is about $10 for adults and about $6.50 for children. Other cruises allow time for swimming and lunch on a deserted beach. Sailing trips can be arranged through hotels. *Check hotel tour desks for further details.*

Golf • There are six golf courses in Freeport/Lucaya: Bahama Reef, 9 holes, is not far from the Holiday Inn; Lucayan Park Golf & Country Club, 18 holes, caters to guests of the Atlantik Beach Hotel; Fortune Hills Golf & Country Club is a 9-hole course; Princess Ruby is one of two courses operated by the Princess hotels and has 18 holes; Princess Emerald, the other one, was designed by Dick Wilson and has 18 holes; and Jack Tar Village, a 27-hole course, is in the West End resort 45 miles outside Freeport.

Horseback Riding • Pinetree Stables takes groups out at 9 a.m., 11 a.m., and 2 p.m. every day except Monday. Riders have a choice of English or Western saddles. *Adults $20 per hour.*

Tennis • Courts are at the Princess hotels, the Holiday Inn, the Shalimar Hotel, Silver Sands Sea Lodge, and Jack Tar Village.

Parasailing and Windsurfing • These sports are available at the Atlantik Beach Hotel and the Holiday Inn.

Waterskiing • The Princess hotels, Holiday Inn, and Jack Tar Village all have waterskiing.

NIGHTLIFE

Freeport Inn is the nightspot to go to if you want to party with an almost completely Bahamian crowd. The live band plays Bahamian music as well as disco, and the club attracts mainly young people. Many visitors go to the **Sandpiper,** the disco in the Coral Beach Hotel. While people tend to dress up to go dancing at **Studio 69** on Midshipman Road, jeans and sneakers are the attire for many at **Sultan's Tent** in the Princess Tower, which plays more calypso than most other clubs. **Yellow Bird,** at Castaways Resort, features Bahamian music. You can listen to live jazz at **Skipper's Lounge** in the Paradise Island Resort's Country Club.

There is always a flurry of activity in The **Princess Casino,** adjoining the tower of the Bahamas Princess Resort. Visitors to the casino's nightclub are treated to a Las Vegas–style act complete with magicians, comedians, and glittering, scantily dressed male and female dancers. Although not yet as busy, the **Lucayan Beach Hotel Casino** attracts guests from the beach area.

DINING OUT

NOTE · · · Some restaurants will add a service charge to your bill if you pay with traveler's checks.

EXPENSIVE

Pier One • *Freeport Harbour; tel: 352–6674* • The delicious food is the first reason for dining here. The dramatic location is a close second. This breezy, window-filled seafood restaurant stands on stilts and is almost completely surrounded by water. Guests can watch a sunset while having cocktails on the balcony off the bar. Early-bird specials are served from 5 p.m. to 7 p.m. At night, the surrounding waters are brought to life with spotlights. The dark-paneled walls and beamed ceilings are decorated with hanging plants, fishnets, starfish, blowfish, frying pans, and street signs such as "Lovers Lane." A boat filled with flowers and butter sculpture is in one of the dining areas. Uwe Nath, the award-winning chef, will be happy to share some of his secrets—just ask for a copy of his cookbook. Pier One is closed on Sundays.

The Rib Room • *Bahamas Princess Resort & Casino; tel: 352–6721* • The atmosphere of this room is warm in the evening, with candlelight against dark beams, and there is a variety of gourmet dishes on the menu. *Major credit cards.*

Le Cotillion • *Bahamas Princess Resort & Casino; tel: 352–9661* • This dining room has the kind of ambience that makes you feel good you dressed up. The service and the food justify the occasion. In the evening this is a popular stop for hotel guests on their way to the casino.

Escoffier Room • *Xanadu Hotel; tel: 352–6782* • In a flattering and softly lighted setting, a gourmet menu is served in this comfortably decorated room. Bahamian dishes, elegantly presented, are also a part of the offering. *Major credit cards.*

MODERATE TO EXPENSIVE

Guanahani • *Bahamas Princess Resort & Casino; tel: 352–6721* • Guanahani was the Indian name for San Salvador when Columbus "discovered" this Bahamian island. Near the pool, this glass-enclosed, elegant restaurant featuring American, French, German, Italian, Japanese, Mexican, and Bahamian cuisine is surrounded by lush plants and is attractively lit at night. *Major credit cards.*

Ruby Swiss • *John Wentworth Ave., off West Sunrise Highway; tel. 352–8507* • Down the street from the Princess Tower, this restaurant has American, German, and Swiss entrees on its extensive menu. The crab meat Rockefeller is a good choice. Live calypso music accompanies dinner. Reservations are necessary.

Pub on the Mall • *Ranfurly Circle; tel: 352–5110* • Right across from the International Bazaar, this lively pub serves English, Bahamian, and American food as well as a variety of imported beers. Closed Sundays. *Major credit cards.*

The Stoned Crab • *Taino Beach; tel: 313–1442* • In addition to crab dishes, this seafood restaurant on one of Freeport's most beautiful beaches specializes in lobster and steak. Only dinner is served.

Cafe Valencia • *International Bazaar; tel: 352–8717* • This popular restaurant, run by a husband-and-wife team, combines Spanish and Bahamian cuisines. Specialties include paella; snapper for two, baked whole, with garlic, surrounded by vegetables such as casava and plaintain; Bahamian macaroni (with a thick and spicy cheese sauce); lobster salad; johnnie cake; and fresh-baked coconut tarts or guava duff for dessert. While the food is good, the furnishings have become somewhat run down over the years. *Major credit cards.*

MODERATE

Japanese Steak House • *International Bazaar; tel: 352–9521* • The Japanese Steak House is a welcome find in the labyrinth of the International Bazaar. It has a pleasant atmosphere, and food is dramatically prepared at hibachi tables. Closed Sundays.

Harry's American Bar • *Queen's Highway at Deadman's Reef* • This little restaurant, with a view of the sea, becomes a favorite of visitors once they discover it. Fourteen miles out of Freeport, it is away from the heart of tourist activity. Having a drink or a steak, chicken, or seafood meal here can be a welcome break in a day or an evening's rounds.

The Buccaneer Club • *Queen's Highway and Deadman's Reef; tel: 348–3794* • This restaurant is a good reason for getting out of town. It is on the beach and its grounds have lush palms and other foliage. The menu consists of European and Bahamian selections. From November through April, when the restaurant is open, it sponsors beach parties with food, volleyball, and other activities for an all-inclusive price. Call for free transportation from your hotel. Open only for dinner, the Buccaneer is closed on Mondays.

Silvano's • *The Mall at Sunrise Highway; tel: 352–5111* • Homemade pasta, veal, salads, and soups are on the menu at this round Italian restaurant with cozy booths by the windows. Silvano's is across from the International Bazaar. Closed Mondays.

Churchill Pub • *The Mall; tel: 352–8866* • This English-style pub, named for Sir Winston Churchill and next to the straw market at the International Bazaar, serves dishes such as roast beef with Yorkshire pudding, but it is also known for its cracked conch. In addition to a

Happy Hour Monday through Friday, there is entertainment several nights a week. The pub is open until 4 a.m.

La Phoenix • *Silver Sands Sea Lodge; tel: 353–3373* • The menu here ranges from Indian curry dishes, seafood kebabs, and chicken Kiev to conch chowder, steak, and lobster. Early-bird specials are served from 5–6:30 p.m. Near hotels in Lucaya. *Major credit cards.*

Marcella's • *East Mall at Kipling Lane; tel: 352–5085* • Before digging into an Italian meal here, try a frozen daiquiri. Many people consider Marcella's the best place to find authentic Italian food in Freeport.

Captain's Charthouse • *East Sunrise and Beachway Dr.; tel: 373–3900* • In this restaurant the hearty fare runs to steaks, chops, shrimp, lobster, and the like. The decor is tropical, and island music adds to the lively atmosphere. *Major credit cards.*

INEXPENSIVE

The Office • *Logwood Rd.; tel: 352–8997* • The Bahamian specials at this casual dining spot that serves three meals a day include okra soup, curried chicken, steamed mutton, chicken souse, and barbecued ribs. The Office, open daily from 8 a.m. to 5 a.m., has a live band and a disco.

The Pancake House • *East Sunrise Highway; tel: 373–3200* • This popular restaurant specializing in Bahamian home-style cooking has nothing to do with the American chain with a similar name. In addition to 12 different kinds of pancakes, the menu includes stewed fish and grits, shrimp, steak, and sandwiches. Breakfast is served all day.

Scorpio's • *Explorer's Way and West Atlantic; tel: 352–6969* • Cracked conch, steamed grouper, and minced lobster are just a few of the dishes served at this restaurant recommended highly by Bahamians. Take-out service is available from 7 a.m. to 3 a.m. every day and major credit cards are accepted. *Major credit cards.*

Freddie's • *Hunters; tel: 352–3250* • Open from 11 a.m. until 11 p.m., Freddie's serves grouper, steak, minced lobster, pork chops, cracked conch, and other local dishes. Early-bird specials are on the menu from 5 p.m. to 6:30 p.m. Freddie's is closed on Sundays.

Blackbeard's • *Fortune Beach; tel: 373–2960* • The location, right on the beach, makes this an especially pleasant place to have a drink, mingle with locals, and sample Bahamian specialties like peas and rice and cracked conch.

Traveller's Rest • *William's Town, off Beachway Dr.; tel: 353–4884* • This informal restaurant, overlooking a narrow beach, is off the beaten track. Conch is served in burgers, fritters, and salads. Hearty chowders, rice and peas, and fish are also on the menu.

Other good restaurants for Bahamian cuisine are the **Fat Man** on Pinder's Point Road (352–2931), the **Native Hut** on Sergeant Major Drive, and **Peace & Plenty** in Eight Mile Rock (353–1814).

WHERE TO STAY

Freeport

MODERATE

☆☆☆**Bahamas Princess Resort & Casino** • This large resort, on both sides of West Sunrise Highway, results from the combining of Freeport's two grand Princess hotels. Guests enjoy the ample facilities of both establishments which include dining, sports, other recreation and, of course, the casino. Two golf courses are on tap and guests not using either of the two pools have free transportation to a nearby beach. The winding, shop-filled streets of the busy International Bazaar are a step away and the new Port Lucaya shopping center is a short bus ride away. The two hotels, the Princess Tower (where the casino is located), and the Princess Country Club are pleasantly landscaped and are an imposing sight seen together. The domed tower building has a Middle Eastern theme brought together in a lavish, blue tiled Moorish lobby with a grand piano in the center. The country club buildings are spread out, with much activity centered around the pool with its waterfall and swim-under bridge. All rooms are cheerfully furnished, equipped with television, and those in the tower have panoramic views of the city. A selection of restaurants such as Le Cotillion and Guanahani offer gourmet as well as Bahamian menus. There is plenty of outdoor space for sunning, reading, dozing, or just people watching.

☆☆☆ **Xanadu Beach Hotel** • Readily recognizable as the pyramid-topped, beige, high-rise with a cluster of villas at its base, Xanadu was once the hideaway of multi-millionaire recluse Howard Hughes. The hotel is connected with Club Land'or, operated by Resorts Condominiums International on Nassau's Paradise Island. Today's Xanadu is a modern refurbished accommodation with comfortable, well-furnished, balconied rooms and set on a peninsula formed by its own beach and its 72-slip marina on the canal waterway. When not basking on the beach, guests may use the pool where there is a bar and drink service. All water sports are offered, with golf at the Ruby or Emerald courses, short trips away. Tennis is on premises. Dining is offered at several locations, with the Persian Room, hung with handpainted silk as the softly lit, intimate room for Continental cuisine. The Escoffier Room is for gourmet dining as well as for Bahamian specialties. Breakfast and snacks are served in the Tiffany Room. On our most recent visit to this coffee shop, service was extremely slow and the food left much to be desired. Pre-dinner cocktails can be had at one of the bars in either the tower building or the pool wing. Howard Hughes' library is much as he left it. Entered through a wrought-iron gate, the cozy room has wood paneled walls, mirrors and backgammon tables.

INEXPENSIVE

Windward Palms Hotel • Just across from the International Bazaar, this small hotel has a pleasant pool area surrounded by colorful trees and flowers. Guests are given free transportation to a beach.

Castaways Resort • Next to the International Bazaar and the casino, this 138-room hotel has a bright, pagoda-inspired roof. There is a disco, the Yellowbird, and guests who forego the pool are transported free to a nearby beach.

Freeport Inn • Freeport Inn is not far from the Mall where the Bazaar and Straw Market are located. Guests have a choice of rooms with or without kitchenettes. There is free transportation to a beach, and staff can make arrangements for golf and various water sports. This no-frills hotel attracts visiting college students and has a popular disco/night club with live bands.

Lucaya

MODERATE

☆☆☆**Atlantik Beach Hotel** • This hotel has many of the features of larger accommodations and, like its Lucaya neighbors, it is sprucing up. Attractive features are its broad, wide beach and large swimming pool surrounded by terra-cotta tiles. The European management blends a continental approach with local ambience for a happy meeting ground. The gamut of water sports, including windsurfing and parasailing, can be had on premises as well as a variety of other activities. A hotel bus delivers guests to the hotel's 72-hole Lucaya Park Golf Club. A pleasant restaurant is next to the pool. The Sunday buffet remains popular. Although rooms are comfortable and well-furnished, note that they are reached by climbing or descending a short flight of stairs after leaving the elevator. Cars can be rented across the road at Avis and National.

★★★★ **Lucayan Beach Resort & Casino** • This hotel is set on just about the best beach in Lucaya. The low, sprawling resort is noted for its lighthouse tower, which stands above the two and three-story wings. Rooms are spacious with generous walk-in closets and come complete with terry robes. The large baths are marble, but over-the-counter lighting could be brighter, especially for shaving and makeup. All rooms have satellite television and king-size or oversize twin beds, with terraces or balconies, depending upon location. Deep, comfortable lobby chairs define relaxing areas and a bar is nearby. Proceeds from the wishing well leading to the Lucayan Room go to the Grand Bahama Children's Home. The casino is large and bright with all the traditional games of chance along with a bar and a cocktail area. Tennis courts are across the road, as is Reef Tours, which offers boating, sailing, and fishing trips on a glass-bottom boat. UNEXSO, the dive center, is also across the road as well as the new, upscale shopping center. There is free bus and ferry service between this and its sister hotel, the Lucayan Marina.

☆☆ **Holiday Inn** • The Holiday Inn's best feature is probably its extensive beach, where parasailing, waterskiing, and windsurfing are very much in evidence. On the way to the beach is the pool where entertainment seems always to be underway, making for a lively outdoor area, albeit somewhat noisy. The busy lobby has a number of shops and comfortable seating for waiting or lounging. The rooms have been attractively redone but, unfortunately service lags behind. Coffee shop service can be extremely slow and not all members of the reception staff are as pleasant as they might be. Also, for each traveler's check cashed, you pay ten cents, no matter what denomination. The Lucaya entertainment and shopping center is across the road, along with UNEXSO and car rentals.

INEXPENSIVE

Silver Sands Sea Lodge • Modest studio and one-bedroom apartments are available here; all have balconies overlooking the pool, the ocean, or the marina. The beach is within easy walking distance and the lodge has two tennis courts as well as paddleball and shuffleboard courts. The hotel's restaurant, La Phoenix, is popular among both locals and visitors.

☆☆☆ **Coral Beach Hotel** • Only a few of the studios and one-bedroom apartments in this condominium complex are rented to guests.

Facilities include a pool and a stunning beach, where guests can sail and snorkel. Fishing is also available, and golf can be arranged. The Sandpiper, a popular nightspot, is in this hotel.

West End

EXPENSIVE

☆☆**Jack Tar Village** • A vast, sprawling resort at Grand Bahama's West End, Jack Tar Village boasts the world's largest swimming pool. About 25 miles from Freeport, this self-contained complex offers a wide range of facilities. It is set on 2000 acres, has a 27-hole golf course, a private beach, a marina, a shopping area, and an airport. Rates are all-inclusive with free mopeds and bicycles.

Off East End

EXPENSIVE

☆☆**Deep Water Cay Club** • This small lodge, a short flight from Freeport, is the perfect place for divers and fishermen who want to enjoy their sports in seclusion. In addition to great bonefishing, a 20-mile barrier reef offshore, and blue holes to be explored, there are quiet unspoiled beaches where guests can snorkel over shallow reefs. Diving and fishing package deals are available. In a recent renovation the dining room and front patio have been extended, and a game room for cards and backgammon has been added.

THE FAMILY ISLANDS

Many visitors as well as Bahamians consider the Family Islands the most beautiful part of The Bahamas. These islands include all those other than New Providence and Grand Bahama, where Nassau and Freeport are located. The government changed the name from "Out Islands" to indicate that these islands are indeed part of the Bahamian family.

Except for small towns here and there and a few large-scale resorts, nature in these islands has been left almost intact. Countless palm-shaded beaches lapped by clear turquoise waters lie undisturbed. Where there are roads, they are often bordered by nothing but wind-blown pines and bushes for miles. While most fun for visitors revolves around watersports, there are also some natural and historical attractions. For seeing the sights, you can rent bicycles or cars or take taxi tours, but be prepared for bumpy roads and large old rattling cars.

Despite the People-to-People Program in Nassau and Freeport, visitors to the Family Islands have more of a chance to meet and socialize with islanders. Many hotels are the centers of activity for their areas and locals are invited to hotel parties and other events. By the same token, residents often invite visitors to town happenings, such as beach parties, parades, dances, and other celebrations. There is not much nightlife during the week, but on weekends something is always going on somewhere nearby. The Family Islands are not for those who are looking for casinos or hotel boutiques and beauty parlors. Don't expect phones, radios, or televisions in most guest rooms. Many hotels and restaurants communicate by VHF radio instead of phones. Also note that many hotels do not use keys for rooms, but safety deposit boxes are available. On some islands, boats, bikes, mopeds and golf carts are far more popular than cars.

On smaller islands, people may wear several hats, appearing as drivers, waiters, fishermen, carpenters, guides, or hotel workers. One of the popular social events is helping unload mailboats which come in every week or ten days. At airports where planes come in once or twice a week, there is also a gathering of onlookers.

The most developed islands are Eleuthera, Abaco, and Exuma. Off the coast of Eleuthera, Harbour Island is known for its pink sand beaches and picturesque Dunmore Town, reminiscent of New England. Green Turtle Cay, in the Abacos, is another pretty island that, like Harbour

Island, was settled by British Loyalists. In April, George Town, in Exuma, is alive with the colorful Family Island Regatta. Many divers make their way to Andros, where one of the world's largest barrier reefs is just offshore, and Long Island, where they can learn to swim among sharks. Inagua is great for birdwatching and Bimini attracts dedicated fishermen. The other Family Islands with tourist accommodations offer visitors even more opportunities for rest and relaxation.

Resorts on some islands will pick up guests in Florida or Nassau and fly them in on private planes. While some commercial airlines have direct flights from Florida to a few Family Islands, **Bahamasair** flies daily or weekly from Nassau to all of them. You may end up spending more time than planned between connecting flights because Bahamasair flights are often delayed. Bahamians are fond of saying, "If you have some time to spare, be sure to fly Bahamasair." However, Family Islands are worth the wait.

Attractions at a Glance

	Place	Page
The Abacos		
*New Plymouth	Green Turtle Cay	222
*Albert Lowe Museum	New Plymouth, Green Turtle Cay	222
Hope Town Lighthouse	Elbow Cay	223
Cholera Cemetery	Elbow Cay	223
Wyannie Malone Museum and Garden	Elbow Cay	223
Local Shipbuilding	Man-O-War Cay	223
*Sea and Land Park Preserve	Fowl Cay	223
Great Guana Cay	Between Treasure Cay and Marsh Harbour	223
Acklins/Crooked Island		
Bird Rock Lighthouse	Crooked Island Passage	231
*Crooked Island Caves	Crooked Island	231
Marine Farm	North End of Crooked Island Passage	231

THE BAHAMAS

	Place	Page
Castle Island Lighthouse	Castle Island, Acklins	233
*Southwestern Beaches	Crooked Island	231
*French Wells	Crooked Island	231

Andros

*Andros Barrier Reef	Parallel to the East Coast of Andros	240
Andros Reservoir	Nicholl's Town	242
*Ocean and Inland Blue Holes	Throughout the island	241
Atlantic Undersea Testing and Evaluation Centre (AUTEC)	Fresh Creek	241
Bahamas Agricultural Research Centre (BARC)	South of Nicholl's Town	242
Morgan's Bluff	North Andros	241
San Andros Pines	North Andros	241
Androsia Batik Works	Fresh Creek	241
Turnbull's Gut	Off Small Hope Bay Lodge	241
The Barge	Small Hope Bay Lodge	242

The Biminis

The Fountain of Youth	Near South Bimini Airport	249
Blue Marlin Cottage	Alice Town, North Bimini	249
*Hemingway Memorabilia	Compleat Angler Hotel, Alice Town	249
Straw Market	Alice Town	249
*Hall of Fame	Anchors Aweigh Guest House, Alice Town	249

	Place	Page
The *Sapona*	Between South Bimini and Cat Cay	249
The Lost Continent	Off North Bimini	249

Cat Island

Mt. Alvernia	Town of New Bight	252
The Hermitage	Town of New Bight	252
Deveaux Plantation	Town of Port Howe	252
Armbrister Plantation	Near Port Howe	252

Eleuthera

Gregory Town Plantation	Gregory Town	261
*Ocean Hole	Tarpum Bay	262
Preacher's Cave	Bridge Point	262
*Glass Window	Upper Bogue	262
Hatchet Bay Plantation	Hatchet Bay	262
Hatchet Bay Cave	Hatchet Bay	262
Titus Hole	Dunmore Town	262
Harbour Island Churches	Harbour Island	262

The Exumas

*The Exuma Land and Sea Park	North Exuma Sound	271
*Stocking Island	Exuma Sound, off George Town	271
St. Andrew's Church	George Town	272
The Hermitage	near George Town	272
Thunderball Grotto	Staniel Cay	272
Rolle Town Tomb	Rolle Town	272
Tropic of Cancer Marker	Little Exuma	272
Williams Town Salt Marsh	Williams Town	272
Patience House	Little Exuma	273
*Family Island Regatta	George Town	273

	Place	Page
Inagua		
*Inagua National Park	Matthew Town	275
The Lighthouse	Southwest Point	275
Salt Factory	Matthew Town	275
Long Island		
*Dunmore's Cave	Deadman's Cay	280
Dunmore Plantation	Deadman's Cay	280
Father Jerome's Churches	Clarence Town	280
Spanish Church	The Bight	280
Conception Island	Off Stella Maris	280
Deadman's Cay Caves	Deadman's Cay	280
Adderley Plantation	Cape Santa Maria	281
San Salvador		
Observation Tower	Near Riding Rock Inn	285
New World Museum	Cockburn Town	285
Columbus Monuments	Long Bay, Fernandez Bay, Crab Cay	285
Dixon Hill Lighthouse	Dixon Hill	285
Watling's Castle	Sandy Point Estate	286
Farquharson's Plantation	Pigeon Creek	286
Big Well	Sandy Point Estate	286
Dripping Rock	Sandy Point	286

THE ABACOS

Often referred to as Abaco, this is actually a cluster of islands and islets. Together these islands, The Bahamas northernmost, form the second largest grouping in the country, with some 650 square miles of land.

As in nearby Eleuthera, 18th-century colonial Loyalists from New England, North Carolina, and other parts of the Colonies fled the American Revolution and settled here. They were joined later by Englishmen and, during the Civil War, by American Southerners and their slaves. As on Eleuthera's Spanish Wells, today the populations of Man-O-War Cay, Elbow Cay, and Great Guana are predominantly white. The people have remained clannish and, until not too long ago banned blacks from the islands after the end of a working day.

Remnants of old loyalties seem persistent. In 1967, with the victory of the black-dominated Progressive Liberal Party, Abaco, which is about 50% white, voted to prevent such a win. Later, when the dominant party petitioned for independence, much of Abaco opposed the move and sought separation from The Bahamas to continue as a British Crown Colony. The effort failed, and the island seems to have come to terms with progress.

The Abacos are thick with an extensive growth of tropical pines, especially the feathery-needled casuarinas. Wild boar still roam some of the forests, providing meat for local tables, and often for festive barbecues at resorts. Most settlements have grown up on the east side of the island facing the Atlantic, protected by offshore cays and reefs and with magnificent views. Since many of the accommodations have housekeeping units in addition to individual rooms, families enjoy vacationing here. Ferries from Marsh Harbour take passengers to Elbow Cay and Man-O-War Cay.

Despite growing development to attract tourists, much of the untouched beauty of Abaco remains. There are long stretches of tropical trees and flowering shrubs. Local women still stroll gracefully along treeshaded lanes bearing trays of fruits and vegetables on their heads.

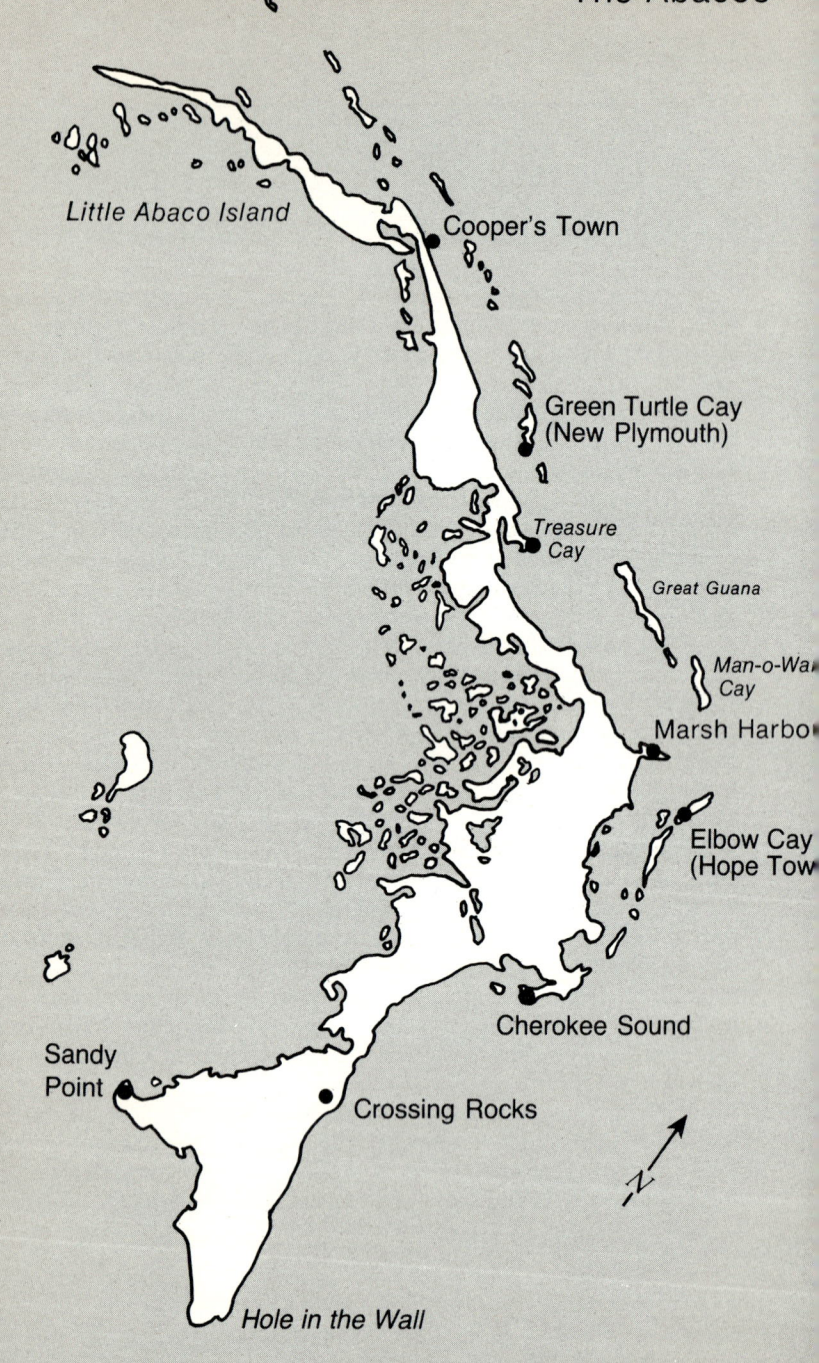

The Abacos

Walker's Cay

Little Abaco Island

Cooper's Town

Green Turtle Cay
(New Plymouth)

Treasure Cay

Great Guana

Man-o-War Cay

Marsh Harbor

Elbow Cay
(Hope Town)

Cherokee Sound

Sandy Point

Crossing Rocks

Hole in the Wall

Marsh Harbour

Marsh Harbour, nearly central, is the Abacos' chief town. Visitors will discover its supermarket, restaurants, and other conveniences. The airport at Marsh Harbour has an accompanying taxi stand with a dispatcher, and a restaurant and bar with snacks and drinks for travelers. Two other airports, at Treasure Cay and Walker's Cay, serve the Abacos' north and extreme northern ends.

Twice a week, the mailboat from Nassau ties up in town, bringing visitors, replenishing stores, and unloading materials for building, living, furnishing, and merely carrying on life in the Abacos.

Ferry services operate among Marsh Harbour, Treasure Cay to the northwest, and the offshore Elbow and Man-O-War cays.

Avid boaters, on craft of all sizes and descriptions, stream into the Abacos, with a good proportion winding up at Marsh Harbour for rest, food, and fuel. The settlement is also a center for those who prefer to charter a bareboat—a fully equipped yacht without a crew. If needed, you can hire a captain to go with the boat. If the boat is big enough, it is also possible to hire a crew. Almost any combination is available from the Bahamas Yachting Services (BYS), which does a brisk business.

Those with a thirst for the sea go to Marsh Harbour to be trained as sailors to navigate the surrounding waters. The BYS course is well defined and trainees are never sent out alone until fully ready. Even then, fast boats that can be alerted by radio stand by to assist anyone in trouble.

As you roam around the settlement, you may discover that an arresting aroma of baking bread comes from Keys Bakery, the oldest in the Abacos. More than 60 years old, the bakery is operated by Bunyan Keys, a retired justice-of-the-peace, and his daughter. They supply resorts and restaurants as well as locals and visitors.

Along with the resorts in Marsh Harbour, there is also a time-sharing development, Abaco Towns. This Mediterranean-style complex offers a touch of luxury in the midst of this mostly boating and fishing settlement.

Most visitors stay at the Conch Inn (pronounced "conk"). With its 67-slip marina, the inn is sea oriented, and its unique dining-front deskbar-game-reading room has a ship-to-shore radio that gets full use from a preponderance of boat-owning guests. People in from the off-island cays drop by for lunch when doing business in town. Each afternoon, sometimes until dusk, the elevated swimming pool and patio echo with splashing and shouts of the "wolleyball" game. When the game ends, the players, of both sexes, climb from the pool making for the showers and a drink before dinner at the convivial bar.

Most visitors who dine out in Marsh Harbour come off the boats that dock in the marinas, and many find their way to the Conch Inn. For good, local cooking, food at two in-town restaurants should be sampled. The popular **Cynthia's Kitchen** is in the center of town and has a bar. The dining room is informal, with hanging plants and plastic tablecloths. Diners can try the curried goat or fried grouper. Other delicacies on the menu are turtle steak, turtle pie, baked stuffed crabs, and Cynthia's own johnny cakes. On nights when the Conch Inn's restaurant is closed, guests walk over here. At **Mother Merl's** the fare also includes dishes not found on hotel menus, such as wild boar, goat, and turtle. **Wally's Restaurant** is open only on Monday nights and reservations are a must. **Vanessa's,** another local eating place, is on Forest Drive.

Treasure Cay

Despite its misleading name, Treasure Cay is on the mainland and is second to Marsh Harbour as an Abaco entry point. Like Marsh Harbour, it is easily reached from most of the Abacos. The Treasure Cay Beach Resort, with its inviting coastline, is the out-island center for golf and tennis enthusiasts.

Great Guana and Man-O-War Cays

North of Marsh Harbour are Great Guana and Man-O-War Cays. Great Guana has wide beaches with offshore reefs attractive to snorkelers and divers. Man-O-War Cay has long been a shipbuilding center. In season, the cay bustles with the activity of boats putting in for refueling, provisioning, sightseeing, or just to rest. There are few cars on the island and no hotels, liquor, or police.

Elbow Cay

Elbow Cay, a quiet and serene piece of land, also lies off Marsh Harbour. It is noted for its much-photographed red-and-white-striped Hope Town lighthouse, which can be seen from almost anywhere on the island. Before the installation of the lighthouse in the middle 1800s, many of Hope Town's inhabitants made a good living luring ships toward shore to be wrecked on the treacherous reefs and rocks so that their cargoes could be salvaged for cash. Visitors may climb the 130-foot lighthouse for views and photographs. **Rudy's Restaurant** is a good place to eat—try the delicious, imaginatively prepared lobster.

The main street, Queen's Highway, curls through Hope Town, following the land's configurations and passing white clapboard houses with a profusion of vines and flowers tumbling over picket fences. Were it not for the palms and other tropical vegetation, Hope Town might be a New England fishing village. The sea is never far from view, whether it is the pounding, crashing ocean, the calmer bay, or the serene harbor with its bobbing forest of masted boats.

The garden of the Wyannie Malone Museum is filled with plants and trees common to town. Set within the low, stone-walled garden are coconut palms, hibiscus, Norfolk pine, crotons, and sea grape, among other plants. It is startling to see an empty area here, a former cemetery closed many years ago after a cholera epidemic. There are no graves or headstones in evidence and the land is aptly called the Cholera Cemetery.

At first glance Hope Town Harbour Lodge seems just another of the white, clapboard houses along Queen's Highway. Then you notice that one wing is three stories, the only building that tall in the Family Islands. Across the road is the hotel's 175-year-old Butterfly House, adjoining the swimming pool.

Walker's Cay and Grand Cay

Walker's Cay and Grand Cay are two tiny islands seemingly cast off by Abaco and left to drift into the Atlantic. Walker's Cay attracts fishermen who come in search of the abundant variety of marine life and boaters who come to enjoy these small islands and others in the Bahamas chain. The island has one hotel and that's where the visitors stay if they're lucky enough to get accommodations.

Most of the hotel's workers live across the water on Grand Cay, where everyone has a boat instead of a car. The popular **Island Club Bar and Restaurant,** also known as Rosie's, brings visitors across in their own boats for lunch and dinner, or by Rosie's water taxi. Rosie Curry owns the restaurant as well as a modest motel. Also on the island is the **Seaside Disco and Bar,** near a cut bordered by a tangle of mangroves. The bar's walls are decorated with the nicknames of such patrons as "Thatch," "Hitman Rev," "The Sea Wolf," and "Flash Dancers." When they want a good beach, the locals, again by boat, take off for nearby Whale Bay Island, another minuscule dot in the Atlantic.

Green Turtle Cay

Green Turtle Cay, northwest of Marsh Harbour, is one of the most charming islands in The Bahamas. Like Hope Town, New Plymouth, its tiny town, resembles areas of Cape Cod and is reminiscent of those New England Loyalists who would not face the consequences of the American Revolution. You'll see goats and roosters as you walk along narrow, paved roads and hear children spelling in unison in a one-room schoolhouse. Barclay's, the lone bank, opens only once a week.

Lobsters trapped offshore have become a thriving local export business for American restaurants. If you're staying somewhere with kitchen facilities, this is a good place to buy fresh lobster for dinner.

At **Sea View Restaurant,** you can have a hearty, inexpensive Bahamian meal before strolling down to the beach. The casual, friendly restaurant has patrons' business cards, photographs of visitors, and dollar bills plastered to the walls. Other popular local restaurants are **Rooster's Rest,** next door to the **Gully Rooster,** where there are live bands on weekends, and **Sea Garden Restaurant. Miss Emily's Blue Bee Bar,** with a jukebox, is a good place to stop for a drink.

Visitors interested in history may stay at the restored New Plymouth Inn, a former private home dating back to the mid-19th century. The inn's lively restaurant is a popular spot. More history is found at the Albert Lowe Museum, which has a collection of hand-carved ships as well as information about the little island's early settlers.

For more good food, try Green Turtle Club and Bluff House. Reservations are recommended for dining at these two hotels, where restaurants specialize in seafood. The Green Turtle Club also has good beef dishes. The manager of the Green Turtle sparked the now popular annual sport fishing tournament held in April at the Green Turtle Club.

WHAT TO SEE AND DO

Sports • Serious divers go to Marsh Harbour, Walker's Cay, Elbow Cay, Green Turtle Cay, and Treasure Cay. Anglers and boaters have the run of the cays, with rewarding deep-sea fishing and convenient marinas. Tennis buffs can choose among Marsh Harbour, Treasure Cay, Green Turtle Cay, and the tonier Walker's Cay up north. Treasure Cay also has an 18-hole Dick Wilson–designed golf course. Windsurfing is available on Walker's Cay, Great Guana Cay, Elbow Cay, and Treasure Cay.

***New Plymouth** • *Green Turtle Cay* • This old and colorful village is much like a New England town except that the houses are pastel colors instead of white and gray, and there are palms and tropical flowers instead of ivy and geraniums. The entire cay is a must for visitors, particularly because it can be explored and appreciated on foot.

***Albert Lowe Museum** • *Green Turtle Cay* • This museum is in New Plymouth town and housed in one of the village's historic buildings. Exhibits go back to the early Loyalist settlers and include much other Bahamian history. There is a collection of model ships built by the late Albert Lowe, for whom the museum is named. The artwork of his son, Alton Lowe, one of the Bahamas' best-known artists, is on display, and you can purchase prints of his paintings.

Hope Town Lighthouse • *Elbow Cay* • Many visitors wind up at Elbow Cay to see and photograph the lighthouse. Beyond the candy-striped lighthouse are fantastic stretches of beach and seascape well worth investigating.

Cholera Cemetery • *Elbow Cay* • This lush, picturesque cemetery can be seen from the main street. Now without visible tombstones or gravesites, it was closed after a cholera epidemic in the last century.

Wyannie Malone Museum and Garden • *Elbow Cay* • The museum is a tribute to the South Carolinian woman who founded Hope Town in 1783. It gives some interesting details of the cay's history. The garden displays indigenous plants and trees. *Open 10 a.m.–noon.*

Local Shipbuilding • *Man-O-War Cay* • This cay was once one of the strongest contributors to the Bahamian economy as a center for shipbuilding. Although that industry has waned, some shipbuilding continues, and visitors may watch craftsmen at work. A sunken ship of the Union Navy, the *U.S.S. Adirondack,* lies off Man-O-War Cay. It was wrecked on a reef in the middle 1800s and can now be explored by divers.

*Sea and Land Preserve • *Fowl Cay* • North of Man-O-War Cay, Fowl Cay is a Bahamian government sea and land park reserve. Divers can explore undersea caves and the shallow reefs that are also accessible to snorklers.

Great Guana Cay • Divers and snorklers are enthusiastic about Great Guana Cay for its beaches and the coral and marine life seen in its clear waters. The Treasure Cay Resort uses part of the island as a playground.

WHERE TO STAY

Marsh Harbour

INEXPENSIVE

☆☆ **The Conch Inn** • This hotel is only 10 minutes from the airport but its most enthusiastic guests are the boaters who come to tie up, have a drink at the bar, and join in the "wollyball" game that takes place in the pool with the guests. In addition to using its 67 slips, boaters who do not take rooms get everything from berths to baths as well as laundry services, mail, and messages. The needs of guests are seen to under the watchful eyes of the managers, who are always nearby when needed. Most rooms, furnished in sunny yellows and apple greens, have small terraces overlooking the harbor and its moored boats and, sometimes, a spectacular sunset. Across the road are a couple of air-conditioned housekeeping units with kitchens and screened porches. The convivial dining-reception-lounge-bar-and-ship-to-shore-radio room, done in a nautical theme, is the gathering place for breakfast and lunch. It also attracts locals and others from the offshore cays who are in town on business and other errands. The more formal restaurant, down the path, is open in the evening and presided over by the maitre d'. This pleasant dining room also has a view of the harbor and its twinkling night lights. There are three areas on two levels with color-splashed Haitian paintings hung against stark white walls. Corner tables have large rattan fan chairs.

Ambassador Inn • This modest accommodation is for those with very modest budgets. In the middle of Marsh Harbour, it is near shopping, banks and other services. Rooms are air-conditioned. The beach and boating facilities are a short walk away.

☆☆☆ **Great Abaco Beach Hotel** • This, the most modern hotel in Marsh Harbour, faces its own beach, which is viewed from the terraces of all its rooms. There are five two-bedroom villas as well. The rooms have king and queen sized beds, white wicker furnishings, telephones, television, and baths with dressing areas. Meals are served in a round dining room with a bar at its center. One side looks out to the beach and the palm shaded lawns. There is a small lobby gift shop, a 120-slip marina, a pool and a Jacuzzi. On weekends there is local entertainment and a live band two nights a week. The ferries to Elbow Cay and Man-O-War Cay are a short walk away.

☆☆ **Lofty Fig Villas** • Lofty Fig's six green painted units are ranged about a kidney-shaped swimming pool. All have screened-in porches and there are spacious rooms with double beds and a sofa bed. There are also kitchens, dining areas and baths. The carpeted units have ceiling fans as well as air conditioning.

Treasure Cay

MODERATE

☆☆☆ **Treasure Cay Beach Hotel & Villas** • Treasure Cay Beach Hotel & Villas, a small village in itself, has developed as one of Abaco's unique vacation resorts. It is served by the island's northern airport, about fifteen minutes away. In addition to Bahamasair flights from Nassau, Aero Coach, Gull Air, Helda Air and Lucayan Air Service fly guests in from Fort Lauderdale, Miami, Palm Beach and Freeport.

Because of the size of this all-inclusive resort, guests are given maps showing the location of places such as the grocery store, liquor store, the bank and post office, the doctor's and dentist's offices, the pharmacy, the beauty salon, the boutique and other services.

Rooms and suites in the double-story hotel and villas are pleasant and comfortably furnished. None of the hotel rooms are beachfront. All are air conditioned and all but those in the villas have cable TV. Landscaped grounds and paths lead to well-placed time share units and the villas. An especially attractive group of villas called Harbour House contains strikingly furnished rooms with walls hung with tropic-colored Dong Kingman water colors. These villas face Clipper Cay across a lagoon and the 150-slip marina is nearby.

A deeply curved, 3½ mile, white sand beach offers such attractions as fishing, sailing, scuba, snorkeling and aqua biking. The Sandbar restaurant and Boat Bar provide snacks and drinks for bathers. Toward the boat-filled marina is one of the resort's three swimming pools and the Tipsy Seagull bar with its adjacent grill. Next door is the dive shop providing the full range of waterside equipment and snorkeling gear.

An 18-hole Dick Wilson–designed course attracts golf enthusiasts at one of the few Family Island courses. There are both hard and soft tennis courts as well as four for night games. A night club is on premises and a separate disco often brings in live musicians.

Cars and bicycles can be rented for exploration of the island's undeveloped areas beyond the resort. Guests can find secluded, pristine beaches and tiny, colorful settlements waiting for discovery, making them feel like modern Columbuses. Ferry service can be arranged for trips to offshore points such as Green Turtle Cay, Man-O-War Cay and Elbow Cay.

Full meals are served in the resort's dining room. For a change of pace, some adventurous visitors, seeking "native" food, try **Touch of Class** or **Traveller's Nest,** nearby local restaurants.

Green Turtle Cay

MODERATE

★★★**Green Turtle Club** • Over the years, this casually elegant resort has drawn guests from Dr. Joyce Brothers and Kenny Rogers to Jimmy Carter and Charles Schultz. The low gray villas and the white clubhouse with its green awning are strikingly attractive from the water, especially in the late afternoon when they are sparkling in the orange glow of the sun. Boats always fill the new-looking marina. Upon arrival, guests are greeted with "Tipsy Turtles," the hotel's legendary potent fruity concoction. In the bar/lounge in the clubhouse, yachting club flags hang from the ceiling beams and the walls are papered with dollar bills. During the days when commercial flights to the Family Islands were limited or nonexistent, private pilots, many of whom had flown in WWII, would write their names on dollars, paste them to the walls, and say, "If I don't come back, have a drink on me." Other visitors have carried on this old wartime tradition (and taken it a bit further). While people gather in the lounge for cocktails, it is not unusual to see a man hoist a woman onto his shoulders so that she may stick a bill on the ceiling. If you play the piano or a guitar in the lounge, your drinks are on the house.

Managers Bill and Donna Rossbach run Green Turtle Club as if they were entertaining friends in their home. There is one seating for dinner, and Donna leads guests into the dining room table by candlelit table. The delicious food is beautifully presented. Individual rooms, suites, and villas with private marinas are available. All units are spacious, with paneled walls, carpeting, sliding glass doors, and air conditioning. The ocean beach is about a 10-minute walk away from the clubhouse, and the one on the bay is about five minutes away. The reef just 50 yards off the beach makes for excellent snorkeling. Brendal's Dive Shop has a very good diving and snorkeling program. There is a large pool as well as tennis courts. Guests have free use of snorkeling gear, fishing tackle, and windsurfers. Those who aren't in the mood for the long walk into town may take the complimentary boat ride. Once a week, the hotel takes guests on a boat trip to Man-O-War Cay and Marsh Harbour (about $25). Green Turtle Club provides charter air service from Palm Beach and Ft. Lauderdale. Make arrangements by contacting the club.

★★★ **Bluff House Club & Marina** • Many people make a habit of returning to this beautiful hotel perched high above a private beach. Guests are picked up by ferry at Treasure Cay and brought to suites, villas with full kitchens, and individual rooms. Over the years, Bluff House has expanded from 8 guest rooms in the main house to more than 30 in various wings. All have private porches. Some of the modern, air-conditioned units are duplexes. Appointments include wicker chairs, floral conches, ginger jar lamps, weathered wood paneling, and wall-to-wall carpeting. Guests no longer stay in the main house, where sliding glass doors open onto a wooden patio and the pool. The sunny split-level lounge, overlooking the pool and the ocean, is decorated with tiles, a driftwood coffee table, paintings, and framed posters. In the dining room, which draws a steady stream of outsiders, many guests ask to be seated at the huge round oak table in the center, with its highbacked chairs. Ferry rides to the town of New Plymouth as well as tennis and tennis racquets are free to those staying here. The staff will arrange fishing and snorkeling excursions.

★★ **Linton's Beach and Harbour Cottages** • There are only two rental cottages here, with two bedrooms each, and they are on a long quiet beach. This is a good choice if privacy and complete comfort are what you want. With high-beamed ceilings, walls paneled in rich brown Abaco pine, ceiling fans, rattan furniture, and screened-in porches with hammocks, each is quite attractive. Linens and all kitchen utensils are supplied. Maid and cook service is available for an additional $45 a day. Many palmettos, seagrapes, white lilies, avocado trees, and huge casuarinas surround the cottages. Near the manager's house on the bay side you can relax in a hammock in a small screened-in cottage called "the Conch Out Lounge."

MODERATE–INEXPENSIVE

☆☆**Coco Bay Club** • These three rental cottages, with fully equipped kitchens, are in an excellent location. The land is so narrow here that guests are right near both the ocean and the bay. The two small two-bedroom cottages are paneled in dark pine. Louvered doors divide the bedrooms from the kitchens. Although the three-bedroom cottage is not always available for rent (the owners often use it), it's definitely worth asking about. It has a huge modern kitchen/dining/living room with bright white cabinets, rattan furniture, and a wonderful ocean view. Many fruit trees grow on the grounds, including those bearing sweet and sour oranges, mangos, papayas, and tangerines. Guests are welcome to help themselves (as long as they aren't gluttons, the managers say). Boat rentals and fishing trips can be arranged through Coco Bay.

INEXPENSIVE

★★**New Plymouth Inn** • Staying at this old home with high ceilings and antique furniture may make you think you've slipped back in time. The 10 inviting guest rooms, all with private baths, have old-fashioned quilts on the beds, attractive floral wallpaper, and handsome chairs and chests. Books line shelves in the hallway. A large octagonal Mexican brasero table sits in the center of the living room. Instead of coals in the center, you'll see fresh hibiscus. The shell of a giant turtle hangs on a wicker partition in the bar area. Paintings decorate the walls, and lanterns hang from the ceiling. The inn was once the home of Captain Billy Roberts, whose ghost is said to appear from time to time. But don't let that scare you away from this charming place. While New

Plymouth is in town, it has a pool, and beaches are not far. Guests can also arrange to go boating, diving, and fishing.

☆ **Sea Star Cottages** • These four housekeeping cottages are in extensive shady grounds along a long narrow beach. You'll see breadfruit trees, pigeon plum trees, and even bamboo. Fishing groups not looking for posh accommodations are attracted to these simple cottages, which are generally rented by the week. Town is about a 15-minute walk away.

Elbow Cay

MODERATE

★★★**Abaco Inn** • This resort is for sybarites fleeing daily chores and cares who are ready for pampering and fine dining. Getting away from it all at Abaco Inn means no radios, televisions, or newspapers. All rooms have books, however. They are numerous and apparently well read. Pampering comes with a variety of gourmet meals including five-course dinners. Among the main courses are Cornish hen, tenderloin, crawfish, duck, and that Bahamian specialty, grouper. Mouthwatering desserts like chocolate peppermint silk, hot apple coconut crisp, and key lime pie delight the palate. Hot cinnamon rolls might turn up for breakfast and a crawfish quiche might be on the lunch menu. There is a rustic touch in the furnishings of the 10 cottages, but comfort is not sacrificed to decor. All rooms are air-conditioned and there are ceiling fans as well. A hammock big enough for two is strung outside each cottage, for lounging, reading, or dozing. The inn stands on a narrow strip of Elbow Cay where the ocean's froth-crested surf washes the beach on one side while the tranquil waters of White Sound bathe the other. Overlooking the ocean is a sun-bleached gazebo and a salt-water swimming pool. Tucked away, a bit up the beach, is a secluded area for guests who prefer taking full advantage of the sun by nude bathing. Ruth Maury, the on-premises host, goes out of her way to create an ideal resort.

MODERATE TO INEXPENSIVE

★★ **Hope Town Harbour Lodge** • With individual rooms, cottages, and a historic dwelling, Butterfly House, for rent, this comfortable hotel in the center of Hope Town appears to be just another New England–like dwelling on a street with similar homes. But when you view it from the rear, you'll see that this charming lodging sits high on a promontory overlooking the harbor and the Hope Town lighthouse. An outdoor terrace on this side makes for dramatic dining and drinking. Historic Butterfly House, across the main road, accommodates families or groups. There is a fresh-water swimming pool as well as the ocean, and a variety of watersports can be arranged. Norris Smith, the young, European-trained Bahamian chef adds an international flair to Bahamian/continental favorites.

Elbow Cay Beach Inn • This hotel, set on 100 acres, is the oldest on the island. A Danish couple, Annie and Robert Maltarp, have operated it since 1970. There is a miniature beach on the bay and excellent snorkeling. The hotel will arrange for windsurfing and its own 38-foot cruise craft will take guests to Sandy Cay (also called Pelican Cay) and Tiloo Cay for picnics, snorkeling and conching trips. The Maltarp son takes guests on scuba excursions. The rooms, some of which were undergoing renovation at press time, were somewhat run down on our last visit. Hope Town is about a mile and a half away and you can walk there along the beach. On Friday nights, almost all the young people from Elbow Cay and Man-O-War Cay descend upon the hotel to dance to the live band.

Walker's Cay

MODERATE

Walker's Cay Hotel & Marina • This is the only hotel on this minute island. When the plane lands, it seems to be headed directly for the other side of the island and into the water. Boaters and fishermen come to the hotel in droves. Other guests are not always as enthusiastic; the hotel is not on a beach and what beaches there are are unmemorable. The hotel has modern rooms in two buildings as well as separate villas. The rooms are spacious and comfortable, with balconies. Rooms in the Hibiscus wing are motel-like, while those in the Coral wing are more upscale. The fishing orientation is reflected in the bar-lounge, where the walls are adorned with giant barracuda, bonefish, sharks, and marlin. There are also photographs of fishermen posing with their catches. The energetic head for the two swimming pools, one salt and the other fresh, and the multipurpose Sport Court where guests can have a go at tennis as well as paddle tennis, pickle ball, basketball, hockey, "wacketball," and soccer tennis. The Lobster Trap, the bar, billiard room, and disco at the marina, is the place to go on weekends. The marina also has showers and a grocery and supply store. Nearby is Aqualife, where visitors can see tropical fish, mainly from the Pacific, in large open tanks going through varying stages of development. Wondrous to see are black, iridescent fish with bright blue and purple stripes or orange and red tiger stripes. The fish appear to be thin neon lights flashing back and forth in the dark tanks. In this commercial undertaking the fish are sold to wholesalers who, in turn, sell them to pet stores. Free tours are conducted in season. Arrangements for tours can be made at the hotel's front desk.

ACKLINS/CROOKED ISLAND

Together Acklins and Crooked Island comprise an almost 200-square-mile area and are about 223 miles southeast of Nassau. The islands, separated by the narrow Crooked Island Passage sprinkled with tiny cays, is still an important sea lane on the southern route. Twice a week, planes visit Spring Point on Acklins and Colonel Hill on Crooked Island.

The islands are a point of interest for fishermen, boaters cruising the southern Bahamas, and devoted divers, all of whom are attracted to the fishing and diving possibilities off Landrail Point on Crooked Island. Since the islands do not swarm with tourists, those who do come can expect leisure and serenity at one of the few places of accommodation.

The first known settlers of these islands were Loyalists who arrived toward the end of the eighteenth century. Soon almost 50 plantations had sprung up, with hundreds of slaves working the fields. But by the 1820s most of the plantations lay in ruins, the crops having been destroyed by blight.

Most activity is centered on the smaller, 70-square-mile Crooked Island. This is where visitors find the one resort, Pittstown Point Landing, and a few guest houses. The mailboat from Nassau makes the overnight trip twice a month. Small farming and fishing are the principal industries and a fish processing plant is under development. There are few telephones and communication is mainly by CB and marine radio.

The capital is Colonel Hill, a small settlement with colorful, painted wood and cement buildings. In Church Grove stands tiny **Tiger Bar,** the first drinking establishment on the island. Every Friday night, dances are held at the **Bloom of the Valley** bar and pool hall, across the street from the **Hillside Grocery** store. There are other minute settlements like Cripple Hill, with about a dozen residents; Moss Town, with the houses clustered around the Anglican church, and, to the northeast, Landrail Point where nearly all the residents are Seventh Day Adventists.

Beyond Landrail Point are several private, beachfront homes owned by Americans and other foreigners. At a salt pond, just outside of town, you'll see flamingos, tropical birds with long, thin tails, mocking birds, finches, wild canaries, and humming birds. The 33 miles of barrier reef off the islands make for excellent diving and snorkeling. Boats are unnecessary for seeing the exciting coral formations and colorful fish. Masks and fins are all that are needed.

Pilots were the first to "discover" Crooked Island in the fifties and built some of the early beachfront homes. One American describes the island as "the kind of place where, if I lost my wallet, someone would look inside to see who it belonged to, then walk two miles to return it."

A government-provided "ferry" at the southeast tip of Crooked Island takes visitors across to Lovely Bay on Acklins. Driving from Pittstown Point Landing to the ferry takes about an hour and a quarter. Hard woods such as mahogany and lignum vitae are found on Acklins, as well as the bark used to make Campari. Many of the houses on the island have dirt-floored, separate kitchens. In some, a corn grinder, used for making one of the staples, grits, stands in the corner.

WHAT TO SEE AND DO

Bird Rock Lighthouse • *Crooked Island Passage* • If there were more visitors, the gleaming-white Bird Rock Lighthouse guarding Crooked Island Passage would be as famed and photographed as the lighthouse at Hope Town in the Abacos.

***Crooked Island Caves** • Like many other islands in The Bahamas, Crooked Island is riddled with caves. These look like majestic, ancient cathedrals, or medieval castles that have fallen into ruins. It is best to explore them with a Bahamian guide. Harmless bats cling to cave ceilings and, in some, sunlight streams through in bright fingers.

***Southwestern Beaches** • *Crooked Island* • Snorklers head for Shell Beach, with its underwater coral heads. Bathing Beach offers an expanse of smooth sand below translucent water. Schools of flying fish sail through the air. On nearby shores slabs of coral look strangely like ancient stone steps. Arrange boat trips at Pittstown Pt. Landing.

***French Wells** • *Crooked Island* • Flamingos beach here but swimming is not recommended because sharks have been sighted. Take a boat trip up a mangrove-lined cut to see barracudas and other fish through the calm, crystal water.

Marine Farm • *North end of Crooked Island Passage* • This is the ruin of a Bahamian fort. It was built by Britain to guard Crooked Island

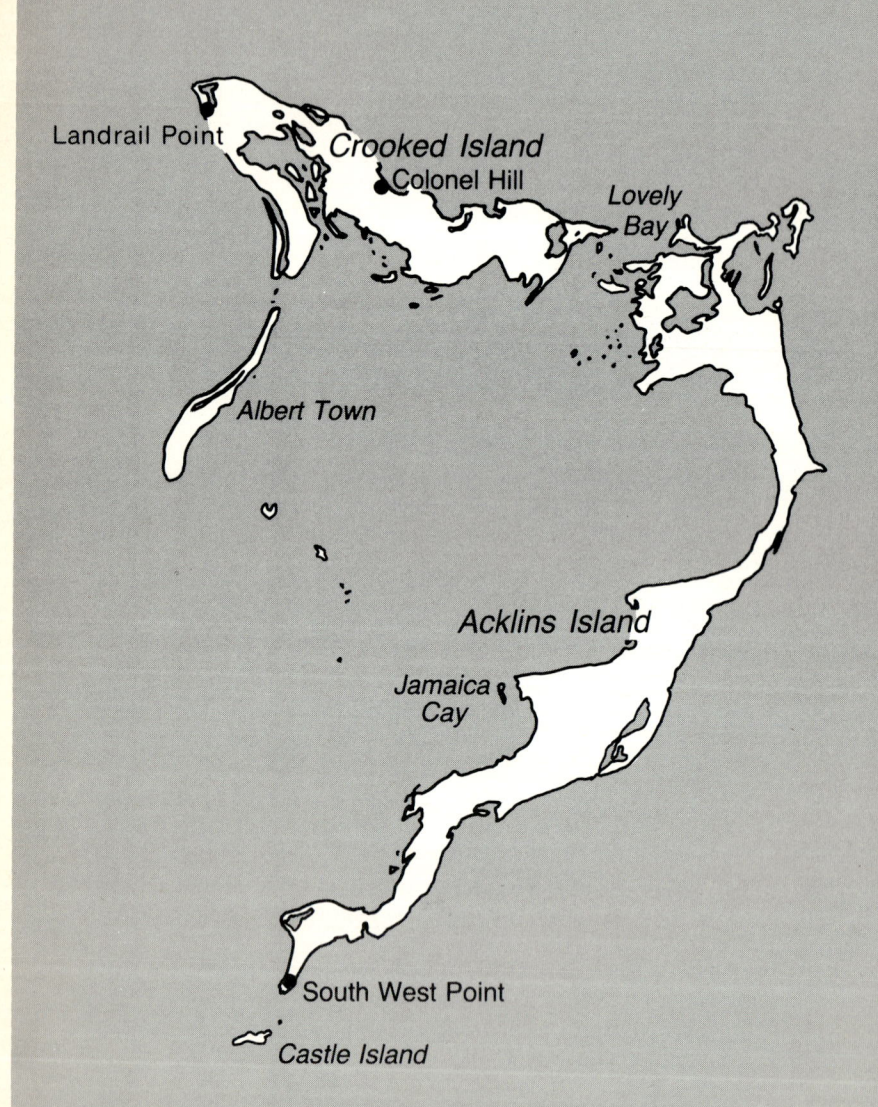

Acklins-Crooked Island

Passage against marauding pirates. Although rusted, markings on the cannons are well-preserved.

Castle Island Lighthouse • *Castle Island, Acklins* • This lighthouse, built in 1867, guides shipping through a passage that was once used by pirates escaping pursuit.

Mayaguana • *across the Mayaguana Passage, and flanked by Acklins and Crooked Islands as well as Inagua* • The 24-mile long island has few more than 400 inhabitants, who are almost completely out of touch with the capital at Nassau. The forests are rich in hardwoods, especially lignum vitae. The U.S. had established a missile-tracking station on the island. There are two acceptable harbors, inviting beaches, and astounding vistas. Because there are no accommodations for tourists, Mayaguana is visited mainly by boaters. It remains quiet, undeveloped, and undisturbed.

WHERE TO STAY

INEXPENSIVE

☆☆☆ **Pittstown Point Landing** • This hotel is 16 miles from the Colonel Hill airport. If there are no taxis, by asking at the airport you'll find a driver who'll charge from $25 to $40 for the trip to the hotel. The hotel has its own airstrip and most guests arrive in their own private planes. The management will arrange for guests to be flown in from Florida, Nassau, or George Town in Exuma. The rooms, with two double beds, bright baths, and good reading lights are comfortable but somewhat spartan. The bar, separated from the dining room by the kitchen, is built around what is said to be the first post office in the Bahamas. Guests get to know each other over meals, games, drinks, discussions about birds sighted during the day, and, of course planes. Guests also get to know the staff. The cook often doubles as a waitress; the bartender might take a group on an excursion to the caves, or the assistant manager might take guests bonefishing. The gift shop, where the register is signed, sells Androsia batik resort wear as well as T-shirts, books, film and toilet articles. Things are casual, although house rules are outlined in a booklet found in your room. In regard to proper dinner attire, for example, it says, "Hair on the chest and low cleavage are great but distract the attention from things on your plate."

Crooked Island Beach Inn • *Colonel Hill* • Owned and operated by Ezekial Thompson, a Bahamasair agent, this comfortable rustic inn has eleven rooms and is near the airport. Guests can arrange for meals, although there are kitchens, and cars can be rented for about $50 per day.

ANDROS

Andros, 108 miles long, about 40 miles across at its widest point, and covering 2300 square miles, is the largest of the Bahama islands. It is interlaced with channels, bays, bights, and inlets. These waterways, called creeks by locals but seeming more like bays and rivers to outsiders, divide the island into three main sections.

Running almost parallel to the east coast is the awesome 120-mile-long Andros Barrier Reef, which is in the league of Australia's Great Barrier Reef. Multicolored marine life of all kinds is found in these waters.

Ocean blue holes, fathomless fresh-water columns of deep cobalt and ultramarine rising from the depths are also offshore. Benjamin's Blue Hole is one that has attracted wide interest. In 1967 Dr. George Benjamin found stalactites and stalagmites 1200 feet under the sea. His conclusion was that The Bahamas are really the peaks of former mountains, since such formations never occur under water. Benjamin's Blue Hole and Uncle Charley's Blue Hole have been featured in the Jacques Cousteau television series on oceanic exploration. In addition, more than 100 inland holes have also been found on the island. Examples are Captain Bill's, near Andros Town and Evansville, not far from Nicholl's Town. The island is also riddled with intricate underground caves such as those at Morgan's Bluff.

Andros has the best farming land in The Bahamas as well as an abundance of plant life found nowhere else. It is said to be the home of nearly 50 kinds of wild orchids. A new species of peony, the white-petaled P. *mascula* subspecies *hellenica,* was recently discovered here, according to Niki Goulandris, a botanist and botanical painter.

Some seven miles south of the San Andros airport is The Bahamas Agricultural Research Centre. Presently headed by Dr. Godfrey Springer, a Tuskegee Institute–trained veterinarian, BARC advises and assists local farmers in obtaining maximum production from their land. The center was established in 1973 through the cooperation of the U.S. agency for International Development and the Bahamian government. Visitors are welcomed to the facility and given interesting and informative tours.

At the center's large packing house hangar, vegetables such as potatoes, okra, cucumbers, cabbage, tomatoes, and some grains are brought in for sorting, grading, packing, and shipment to Nassau. Other products grown on Andros are papayas, cantaloupes, strawberries, and a variety of citrus fruits.

Another section of the center is devoted to breeding and raising improved strains of horses, cattle, and other livestock such as sheep, hogs, and poultry. Dr. Springer attests that there is no rabies in The Bahamas and that a rigid inspection program is in force for meats such as beef and mutton.

Andros supplies much of the nation's fresh water. A reservoir can be seen along the Queen's Highway on the way to Nicholl's Town from the San Andros airport. Almost three million gallons of water are shipped by barge each day from the port at Morgan's Bluff to New Providence, just 20 miles across the channel. Because the deep Tongue of the Ocean divides the channel, barges are the only way of transporting fresh water across. One of the engineers says that bad weather sometimes interrupts water shipments and worries that continued development and growth in Nassau might soon overtax the supply.

Some of this feeling probably accounts for plans to increase tourism on Andros itself. As the largest of the islands, there is lots of room for development, some interesting, tourist-worthy sights, as well as attractive and varied landscapes. A hotel is proposed for a site high on Morgan's Bluff, overlooking the channel from which, at night, the sparkling lights of Nassau can be seen. Another plan is to rebuild and refurbish a superbly situated former luxury resort at Fresh Creek called The Lighthouse Club and Marina.

A station of the Atlantic Undersea Testing and Evaluation Center (AUTEC) is also located at Fresh Creek. This research station is jointly operated by the British and U.S. governments. It was established in 1966 as an antisubmarine research center and is protected from heavy ocean traffic by the offshore Tongue of the Ocean chasm.

Northern Andros has a rocky shoreline with froth-crested waves dashing against its cliffs. Its southern shores are less rocky, with great stretches of empty, palm-fringed, sandy beaches that can make visitors feel like modern-day Robinson Crusoes.

About two miles south of Nicholl's Town, at Conch Sound, is a tiny settlement devoted to fishing and boat repair. It was once the site of a thriving local boat construction industry. The boats were then used primarily for spongers.

If on schedule, the mailboat stops weekly at Morgan's Bluff, Mastic Point, Stafford Creek, Fresh Creek, and Mangrove Cay. The boat brings supplies to the various points and returns with deliveries and passengers. The arrival of the mailboat is a signal for a social occasion, with locals suspending their activities to see who and what is arriving and to catch up on bits of news and gossip.

Similar gatherings also take place at the airports of Andros, which are located in the north at San Andros, farther south at Andros Town, and still farther south at Moxey Town and Congo Town. Very often visitors arrive at an Andros airport wondering what awaits them on this new island. These very same visitors later leave feeling that old friends are being left behind and vowing to return. Some experiences have reinforced a belief among visitors that Family Island Bahamians are some of the most pleasant and hospitable people ever encountered during their travels.

Fishing and Hunting

Andros is known as the bonefish capital of the world. Marlins and tarpons are found in the surrounding waters as well as reef-seekers such as snapper, amberjack, yellowtail, and grouper. During the tourist off season, from about June until September, land crabs crawl across the beach to lay their eggs. Beachcombers can simply pick up the crabs and have one or two for dinner.

The forests are thick with pine, mahogany, and other tropical trees. These woods are an excellent habitat for quail, ducks, partridges, marsh hens, and parrots, which are hunted by enthusiastic nimrods during the September through March season. In September and October, hunters in camouflage fatigues hunt white crown pigeons in the forests of South Andros.

History and Folklore

Andros, then populated by Lucayan Indians, is said to have been visited by the Spaniards in search of slave labor to work in Hispaniola. Both during and after the Seminole Wars in the United States, Seminole and Creek Indians, African slaves, and escaped slaves who had intermarried with Native Americans fled Florida to northern Andros. They landed at Joulter Cays and later filtered south to the mainland at what is now Morgan's Bluff and Red Bay. Other former slaves, freed by the British, came from Exuma and Long Island on the other side of the Tongue of the Ocean, settled in southern Andros, and took up farming.

Later in the 19th century, sponging became a thriving and lucrative industry in Andros. This undersea organism was found in abundant supply off the mud flats of the southwest coast. Until then, the chief industry had been ship wrecking for often very valuable cargoes. Sponging continued until the late 1930s, when an unknown blight killed only the sponges and no other marine life. Another profitable industry was sisal production, the plant used in rope making. Sisal grew well in the Andros soil, but this industry also waned in the early 1920s. From the sixties until well into the seventies, the U.S. company Owens-Illinois harvested Andros timber for pulp production. To facilitate shipment, a system of crushed limestone roads was built by the company. The roads remain, now somewhat in disrepair, but that industry, too, departed leaving a pocket of unemployment.

Sir Henry Morgan, the notorious pirate, is said to have established his headquarters in north Andros at the point now called Morgan's Bluff, which looks out toward the Berry Islands. According to legend, Morgan buried some of his ill-gotten treasure near the site. However, searches both serious and frivolous have uncovered nothing.

Another persistent legend tells tales of chickcharnies. These are impish, mischievous, red-eyed, feathered creatures with three-toes and three-fingers and a long, prehensile tail. Some say chickcharnies have the ability to turn their heads completely around. They are said to live in the pine and hardwood forests of Andros and are not found on any of the other islands.

If a wanderer happens upon a chickcharney and treats it well, then blessings and good fortune follow. However, if the chickcharney is mistreated, the wanderer can be struck by the direst misery, which can last a lifetime. Having done its mischief, the chickcharney scampers merrily off into the forest. Today, locals with a twinkle in their eyes warn each other of the wrath of mischievous chickcharnies and frighten naughty children into obedience.

Red Bay Village is said to be near the home of a primitive people who maintain old tribal traditions, still use bows and arrows, and dwell in the forests. Although this belief persists, no evidence of such people has been found. Some believe that the legendary tribe are descendants of the mixed Africans and Seminoles who fled slavery and war in Florida.

Exploring Andros

In North Andros the unusually tall, straight pines look like telephone poles with trees stuck on top. Most of the action is in Nicholl's Town. Many divers and other vacationers stay here at the Andros Beach Hotel, where the staff will be happy to arrange guided trips to see the tallest pines or to the caves in nearby Morgan's Bluff. The hotel bar is a popular hangout for locals and tourists. Formerly part of the hotel, the 40 modern villas bordering the two adjacent streets are now owned by Americans, Canadians, and other foreigners. A small shopping center, with a bank, a drugstore, a liquor store, and a grocery store, is just down the street.

The residential road leading to the tiny town is filled with the sound

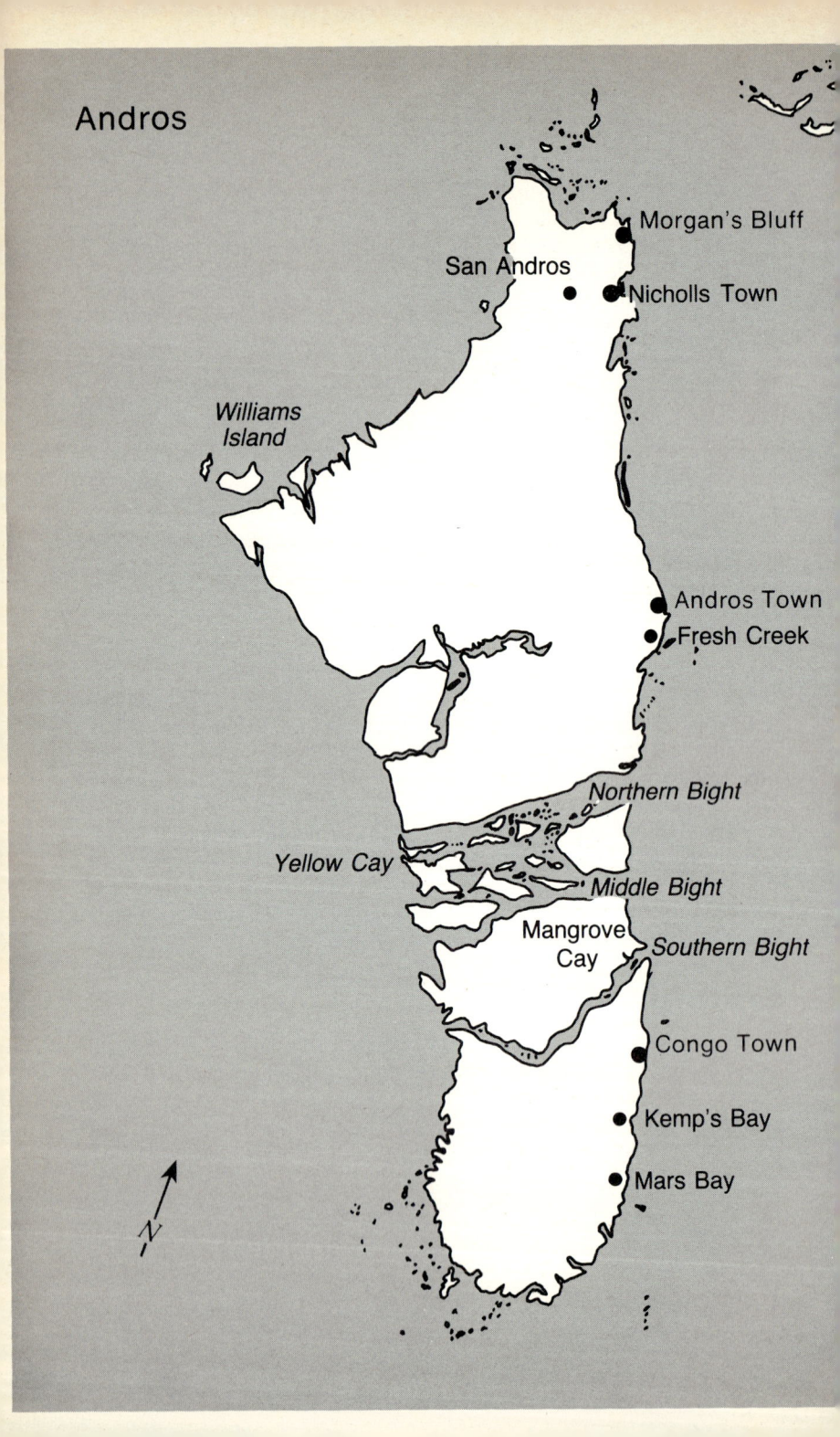

Andros

- Morgan's Bluff
- San Andros
- Nicholls Town
- Williams Island
- Andros Town
- Fresh Creek
- *Northern Bight*
- *Yellow Cay*
- *Middle Bight*
- Mangrove Cay
- *Southern Bight*
- Congo Town
- Kemp's Bay
- Mars Bay

N

of roosters crowing to each other. The small, colorfully painted wooden houses are overhung with palm fronds and the bright green leaves of banana trees. A 15-minute walk to town will take you past stores such as **Curry's Grocery** and **Wellie's Variety,** and the popular **Picaroon Restaurant** near the beach. Mr. and Ms. Henfield have run the restaurant, affectionately called Picaroonie's by locals, for over 25 years. They serve chicken, ribs, and fish Bahamian style. Next door at the Henfield's gift shop, you can rent bicycles for about $12 a day.

Other good restaurants in town are **Hunter's** with a bar and satellite television, and **Donna Lee's.** Both also have inexpensive guest rooms and often give parties on weekends to which everyone, including tourists, is invited. If you didn't rent a car at the airport or through the Andros Beach Hotel, you can rent one at Hunter's. **Pinewood Cafeteria** and **Paula's Inn** also serve homestyle food.

Not far from Nicholls Town, in the Pleasant Harbour area, are nicely landscaped beachfront homes owned by foreigners. When the tide is low you can walk out to uninhabited Money Cay to collect colorful shells.

A Bahamas Agricultural Research Demonstration Project at North Andros carries out experiments for the development of Andros as a farming and livestock-raising area. The two-million-gallon reservoir, also at North Andros, produces more than six million gallons of fresh, potable water each day, a record for the islands of The Bahamas.

Most visitors to Andros Town, south of Nicholl's Town, stay at Small Hope Bay Lodge. Before the lodge was built in 1960, this area had no roads, electricity, or running water, and only one telephone. While this part of Andros has come a long way since then, it is still mainly undeveloped, with just a few small settlements here and there. If you go bike riding, you'll notice that people in cars will wave to you as they pass.

Many locals consider the beaches in Staniard Creek, about 10 miles north of Andros Town, the nicest around. **Prince Monroe's** is a popular restaurant here. **Androsia Batik Works,** which began in 1973 at Small Hope Bay Lodge, is now in nearby Fresh Creek. This factory, which produces brightly colored resort wear and decorative batiks, has been a real boon to the island's economy. It is on the grounds of the Lighthouse Club, a luxurious resort built by a Swedish millionaire in the '50s. Although the club is now closed, the Bahamian government has plans to restore it to its original splendor and reopen it. In its heyday, peacocks strolled through the attractive grounds. Royal palms and lush colorful plantings still remain. The club sits on the shore of a wide creek and, with masted houseboats bobbing just outside, from a distance it doesn't appear to be abandoned.

Good local restaurants in Fresh Creek include **Papa Gay's** on the waterfront, which sells chicken in a bag; the dining room in tiny **Chick-**

charnie's Hotel; **Skinny's Landmark Restaurant;** and the **Bridge Inn,** which serves snacks. In this drowsy town where the quiet is punctured by crowing roosters, you'll also find stores such as **Turpi's Straw Market** and **Rosie's Gift Shop,** which sells T-shirts and other items.

The peaceful town of Calabash Bay is within walking distance of Small Hope Bay Lodge. On weekends, the Samson Center opens as a bar and disco, where many teenagers gather. On nights when the moon is full, the walk along the beach to Calabash Bay is especially pleasant. **Minnes' Diamond Bar** is one of the oldest bars in the area. Cyril Minnes, the owner, is nicknamed "Twenty-Four Hours" because he can almost always be seen sitting outside watching everything that happens. During the summer, there are church fairs practically every weekend to raise money for various causes.

On the way to the freshwater Captain Bill's Blue Hole from Small Hope Bay Lodge, you'll pass bushes that partially obscure "pothole" farms, where corn, cassava, pigeon peas, sugar cane, and bananas are grown. These farms are called potholes because the soil has accumulated in small depressions in the land. You'll also pass the pretty settlement of Love Hill, where there are several churches, but no bars (usually it's one for one).

Divers appreciate the proximity of the Andros Barrier Reef to shore. Many are enthusiastic about the extensive dive programs offered by Small Hope Bay Lodge and the Andros Beach Hotel. So much marine life lies close to beaches that even snorkelers rave.

The central and southern parts of Andros are even less built up than the north. Towns, few and far between, are smaller and quieter. In Mangrove Cay there are several very inexpensive guest houses that are very modest as far as comfort goes.

WHAT TO SEE AND DO

Sports • Small Hope Bay Lodge near Andros Town and the Andros Beach Hotel in Nicholl's Town both offer diving. For fishing and boating, the places to stay are Charlie's Haven in Behring Point, Las Palmas in Congo Town, and the Chickcharnie Hotel in Fresh Creek. Andros is in one of the world's most famous areas for bone fishing.

***Andros Barrier Reef** • *off the east coast* • At this natural wonder, the third largest reef in the world, divers can swim through caves and tunnels to get a close look at some spectacular marine life, including brilliantly colored (and friendly) fish and many kinds of coral and sponges. Small Hope Bay Lodge, outside Andros Town, specializes in diving excursions to a depth of from 10 feet on one side of the reef to 185 feet "over the wall," where the reef plunges into the 6000-foot Tongue of the Ocean.

*Blue Holes and Inland Ocean Blue Holes • *points throughout the coast and island* • Ocean blue holes, the 200 feet and more fresh water wonders arising from the briny deep, may be visited by either rented or tour boats. Some of these holes have been featured in a Jacques Cousteau TV program. Diving expeditions off Andros give visitors another way to see these majestic undersea phenomena in the waters surrounding the island. Inland ocean holes are tucked away in the woods throughout Andros. With steep, porous limestone walls that catch the dancing reflection of the sun on the water, Captain Bill's Blue Hole, near Small Hope Bay Lodge, is a tranquil place for a private swim. Many birds, including great blue herons, snowy egrets, and humming birds, come through this area.

Atlantic Undersea Testing and Evaluation Centre (AUTEC) • *Fresh Creek* • This center is operated jointly by the U.S. and Britain, and is located in Andros Town. Researchers conduct oceanographic and antisubmarine studies.

Morgan's Bluff • *North Andros* • This is a site where pirate Sir Henry Morgan's treasure is said to be buried. Visitors are not barred from seeking clues. At the Andros Beach Hotel arrange to explore caves here.

San Andros Pines • *Northern Andros* • Giant pine trees, for which Andros is famous among the islands, grow in the north. Other attractions to look for while here are hidden inland blue holes.

*Androsia Batik Works • *Fresh Creek* • Started by Rosi Birch, the co-owner of Small Hope Bay Lodge, Androsia began in the early '70s with a staff of three who worked out of bathtubs on the lodge's property. The batik factory employs about 70 people who design, dye, and sew the colorful wall hangings and resort wear that is sold throughout the Bahamas. The clothing, for both men and women, ranges from shorts, jackets, and dresses to bathing suits. Visit Androsia to see how the material is made.

Turnbull's Gut • *off Small Hope Bay Lodge* • This is a coral and sun-filled underwater tunnel that opens onto a thrilling vertical drop to the depths, where divers encounter awesome undersea life.

The Barge • *Small Hope Bay Lodge* • This navy landing-craft from World War II was sunk by the owner of Small Hope Bay Lodge to enhance underwater adventure for his guests. Curious fish join the divers in this protected area.

Andros Reservoir • *Just south of Nicholl's Town* • Although the water cannot be seen in the mounded reservoir as you drive by on the road, 3 million gallons of it are shipped 20 miles across the channel to Nassau each day.

Bahamas Agricultural Research Centre (BARC) • *7 miles south of San Andros airport* • This center, begun as a joint venture between the governments of The Bahamas and the United States, advises and assists local farmers on raising and producing improved livestock and agricultural products. Visitors are warmly welcomed to view the produce and visit with a variety of livestock.

WHERE TO STAY

MODERATE

★★★**Small Hope Bay Lodge** • *outside Andros Town* • Many guests have remarked that this family-run resort has the casual, convivial atmosphere of summer camp. Leave your jackets, ties, and evening wear at home when you come to this rustic beachfront lodge that specializes in diving. Less than 15 minutes from shore is one of the world's longest barrier reefs, and snorkelers need only swim under the dock to see some of the most exciting marine life around. The first resort in the Bahamas to make diving the main attraction, the Small Hope Bay Lodge was begun in 1960 by Canadian-born Dick Birch, a record-breaking diver himself. He was largely responsible for having the Bahamian government declare the Andros Barrier Reef a national reserve. Nondivers and nonsnorkelers don't have to miss the wonderful underwater displays. Expert dive masters will teach them how to snorkel or dive—at no cost—and will allow them to learn at their own pace. Because the reef is so extensive, dive masters are always finding new sites for visitors to explore. The lodge's 20 pine and coral stone cabins (which aren't particularly soundproof) are spread out along an expansive beach shaded by tall coconut palms. (You won't see very many people wearing shoes here.) Some cabins have picture windows. All are cooled by ceiling fans and are colorfully decorated with wall hangings, pillows, and curtains made of the distinctive batik cloth created at Androsia, the factory begun by Dick Birch's wife, Rosi. Families with children often request the cabins with two rooms and a shared bath. No room keys are provided, but you can lock up your valuables in the office. Hammocks wide enough for two are strategically located throughout the grounds so that guests can stretch out while gazing at some of the best views of the water. This is probably not the kind of place where you'd expect to find a hot tub, but one is right on the beach. You can even arrange to have a massage here. Complimentary bicycles are available for trips to nearby settlements or Captain Bill's Blue Hole, a secluded inland body of fresh water about 5 miles away. Deep-sea fishing, birdwatching, shell collecting, examining unusual species of wild orchids, finding plants used for bush medicine, and shopping at the "batik boutique" are some of the ways guests spend their time when not diving. Cocktails, along with conch fritters that go quickly, are served every evening before dinner. In the main building, the lounge and dining room are separated by a huge batik wall hanging. Guests dine at large tables with the Birches, whose children are now running the lodge. Young children, who are well taken care of while their parents are off diving, eat in the game room. On barbecue nights, meals are served on the waterfront by the outdoor bar. The menu ranges from cracked conch and broiled lobster to roast beef and spare ribs, and the fresh vegetables come from the lodge's own small farm. The Birches try to tailor evening entertainment to the whims of the guests who happen to be with them at the moment. There might be an impromptu party or a showing of underwater slides in the lounge, with its overstuffed pillows and gaping fireplace. Or a staff member might simply give guests directions to the disco in nearby Calabash Bay. Be sure to go into the lodge's "glass room," which has a chess set and a palm growing through its ceiling. Here you can flip through albums of photographs of important events in the lives of the Birches. The lodge runs a charter air service between Andros Town and Fort Lauderdale. (Contact the hotel's Florida office at P.O. Box 21667, Ft. Lauderdale, FL 33335–1667; (800)223–6961 toll free or (305)463–9130 in Florida).

INEXPENSIVE

☆☆ **Andros Beach Hotel** • *Nicholl's Town* • On a powdery four-mile stretch of beach, this casual hotel attracts many divers. Deep-sea and bone fishing, snorkeling, and trips to deserted islands can be arranged. By the pool area, which overlooks the beach, guests may relax in a hammock between two palm trees. Ten spacious ocean-front rooms with terraces and ceiling fans are available along with three private cottages. On short notice, sometimes overnight, the on-premises boutique will run you up a shirt or a dress in Androsia fabric or another of your choice. In the bar where people from town mingle with visitors, try your hand at the famous "Ring Game." Ask at the front desk about baby-sitting.

Bannister's Cottages • *Mangrove Cay* • This small, no-frills accommodation is known for its good homestyle food, particularly the fresh seafood. Only one of the rooms in the group of stone buildings is air conditioned. Most of the guests are avid fishermen, hunters, and boaters.

Moxey's Guest House • *Mangrove Cay* • Visitors are taken into the family at this six-room guest house. In the best Bahamian People-to-People tradition, you can become involved in local activities such as church suppers, barbecues, and chorales.

Movashti Hotel • *Lowe Sound* • Just north of Nicholl's Town, this 30-room hotel looks out on the sound. All rooms are air-conditioned and have TV. There is a restaurant and bar on premises. Because of the hotel's small size, guests get to know each other and often join up for sightseeing and beach trips.

THE BERRY ISLANDS

The 12 square miles of the Berry Islands are a series of small cays just north of Andros and New Providence. The population of a little over 500 is concentrated on Great Harbour Cay, the largest of the islets. Most of the cays are privately owned.

Great Harbour Cay, 7 miles long and 1½ miles wide, was opened in the wake of aggressive developers, and attracted the international wealthy. Where the wealthy go, golf seems to follow, and Great Harbour Cay's clubhouse sits on a rise overlooking the carpetlike course with the sea as a background. Douglas Fairbanks, Jr. was once chairman of the development company's board. His presence drew film people and jet setters eager to catch a glimpse of and be part of the new "in" place.

Some of the tiny southern cays are privately owned, accessible by boat and without tourist accommodations. They have colorful names such as Cat, Crab, Cockroach, Fish, Whale, Goat, and Hog. Bebe Rebozo, remembered from the Nixon years, has a home on Cat Cay. A private bird sanctuary is on Bond's Cay and a private airfield on Hog Cay. The remnants of a farming community, established for freed slaves, still exist on Whale Cay. Many of the smaller islets are the homes of sponge fishermen.

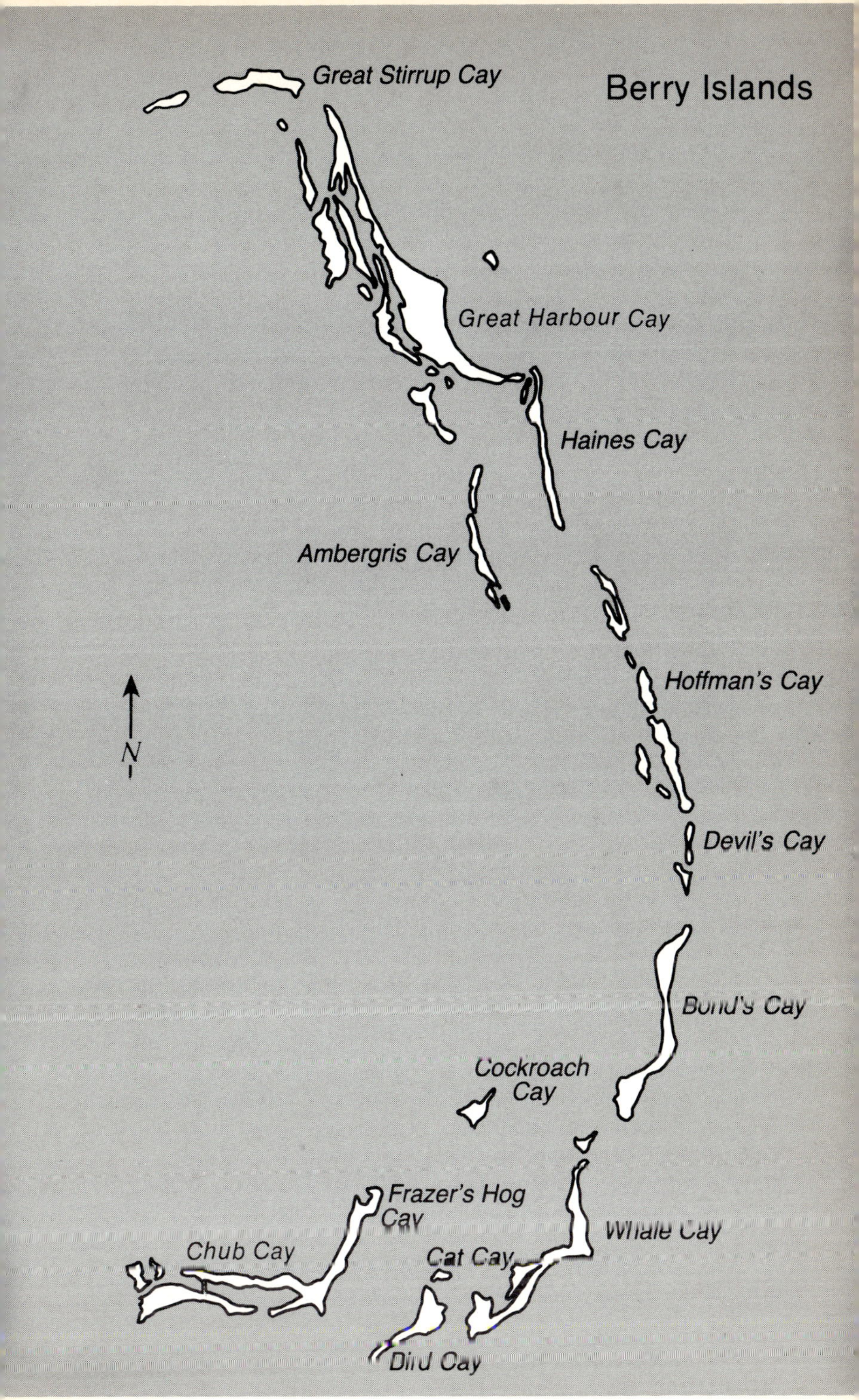

Berry Islands
Great Stirrup Cay
Great Harbour Cay
Haines Cay
Ambergris Cay
Hoffman's Cay
N
Devil's Cay
Cockroach Cay
Frazer's Hog Cay
Whale Cay
Chub Cay
Cat Cay

Chub Cay, the southernmost cay of the Berry Islands, is across the channel from Andros and has the Chub Cay Club, the only resort that takes guests. The main airport is at Chub Cay with the other airport at Great Harbour Cay in the north.

The Nassau mailboat makes the weekly trip to Chub Cay, where there is a marina with 76 slips, full boating services, and a commissary.

WHERE TO STAY

MODERATE

☆☆☆**The Chub Cay Club** • This club offers scuba and tennis as well as a swimming pool, a beach, and all the fishing anyone could want. A yacht can be chartered for deep-sea fishing. Although Chub Cay is also a private club, it welcomes a limited number of nonmembers. There are some air-conditioned oceanside guest rooms. Other rooms overlook the marina. There are also two- and three-bedroom villas, and a permanently docked houseboat, ideal for families.

THE BIMINIS

From just about all points along the narrow North Bimini, the ocean can be seen. There are seven miles of beach on one side and marinas and other boating facilities on the other. The best beaches are in northernmost North Bimini and visitors can rent motor scooters or get taxis to take them there. On one side of the island is King's Road and on the other, Queen's Road. Which is which is determined by whether a male or female is monarch, with the larger road named for Britain's ruler.

Chalk's seaplane lands at Alice Town near the Customs building and mini-buses transport passengers to hotels. If you don't have much luggage, all hotels are within walking distance, except the Admiral in Bailey Town. Visitors and residents seem more reserved and less outgoing than on other Family Islands. Some say this stems from the island's Americanization, in terms of proximity and a long history of tourism.

The main settlements are Alice Town, the capital, and Bailey Town to the north. Going north, the paved road ends, taken over by a pine needle covered dirt road. Pines, leaning toward each other, make a leafy canopy over the road. The Biminis are for people who are dedicated to the sport of big game fishing. Some avid anglers swear these islands are *the* place to go for serious big-game fishing. They are *not* the place to go if you're looking for glamour or fine dining.

Ponce de Leon visited the islands during his fruitless search for the Fountain of Youth. A spot said to be the fountain is located near Bimini's only airport in South Bimini, one of the two main islands. The other island, hook-shaped North Bimini, 50 miles east of Miami, has most of the hotels, restaurants, and the action.

During U.S. Prohibition, the Biminis were a refuge for bootleggers and rumrunners who took advantage of its close proximity to Florida. They used its cays and inlets as shelters and ways of eluding and foiling pursuit, as their piratical predecessors had.

The Two Americans

Two Americans, Ernest Hemingway and Adam Clayton Powell, Jr., have put their stamps on the Biminis. Hemingway, an avid fisherman, spent his time away from the water at the bar of the Compleat Angler Hotel. At one time he lived in a cottage called The Blue Marlin, which still stands as a sight for Hemingway fans. The lobby of the Compleat Angler Hotel is filled with Hemingway memorabilia, and there is a rentable guest room where sections of *To Have and Have Not* are said to have been written.

Adam Clayton Powell, Jr., the New York congressman, could be found in Alice Town's "End of the World" bar, where he was a favorite among residents who admired him as the black man who, with satire, wit, and good humor, could tell off white Americans. Powell, too, fished enthusiastically. Every December, Bimini holds the Adam Clayton Powell Memorial Fishing Tournament.

WHAT TO SEE AND DO

Sports • Deep-sea fishing records are held by many who have fished Bimini waters. The walls of the Bimini Hall of Fame are covered with photographs of fishermen displaying their catches. Veteran fishermen wax ecstatic about the seas swarming with giant tuna, tarpon, dolphin, snapper, bonefish, amberjack, bluefish, white and blue marlin, swordfish, sailfish, bonito, mackerel, barracuda, grouper, and shark. Make fishing and boating arrangements through the Big Game Fishing Club

The Biminis

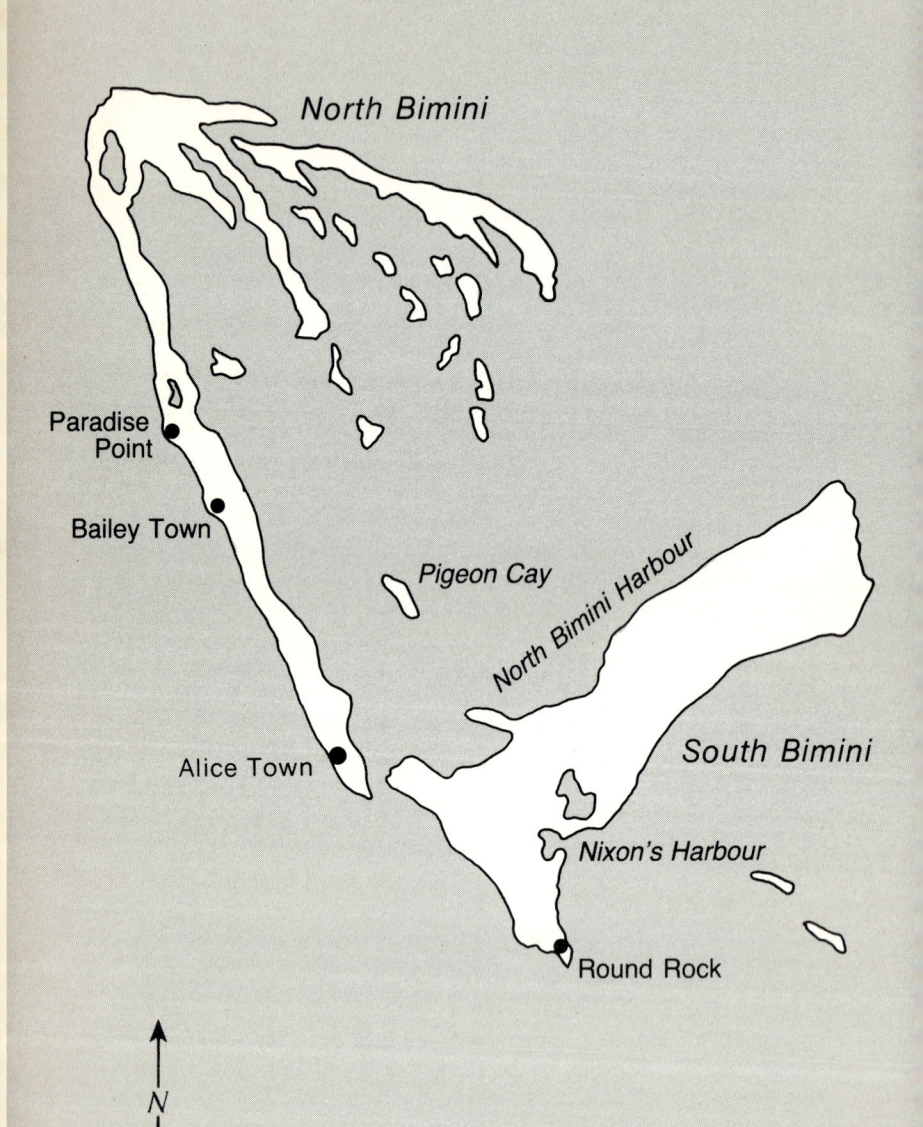

& Hotel, Bimini Blue Water Ltd., Brown's Marina, or Weech's Bimini Dock. Brown's Hotel also has a dive program.

For diving, contact Bimini Undersea Adventures or Brown's Hotel. Tennis Courts are at the Bimini Big Game Fishing Club.

The Fountain of Youth • *Near the South Bimini Airport* • Although Ponce de Leon never found the Fountain of Youth, its position is invariably pointed out to visitors as they pass through South Bimini.

Blue Marlin Cottage • *Bimini Blue Water Marina, Alice Town, North Bimini* • This house was lived in by Ernest Hemingway during his writing and fishing visits to the Biminis.

*Hemingway Mcmorabilia • *Compleat Angler Hotel, Alice Town* • The lobby of the Compleat Angler Hotel has a display of mementos associated with Ernest Hemingway, including manuscripts, photographs, and paintings.

Straw Market • *Alice Town, North Bimini* • The selection here is not as extensive as in Nassau or Freeport. But if neither city is on your itinerary, then Alice Town is the place to shop for these Bahamian products.

*Hall of Fame • *Diandrea's Inn* • Proud anglers, from around the world, pose in photographs displaying their prize-winning catches in this fisherman's hall of fame. Some of the beaming exhibitors are celebrities.

The *Sapona* • *Between South Bimini and Cat Cay* • During the first World War, the automobile magnate Henry Ford built a large, concrete ship, the *Sapona*. No longer his during Prohibition, it was anchored off South Bimini for a private club much used by rumrunners. In 1929, it was wrecked and blown toward shore during a hurricane. It is now a dive site as well as a reminder of the Bimini's adventurous past.

The Lost Continent • *Off North Bimini* • This group of large, flat rocks juts from 20 to 30 feet out of water at Paradise Point. Because the rocks seem hand-hewn, it is claimed that they are part of the road system of that fabled lost continent, Atlantis.

WHERE TO STAY

INEXPENSIVE

☆☆**The Compleat Angler Hotel** • With 15 rooms, the Compleat Angler Hotel seems an overgrown private home. It is proud of the dark bar where Hemingway drank, which is made of old rum-barrels. The restaurant serves Bahamian meals and is open to nonguests. A library has a collection of well-worn books and a display of big catch photos. The room where Hemingway worked is sometimes available for guests.

☆☆**Bimini Big Game Fishing Club** • This hotel, with 35 rooms, 12 cottages, and two penthouses, is the largest in the Biminis. It is operated by Bacardi International, the rum people, and is headquarters exclusively for serious sport and game fishermen. This is where they find comfort after their boats are tied up in the hotel's marina. The marina accommodates up to 60 boats. There is also a swimming pool, two dining rooms, a bar, and the beach is not far.

Brown's Hotel • At Brown's modest 28-room hotel and marina, divers will find Bimini Undersea Adventures, an enterprise working to popularize diving as an attraction in Bimini. It caters to guests at the Big Game Fishing Club as well as to others interested in diving.

★★ **Bimini Blue Water Marina** • Nicely landscaped, with a picket fence out front, this 12-room establishment has a welcoming dining room and bar. It has its own beach and two pools. Most rooms overlook the sea and sunset views can be spectacular.

★★ **Diandrea's Inn** • The thirteen rooms in this small hostelry all have color televisions. Some have double beds and others, twin. The one-room "suite" with two double beds, is huge and the cottage has cooking facilities. There is a front porch and a sunny, outside reception area. Although no meals are served at present, a new 30-room addition, now underway, will bring a bar and dining room.

☆ **Seacrest** • This small hotel has ten rooms, all with television. Each room has a single and a double bed and rooms are surrounded by outside corridors. The spacious rooms, which can be adjoining, are good for families. There is neither a pool nor a restaurant, but the beach is across the road and good, local restaurants are nearby.

☆ **Admiral Hotel** • Farthest from the Alice Town seaport, the Admiral Hotel is in residential Bailey Town. Reached by taxi or mini-bus, the 24 rooms have television, air-conditioning, and two double beds. A favorite with vacationing Bahamians, the hotel offers doubles, suites, and efficiencies.

CAT ISLAND

Across the sound from the Exumas, Cat Island has the highest elevation of all The Bahamas. Like many Bahamian islands, it is long and thin, 50 miles in length, and varies from one to 4 miles across. The one airport is at Arthur's Town in the north where Bahamasair has two flights a week. Despite its natural beauty and near pristine beaches, Cat Island is not a major stop on the tourist path. It is a nice island for walking trips and bicycling.

Atop the island's 206-foot Mount Alvernia is the Hermitage, built by Father Jerome Hawes, a revered Catholic missionary who died in 1956. As in many such communities, his untiring efforts did not succeed in wiping out century-old practices such as Obeah, a mixture of African and Caribbean ritual.

There are still the remains of colonial plantations on the island. One, built by the slaves of another loyalist from the colonies, Colonel Andrew Deveaux, lies in ruins near Port Howe.

Cat Island is slow-paced, far removed from the frenetic tourism of Nassau and Freeport. Some people have no electricity, cook outside, and draw water from wells, just as their ancestors did centuries before them. Cat Island's population, something over 4000, lives by limited farming and fishing. Young people tend to seek more lucrative ways of making a living on other islands or in the U.S. One of the island's native sons, the actor-director Sidney Poitier, did just that, leaving Arthur's Town as a youth.

As with other Bahamian islands, there are stories of pirates having come this way. But unlike other islands, treasure was actually found here. This gave rise to a belief that there is still more awaiting discovery somewhere on land or sunken offshore.

WHAT TO SEE AND DO

Mount Alvernia • *Town of New Bight* • At 206 feet above sea level, Mount Alvernia is the highest point in The Bahamas. It can be seen from several miles away, crowned by the Hermitage.

The Hermitage • *Town of New Bight* • This structure, at the pinnacle of Mount Alvernia, is a small abbey with a miniature cloister and a round corner tower, all of gray native stone. The Hermitage commands a sweeping view of Cat Island, taking in the Bight as well as Fernandez Bay to the north. It is reached by turning off the main road at New Bight and following the dirt road to the foot of the rise. Here, you'll have to abandon your car. A free-standing arch marks the beginning of the foot path up the hill. Rubber-soled shoes are recommended for the tricky climb to the top. Where he could, Father Jerome Hawes, who built the abbey, carved steps into the existing stone and also carved stations of the cross along the way. Just to the right of the main road leading up to Mount Alvernia, standing like a forgotten movie set, is the ruined stone facade of a structure from the Ambrister Plantation.

Deveaux Plantation • *Town of Port Howe* • This plantation was constructed for Colonel Andrew Deveaux by his slaves when he settled on Cat Island after leaving the Colonies. It is reputed to have been beautifully furnished and the scene of much entertainment, but is now in ruins.

Armbrister Plantation • *Near Port Howe* • This is another reminder of colonial life in The Bahamas. Crumbling stone fences and the remains of walls are all that is left of this plantation.

WHERE TO STAY

MODERATE
★★★**Fernandez Bay Village** • Charming, rustic, and laid-back, this resort is on a curving stretch of dreamed-of beach, fringed with feathery casuarinas. You'll almost have the beach to yourself. Tony Armbrister, the multitalented proprietor, will pick you up in Nassau or elsewhere, if you so arrange, and fly you to the island in his Beechcraft.

Cat Island

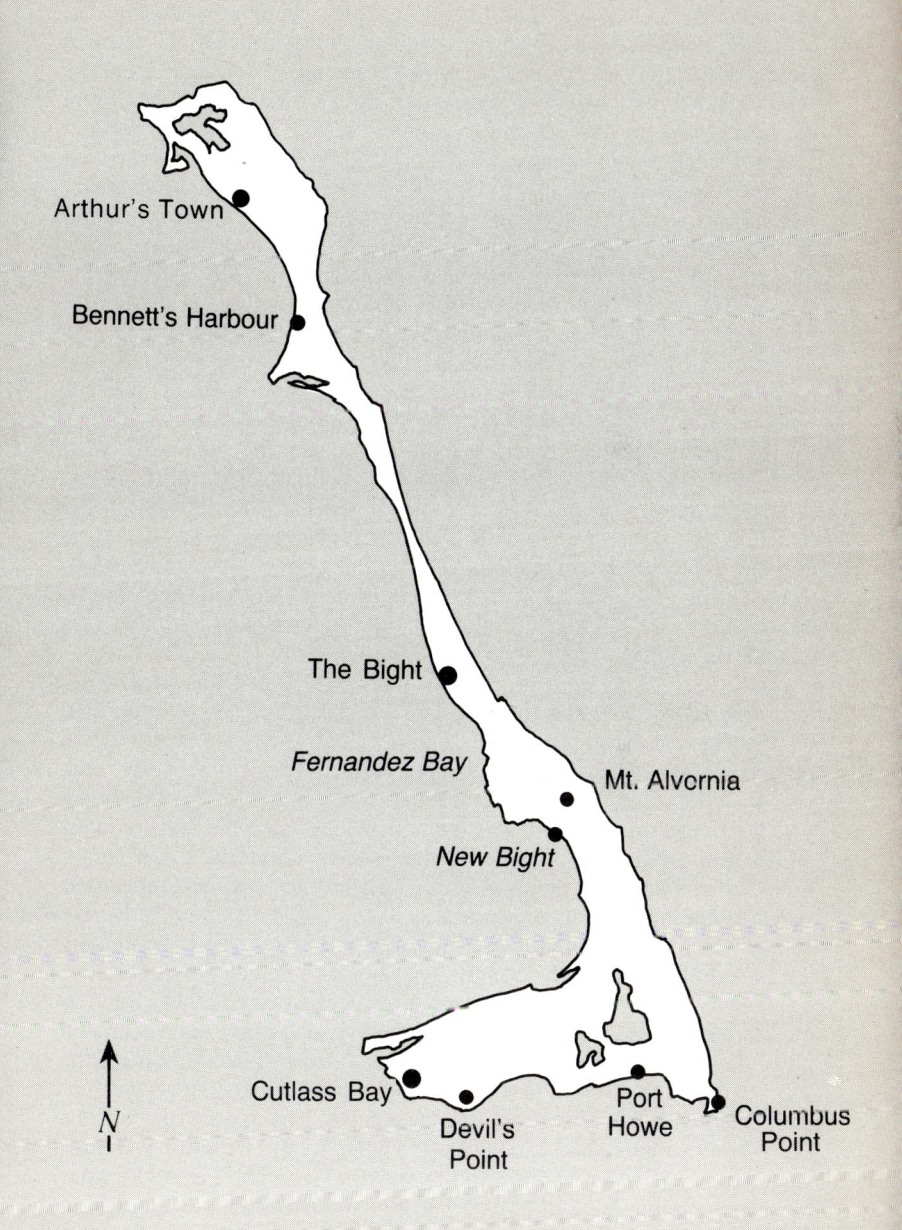

From Nassau, flying time is just under an hour. The "village" consists of six villas, each sleeping up to eight people. The houses, constructed of native stone, have glass-window walls opening to individual terraces facing out to the sea. Three craggy outcroppings of rock rise from the center of the cove, which is Fernandez Bay, on Exuma Sound. From the beach or from their sweeping window views, guests can watch occasional small planes as they come in to land on the tiny airstrip beyond the trees. A special feature of the villas is the indoor-outdoor showers, which, surrounded by tropical vegetation and protected from viewers, are open to the outdoors with sky overhead. Some of the villas are duplexes with cathedral ceilings and overhead fans. Most watersports are at beachfront, and there are bikes and cars for those who want to visit nearby settlements or landmarks, such as Mount Alvernia. Books are found in the lounge area and in villas for those who prefer to curl up in the shade. Radio, television, and newspapers are out. This is the place for total escape. Guests become a congenial group, which gathers for pre-meal drinks and dines on the honor system by signing for what they take or are served. The home-cooked food is ample and delicious. A hefty dose of will power is needed to resist the slabs of daily baked bread, which turns up toasted at breakfast. Armbrister, who is of local descent, often strums the guitar and sings folk songs at evening bonfires if he is not off tinkering with a machine or seeing to your comfort. Many guests are repeaters who swear by this resort and pray that Fernandez Bay Village remains an unspoiled secret.

★★ **Hawk's Nest** • If you arrive by private plane, you can land on the Hawk's Nest private airstrip. By boat, you can tie up at the private, 10-berth marina. If you have neither, Hawk's Nest will pick you up and fly you in from several points in Florida or in Nassau. When you land, you are at the resort, without having gone through the wear and tear of getting in from the airport. The 10 comfortable, air-conditioned rooms can also be cooled by overhead fans but the gentle trade winds often make both unnecessary. Just outside the pleasantly furnished, cool ceramic-tiled-floored rooms are private patios overlooking the incredibly blue Exuma Sound. The sunsets here can be spectacular. Car rentals are available on premises for visiting nearby sights, such as the Hermitage and plantation ruins. Boats for exploring the Sound and other points of interest are complimentary. A well-stocked bar is off the sun-washed dining room, and the excellent home-cooked meals are supplemented with fresh fish from the day's catch. The marina store carries everything from fuel and candy bars to suntan lotion. Favorite purchases are T-shirts and sweat shirts with the resort's logo. The Turners, former Floridians, are on hand to provide information and are expert at making each guest feel comfortable and completely relaxed.

INEXPENSIVE

☆☆**Cutlass Bay Club** • sits at the southern foot of Cat Island near Dolphin Head, where Exuma Sound meets the Atlantic. A long, wide veranda greets guests, offering unsurpassed views of the sea. Like most Cat Island resorts, Cutlass Bay has its own airstrip. The attractive decor of the lounge and bar is an adventurer's idea of a tropical hideaway. A two-mile offshore coral reef ensures some rare swimming in the clearest of waters, and the Tartar Bank, four miles out, beckons fishermen. Guest villas are strewn throughout the property, and there is a dive center as well as boats for fishing. Tennis buffs can play on the property, and transportation is available for visiting the island's sights.

☆ **Greenwood Inn** • This modest resort is on the south coast where Exuma Sound and the Atlantic meet. Cottages make up the 16-room accommodations and their terraces face the sea. A long stretch of pristine beach invites swimming and sunbathing. There is a pool and two boats are available for fishing as well as scuba diving and snorkeling excursions. Greenwood Inn flies guests in to the island, landing on its nearby airstrip.

☆**Bridge Inn** • Nearer to the island's center is The Bight where the Bridge Inn is located. There are 12 rooms, and beaches are not far.

ELEUTHERA

Some visitors say that Eleuthera, the most developed Family Island, is also the most beautiful Bahamian island. It certainly competes with New Providence and Grand Bahama for some of the most upscale resorts. This island was host to the first Bahamian settlers, sometimes called the Eleutherian Adventurers, who came from Bermuda in search of religious freedom. Spanish Wells, Harbour Island, and the cay called Current are tiny islands just offshore.

About 5 miles at its widest point, the island is a long, thin arc, curling southward from New Providence for 110 miles toward Cat Island and the cays of the Exumas. Despite a coral and limestone surface, which might seem forbidding to farmers, Eleuthera is the agricultural center of The Bahamas. In the late 1800s, it dominated the pineapple market with its luscious fruit of a special sweetness without a tart aftertaste.

Like most of the other Family Islands, Eleuthera has few large trees. Its thin but rich soil crust bears mainly small trees and shrubs. Along its main north-south road, you are seldom able to see over and beyond the hedgerows to the rocky fields where the island's rich crop of fruits and vegetables grow. You can drive for miles between towns. Beautiful, deserted and endless beaches, some palm-shaded and with pink sands, border Eleuthera.

Rough coral caves are found throughout the island, with one of the largest at Hatchet Bay, located in the north. Awesome ocean holes, or blue holes, which are seemingly bottomless inland salt-water tidal pools, are a constant surprise, where fish in all their tropical splendor swim to the surface to be fed by visitors. Bahamian waters maintain their crystal clarity because they are virtually unpolluted. Also, the islands are without streams and rivers and no silt or sediment collects to cloud them.

Some of Eleuthera's most arresting attractions are under water. The Devil's Backbone off the northern coast, for example, is a spine of reefs that in the past caused many shipwrecks that still lie below the surface awaiting exploration by divers. A Civil War train that was being transported to Cuba by barge lies wrecked in the middle of the Devil's Backbone. The Union locomotive came to grief during an 1865 storm and now lies among coral and rusted wreckage. A wrecked steamship, the *Cienfuegos,* lies nearby. It went down in 1895, with all passengers surviving. The treacherous Devil's Backbone has claimed still other victims that remain visible to divers, including the freighters *Vanaheim* and *Carnarvon.* Current Cut, between Eleuthera and the cays off Current island, is rich in undersea life, which can be seen over 50-feet down. Six Shilling Channel, separating Eleuthera from Nassau, is a coral reef system among the cays of Current Cut. Underwater photographers have captured magnificent views of exotic creatures making for the depths of Tongue of the Ocean to the south.

The island's three airports are in North Eleuthera, Governor's Harbour, and Rock Sound. In addition to Bahamasair flights from Nassau there are also direct flights from Miami to all three airports. Nassau mail boats make weekly trips to various points throughout Eleuthera.

Eleuthera now participates in the People-to-People program. For information, contact the Ministry of Tourism in Governor's Harbour, 809–332–2142, and give at least four day's notice.

A Little History

When Captain William Sayles and 70 other Englishmen came south from Bermuda in search of religious freedom in 1649, they settled on Cigatoo, as the Arawaks (whom they replaced) called the island. They

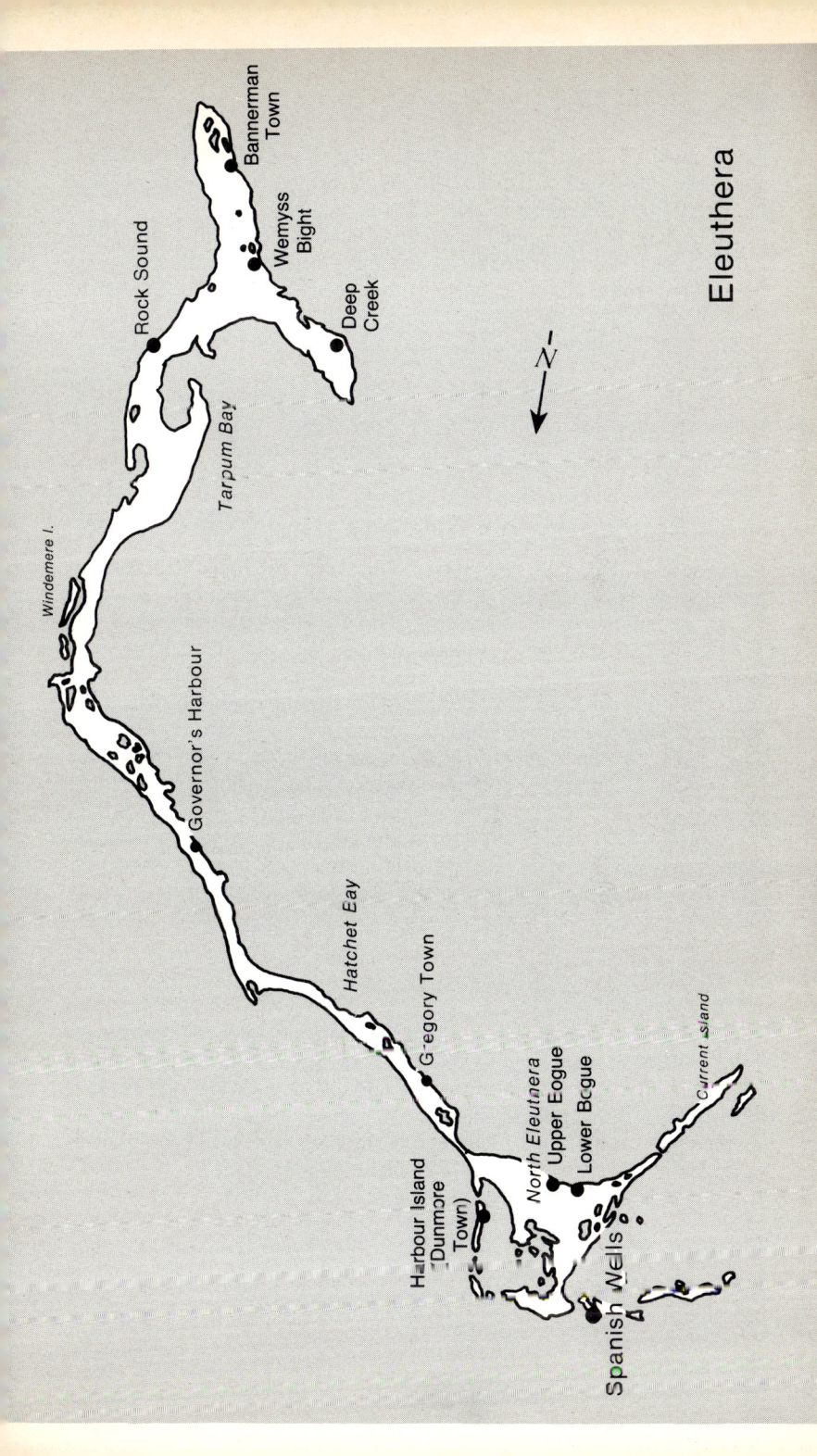

Eleuthera

were joined by New England Puritans, also in search of religious freedom. The island had been called Alabaster, but the new colonizers chose the Greek word for freedom and called it Eleutheria.

The early New England settlers continued contact with their fellow Puritans back home. In 1650, for example, a rare and valuable wood found on Eleuthera was shipped back to New England to be sold to raise funds for the new Harvard College. This was in payment for provisions that the New Englanders had previously sent the hard-pressed settlers.

By 1831 white settlers had been outnumbered three to one by 12,000 slaves and free blacks. Three years later, Queen Victoria issued the proclamation that set slaves free throughout the islands.

Rock Sound, Tarpum Bay, and Windermere Island

Rock Sound, it is said, was once called "Wreck Sound." It has replaced Governor's Harbour as the island's leading settlement. Its small village has a liquor store, a grocer's, and very little else. Although some resorts use a Rock Sound mailing address, they are all really outside town.

Just north of Rock Sound is Tarpum Bay. A bridge connects the mainland with Windermere Island, long a favorite resort and getting-away place for the affluent. The Windermere Island Club, which has had royalty as guests, is considered one of The Bahamas most prestigious resorts.

Tarpum Bay has a thriving, if minute, art colony. Transplanted Americans Mal Flanders and his wife, Kay, paint tropical seascapes, scenes of island life, and portraits of its people. Some of their works have been collected by visitors passing through Tarpum Bay.

South Eleuthera

South of Rock Sound, Eleuthera has settlements such as Bannerman Town, Wemyss Bight, and Deep Creek, which shelter local populations where children are seen in uniform colors of their various schools and tourists pass through as sightseers. At Powell Point, on the island's southern tip, is the Cape Eleuthera Yacht Club which, although not in full operation as a resort, does have facilities for boaters.

Governor's Harbour

Governor's Harbour, at Eleuthera's center, away from the ocean on the bay side of the island, is thought to be one of the earliest settlements and seat of government. While this picturesque town with well-restored homes—some of them guest houses—may seem quiet now, for many years it was an active port. Just north is a U.S. missile tracking station, which works in conjunction with others on Grand Bahama, San Salvador, and Mayaguana. The second Club Med in the Bahamas is at Governor's Harbor on a wide, pink sand beach.

With beautiful, wide, pink beaches (tinted by powdered coral and shells), this hilly town is considered a real find by most visitors. Tourists, few and far between, are often unhappy to run into each other. In town, attractive pink and white government buildings face the water near a much used basketball court by a long, narrow cemetery. Many streets are shaded with tall palms and pines. The waterfront, with its handsome Victorian houses, is one of the nicest places to spend time, especially at sunset. A leisurely walk along the shore will take you across a bridge to Cupid's Cay, where you'll see **Mamie's Bakery** next to the old fire station.

Ask someone to show you Twin Coves, a secluded private estate that welcomes visitors who want to relax or snorkel at the quiet northshore beach. You'll drive through a lush, wonderfully landscaped palm grove.

Ronnie's Hi-D-Way is a restaurant and bar where parties often take place on weekends. Many visitors and locals spend their evenings at the bar at the **Buccaneer Club.** The outdoor cafe at the Buccaneer is a pleasant place to have an inexpensive lunch. The swivel chairs around the umbrella-covered tables are made from old wooden casks. **Mate 'n Jenny's,** a bar and restaurant in Palmetto Point, about five miles outside Governor's Harbour, specializes in Bahamian pizza and is another local hang-out in the evening.

Rodney Pinder, the maitre d' at the Windermere Island Club, runs his own restaurant in Palmetto Point. Called **La Rastic,** it specializes in home-style Bahamian dishes including mutton, cracked conch, grouper, and pork chops. He does not serve alcohol, but you can bring your own bottle. At **Sandy Beach Inn,** a stone's throw from **Mate 'n Jenny's,** George Deal is known for generous portions of grouper, conch, and crawfish, which he catches himself. He also grows his own vegetables. The huge tail of a 500-pound marlin caught by his cousin adorns a wall. Deal dares you to ask for a drink for which his bar does not have the ingredients. The omelet chef at the Windermere Island Club operates her own restaurant outside of Savannah Sound. It is called **Big Sally's,** located on the mainland near the bridge to Windermere Island, and serves up hearty local dishes.

Hatchet Bay

At Hatchet Bay, to the north, there is an old plantation where prize Angus cattle were once raised. Instead of cattle, poultry and dairy products comprise its present output. At Shark Hole, these hungry fish devour the unused chicken parts thrown into the Atlantic several times a day. Locals now live in the homes built by employees of the once prosperous plantation.

Gregory Town

Gregory Town is the pineapple capital of the island. If you go beyond the shrubs along the main road, you'll see fields of the fruit. Pineapple rum is a favorite among visitors as well as locals. Eleuthera's highest hill, near the Cave and Glass Window, which will give you a wonderful panoramic view of the area, is also here. Near some houses, you'll notice outdoor ovens for baking bread. For a fresh-baked treat, stop at Thompson's Bakery. The Thompson's take guests in their home for about $35 a night per person, including two meals. This town caters to young surfers, many of whom are convinced that its beaches have some of the best waves around.

Harbour Island

Called "Briland" (with a long "i") by residents, Harbour Island is a ten-minute ferry ride from Three Island Dock, which is near the North Eleuthera airport. Once visitors see this breathtaking oasis, many return year after year. Its pink shores have some of Eleuthera's most beautiful beaches.

Not even two square miles, the island can be explored on foot. Dunmore Town, its principal settlement, is one of the Bahamian villages with New England charm as its legacy. White picket fences surround brightly painted houses along streets shaded with fig trees, coconut palms, and casuarinas. Located on the harbor side of the island, the town is named for Lord Dunmore, who built Nassau's Fincastle and Charlotte forts. Two of the oldest churches in The Bahamas stand here. The oldest Anglican church, St. John's, was erected in the mid-1700s and Wesley Methodist Church sometime around 1846.

Visitors looking for homestyle Bahamian meals should not leave the island without eating at **Angela's Starfish Restaurant.** Plentiful specialties include pork chops, cracked conch, lobster, and peas and rice. Go easy on the hot sauce. A sign here requests that patrons refrain from swearing or wearing bare-backed clothing.

The names of other establishments, such as **George's Night Club, Willie's Tavern, Shirley's Dressmaking Shop,** and **Frank's Art Gal-**

lery and Souvenirs, also give an indication of the friendly familiarity of small island life. At the **Vic-Hum Club,** where Brilanders hang out to watch TV and relax, visitors can occasionally hear live bands. Near the tree lined entrance to the Runaway Hill Club is **Three Sisters Restaurant.** Stop by in advance to make arrangements for the women to prepare a meal. **Casablanca Bar and Restaurant** is another dining spot where arrangements should be made in advance.

Spanish Wells

Also off the north coast is Spanish Wells. Spanish explorers are said to have used the small island as a final point to take on fresh water before beginning the long, arduous voyage back to Spain. The wells were dug only to a certain depth because, beyond that, salt water would be struck, spoiling the cargo. Somewhat more developed than Harbour Island, this pretty cay also resembles a New England town and is known for its booming crawfish (or lobster) business. In a predominantly black country with a black government, Spanish Wells is unusual in that its population is virtually all white. Some say this is because the original settlers opposed slavery and never brought slaves to the island.

Current

Another tiny cay off Eleuthera's north tip, Current is reputed to be the island's oldest settlement. The story goes that a group of North American Indians were exiled to Current after a so-called massacre of white settlers on Cape Cod. Today, there is no trace of exiled Indians, and Current's present inhabitants are mainly black.

WHAT TO SEE AND DO

Sports • Diving expeditions may be arranged on Harbour Island through the Romora Bay Club or Valentine's Yacht Club; in Rock Sound, through the Winding Bay Dive Center; and on Spanish Wells, through the Spanish Wells Beach Resort and the Harbour Club. For fishing and boating on Harbour Island, contact the Coral Sands Hotel, Romora Bay, or Valentine's; near Rock Sound, the Cotton Bay Club, and on Spanish Wells, Sawyers Marina or Spanish Wells Beach Resort. Eleuthera's golf course is at the Cotton Bay Club near Rock Sound. Tennis courts are in Governor's Harbour, Rock Sound, Harbour Island, and Spanish Wells.

Gregory Town Plantation • *Gregory Town* • This ancient plantation is a reminder of Eleuthera's days of leadership in pineapple production. One of its current products is pineapple rum, which visitors may sample and even take home for a treat.

*Ocean Hole • *Tarpum Bay* • Among several "holes" on the island, this one, just north of Rock Sound and also called "blue hole," is just east of the main road, and teems with a variety of tropical fish eager to be fed.

Preacher's Cave • *Bridge Point* • Shipwrecked settlers, the Eleutherian Adventurers, sought shelter in this cave near Bridge Point in the north. A rocky pulpit formation gives a churchlike feeling, which generated the cave's name.

*Glass Window • *Upper Bogue* • Just south of Upper Bogue, at a spot where the island is almost divided, this windowlike formation was created by erosion from the sea and the wind. It provides a spectacular view both east and west, from the ocean to the bay. The deep blue of the ocean's water on one side of the island contrasts with the bright turquoise of the more shallow water on the other.

Hatchet Bay Plantation • *Hatchet Bay* • This plantation was once the center for raising prize Angus cattle. Its present output is poultry and dairy products.

Hatchet Bay Cave • A giant fig tree marks the entrance to this cave. The tree was supposedly planted by pirates. The cave itself is more than a mile long and harmless bats live in its interior. Because there are no guards, visitors are warned against exploration without the company of an islander who knows his or her way about the cave.

Titus Hole • *Dunmore Town* • This cave, on the harbor at Dunmore Town, is said to have been Harbour Island's first jail.

Harbour Island Churches • *Harbour Island* • St. John's Anglican Church on Harbour Island dates from the 1700s and is the oldest in The Bahamas. Wesley Methodist, built in 1845, is the largest of that denomination in The Bahamas. You'll find a surprising number of other churches for such a small island. Near Wesley Methodist Church is flower-filled St. Catherine's Cemetery.

WHERE TO STAY

Spanish Wells

INEXPENSIVE

☆☆ **Spanish Wells Beach Resort** • Fishing and diving are the specialties at this small beachfront hotel. All of the superior rooms and cottages face the ocean. Sliding glass doors lead to balconies, and rooms are kept cool with ceiling fans. Weekend entertainment takes place at the waterfront bar. This hotel has the honor of being the home of the island's only tennis court. Volleyball and shuffleboard also keep guests active.

☆ **Spanish Wells Harbour Club** • This large resort also caters to those who thrive on water sports and fishing. Pleasure and fishing boats tie up at its marina. There are 20 guest rooms.

Sawyer's Marina • Sawyer's has 8 guest rooms and cottages and apartments. It has its own beach and swimming pool. Most sea sports are offered at its marina and dock.

Current

MODERATE

☆☆**Sea Raider** • Although the sea is also the focus at this small resort with a beach, the management can arrange tennis. Apartments and individual rooms are available. Cars can be rented here and Sea Raider also has bicycles.

Harbour Island

MODERATE

★★★**Dunmore Beach Club** • The elegant Dunmore Beach Club looks out toward the Atlantic and has cottages amid lush vegetation. Whether served in the airy dining room, decorated with paintings and potted plants, or on the garden terrace overlooking the beach, the European and Bahamian food is delicious. Tennis courts are available and fishing expeditions can be arranged.

★★★★**Pink Sands** • The resort's name aptly describes the wide quiet beach, which you approach from above. The stone cottages, each with a name, ceiling fans, kitchens, bottled water, the makings for coffee or tea, dining, sitting, sleeping, and dressing areas, are pleasantly furnished and quite comfortable. Patrons come year after year, many asking for the same cottage. Since there are no cottage keys, you may lock any valuables in a safe-deposit box at the front desk. The property stretches over 40 acres, and guests are given flashlights upon registering. Soft chimes summon guests to dinner, and they dress for the meal served in the large, open-to-the-air dining room with a fireplace. Next door is a small, comfortable library, lined with books for borrowing as the mood hits. The property, designated a bird sanctuary, has tree-shaded, flower-lined winding paths; hence, the flashlights for night. If you become hopelessly lost, a security guard is on the premises to assist. Tennis is available, as well as watersports.

★★**Romora Bay Club** • This colorful, flower-filled resort is a favorite with honeymooners. Bordering both the harbor and the beach, it has an X-rated island where couples can be marooned all day. They are given a lunch and boats are warned off. When guests are not marooned, they can enjoy watersports.

☆☆☆**Coral Sands Hotel** • Located on 14 hilly acres stretching from the pink sand beach to Dunmore Town, Coral Sands has 33 rooms. Its tennis courts can be used at night. Sailboats, rowboats, surf riders, ping pong, badminton, and shuffleboard are also available to guests. Many visitors enjoy the bar overlooking the beach.

★★★**Runaway Hill** • Staying at this secluded inn overlooking a pink sand beach is like visiting old friends. The homey atmosphere is a pleasant reminder that the inn was built as a private home. The dining/lounge room is furnished in wicker and black and white tiles pave the floor. From the books in the guestrooms to handwritten menus, the personal attention of the managers, Carol and Roger Becht, is apparent. Carol and Roger always make sure that visitors are informed of all the social events that take place on the island. People staying at other hotels often stop by for drinks and excellent meals served on the veranda above the small swimming pool or in the airy, attractive dining room. Guests dress for dinner (reservations are essential).

☆☆**Valentine's Yacht Club** • When not indulging in the wide range of watersports Valentine's offers, guests play tennis or relax in the hot tub. The staff of this family-operated inn on the harbor can also arrange for guests to be marooned on a deserted island.

INEXPENSIVE

★**Rock House** • overlooks the harbor on Bay Street near the Customs House. Guests dine on a sun porch that also has a view of the water. The five large, airy rooms are colorfully decorated and breezy. The sitting room has bright wicker furniture set on bold black-and-white floor tiles. A penthouse suite has a king-size bed as well as a queen-size sleep sofa. Guests can watch the comings and goings of the island's visitors and locals.

Gregory Town
MODERATE

☆☆☆**Oleander Gardens** • These white, red-roofed villas are perched on the shore overlooking the beach. Each attractively furnished villa has two bedrooms, two baths, a living room, a dining area, a kitchen, and two terraces. Tennis, fishing, and watersports are available.

☆**Caridon Cottages** • This accommodation offers one- and two-room cottages. Bicycles and motor scooters can be rented and there is a gift shop.

Governor's Harbour
INEXPENSIVE

☆☆**Cigatoo Inn** • An attractive, family-run hotel, Cigatoo sports a pool, tennis court, and a bar and restaurant where locals often stop for drinks. Guest rooms, with terraces surrounded by flowering plants, are small but comfortable. All the rooms have TV and refrigerators. Families with young children can arrange for baby-sitting. A short walk will take you to a broad, pink sand beach not far from Club Med. Guests are quickly drawn into the life of the town. One of the best things about the Cigatoo is the lively, warm, and congenial atmosphere.

Tuckaway • This pleasant guest house in a residential neighborhood is run by Carmen and Richard Rolle, who live across the street. There are six rooms in three cottages and all are air-conditioned, with refrigerators and shady front porches. A crib is available should a young one turn up. All the front yards are alive with colorful vegetation. Guests will be able to pick pineapple and other fruit when the plants mature. An unspectacular beach is a 2-minute walk away. For a better pink-sand beach on the north shore, a 20-minute walk is required.

Laughing Bird Apartments • These are all comfortable air-conditioned, 1-bedroom efficiency units. They are sometimes referred to as "Nurse Jean's apartments," since this Bahamian nurse owns them with her English husband, Donald Davies, an architect. The units consist of two apartments, each sleeping up to six people. Each has living-dining areas with separate bedrooms and baths. The houses are near to town and front an adequate beach. Markets and other services are close by. Maid service is available at a small extra charge.

Windermere Island

EXPENSIVE

★★★★★ **Windermere Island Club** • This resort is on a 5-mile-long island connected to mainland Eleuthera by a bridge. Quiet Savannah Sound is the closest town. Windermere's high rating is not for its club rooms, which, although comfortable and with ocean-view balconies, are surprisingly small and modest. The rating is for the attentive, unobtrusive, and courteous service and the other units: the 1-bedroom suites, the 2-bedroom apartments, 2- and 3-bedroom cottages, and the 1–5-bedroom villas, many of which are breathtaking in design and appointments. Men are required to wear jackets for dinner every night, but on Saturday night and gala nights they also don ties, and the women appear in cocktail dresses. Guests gather in the lounge, formed by two adjoining octagonal rooms near the pool patio. The Saturday night buffet is spectacular in presentation and taste. Among the offerings might be smoked trout and salmon, chicken-stuffed pastry, roast turkey, soups, and salads. There are rich desserts, fruits, and cheese platters. Off on the patio a combo plays, and there is dancing. The guest rooms have fresh flowers and telephones, but no radios or TV. There are two beaches, one on the ocean side and the other, protected and calm, facing the mainland. Breakfast brings fresh-squeezed orange juice, made-to-order omelets, fresh fruits, hash browns, and other morning delights. Guests beg the recipe for the French toast, which is crunchy brown on the outside and soft inside. Cars may be rented through the hotel, taxi drivers, or the maitre d'. Bikes can be borrowed to ride the main road, where the branches of tall pines provide a shady roof. Set back from the road are many private homes with names such as Cherokee, Dolphin House, and Beaumaris. The Windermere Island Club closes from the end of May to the beginning of November.

Rock Sound Area

EXPENSIVE

★★★★★**Cotton Bay Club** • This resort, developed as a retreat for millionaires, continues to be one of the finest in The Bahamas. From the road it is reached by a winding driveway shaded by palms and Norfolk pines. The pink cottages have stair-stepped roofs like those used in Bermuda for catching rainwater. The rooms, most with outdoor terraces, are tastefully furnished with rattan, and have ceiling fans, white-tile floors, and shutters at tall windows. The baths all have useful grab bars, and there are safe-deposit boxes in the closets. The pristine white-sand beach arcs off in each direction against a coastline of palms and casuarinas. There is an 18-hole Robert Trent Jones golf course and tennis courts. The grounds are landscaped with lush tropical plantings dominated by huge aloes. The dining room goes mainly unused because most dining takes place outside, beside the pool, under tall palms that lean protectively. There is a singer each night during season and, on buffet nights, a live band. Guests are expected to dress for dinner. As they check out, many make reservations for the following year.

INEXPENSIVE

Hilton's Haven • This ten-room guest house is run by a former public health nurse, celebrated for her past contributions to the nation's health and her present hospitality. Although her service is not as lavish as Rock Sound's larger resorts, it is much more personal.

THE EXUMAS

The Exumas are a chain of 365 tiny islands and cays strung out for 100 miles from New Providence and Eleuthera to Long Island. They lie between Exuma Sound on the east and the awe-inspiring Tongue of the Ocean to the west. Out in Exuma Sound near Sampson Cay is the Exuma National Land and Sea Park, 177 miles of undersea wonders, many of which can be clearly seen from three to ten feet down. From the air, the water and surrounding cays of Exuma is one of the most memorable sights of the Bahamas. A giant hand seems to have done a whimsical finger painting, leaving sand whorls and ripples clearly visible beneath the turquoise and jade sea.

These islands are served by the airport at George Town. A new international airport is under construction at Moss Town, to the north, and is scheduled to open early in 1989. The mailboat comes in weekly, making stops at George Town, Staniel Cay, and several other islets in this chain. Taxis are always at the airport, and some drivers will conduct tours. Hotels either rent or have access to motor scooters and bicycles. You can also rent cars (for about $70 a day!) through hotels or in town.

George Town

George Town, Exuma's picturesque capital, lies on the island of Great Exuma, looking out to Stocking Island, which encloses Elizabeth Harbour. The largest structure in town is the impressive Administration Building, where the post office is located. Its architects strove mightily to duplicate Nassau's Government House.

Under the shade of an enormous fig tree near the administration building, women sell a variety of straw products, from rugs to dolls. Across Lake Victoria, which covers two acres in the center of town, you can sample fresh, delicious Bahamian food at the **Sunrise Cafe** or **Eddie's Edgewater.** Eddie's is a friendly, informal restaurant where Bahamians and visitors relax at the bar. Stop by in advance to make reservations.

Local George Towners can be found socializing at the Peace and Plenty Hotel, named for the ship on which the American settler Lord Rolle arrived in the Exumas. Locals as well as guests of other hotels frequent the lively parties given here. The community center next to St. Andrew's Anglican Church, which overlooks Victoria Lake, hosts weekend dances for young people.

The Exumas are bliss for confirmed sailors who say that the cruising is unequaled anywhere else. Veteran boaters insist that if you have not sailed the Exuma waters and seen its quiet coves and inlets, you have neither sailed nor lived.

Each April, the Exumas close down for a week. Fellow Bahamians, cruising yachtsmen, boaters, visitors, and landlubbers all make their way to George Town to watch and take part in the festivities surrounding the annual inter-island "Family Island Regatta." The festivities include a parade and a variety of other special events, as the hand-crafted work sloops, owned and operated by Bahamians, compete out in Elizabeth Harbour. The regatta signals non-stop eating, drinking, and all-round partying. Some are prompted to refer to the boat races as the "Regretta." Accommodations are difficult to come by for outsiders and some make their reservations a year or so in advance.

Food stalls are set up along the waterfront selling fresh pineapples, cooked chicken, fish, and conch in all its incarnations. Reggae throbs from the stalls and long lost friends greet each other with embraces and beer. Domino-playing men slap the tiles on tables with sharp clicks, pulsing drums and clanking cowbells, blaring horns and shrill whistles accompany a Junkanoo band down the center of the street.

Like birds lined on telephone wires, people sit on the low walls in front of the administration building to watch the passing line of honking cars decorated with colored streamers. Children in their Sunday best sit on hoods or poke their smiling faces from sun roofs. When the Police band performs in Regatta Park, everyone surges onto the steps of the

Exume Supplies building and nearby footholds for a better view. The band, in sparkling white tunics, wide red belts, hats with red bands, and black trousers with red side stripes, moves children and their elders to dance and move with the beat.

On Emancipation Day, celebrated on the first Monday in August, another regatta is held at Rolleville.

Outside George Town

Many people in the Exumas make their living from farming. Two former plantations, Rolleville and Rolle Town, are named for John Rolle, an American Loyalist who, with his slaves, settled in the Exumas after 1783. He acquired extensive landholdings in the Exumas, and the British later rewarded him with a knighthood. Lord Rolle's will left his land to his slaves whose descendants still live in the two villages. Some visitors find that almost every person they meet in Exuma is a Rolle. The parents of Esther Rolle, the actress, moved to the United States from here before she was born. The Rolle land cannot be sold, and passes from generation to generation.

A ride northwest along Queen's Highway, flanked by banana trees, coconut palms, sea grapes, mango trees, and farmland, will take you to a number of small settlements. About seven miles from George Town, **Iva Bowe's Central Highway Inn** serves good homestyle food.

Mt. Thompson is a pretty, hilly town with a packing house for onions and other produce. Even if you're not hungry or thirsty, stop at **Three Sisters Club**, a restaurant owned by John Rolle, who is also a taxi driver. When you go out back to the gorgeous beach, you'll see the "three sisters"—three huge rocks in the water. About a mile north is Ocean Bight, a large, sparkling, white sand beach that is a wonderful place for snorkeling and swimming. In Farmer's Hill and Roker's Point, you'll see goats, pigs, lambs, and chicken in yards.

Rolleville, about 30 miles from George Town, is the westernmost settlement. The largest of the Rolle plantations, this town has low, thatched-roof shelters where vegetables like pigeon peas are stored. **Kermit's Hilltop Tavern**, a bar and restaurant, overlooking the bay is popular with visitors as well as locals. (Kermit Rolle, another restaurateur/taxi driver, also has a restaurant called **Kermit's** at the airport.) In Barry Tarry, north of Rolleville, the **Fisherman's Inn** restaurant and nightclub is especially busy on weekends.

Little Exuma, south of George Town, is much less developed than its sister island. Once over the small bridge connecting the two islands, you'll come to a small settlement called The Ferry. This is the home of Gloria Patience, commonly known as "The Shark Lady of the Exumas." If there were any Exumians who hadn't heard of women's lib before she arrived, there certainly aren't any now.

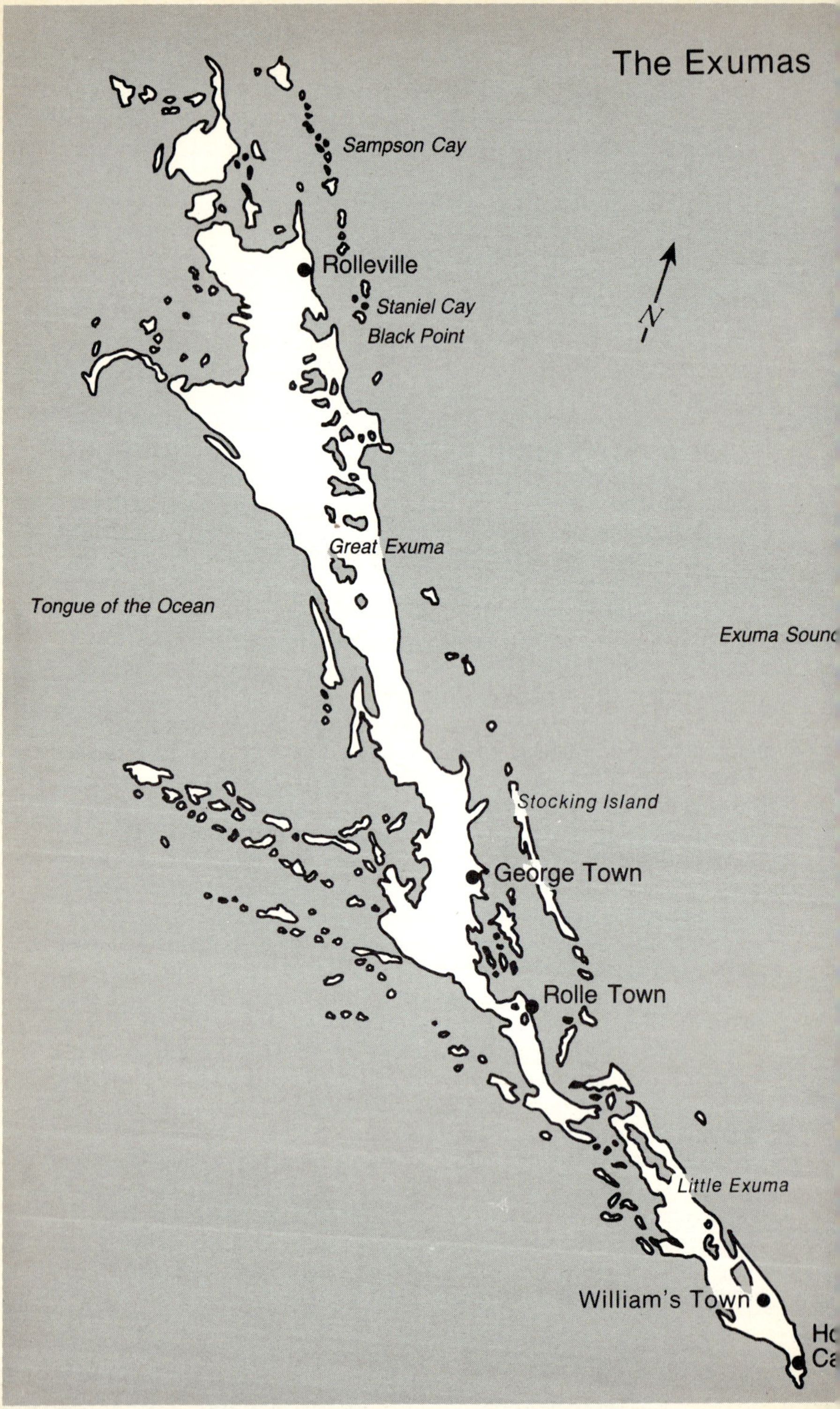
The Exumas
Sampson Cay
Rolleville
Staniel Cay
Black Point
N
Great Exuma
Tongue of the Ocean
Exuma Sounc
Stocking Island
George Town
Rolle Town
Little Exuma
William's Town
Hc
Ca

After traveling around the world, then returning to Nassau to raise nine children, Ms. Patience moved to Little Exuma and began making a living catching sharks. As if this weren't enough, she also became the first woman to skipper a boat in the Family Island Regatta.

Now in her sixties, she hauls the snared sharks, most weighing hundreds of pounds, into her boat herself. She makes necklaces from their spines and sells their teeth to Nassau jewelry stores. At her house, you can buy shark teeth as well as shells, paintings, old sea bottles, and driftwood.

Not far from here is the now closed Sand Dollar Beach Club on Pretty Molly Bay. There is a legend that one of the slaves on a plantation near this bay was a beautiful young woman named Molly. Melancholy about her barren life and a future of continued servitude, she drowned herself one moonlit night in the bay that was given her name. If you look carefully, you may catch a glimpse of Molly, who is said to roam the beach by moonlight.

Black Bahamians swear by the legend and dismiss another version of the story in which Molly is a young white woman who was transformed into a mermaid and sits on a rock in the bay combing her hair by moonlight.

WHAT TO SEE AND DO

Sports • Diving and snorkeling, including several very different dive sites, can be arranged in George Town at Exuma Divers, down a short hill across from the Peace and Plenty Hotel. In Staniel Cay, make arrangements at the Staniel Cay Yacht Club. For fishing and boating in George Town, contact Exuma Docking Services or Minn's Watersports; in Staniel Cay, contact Exuma Flotilla Ltd., Happy People Marina, or the Staniel Cay Yacht Club. Tennis courts are at the Out Island Inn in George Town.

*Exuma Land and Sea Park • *North Exuma Sound* • This Bahamian government-protected national park is unique in that it is mainly under water. It is reached only by boat for thrilling sights of unusual undersea landscapes, coral formations, and myriads of sea creatures. Diving is permissible, but any hunting or fishing is strictly forbidden.

*Stocking Island • This long, narrow island, with three hills in the center, is in the sound off George Town. Hotels run guests out for isolated sunbathing. It's easy to find a secluded spot here for skinny dipping. The boat will drop you off on the calm bay side, where red and black starfish float at the water's edge and a huge sandbar stretches out for half a football field. Try bonefishing right off the dock. Follow a path by the Peace and Plenty "Beach Club" (really a snack bar) across the narrow island to the ocean side, where the water is rougher and rockier in places. You'll find all kinds of shells in deserted coves. For a small fee, you may be able to talk the man who brings you here into taking a detour to Sand Dollar Beach at the southern end of the island. Here you can walk to the end of another sandbar, then swim to Elizabeth Island. And, of course, you'll have no trouble finding sand dollars.

St. Andrew's Church • *George Town* • St. Andrew's Anglican Church, with its graveyard, sits on a rise across from Government House. At its rear is Victoria Lake. It dates from 1802, and was erected for early settlers of British background.

The Hermitage • *Jimmy Hill, Great Exuma, down a narrow road off Queen's Highway* • It's probably best to let a Bahamian show you the way to the crumbling tombs at the Hermitage, about eight miles from George Town. Dating back to the 1800s, the three tombs of slavemasters lie next to the grave of one of their servants.

Rolle Town Tomb • Off the main road at Rolle Town and up the hill to the right of the Baptist church is a burial ground. At its center is a large, crumbling tomb of limestone and brick holding a marble slab bearing the following inscription:

> *Within this tomb lie interred*
> *the body of Ann M. Kay the wife*
> *of Alexander M. Kay who departed*
> *this life the 8th of November 1792*
> *Aged 26 years and their infant child.*

Thunderball Grotto • *Off Staniel Cay* • This grotto is pierced by shafts of filtered sunlight that illuminate its rock and coral formations. The grotto was used for scenes in *Thunderball*, the James Bond film.

Tropic of Cancer Marker • *Little Exuma, near the Sand Dollar Beach Club* • The Tropic of Cancer marks the separation of the tropics from the temperate zone. Its northern limit cuts through Little Exuma. A marker shows where the imaginary line is drawn.

Williams Town Salt Marsh • *Near the Sand Dollar Club* • The site and other traces of Exuma's once-thriving salt industry are still apparent at Williams Town in Little Exuma. The best way to view the salt pond is to climb the rise to the single concrete column overlooking the flats. With the sea at your back, the entire marsh is visible.

Patience House • *The Ferry* • Gloria Patience's home has become a stop for tourists on their way to the Williams Town Salt Marsh. This colorful woman has collected china, glassware, silver, and other items, which fill every surface in the house. Her main attractions are the souvenirs she sells, which she has fashioned from shark's teeth. The fine pieces of china and glass are for display only. Ms. Patience, always barefoot, will give a tour of the house.

*Family Island Regatta • If in George Town or on one of the nearby cays in April, don't miss this annual race among sailors of several islands. The competition is keen and George Town is crowded and festive when everybody turns out for the occasion.

WHERE TO STAY

MODERATE

★★**Staniel Cay Yacht Club** • This hotel is on a small island north of George Town, and has only 6 guest rooms. The club centers around its marina, and guests staying more than three days have free use of a 13-foot Boston whaler. The club is also a vantage point for watching the Family Island Regatta and the Emancipation Day races. A nearby 3000-foot runway puts private planes almost at its doorstep

☆☆ **Happy People Marina** • Happy People is almost next door to Staniel Cay Yacht Club, and has 14 guest rooms. It, too, looks out toward the sea, and rents bare boats from its marina for exploring the cays and inlets of the Exumas.

INEXPENSIVE

★★★**Peace and Plenty Hotel** • This is where all of George Town gathers for drinks, to swap gossip, to see who's in town, and to catch up on the latest. It was once a sponge market and private home. Two rooms that served as a kitchen during slavery have been converted into the bar. Visitors are treated like locals and are soon adopted into the little George Town community. A popular breakfast specialty is grits and boiled fish. Try the pumpkin soup for dinner. Rooms are large and have wonderful views of the bay. Entertainment at night includes parties by the pool. Twice a day, guests are taken by ferry to the beaches on Stocking Island, where there's an unobtrusive snack bar.

☆☆ **Pieces of Eight** • Not far from the center of George Town, this lively hotel is known for its good food and popular bar. All rooms have views of the ocean, across the road. Guests may use the beautiful Out Island Inn beach or take a complimentary ferry ride to Stocking Island beaches. If there's nothing going on at night at Hotel Peace and Plenty, there's probably some kind of entertainment near the pool here.

★★ **Out Island Inn** • Small buildings made of stone and wood sit along an inviting beach at this hotel, which is the largest in Exuma. The lush, colorful grounds are a pleasant place to wander. The dining room is very attractive. Guests may play tennis or arrange water sports.

★★ **Regatta Point** • This guest house in George Town is on a 1½-acre cay out in Elizabeth Harbour, making it ideal for viewing the regattas. It is connected to the mainland by a causeway, enabling guests to walk or drive to town. The large rooms are very attractive.

INAGUA

The most southerly island of The Bahamas, Inagua thrusts southward toward the Windward Passage and northern Haiti. Sometimes called Great Inagua, it is the third largest of the islands. Its sister island, Little Inagua, lies to the northeast, and is uninhabited.

Inagua is not for avid fishermen, divers, golfers, or tennis players. However, for nature lovers and those seeking complete peace and quiet, it can be all they need. Lake Windsor in the interior attracts the largest colony of flamingoes in the world. In surrounding Inagua Park, protected by the Bahamas National Trust, there are more than 200 species of birds. Among them are the roseate spoonbill, herons, egrets, and hummingbirds. Green turtles, wild boars, and donkeys are also found roaming unhampered on the island.

Because of its salt industry, Inagua, so remote from Nassau, is relatively prosperous. Mounds of salt are a prominent feature of the island's landscape. The Morton Salt Company still dries its salt mined from the sea, here, and many of Matthew Town's 900 or so inhabitants are employed in the industry. The dried salt is shipped from Matthew Town to the U.S. for processing. Earlier, when the industry was larger, Inagua had a railroad to transport the salt.

One of Inagua's legends is that Henri Cristophe, the 19th-century

Haitian revolutionary leader who crowned himself king, escaped to Inagua and hid in its dense forests. Eugene O'Neill drew upon this theme for his play, *The Emperor Jones*.

The airport is at Matthew Town, the island's only developed area. Bahamasair sends in two flights a week, and the Nassau mailboat puts in once a week.

There are no car rentals in this little settlement. But if you're persistent, you may be able to arrange something through one of the resorts. Motor scooters can be rented in town.

WHAT TO SEE AND DO

***Inagua National Park** • *Matthew Town. Tours arranged through the National Trust Office in town.* • This park is one of the world's most famous for tropical bird life. The preserve is protected by the Bahamas National Trust. On the shores of Windsor Lake is the world's largest assemblage of pink flamingoes, the national bird of The Bahamas. Two tours are available, one to see the flamingoes, and the other for the remainder of the birds, plus flora and fauna.

The Lighthouse • *Southwest Point* • This lighthouse, at Southwest Point, not far from Matthew Town and erected in 1870, guides ships using the Windward Passage channel between Inagua and Hispaniola, the island of Haiti and the Dominican Republic.

Salt Factory • *Matthew Town. Inquire at hotel, since these tours are not regularly scheduled.* • The Morton Salt Company plant conducts tours from time to time, demonstrating the process of drying and refining sea salt for commercial use.

WHERE TO STAY

INEXPENSIVE

Ford's Inagua Inn • A tiny building close to the airport, this inn is known for its delicious local cuisine. At this writing, it was closed temporarily.

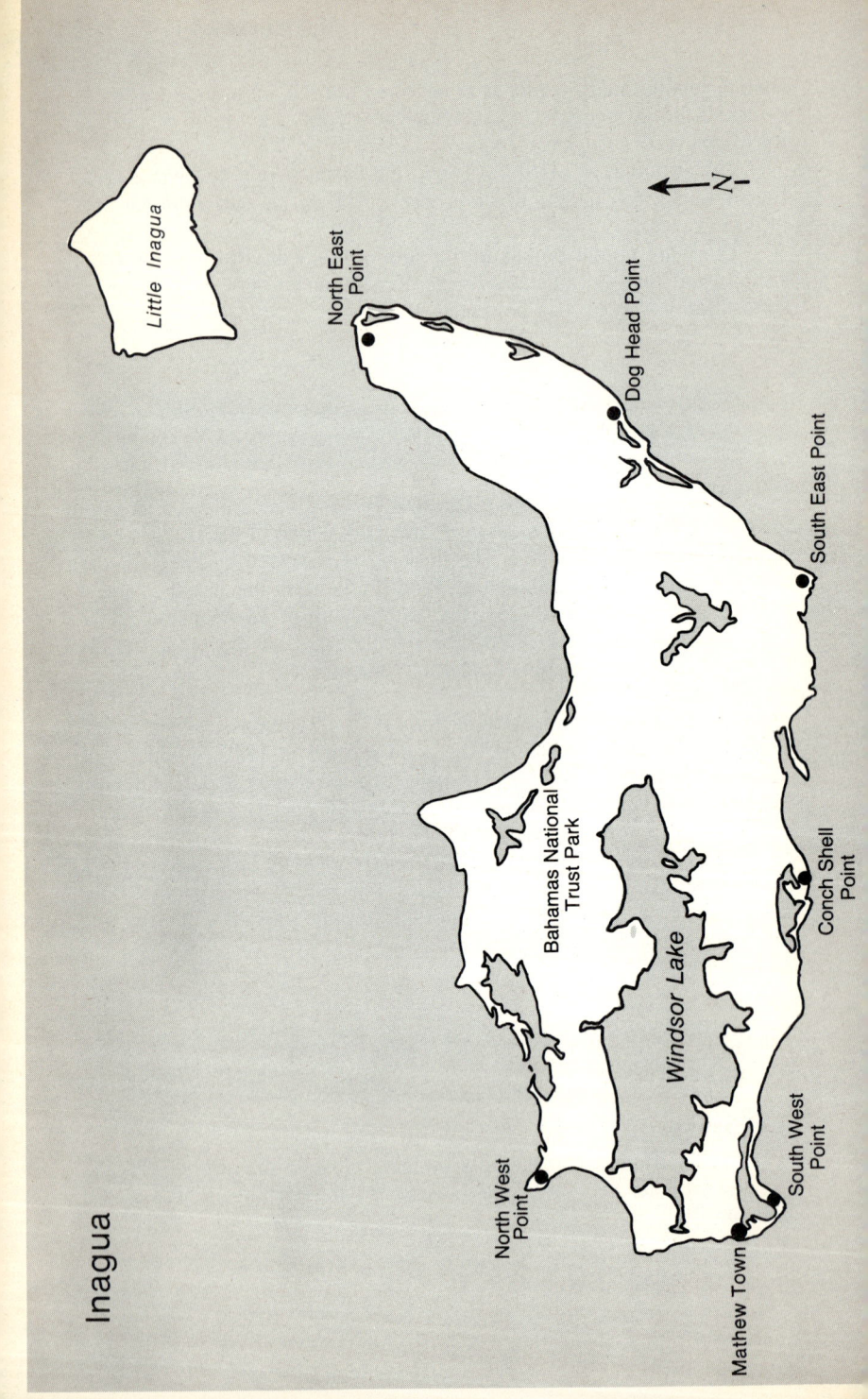

Inagua

- Little Inagua
- North East Point
- Dog Head Point
- South East Point
- Bahamas National Trust Park
- Windsor Lake
- Conch Shell Point
- North West Point
- South West Point
- Mathew Town

LONG ISLAND

A narrow sliver of land with its top pointing northwest toward the Exuma Cays, Long Island is said to stretch anywhere from 60 to 100 miles. Curiously, there seems to be some question about its length, but no dispute about its being long. It is a little more than a mile wide and, at some of its hilly points, you can see the Atlantic to the east crashing against the craggy rocks and, to the west, the calmer blue waters of Exuma Sound. The hills almost reach the height of Cat Island's highest and, on the ocean side, sharp, jagged coral cliffs drop steeply to the sand-bordered beaches below. The Tropic of Cancer slashes through the island's northern quarter.

This island has some of the most beautiful and deserted beaches in The Bahamas. Some seasoned travelers call the beach at Cape Santa Maria one of the world's best. Located at the northwest tip of the island, it is a 3-mile cove of cerulean water and deep, powdery white sand. Other fine beaches dot the coast, and ardent swimmers and sun lovers can stumble upon one after another.

Diving, snorkeling, and shelling are ideally suited to the waters and beaches fringing the island. Scuba divers have an almost limitless list of interesting sites including a blue hole and an undersea visit to a colony of tame groupers. A local guidebook lists almost 30 different dive sites. Fishing is another island attraction, and guides take visitors to places teeming with the kind of fish and fishing they seek, whether from land, inland, or offshore. Stella Maris Inn at the north of the island arranges both diving and fishing expeditions.

Long Island was a stopping-off point for Columbus on his voyage to the "New World." He called it Fernandina after Ferdinand, the Spanish king. The island is riddled with ominous caves and mysterious ocean holes. The Stella Maris Inn has fashioned one of these grottos into an attractive entertainment setting—"party cave."

At the south of the island, near Clarence Town, the Diamond Crystal Salt Company operates a solar evaporation plant that provides some local employment. Many settlements such as Simms, Deal, and others were named for leading families. The people of Long Island fish and farm on land considered fertile compared to the other islands. Some of their houses bear a kind of hex sign painted near the roof line. Religion plays an important role in their lives. In addition to well-attended local church services, traveling, revivalist-type preachers visit up and down the island and Obeah, a variation of religious practices from West Africa, is still in evidence.

Father Jerome, the priest who built The Hermitage at the highest point on Cat Island, is also responsible for several churches on this island. One of the oldest in The Bahamas, a gleaming white, Spanish-style structure, is at Clarence Town on southern Long Island. Examples of early native architecture are evident in a sprinkling of the square stone houses with wood rafters and pyramidal, thatched roofs. Many of the older buildings stand in ruins, but the basic design is reflected in later but similar styles built of cinder block.

Two airports serve the island, one at Stella Maris in the north and the other at Deadman's Cay, almost central. A highway, Government Road, runs the island's length.

Clarence Town receives the Nassau mailboat once a week. The boat puts in at Stella Maris or Deadman's Cay once or twice a week. Because of weather conditions and other hazards, the schedule is not always strictly adhered to. Cars can be rented at Stella Maris or at the **Thompson Bay Inn,** which is also a good place for fresh seafood and other inexpensive meals.

History

The ruins of the Adderley plantation stand at the northern end of the island, not far from the Stella Maris Inn. The remains of three roofless buildings still stand, with a tall stone chimney much in evidence. Large, hand-hewn stones are strewn about, and traces of stone fences can still be seen. Many stout cedar frames clinging to some windows and doors are still intact and give off their fragrant scent.

Near the plantation is the Adderley slave burial ground. It is off the beach near a stand of tall trees, but difficult to get to because of the thick, scratchy underbrush. Once through, however, the mounds of graves can be seen, but they are slowly disappearing from erosion and neglect.

The original Adderley apparently fled the United States with his slaves at the end of the Revolution. He established a cotton plantation and also did subsistence farming. He is said to have been prosperous in his new home. According to his black descendants, Adderley committed suicide upon discovering that his favorite son had formed a liaison with one of the female slaves. The liaison continued, nevertheless. By the time abolition came to The Bahamas, white Adderleys were hard to come by. Many Adderleys and Taylors still live on the island, and the name is a common one throughout The Bahamas.

Mrs. Adderley, the late matriarch and great-grandmother of present-day island Adderleys and Taylors, lived to the age of 130. She never once traveled by boat, automobile, or airplane. She felt that the Lord

Long Island

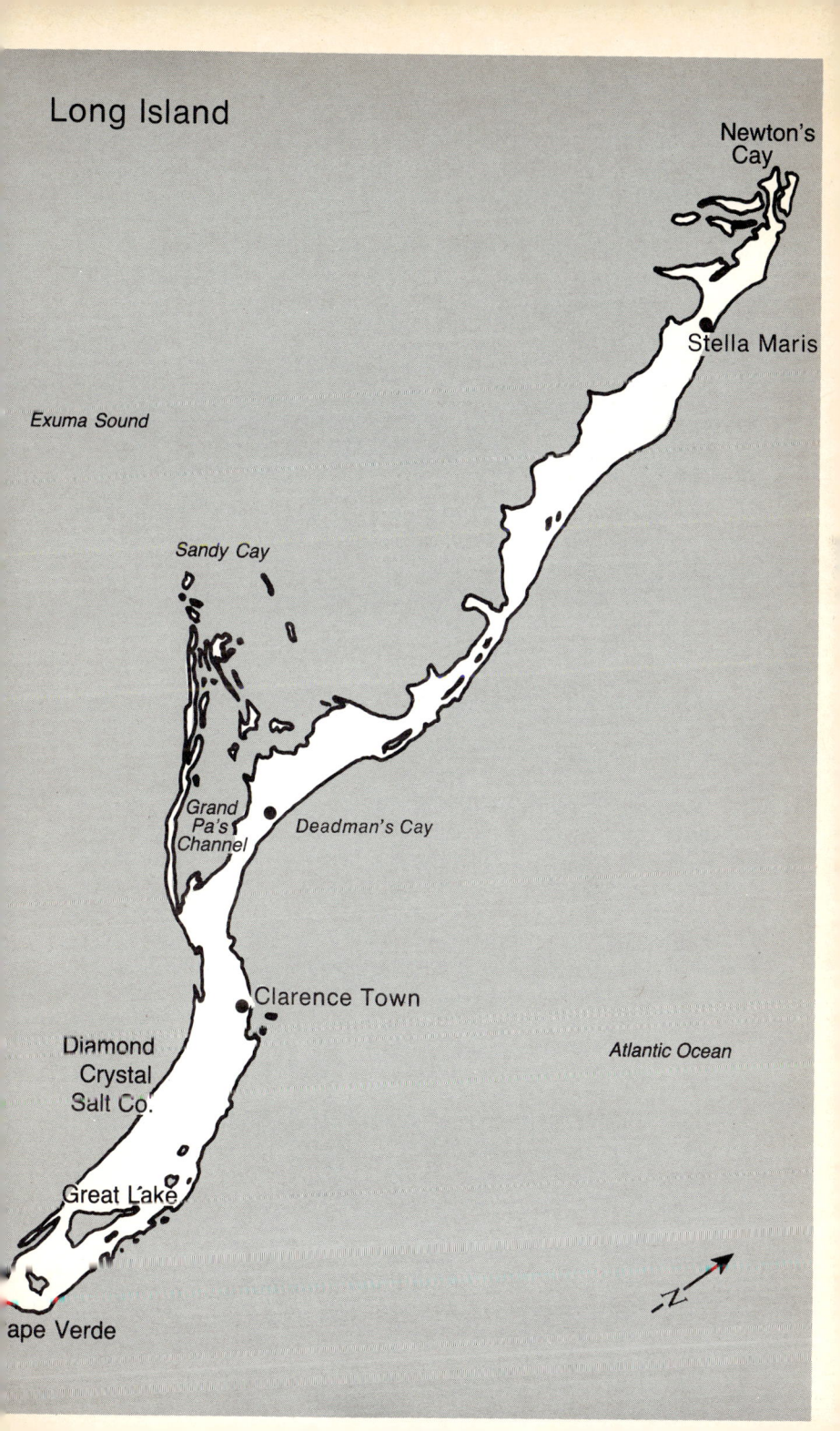

- Newton's Cay
- Stella Maris
- Exuma Sound
- Sandy Cay
- Grand Pa's Channel
- Deadman's Cay
- Clarence Town
- Diamond Crystal Salt Co.
- Atlantic Ocean
- Great Lake
- Cape Verde

-N-had provided feet as the means of transport and there was no need for artificial, man made devices. As the oldest living person on the island (and probably in The Bahamas), she was selected to be guest of honor and ribbon cutter at the gala opening of the tennis courts at Stella Maris Inn. The ceremony was attended by local officials and dignitaries as well as representatives from Nassau. Mrs. Adderley's descendants, who live in nearby towns such as Burnt Ground, Clinton, and Seymour, will proudly relate the story.

WHAT TO SEE AND DO

Sports • The Stella Maris Inn has a very good diving program with one of the best dive masters in The Bahamas. The adventurous go to a reef where they swim among black-tip, lemon, and bull sharks. (According to the instructor, who even pets the sharks, people who fear sharks don't know much about them.) Rum Cay is also a popular diving site. Fishing, boating, and tennis are available at Stella Maris.

*Dunmore's Cave • *Deadman's Cay* • There is convincing evidence that Arawak Indians used these caves and that, later, pirates made use of them for cargo storage as well as for hiding places.

Dunmore Plantation • *Deadman's Cay* • Lord Dunmore, an early Bahamian governor, had large landholdings here. His estate, commanding a view of the sea, is in ruins, but gateposts remain to mark the entrance to his mansion.

Father Jerome's Churches • *Clarence Town* • The Catholic missionary, Father Jerome, who also left his mark on Cat Island, built two of the town's churches, one Catholic and the other Anglican.

Spanish Church • *The Bight* • The oldest Spanish church in The Bahamas dates from the time of an early Spanish settlement.

Conception Island • *Off the town of Stella Maris* • This island, reached by boat, is northeast of Long Island's north tip. Protected by the Bahamas National Trust, it is a sanctuary for tropical and migrating birds, and for the protected green turtles of The Bahamas.

Deadman's Cay Caves • *Deadman's Cay* • These fascinating caves have never been completely explored and continue to reveal new findings. They have stalactites and stalagmites, and Indian drawings are found on the walls. One of the caves has a tunnel that leads out to the ocean.

Adderley Plantation • *Off Cape Santa Maria* • The plantation stands in stately ruins, showing its thick walls of hand-hewn stone, its tall chimney, and the stone fence that once defined the manor's limits. The remaining pieces of cedar window and door frames are still fragrant. The various houses are difficult to reach because of overgrown vegetation and neglect. Even more difficult to see is the old slave burial ground, which is a short distance north just off the beach. Scattered mounds can be discerned if you brave slashes and scratches reaching the area through the underbrush.

WHERE TO STAY

MODERATE

☆☆☆**Stella Maris Inn** • The largest of the the Long Island hotels, Stella Maris has cottages, apartments, and individual rooms. The hilly, sprawling grounds provide beautiful views of the beach. Just about all watersports are available here, including fishing, boating and an exceptional diving program. This German-owned inn is popular for its "rake-and-scrapes," when local musicians play up a storm. As with many Family Island hotels, no keys are used for guest rooms, but there are safety deposit boxes for those who choose to bring the family jewels. Along the road overlooking the shore are the inn's dramatically perched luxurious villas as well as private homes owned mainly by Germans. Don't forget to bring bug repellant, which is needed especially in the late afternoon.

SAN SALVADOR

Called Guanahani by its early Indian inhabitants and Watling's Island until 1926, San Salvador sits 200 miles southeast of Nassau. It is known world wide as the place Columbus first set foot in the New World. However, a recent replotting of his voyage by a *National Geographic* team places Columbus' landing some 65 miles to the south at

Samana Cay, another Bahamian island. As one government official put it, "I have no concern for the particular island as long as it's in the Bahamas." The Bahamian government is busily preparing to celebrate the cinque-centennial of the landing in 1992.

Not one, but three Columbus landing monuments mark the disputed event. The most easily seen is a white cross standing on the sandy shore at Long Bay. Nearby is a second monument commemorating the 1968 Olympic Games in Mexico. Set on a raised platform, the center bowl of this dark metal structure held the Olympic flame, which had been brought from Greece and burned here until the games opened in Mexico City.

The waters around San Salvador, with reefs, shoals, and crashing surf, teem with marine life and are ideal for fishing, snorkeling, and diving. A full-fledged dive center is located at Riding Rock Inn, the island's sole hotel, where you can book dive packages.

Like most Bahamian islands, San Salvador's crust is limestone and coral, topped with a variety of low-growing tropical brush. In addition to palms, the feathery casuarinas provide a deep green background. Girding the five-by-twelve mile area of this seldom visited island is the Queen's Highway, a 35-mile stretch of limestone-dusted road. The interior is laced with a network of lakes, ranging from Great Lake, the largest, to smaller ones including Granny Lake, Little Lake, and Long Lake, which connects the northeast and northwest arms of the system.

The terrain is somewhat rolling and, at the northeast, the island boasts a hill crowned by gleaming white Dixon Hill Lighthouse. From the top, you can take in the network of lakes and the settlement called United Estates. Offshore, Golding Cay and Man Head Cay, their bleached limestone terrain chalky against the blue-green water, are also visible, along with verdant Green Cay.

An oldtimer remembers when, as a small boy, oil for the lighthouse was unloaded from boats docked at Cockburn Town and transported over land and, by way of the lakes, to Dixon Hill. With other boys his age, he helped men roll the heavy oil casks from the dock and along the primitive road to Long Lake. There, the barrels were again loaded onto small rowboats and ferried through the lake passages to the lighthouse. The boys who helped with this task were rewarded with British coins, which they quickly traded for candy and other treats.

The administrative seat of the island is Cockburn Town (pronounced Coburn) where the only airstrip and the one tourist accommodation are located and where the mailboat docks. Although a sizable portion of the island's small population lives in Cockburn Town, the largest and most robust settlement is at United Estates (referred to by locals as U.E.), at the northeast edge.

Cockburn Town has the Commissioner's office, post office, library, police station, courthouse, and jail, which has neither prisoners nor locks. A likeness of Columbus over the door of the little Catholic church greets visitors and the Anglican church is not far off the highway. Nearby are the public and Catholic cemeteries.

The remnants and ruins of former plantations remain as reminders of what used to be. The most notable, Watling's Castle, stands on a rise at Sandy Point Estate. The eighteenth century plantation house was owned by George Watling, a slaveholder and reputed pirate, for whom the island was once named. Many of the stone walls, with empty window openings, still stand, including the cook house chimney and boundary fences built by slaves. Much of the site is overgrown and inaccessible.

To the east is Farquharson's plantation, another ruin. Charles Farquharson was a justice of the peace for the island and his journal covering the years 1831 and 1832 is one of the few remaining documents of plantation life at the time.

During World War II, there were both British and American installations on the island. The Royal Air Force had a submarine watching station and the United States had a naval base and a coast guard station. Later, the U.S. also maintained a missile tracking station on the island. The naval base now houses students of the College Center of Finger Lakes, a consortium of upstate New York colleges (Elmira, Corning and Hartwick) for the study of marine life and the environment.

At Sandy Point, not far from Watling's Castle, a number of well-appointed private homes are owned by foreigners and built on one of the most beautiful stretches of beach on the island. Not far off, but in a less ideal area away from the beach, is a more modest development of condominiums, also housing non-Bahamians who use them as vacation homes. Near these developments, an interesting place to visit is Dripping Rock, one of the limestone caves that riddle the island.

Rum Cay, located between San Salvador and Long Island, is under the same jurisdiction as San Salvador. The island boasts rolling hills, miles of empty beaches, and caves with pre-Columbian drawings. Its chief town is Port Nelson and its only resort is the Rum Cay Club, where the specialty is diving.

WHAT TO SEE AND DO

Cockburn Town • Starting out from Riding Rock Inn, much of this tiny Family Island settlement can be seen on foot. A sign across the road from the Inn's entrance points directions to several of the not-to-be-missed sights. The administration buildings, churches, and cemeteries are clustered along and just off the main road (Queen's Highway) and within view of the sea. Some steps off the road and heading inland

San Salvador

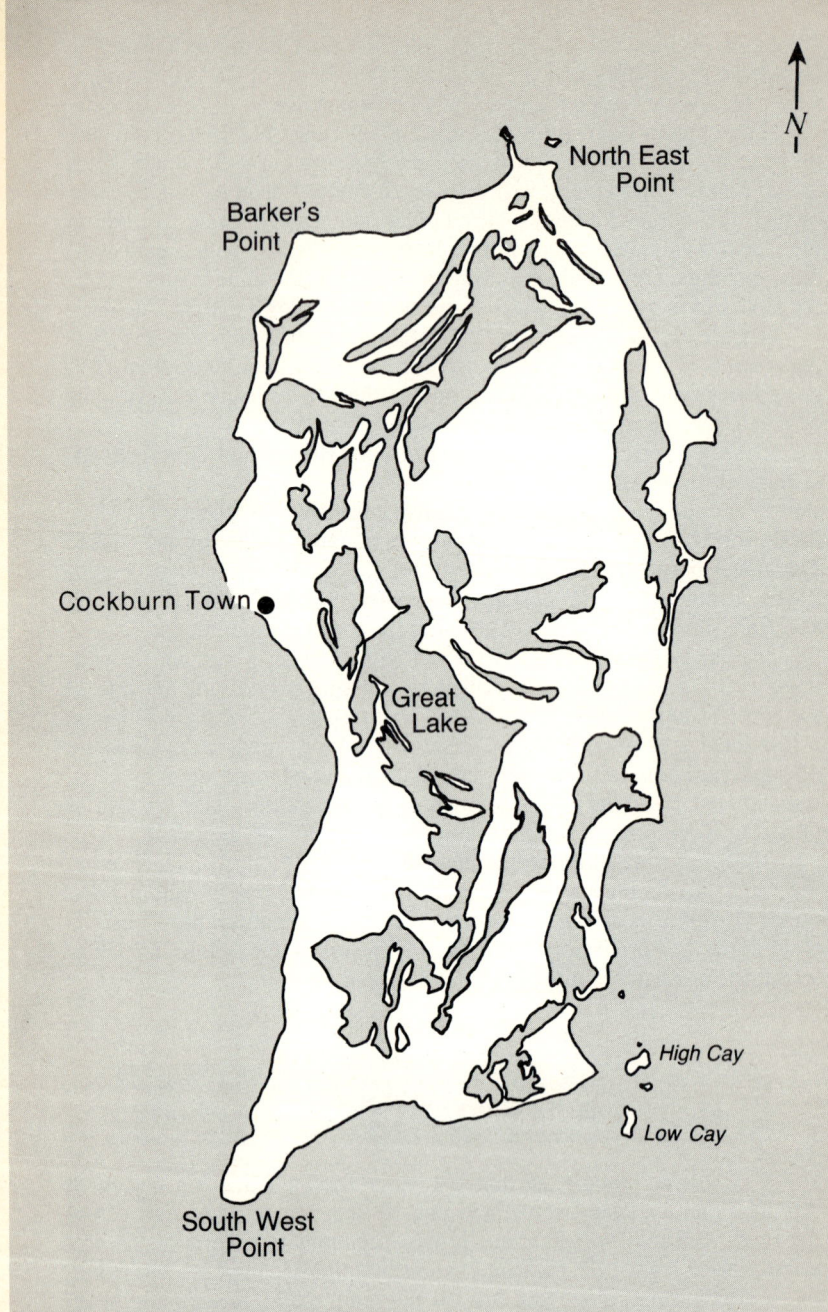

are the local grocery store, the crafts shop, and other services for residents. The Harlem Square Club, the local music and drinking night spot, is at its liveliest on weekends.

Observation Platform • *near Riding Rock Inn* • The view from the Observation Tower platform will give you a good idea of the island's inland lake network. Walking about two miles straight ahead from the Inn, past an abandoned military installation filled with rusted, discarded vehicles, visitors can reach the wooden tower. The platform is in need of repair, so sightseers are warned to be careful.

New World Museum • *just north of Cockburn Town* • This small museum by the sea is operated by Ruth Wolper, who has a keen interest in the history and development of the island. Because she is often out unearthing additional history and artifacts on San Salvador, the museum is not always open. However, because the community is small, it is relatively simple to find out when she will be around.

Columbus Monuments • Three monuments commemorate the landing of Christopher Columbus in the New World. This claim has been recently disputed by a team from the National Geographic Society. After remapping Columbus' voyage, their finding, published in the November 1986 *National Geographic,* puts the landing farther south, on the Bahamian island of Samana Cay.

On nearly inaccessible Crab Cay in the northeast, one marker was placed by *The Chicago Herald* newspaper in 1892, when the city of Chicago was chosen as the center to celebrate the 400th year of Columbus' landing. At Fernandez Bay, to the south of the west coast, is the Heloise monument. This obelisk-shaped column is off the roadway, near the beach, and reached by an overgrown path. The marker was put here in 1957 by a small boat, the *Heloise,* after a round-the-world cruise. The island's most famous and most photographed monument is a tall, white cross planted in the sand at Long Bay. Yet another monument lies hidden here on the ocean floor.

United Estates • The largest and most populated settlement on San Salvador, United Estates lies within the shadow of the Dixon Hill Lighthouse. From the settlement, visitors can easily walk to such places as the College Center of Finger Lakes, the U.S. Coast Guard station, or to East Beach for swimming, snorkeling, or shell gathering.

Dixon Hill Lighthouse • *Dixon Hill* • Twice every 25 seconds, this sparkling white lighthouse, built in 1856, sends out a 400,000 candlepower beam that can be seen for 19 miles. The lighthouse is 160 feet high, still hand operated, and uses oil. Visitors climbing to the top are astounded by the tiny light source and then transported by the spectacular view of surrounding cays, inland lakes and, far in the distance, *The Chicago Herald* marker on Crab Cay in memory of Columbus' landfall. The lighthouse keeper's house is next door and, if asked, he will show you the inspector's book with signatures dating back to the Queen's rule.

Watling's Castle • *Sandy Point Estate* • The folorn remains of a group of stone plantation houses known as Watling's Castle are planted on a rise overlooking the sea. Named for George Watling, a one-time pirate whose name the island bore for a time, the crumbling walls still stand as well as stone boundry walls and the cookhouse oven. Much of the site is inaccessible because of the surrounding overgrown vegetation. As time-worn as they are, the ruins are quite impressive, especially when the empty stone shells are seen from below.

Farquarson's Plantation • *Pigeon Creek* • On the eastern side of the island, this old estate, once owned by Charles Farquarson, the island's justice of the peace, is now in ruins. You'll see the remains of the main house, slave quarters, fireplaces, and ovens.

Big Well • *Sandy Point Estate* • Big Well is south of the Columbus monument at Long Bay. The well is almost 150 years old and was an early source of fresh water for locals.

Dripping Rock • *Sandy Point* • This is one of the many limestone caverns at the southern end of the island. There are fruit trees in this fertile aea and the cool cave encloses a fresh water well.

WHERE TO STAY

☆☆ **Riding Rock Inn** • *Cockburn Town* • Named for offshore boulders that once rolled on the ocean floor, Riding Rock Inn is the only tourist accommodation on San Salvador. Although located a stone's throw from the island's only airstrip, noise is never a problem since planes fly in and out infrequently. The inn's 24 rooms, all on one level, are ranged along the rim of the rocky shore. Some rooms look out to the ocean, and the remaining face inland with views of the swimming pool, the main road and the lush island foliage. Cozy and air-conditioned, the rooms all have private baths and are comfortably furnished with outside patios and chaises that invite sprawling. The patios on the seaside are ideal for lounging and watching the often glorious sunsets.

The sound of the sea at night induces sleep and can be great for insomniacs. Some 50 yards south of the inn, the rocks have been cleared away for a serviceable, sandy beach with a panoramic view to the north and south. In addition to the pool, there are tennis courts, which are almost always free for playing. For sightseeing, rental motor bikes, bicycles, and cars are available just outside the main office. A major attraction at the inn is its dive program run by Guanahani Dive, Ltd. Package rates are available by prearrangement as well as daily rates. Just about everything needed for diving is on tap, from lessons to rental of masks, wetsuits, underwater cameras and film processing. Marina services are also available for boating and sports fishing. Advance reservations are recommended. Because there are no local restaurants, the inn provides three meals. Bahamian specialties are served as well as American and Continental cuisine. Among the local dishes are conch chowder, okra soup, peas and rice, and turtle steak. Especially mouthwatering when toasted and laden with butter at breakfast, home baked bread is served at all meals. The inn's main building houses the registration desk, a modest lounge, the dining room, the bar, and an oceanside veranda that runs the length of the building. The Driftwood Bar, with taped background music and decor to echo its name, is the inn's focal point. Here, visitors get a chance to mingle with other guests, hear tales of diving and sailing exploits, and get to know the friendly cooperative staff.

☆☆☆**Rum Cay Club** • This resort is located on a small island between San Salvador and Long Island. Although most of its patrons are avid divers, there is a sprinkling of honeymooners, boaters, and those drawn by the serene surroundings. Beautiful empty beaches rim the island, and the resort rents bikes and jeeps for exploring the other side of the island, 5 miles away, and its stunning, deserted beaches. You fly into the club's landing strip, an unpaved slash in the grass and a short walk or a bumpy ride from the hotel. Someone from the hotel meets the plane. If traveling light, you can walk the distance in minutes. The Flying Physicians, an organization of doctors who all dive and have their own planes, come once a year around the end of November or early December, so you may have a difficult time booking during their stay. The Club House is the focal point of the resort. That's where guests gather for pre-dinner drinks, sunbathe during the day on one of the multi-level decks, or soak in the ocean-view hot tub. On barbecue night, guests eat here rather than in the dining room. You can leave film here for overnight development. The hotel rents cameras for underwater photographs. Dive sites include sheer walls and tunnels as well as a shipwreck more than a century old. The guest rooms, in 2-story wooden buildings, are large, with balconies, refrigerators, dressing alcoves, and light boxes for viewing slides. Instead of TV, telephones, radios, or room keys, guests have the sound and sight of the ocean outside their sliding doors. Monday night is "Island Night," when guests go to town for local food at Kay's Bar or the Ocean View Restaurant. Port Nelson, the small, friendly town, is a 15-minute walk away. Dress is casual whether at the club or in town. The only telephone on the island is outside of town and operative for about an hour three times a day. Hotels, bars, and boats communicate with VHF. Rum Cay is reached by charter flights from George Town, Exuma, and other islands, or from Fort Lauderdale. Most guests come by way of Fort Lauderdale and stay from Saturday to Saturday.

HOTEL QUICK-REFERENCE CHARTS

Key

Facilities

BP	Beach Privileges		MP	Mopeds
BT	Boating		S	Waterskiing
F	Fishing		M/D	Marina-Dock
G	Golf		HC	Health Club
PB	Private Beach		HB	Horseback Riding
SC	Scuba		CA	Casino
T	Tennis		BA/B	Barber-Beauty Salon
WSF	Windsurfing		BA/S	Baby-sitting
PS	Parasailing		DI	Disco
P	Swimming Pool		TV	Television

Credit Cards

A	American Express		C	Carte Blanche
B	Barclays		D	Diners Club
BA	Bankamericard		M	MasterCard
TF	Trust House Forte		V	Visa
T	Texaco			

Meal Plans

CP	Continental Plan: Light Breakfast		MAP	Modified American Plan: Breakfast & Dinner
EP	European Plan: Room only			
FB	Full American Breakfast		FAP	Full American Plan: Three meals

The following approximate rates are all daily, in-season (December through April). For MAP, add from $20 to $30 per person, per day.

Nassau
Hotels

Page	Establishment	Meal Plans Offered	No. Rooms	Double Room (Per Person in Season)	Credit Cards	Facilities	Other
187	Ambassador Beach Hotel (Wyndham) P.O. Box N–3026, Nassau (809) 327-8231	EP, MAP	480	$75–135	A, M, V, B, C	PB, P, T, BT, SC, WSF, PS	
190	Buena Vista Hotel P.O. Box N–564, Nassau (809) 322-2811	EP	6	$40	A, M, V, D		downtown, 19th-century mansion
187	Cable Beach Hotel & Casino P.O. Box N–4914, Nassau (809) 327-6000, (800) 822-4200	EP	700	$77–105	A, M, V, D	PE, P, CA, G, T, PS, S, SC, WSF	theater, rooms for handicapped
188	Cable Beach Inn W. Bay St., Nassau (809) 327-7341	EP	114	$50	A, M, V	PB, P, T, HC	
189	Cable Beach Manor P.O. Box N–8333, Nassau (809) 327-7785 (800) 327-0787	EP	44	$77–105	A, M, V, D		
	Coral Harbour Beach Club P.O. Box N–4808, Nassau (809) 326-1144	EP	35	$40–50	A, M, V	PB, BT, F, WSF, G	
196	Coral World P.O. Box N–7797, Nassau (809) 328-1036, (800) 221-0203		22				Each room has private pool

Nassau (cont.)
Hotels

Page	Establishment	Meal Plans Offered	No. Rooms	Double Room (Per Person in Season)	Credit Cards	Facilities	Other
187	Crystal Palace Resort & Casino P.O. Box N-8306, Nassau (809) 327-7341, (800) 453-5301		872		PB, P, T, G, HC		
194	Divi Bahamas Beach Resort P.O. Box N-8191, Nassau (809) 326-4391, (607) 277-3484 (800) 333-3484	EP	120	$80	A, M, V, D	PB, P, T, G, SC	
191	Dolphin Hotel P.O. Box N-3236, Nassau (809) 322-8666 (800) 432-5594	EP, CP, FB	66	$35-40	A, M, V	P	beach across street, pool on premises
191	El Greco Hotel P.O. Box N-4187, Nassau (809) 325-1121	EP	26	$45	A, M, V, D	P, BA/S	close to downtown
	Grand Central Hotel P.O. Box N-4084, Nassau (809) 322-8356	EP	35	$40	None		
189	Graycliff Hotel P.O. Box N-10246, Nassau (809) 322-2796	CP	21	$80-100	A, M, V, D, C, B	P	good food, old mansion
191	The Harbour Moon Hotel P.O. Box N-646, Nassau (809) 323-7330	MAP	30	Rates on Request	A, M, V		downtown on Bay St. overlooking Paradise Island

	Hotel	Plan	Rooms	Rate	Cards	Features	Notes
190	Henrea Carlette Hotel P.O. Box N-4227, Nassau (809) 327-7801	EP	20	$66–$70	A, M, V		
	Lighthouse Beach Hotel P.O. Box N-915, Nassau (800) 322-4474	EP	90	$44	A, M, V,	P, BP	across street from beach, near downtown shopping
191	Marietta's Hotel P.O. Box 5053, Nassau (809) 323-2395	EP	42	$35	A, M, V	P	near beach, good food, cable TV in all rooms
188	Nassau Beach Hotel P.O. Box N-7756, Nassau (809) 327-7711 (800) 223-5672	EP, BP, CP, FAP	425	$80–110 Palm Club $499 (4 nights all-inclusive)	A, M, V, D, C, TF	P, PB, BT, F, SC, S, T, PS	shops, entertainment
	Nassau Harbour Club P.O. Box N-3703, Nassau (809) 323-3771	EP	50	$35–45	A, M, V	P, BA/S, BT, M/D	entertainment
191	New Olympia Hotel P.O. Box N-984, Nassau (809) 322-4971	EP	53	$40–50	A, V, D		gift shop, backgammon, near beach and town
191	Ocean Spray Hotel P.O. Box N-3035, Nassau (809) 322-8032	EP	30	$40	A, M, V, D		
190	Parliament Hotel P.O. Box N-175, Nassau (809) 322-2836	EP	16	$40–50	A, M, V, D	MP	downtown Nassau, good restaurant
	Parthenon Hotel P.O. Box N-4930, Nassau (809) 322-2643	EP	18	$30	A, M, V	BA/S	downtown, near beach, breakfast in room or on patio

Nassau (cont.)
Hotels

Page	Establishment	Meal Plans Offered	No. Rooms	Double Room (Per Person in Season)	Credit Cards	Facilities	Other
190	Pilot House Hotel P.O. Box N–4941, Nassau (809) 322–8431	EP, MAP, CP, FAP	124	$50–65	A, M, V, B, C	P, BA/S, BA/B, BT, F, SC	complimentary private ferry
	Poinciana Inn P.O. Box N–7096, Nassau (809) 323–1720	EP	50	$35–45	None		
188	Royal Bahamian (Wyndham) 5775 N.W. 11th St. (Suite 400) Miami, FL 33126 (800) 822–4200	EP	200	$95+	A, M, V, D	PB, P, T, BT	on Cable Beach suites and villas available
190	Sheraton British Colonial Hotel P.O. Box N–7148, Nassau (809) 322–3301/(800) 325-3535	EP, MAP, CP, FAP	325	$55–85	A, BA, B, C, D, M, V	B, P, BA/S, T, BA/B, PB, F, S, SC, MP, DI	shops, shuffleboard, ping pong, restaurants. Downtown
	Towne Hotel P.O. Box N–4808, Nassau (809) 322–8450	EP	47	$35–45	A, M, V		off Bay St.
193	*Paradise Island* Bay View Village P.O. Box SS–6308, Nassau (809) 326–2555/6	EP	75	Rates on Request	A, M, V	PB	apartments, villas, laundry room, 3 pools

193	Club Land'Or P.O. Box ES–6429, Nassau (809) 326–2400	EP	71	$80	A, M, V, D	B, P, BA/S	apartments & rooms
	Grosvenor Court Apts. P.O. Box SS–5151, Nassau (809) 326–2171	EP	35 Apts.	Rates on Request		P, PB	
192	Holiday Inn P.O. Box 6214, Nassau (809) 326–2101	EP, MAP, BP, FAP	535	$70–90	A, M, V, D	BT, DI, PB, F, S, SC, T	rents motor scooters only
194	Loews Harbour Cove P.O. Box 6249, Nassau (809) 326–2561	EP, MAP, FB, CP	250	$70–90	A, M, V, D, C	DI, P, PB, M/D	harbour view of Nassau
192	Ocean Club P.O. Box N–4777, Nassau (809) 326–2501 (800) 321–3000	EP, MAP	70	$75–180	A, M, V, D	P, PB, BA/S, BT, S, SC, M/D, G, T	
194	Paradise Paradise P.O. Box SS–6259, Nassau (809) 326–2541 (800) 321–3000	EP, MAP	100	$70–90	A, M, V, D	PB, BA/S, SC	special sports package deals available
192	Paradise Island Resort & Casino P.O. Box N–4777, Nassau (809) 326–3000 (800) 321–3000	EP, MAP	1300	$85–200	A, M, V, D		complex of several era hotels sharing facilities
193	Sheraton Grand Hotel 1 Fifth Avenue New York, NY 10033 (800) 325–3535	EP, MAP	360	$90–135	A, M, V, D	PB, P, BT, F, T, G, PS	all rooms ocean view, refrigerators in rooms

Nassau (cont.)
Guesthouses/Apartment Hotels (some have fans and/or limited air conditioning)

Page	Establishment	Meal Plans Offered	No. Rooms	Double Room (Per Person in Season)	Credit Cards	Facilities	Other
	Bayshore Inn P.O. Box SS–5318, Nassau (809) 323–2973	EP, CP	12	$35	A, M, V	P	individual attention
	Bel-Air Apartment Hotel P.O. Box N–4428, Nassau (809) 327–7078	EP	10 1-BR Apts.	$37	None	BP	on Cable Beach
189	Casuarina's Apartment Hotel P.O. Box N–4016, Nassau (809) 327–7921	EP	74 Apts.	$30–50	A, M, V, D	BA/S	on Cable Beach
	Seagrape Villas P.O. Box N–3941, Nassau (809) 325–2136	EP	1- and 2-BRs	Rates on Request	A, V		
	The Orchard Garden Apartment Hotel P.O. Box N–1514, Nassau (809) 323–1297	EP	22	$50	A, M, V	P, PB, BA/S	bike & moped rentals, pets permitted
	Family Guest House P.O. Box N–6, Nassau (809) 325–4147	EP	14	$20	None		
	Kelton Lodge P.O. Box N–4019, Nassau (809) 328–1940	EP, CP, MAP	6	$40	A, M, V		near town, some private baths, dinner on request

Klonaris Guest House P.O. Box N-1174, Nassau (809) 322-3888	EP	5	$20	None	closed June–Sept. near beach & center of town
Mignon Guest House P.O. Box N-786, Nassau (809) 322-4771	EP	8	$20	None	
Mitchell's Cottages P.O. Box N-715, Nassau (809) 322-4365	EP	6	$20	None	offers afternoon tea and sympathy
Mondingo Inn P.O. Box N-9669, Nassau (809) 324-3333	EP	8	$30	None	B, DI, BA/S
Morris Guest House P.O. Box N-1077, Nassau (809) 323-6013	EP	5	$20	None	
West Bay Inn Motel P.O. Box N-3222, Nassau (809) 325-8900	EP	6	$25	V, M	

Freeport
Hotels

Page	Establishment	Meal Plans Offered	No. Rooms	Double Room (Per Person in Season)	Credit Cards	Facilities	Other
209	Atlantik Beach Hotel P.O. Box F–531, Freeport (809) 373–1444 1-(800) 327–0787	EP, MAP	175	$60–75	A, BA, M, D, M, V	P, G, T, MP, TV	Situated on beach
208	Bahamas Princess Resort & Casino P.O. Box F-207, Freeport (212) 582–8100 (800) 223–1818 (809) 352–6721	MAP	960	$65–80	A, M, V, D	P, BP, BA/S, DI	free shuttle to beach
209	Castaways Resort P.O. Box 2629, Freeport (809) 352–6682	EP	138	$35	A, M, V, D	PB, P, F	free shuttle to beach
210	Coral Beach Hotel P.O. Box F–2468, Freeport (809) 373–2468	EP	10	$35–45	A	F, SC, BP	golf privileges
211	Deep Water Cay Club P.O. Box 1145 Palm Beach, FL 33480 (305) 684–3958 or P.O. Box F-39, Freeport	FAP	8	$140	M, V	P, DI, BA/S, BP, BT, F, SC, G	East End, own air strip, fishing emphasis
209	Freeport Inn P.O. Box F–200, Freeport (809) 352–6648	MAP	150	$50–60	A, M, V, D	P, DI, BA/S, BP, BT, F, SC, G	use Xanadu Beach, free transportation, bike rentals, pets, some kitchenettes

210	Holiday Inn P.O. Box F-760, Freeport (809) 373-1333 (800) HOLIDAY	EP, MAP, FAP	505	$65–80	A, M, V, D	TV, PB, HC, BT, F, T, G, SC	health club, games room, situated on beach
211	Jack Tar Village 103 South Akard St. Dallas, TX (809) 346-6211 (800) 527-9299	FAP	377	$140 (FAP)	A, M, V, C	T, G, BT, F, W/S, SC, P, B, BA/S	rates are all inclusive
210	Lucayan Beach Resort & Casino P.O. Box F-336, Freeport/Lucaya (809) 373-7777 (305) 463-7760	MAP, EP	168	$65–85	T, G, BT, F, W/S, P, B, BA/S		
	New Victoria Inn P.O. Box F-1261, Freeport (809) 373-3040/2	EP	40	$45	A, M, V	BT, F, SC	
	Sea Sun Manor P.O. Box 125, Freeport (809) 352-2140	EP	64 Apts	$40	A, M, D, C, V	P	parasailing
210	Silver Sands Hotel P.O. Box F-2385, Freeport (809) 373-5700	EP, MAP	164	$60	A, M, V, D, B	TV, BA/S, PB, BT, T, SC, P	apartments & suites
209	Windward Palms Hotel P.O. Box F-2549, Freeport (809) 352-8821/(800) 327-0787	EP	100	$40	A, M, V, D	P, 3P	free transportation to beach
208	Xanadu Beach Hotel P.O. Box F-2438, Freeport (809) 352-6782 (800) 222-3788 (804) 270-4313	EP, MAP	184	$80	A, BA, D, M, V	TV BA/S, T, BT, P	marina on premises and villas

The Abacos

Page	Establishment	Meal Plans Offered	No. Rooms	Double Room (Per Person in Season)	Credit Cards	Facilities	Other
	Walker's Cay						
229	Walker's Cay Hotel 700 S.W. 34 St., Ft. Lauderdale, FL (305) 522–1469 (U.S.)	EP	62	$60–85	A, D	P, DI, BA/S, PB, M/D, BT, F, S, SC, T	
	Treasure Cay						
224	Treasure Cay Beach Hotel & Villas P.O. Box TC-4183, Abaco (809) 367–2570 (800) 432–8257	All-inclusive	250	rates on request	A, M, V, D	PB, P, BA/S, BA/B, M/D, SC, F, BT, G, T	fuel avail. bicycles rented, laundry, TV & card room, shuffleboard, volleyball
	Green Turtle Cay						
226	Bluff House Club & Marina Green Turtle Cay Tel: Green Turtle Cay	EP	32	$35	None	BT	closed Sept.–Oct.
227	Coco Bay Club Box 836, Green Turtle Cay (800) 752–0166	EP	7 Cottages	$50	None	PB, BT	
225	Green Turtle Club P.O. Box 270, Green Turtle Cay (809) 367–2572	EP	30	$50–60	A, M, V	P, PB, BA/S, M/D, BT, F	closed Sept–Oct., hosts annual fishing tournament and annual regatta, units available with kitchens
227	Linton's Beach and Harbour Cottages Green Turtle Cay USA (615) 259–5682	EP	2 Cottages	$60	None	PB	maid and cook service available

227	New Plymouth Inn
Green Turtle Cay
(809) 367-5211	MAP	10	$55 (MAP)	None	BP, BT, F	pets allowed
228	Sea Star Beach Cottages
P.O. Box 282, Gilam Bay
Green Turtle Cay
Tel: Green Turtle Cay 544	EP	14	$40	None	BA/S, BT, SC, F	small pets only
	Great Guana Cay						
	Guana Beach Resort
P.O. Box 455, Marsh Harbour
(809) 367-2207	EP, MAP	18	$40	M, V	PB, M/D, BA/S, BT, S, F	7 miles of beach, pets permitted
	Finder's Cottages
Great Guana Cay, Abaco
Tel: dial Operator	EP	4 Cottages	Rates on Request	None	PB, BT, F, SC	
	Elbow Cay						
228	Abaco Inn
Hope Town, Abaco
(809) 367-2666	EP, MAP	10	$55–65	M, V	P, PB, M/D, SC, F, S, WSF	bicycles and boats rented, pets allowed, closed Sept.–Nov.
228	Hope Town Harbour Lodge
Hope Town, Abaco
(809) 367-2277	EP	21	$40–50	A, M, V	P, M/D, BT, SC, F, WSF	closed Sept–Oct.
224	*Marsh Harbour*
Ambassador Inn
P.O. Box 484, Marsh Harbour
(809) 367-2022	EP	6	$25	None	BP	
223	Conch Inn
P.O. Box 434, Marsh Harbour
(809) 367-2800	EP	14	$45	A, M, V	P, BP, M/D, BT, SC, S	bicycles rented

The Abacos (cont.)

Page	Establishment	Meal Plans Offered	No. Rooms	Double Room (Per Person in Season)	Credit Cards	Facilities	Other
224	Great Abaco Beach Hotel P.O. Box 419, Marsh Harbour (809) 367–2158	EP	20	$50–65		PB, P, BA/S, T	on waterfront

Acklins/Crooked Island

Page	Establishment	Meal Plans Offered	No. Rooms	Double Room (Per Person in Season)	Credit Cards	Facilities	Other
233	Pittstown Point Landing Bahamas Caribbean Intern. P.O. Box 9831 Mobile, Alabama 36691 (205) 666–4482	FAP	12	$40–50	A, M, V	PB, BT, F, WSF, SC	closed Sept., Oct., bicycles rented, airstrip nearby
	T & S Guest House Church Grove Tel: Church Grove	EP	10	$20	None	TV, BP, F	
233	Crooked Island Beach Inn Colonel Hill (809) 336–2096		11	$25	None		Near airport

Andros

Page	Establishment	Meal Plans Offered	No. Rooms	Double Room (Per Person in Season)	Credit Cards	Facilities	Other
	Nicholl's Town						
243	Andros Beach Hotel (309) 329-2582	MAP	24	$40	A, M, V	P, PB, DI, M/D, BA/S, SC, F	pets allowed, 3 cottages
244	Movashti Hotel P.O Box GD, Lowe Sound Andros (309) 329-2331		30			PB, TV, F, DR	Near Nicholl's Town
	Tradewinds Villas P.O. Box 4465, Nicholl's Town (309) 329-2185	EP	16 Cottages	$35	A	BP, BT, F, SC, T	
	Andros Town						
	Chickcharnie Hotel Fresh Creek, Andros Town (309) 368-2025	EP	8	$30	None	BT	
242	Small Hope Bay Lodge Box N-1131, Nassau (109) 363-2014 (800) 223-6961 (305) 463-9130	FAP	20	$50-100	A, V, M	PE, BA/S, BT, F, SC	bicycles rented, pets allowed, closed Sept.–Oct. Androsia works nearby, some shared baths
	Mangrove Cay						
244	Bannister's Cottages Lisbon Creek, Mangrove Cay Tel: 329-4188	FAP, AP, CP	6	$32 (CP)	None	BP, BA/S, BT, F, WSF	bicycles rented, shared baths, adjacent club with fish & turtle pool

Andros (cont.)

Page	Establishment	Meal Plans Offered	No. Rooms	Double Room (Per Person in Season)	Credit Cards	Facilities	Other
	Longley's Guest House Lisbon Creek, Mangrove Cay (809) 325-1581	EP	5	$25	None	PB, BT, F, SC	
244	Moxey's Guest House Mangrove Cay Tel: Mangrove Cay Operator	EP, FAP	6	$27	A	PB, F	pool room, dancing club, some private baths

The Berry Islands

Page	Establishment	Meal Plans Offered	No. Rooms	Double Room (Per Person in Season)	Credit Cards	Facilities	Other
246	The Chub Cay Club P.O. Box 661067 Miami Springs, FL 33166 (305) 445-7830 (809) 325-1490	EP	35	$45	A, M, V, TF	M/D, PB	permanently docked houseboat

Bimini

Page	Establishment	Meal Plans Offered	No. Rooms	Double Room (Per Person in Season)	Credit Cards	Facilities	Other
250	Bimini Big Game Fishing Club P.O. Box 699, Alice Town (809) 347-2391/(800) 327-4149	EP	50	$55	A, M, V	M/D, P, TV, BT, F, S, SC	restaurant, big game fishermen exclusively

	Establishment	Meal Plans Offered	No. Rooms	Double Room (Per Person in Season)	Credit Cards	Facilities	Other
250	Bimini Blue Waters Marina P.O. Box 627, Alice Town (809) 347–2166	EP	12	$50	A, M, V	P, PB, M/D, BT	water view on each side of hilltop building
250	Brown's Hotel P.O. Box 601, Alice Town (809) 34–72227	EP	28	$45	None	DR, B, F, SC, BP	
250	Compleat Angler Hotel P.O. Box 601, Alice Town (809) 347–2122	EP	12	$35	A	TV, SC	Hemingway memorabilia

Cat Island

Page	Establishment	Meal Plans Offered	No. Rooms	Double Room (Per Person in Season)	Credit Cards	Facilities	Other
255	Bridge Inn The Bight, Cat Island (809) 354–5013	CP	12	$35	None		
252	Fernandez Bay Village P.O. Box 2126 Ft. Lauderdale, FL 33303 (305) 764–6945	EP	5 Cottages	$60–80	None	PB, BT	1–2 person and 1–8 person cottages, airstrip
255	Greenwood Inn P.O. Box N-8598, Nassau (809) 32–74453	MAP	20	$50 (MAP)	A	PB	airstrip
254	Hawk's Nest Devils' Point, Cat Island Tel: Devil's Point	EP	10	$60	None	P, BT, F, T	marina, airstrip, food and fuel

Eleuthera

Page	Establishment	Meal Plans Offered	No. Rooms	Double Room (Per Person in Season)	Credit Cards	Facilities	Other
	Spanish Wells						
263	Spanish Wells Beach Resort P.O. Box 31, Spanish Wells Tel: 299, Spanish Wells (800) 327-5118 (800) 432-1362	MAP, EP	21 rooms 6 villas	$50	A, M, V	PB, T, BT, F, SC	free bikes, rooms overlook beach, underwater photo lab
263	Spanish Wells Harbour Club P.O. Box 31, Spanish Wells Tel: 299, Spanish Wells	MAP, EP	14	$35	A, M, V	BP, BT, F, SC, BA/S, T	closed summer, "X"-rated picnic, free bikes, dive shop
	Current						
263	Sandcastle Cottages Current Tel: Overseas Operator	EP	5	$22	None	PB, BA/S, SC	bike rentals
263	Sea Raider Current Tel: Overseas Operator	EP	9	$22	V	PB, BT, F, T	
	Harbour Island						
264	Coral Sands Hotel Coral Sands, Harbour Island (809) 333-2350 1-(800) 327-0787	MAP, EP	33	$60	A, M, D	TV, PB, T, BA/S, F, SC	3 mile beach, closed Sept.-Nov., night tennis, extensive wine cellar
263	Dunmore Beach Club P.O. Box 122, Harbour Island (809) 333-2200	MAP, FAP	14	$75 (FAP)	None	PB, T, F, BT	closed May-July

	Ocean View Club P.O. Box 134, Harbour Island (809) 333-2276	EP, MAP	10	$50	M, V, C	F, SC	
263	Pink Sands P.O. Box 87, Harbour Island (809) 333-2030	FAP	46	$80 (FAP)	None	PB, BA/B, BA/S, T, SC	closed Aug.–Nov., breakfast served in room, 25 acres
264	Rock House General Delivery, Harbour Island Tel: Overseas Operator (809) 333-2053 (800) 327-5581	MAP	6	$53 (MAP)	A, M, V	BP, T, BA/S, WSF	closed Sept.–Oct.; X-rated island, bicycles rented, pets permitted
264	Romora Bay Club P.O. Box 146, Harbour Island (809) 333-2325 (800) 327-8286	EP, MAP	30	$60–90	A, M, V	BP, T, BA/S, M/D, F, SC	"X"-rated picnic closed Sept.–Nov.
264	Runaway Hill Club P.O. Box 31, Harbour Island (809) 333-2150 (800) 327-0787	EP, MAP, FAP	8	$65	A, M, V	P, BA/S, PB	homelike atmosphere, closed day after Labor Day to mid-Oct.
264	Tingum Village P.O. Box 1, Harbour Island (809) 333-2161	EP, MAP	8	$30	None	BP, T, BA/S, PB	good food and parties
264	Valentine's Inn & Yacht Club P.O. Box 1, Harbour Island (809) 333-2080 (800) 327-0787	EP, MAP	24	$50–60	M, V	P, BP, BA/S, BA/B, M/D, WSF	closed Sept. hot tub X-rated island

Eleuthera (cont.)

Page	Establishment	Meal Plans Offered	No. Rooms	Double Room (Per Person in Season)	Credit Cards	Facilities	Other
265	**Gregory Town** Caridon Cottages P.O. Box 5206, Gregory Town (809) 332-2690 Ext. 230	EP, MAP	14 cottages	$12	None	BA/S, BP, T, BT, F, SC	open year round, add $10 MAP, scooter rental
265	**Governor's Harbour** Cigatoo Inn P.O. Box 86, Governor's Harbour (809) 332-2343, (800) 327-0787	EP	26	$35	A	P, BP, BA/S, T, F, BT, SC	
265	Laughing Bird Apartments P.O. Box 76, Governor's Harbour (809) 322-2012						
265	Tuckaway P.O. Box 45, Governor's Harbour (809) 332-2000	EP	6	$20–25		B	
	Rainbow Inn P.O. Box 53, Governor's Harbour Tel: Hatchet Bay 1–(800) 327-0787	EP, MAP	10	$35	A	PB, T, BA/S, P	restaurant closed May–June & Sept.–Nov., hotel open year-round
	Scriven's Villas P.O. Box 35, Governor's Harbour (809) 322-1041	EP	4	$20	None	PB, BA/S, M/D, T, G, SC	

Rock Sound

Cartwright's Ocean View Cottages Tarpum Bay 809) 334-2131	EP	5	$22	None	B	bike & moped rentals
Cotton Bay Club P.O. Box 28 Rock Sound Eleuthera (809) 334-2101	MAP	77	$150–200	A, M, V	P, PB, BA/S, F, T, G	7 miles of beach, 18-hole golf course, bike rentals
Culmer's House & Lodges P.O. Box 50, Rock Sound Tel: Tarpum Bay	EP	6	$22	None	BP	
Edwina's Place P.O. Box 30, Rock Sound (809) 334-2094	FAP	9	$37	None	TV, BP, P, BA/S	closed Sept.
Ethel's Cottages P.O. Box 27, Tarpum Bay (809) 334-2216	EP	18	$33	None	BP, BA/S, F	
Hilton's Haven Tarpum Bay (809) 334-2216	EP, MAP	10	$20	None	BP, BT, F	

Windermere Island

Windermere Island Club P.O. Box 25, Eleuthera (809) 322-2538, (212) 839-0222, 1-(800) 237-1236	FAP	21	$105–150	A	P, BT, F, PB, T	beautiful beach

The Exumas

Page	Establishment	Meal Plans Offered	No. Rooms	Double Room (Per Person in Season)	Credit Cards	Facilities	Other
	Exumas Supplies Apartments P.O. Box 50, George Town (809) 336–2506	EP	4 Apts.	$32	M, V	BP, BA/S, BT, S, F, SC	
273	Happy People Marina Staniel Cay, Exuma Tel: Staniel Cay	EP	14	$35	None	PB, BT, F, SC	
273	Peace and Plenty Hotel P.O. Box 55, George Town (809) 336–2551	MAP, EP	32	$50–55	A, M, V	B, P, BT, F, SC, M/D	bikes rented, free ferry to Stocking Island, no children under 6 years
	Marshall's Guest House P.O. Box 27, George Town (809) 336–2571	EP	12	$30	None	BP, F	
274	Out Island Inn P.O. Box 49, George Town (809) 336–2171	EP	80	$55	A, M, V	PB, BA/S, BT, F, T, P, SC	bikes rented
274	Pieces of Eight P.O. Box 49, George Town (809) 336–2600	EP	32	$40	A, M, V	PB, P, BA/S, BT, F, SC	overlooks site of regatta
274	Regatta Point P.O. Box 6, George Town (809) 336–2206	EP	5	$42	None	PB	on cay with causeway to George Town, good view for regatta

273	Staniel Cay Yacht Club 809) 355-2024	FAP	6	$85	A	BT, F, SC, WS, BP	free sailboats, windsurfing for guests 3 nights & more, dive operation
	Two Turtles Inn P.O. Box 51, George Town (309) 336-2545	EP	16	$35	A, M, V	BP	

Inagua

Page	Establishment	Meal Plans Offered	No. Rooms	Double Room (Per Person in Season)	Credit Cards	Facilities	Other
275	Ford's Inagua Inn Matthew Town, Inagua Tel: 277	EP, MAP	5	$20	None	BP, F, M/D	
	M in House Matthew Town, Inagua Tel: 267	EP	5	$25	None	BP	

Long Island

Page	Establishment	Meal Plans Offered	No. Rooms	Double Room (Per Person in Season)	Credit Cards	Facilities	Other
281	Stella Maris Inn P.O. Box 105, Stella Maris 809) 336-2106	EP, MAP	60	$50	A, M, V	PB, P, BT, F, SC, T, S	exceptional diving program, 3 pools, pets allowed

Long Island (cont.)

Page	Establishment	Meal Plans Offered	No. Rooms	Double Room (Per Person in Season)	Credit Cards	Facilities	Other
	Thompson Bay Inn P.O. Box SM 30–123, Stella Maris Tel: Salt Pond Operator	EP	8	$25	None	BP	some apartments, good food

San Salvador

Page	Establishment	Meal Plans Offered	No. Rooms	Double Room (Per Person in Season)	Credit Cards	Facilities	Other
287	Riding Rock Inn 701 Southwest 48th St. Ft. Lauderdale, FL 33315 (809) 322–2631	EP, MAP	24	$80	V	P, T, PB,	dive packages available, on rocky beach (sandy beach nearby)
286	Rum Cay Club P.O. Box 22396 Ft. Lauderdale, FL 33335 (305) 467–8355 (800) 334–6869	EP	16	$110	M, V	BP, SC, F	special dive package

INDEX

BERMUDA

accommodations, 3, 14–15, 89–125; apartments, housekeeping, 90, 106–09; charts, 110–25; cottage colonies, 90, 99–102; guest houses, 102–06; hotels, 90–91, 91–99; Paget, 37; private homes, rooms in, 91; Warwick, 35
apartments, housekeeping, 90, 106–09; Warwick, 35
aquarium, 52, 53
art, 43–44, 63
Attractions at a Glance, 26–28

beaches, 8, 34, 35, 49, 65
Bermuda Day, 18
Bermuda Kite Festival, 10–11
Bermudians, 3–4, 8, 9–11
botanical gardens, 38–39

caves, 54–55
children, travel with, 15, 90
churches, 33, 36–37, 44, 48, 61–62
climate, 2–3, 8, 16
clothing, 23
College Weeks, 17
communications: cables, 24; postal service, 24, 45; telephones, 24
cottage colonies, 90, 99–102
crafts, 44, 72
cuisine, 3, 9, 11, 73–74
culture, 3, 9
Cup Match, 11
currency, 22, 42
customs regulations, 21–22

departure tax, 21
dress, 23
drugs, 22
duty-free allowances, 21

economy, 13–14
electricity, 24
entry and departure requirements, 21–22

firearms, 22
forts, 33, 46, 64

geography, 1, 8; Devonshire, 47; Hamilton Parish, 52; Paget, 37; Pembroke, 39; St. George's, 56; Sandys, 29; Smith's, 49; Southampton, 34; Warwick, 35
gombey, 4, 10–11
government, 13, 42–43
guesthouses, 3, 102–06

Hamilton, city of, 12, 39–46
handicapped, travel for, 15–16
history, 10, 12–13, 45; Devonshire, 47; Paget, 37; Pembroke, 39–42; St. George's, 55–57; Sandys, 29, 33; Smith's, 49; Southampton, 34; Warwick, 36
holidays, 16–17
hotels, 3, 90–91, 91–99

Indians, 3, 9, 57

language, 9, 22
libraries, 32, 44, 61

medical care, 24
museums, 31, 45, 53
music, 3, 9, 10, 47, 69

nature reserves, 32, 48, 51
night life, 9, 47, 69–71

parishes, 12
parks and gardens, 44, 45–46, 48, 63
pets, 21
private homes, rental of, 91

race, 3, 10
Rendezvous Time, 16, 44
restaurants, 3, 10, 73–89

St. George, town of, 13, 55–63
shopping, 30, 44, 53, 71–73
sights, general information, 2, 8–9, 26–28.
slavery, 9, 36–37, 56, 60
special events, 16–17
Somerset Village, 29–30
sports, 1, 8, 16, 17, 65–69; boating, 8, 30, 66; bowling, 66; fishing, 8, 30, 66–67; golf, 1, 8, 15, 34, 67; jogging, 23, 68; marathon, Bermuda, 65; scuba diving, 8; snorkeling, 8, 68; squash, 68; swimming, 8, 34, 65; tennis, 9, 15, 68–69; waterskiing, 8, 69; windsurfing, 8, 69

time, 24
time sharing, 90
tipping, 22
tours, 4, 9, 37, 64–65

311

transportation: air travel, 15, 18–19; bicycles, 9, 23; buses, 9, 15, 23; carriages, horsedrawn, 9, 24; cruises, 19–20, 35; ferry, 24, 29; mopeds, 9, 15, 23; taxis, 9, 23–24
travel documents, 21

visitor information, 25

Weather. *See* climate.

THE BAHAMAS

Abacos, 217–30; dining, 220, 221; Elbow Cay, 220–21; Great Guana Cay, 220; Green Turtle Cay, 221–22; history, 217; hotels, 223–30; Man-O-War Cay, 220; Marsh Harbour, 219–20; sights, 222–23; Treasure Cay, 220
accommodations, Abaco, 223–30; Acklins/Crooked Island, 233–34; Andros, 242–44; Berry Islands, 246; Biminis, 250–51; Cat Island, 252, 254–55; charts, 289–310; Eleuthera, 263–67; Exuma, 273–74; Grand Bahama, 208–211; Inagua, 275; Long Island, 281; Nassau (Paradise Island), 186–95; San Salvador, 286–88
Acklins/Crooked Island, 230–34; hotels, 233–34; sights, 231, 233
airlines, 141–42
Alice Town, 246
Andros, 234–44; Andros Town, 234; barrier reef, 240–41; fishing, 236, 240; folklore, 237; hotels, 242–44; hunting, 236, sights, 240–42
art, colony (Eleuthera), 258
Arthur's Town, 251
Atlantic Undersea Testing and Evaluation Centre (AUTEC), 241
Attractions at a Glance: Family Islands, 213–16; Freeport, 195–96; New Providence, 157, 167

Bahamians, 3, 4, 133–35, 168, 197
Bay Street, 2, 130, 155, 169, 173
Berry Islands, 244–46; Chub Cay, 246; Great Harbour Cay, 244; hotels, 246
Biminis, 246–51; Alice Town, 246; fishing, 247; hotels, 250–51; sights, 249

casinos, 2, 130, 150, 155, 187, 192, 196, 204, 208
Cat Island, 251–55; Arthur's Town, 251; history, 251; hotels, 252, 254–55; sights, 252
chickcharnies, 237
children, travel with, 137–38
Chub Cay, 246
churches, 244, 262, 272, 280
Clarence Town, 277–78
climate, 2, 138–39
Cockburn Town, 283, 285
Colonel Hill, 230
Congo Town, 236
costs, 137
crafts, 177, 203, 249
cruises. *See* transportation.
cuisine, 3, 135–36
culture. *See* Bahamians.
currency, 148
Current, 261
customs requirements, 146–47

departure tax, 146
dress, 147
drugs, 147
duty-free allowances, 147

economy, 133
Elbow Cay, 220–21
electricity, 151
Eleuthera, 255–67; dive sites, 261; Governor's Harbour, 258–59; Harbour Island, 260–61; Hatchet Bay, 260; hotels, 263–67; Rock Sound, 258; sights, 261–62; Spanish Wells, 261, Tarpum Bay, 258; Windermere Island, 258
Emancipation Day, 140, 269, 273
entry and departure requirements, 146–47
Exumas, 267–74; boating, 271; George Town, 268–69; history, 271, 272; hotels, 273–74; regatta, 268, 273; sights, 271–73

Family Islands, 2, 131–32, 149, 152, 212–16; regatta, 268, 273; sights, 213–16
firearms, 147
Freeport/Lucaya, 2, 126, 130, 135, 149, 150, 152–57, 195–211; *see also* Grand Bahama.

gambling, 2, 130, 150, 155, 187, 192, 196, 204, 208
geography, 1, 126
George Town, 268–69

goombay, 3, 138; festival, 135
government, 133
Governor's Harbour, 258–59
Grand Bahama: history, 199; hotels, 208–11; restaurants, 204–08; sights, 195–96, 199–203
Great Guana Cay, 220
Great Harbour Cay, 244
Green Turtle Cay, 221–22
Gregory Town, 260

handicapped, travel for, 138
Harbour Island, 260–61
Hatchet Bay, 260
history, 132–33, 168–169, 199, 217, 230, 236–37, 247, 251, 256, 258, 271, 274–75, 277–78, 280, 282
hotels. *See* accommodations and individual islands

Inagua, 274–76; hotels, 275; Matthew Town, 275; sights, 275
International Bazaar, 2, 150, 156, 208

Junkanoo, 139; festival, 138; parade, 170

Landrail Point, 230
language, 147
Long Island, 277–81; Clarence Town, 277–78; history, 278, 280; hotels, 281; sights, 280–81

mail boats, 150, 219, 236, 246, 256, 275, 278, 282
Mangrove Cay, 235
Man-O-War Cay, 220
Marsh Harbour, 119–20; diving, 222; ferry service, 219
Matthew Town, 275

Mayaguana, 233
medical care: drinking water, 151; health centres, 151; hospital, 151; vaccinations, 146
mopeds, 149–50
Morgan's Bluff, 235
museums, 176, 200, 222
music, 3, 135, 155

Nassau, 2, 126–27, 130, 149, 150, 152–57, 161–95; history, 168–69; *see also* New Providence.
New Providence, 167–95; history, 168–69; hotels, 186–95; restaurants, 179–86; sights, 157, 167, 172–77
Nicholl's Town, 235
night life, 155

Out Islands. *See* Family Islands.

Paradise Island, 2, 171–72, 185–86, 192–94
People-to-People Program, 4, 126, 134–35, 168, 197
pets, 147
private homes, rental of, 148

race relations, 132–33, 217, 258, 269, 271
Rand Memorial Nature Center, 127, 197, 201
Rawson Square, 176
Red Bay Village, 237
restaurants: Abacos, 220; Andros, 239; Freeport/Lucaya, 204–208; Harbour Island, 261; Nassau, 179–86
Rock Sound, 258
Rolleville, 269

San Salvador, 281–88; Cockburn Town, 283–85; history, 282; hotels, 286–88; mail boat, 282; sights, 283–85
shopping, 155–56, 169, 177, 203
slavery, 132, 174–74
Spanish Wells, 261
special events, 138–40
special services, 138
sports, 126, 152–55; boating, 152–53, 178, 203, 222, 240, 261, 271, 277; diving, 154, 178, 203, 222, 240, 247, 261, 271, 277; fishing, 153, 178, 203, 222, 236, 240, 247, 261, 271, 277; golf, 153, 178, 203; horseback riding, 153, 178, 204; information, 152; parasailing, 153–54; regatta, 268, 273; snorkeling, 154; tennis, 154; windsurfing, 154–55, 179
straw markets, 177, 203, 249

Tarpum Bay, 258
time, 150
tipping, 137
tours, 156–57, 200
transportation, 141–46; airlines, 141–42, 213, 236, 251, 256, 275, 278; automobiles, 149; buses, 150; charter planes, 142; cruises, 142–46; cycles, 149–50; ferries, 150, 219, 227; mail boats, 150, 219, 236, 246, 256, 275, 278, 282; private planes, 142; taxis, 149; yachts, 141
travel documents, 146
Treasure Cay, 220

visitor information, 151
visitor offices, 151–52

Walker's Cay, 221
weather. *See* climate.
Windermere Island, 258